Quantum Computing and Machine Learning for 6G

Scrivener Publishing
100 Cummings Center, Suite 541J
Beverly, MA 01915-6106

Industry 5.0 Transformation Applications

Series Editors: Dr. S. Balamurugan (sbnbala@gmail) and Dr. Sheng-Lung Peng

The increase in technological advancements in the areas of artificial intelligence (AI), machine learning (ML) and data analytics has led to the next industrial revolution, "Industry 5.0". The transformation to Industry 5.0 collaborates human intelligence with machines to customize efficient solutions. This book series covers various subjects under promising application areas of Industry 5.0 such as smart manufacturing, intelligent traffic, cloud manufacturing, real-time productivity optimization, augmented reality and virtual reality, etc., as well as titles supporting technologies for promoting potential applications of Industry 5.0, such as collaborative robots (Cobots), edge computing, Internet of Everything, big data analytics, digital twins, 6G and beyond, blockchain, quantum computing and hyper-intelligent networks.

Publishers at Scrivener
Martin Scrivener (martin@scrivenerpublishing.com)
Phillip Carmical (pcarmical@scrivenerpublishing.com)

Quantum Computing and Machine Learning for 6G

Edited by

Pallavi Sapkale
Department of Computer Science and Engineering, Ramrao Adik Institute of Technology, Nerul, Navi Mumbai, India

Shilpa Mehta
Department of Electrical and Electronic Engineering, Auckland University of Technology, Auckland, New Zealand

and

S. Balamurugan
Albert Einstein Engineering and Research Labs, Tamil Nadu, India

Scrivener Publishing

WILEY

This edition first published 2026 by John Wiley & Sons, Inc., 111 River Street, Hoboken, NJ 07030, USA and Scrivener Publishing LLC, 100 Cummings Center, Suite 541J, Beverly, MA 01915, USA

For more information about Scrivener publications please visit www.scrivenerpublishing.com.

Wiley Global Headquarters
111 River Street, Hoboken, NJ 07030, USA

For details of our global editorial offices, customer services, and more information about Wiley products visit us at www.wiley.com.

The manufacturer's authorized representative according to the EU General Product Safety Regulation is Wiley-VCH GmbH, Boschstr. 12, 69469 Weinheim, Germany, e-mail: Product_Safety@wiley.com.

Library of Congress Cataloging-in-Publication Data

ISBN 978-1-394-23808-8

Cover image: Generated with AI using Adobe Firefly
Cover design by Russell Richardson

Set in size of 11pt and Minion Pro by Manila Typesetting Company, Makati, Philippines

Printed in the USA

10 9 8 7 6 5 4 3 2 1

The editorial team extends heartfelt dedication to their families—parents, spouses, and children—for their boundless support throughout the creation of this work. Additionally, the editors express sincere gratitude to their colleagues at their esteemed institution for their unwavering love, blessings, and encouragement. Finally, this book is respectfully dedicated to the entire research community, whose collective efforts continue to enrich our understanding of the world.

Contents

Preface xix

Acknowledgement xxiii

Part I: Introduction 1

1 **Introduction to Wireless Communication and Transition from 1G to 6G** 3
Krupali Dhawale, Pranali Bhope, Kunika Dhapodkar and Sejal Kumbhare
1.1 Introduction to Wireless Communication 4
1.1.1 Definition and Importance of Wireless Communication 4
Importance of Wireless Communications 4
1.1.2 Role of Wireless Communication in Connecting People and Devices Globally 5
1.1.3 Evolution of Wireless Communication Technologies 6
1.2 Generations of Wireless Communication 8
1.2.1 1G (Analog Cellular) 8
1.2.2 2G (Digital Cellular) 9
1.2.3 3G (Mobile Broadband) 10
1.2.4 4G (LTE and Beyond) 11
1.2.5 5G (Next-Generation Connectivity) 12
1.2.6 Anticipating 6G (Future Evolution) 14
1.3 1G to 4G: Evolution of Wireless Standards 15
1.3.1 Overview of 1G to 4G Transitions 15
1.3.2 Advancements in Digital Modulation and Compression 17
1.3.3 Shift from Analog to Digital Transmission 19
1.3.4 Introduction of Data Services and Mobile Internet 20
1.4 Industry and Research Initiatives for 6G 22
1.4.1 Involvement of Academia, Industry, and Standardization Bodies 22

1.4.2 Research Goals and Technological Roadmaps 24
Conclusion 27
References 27

2 The State-of-the-Art and Future Visioning 6G Wireless Network 29
Payal Bansal
2.1 Introduction 30
2.1.1 Heterogeneous Wireless Networks 31
2.1.2 Vertical Handover 32
2.2 Handover Management in 6G 34
2.2.1 History of Handover System 34
2.2.2 Handover Process 36
2.2.3 Single-Tier Networks with Handover Skipping Process 38
2.2.3.1 Coverage Probability 38
2.2.3.2 Handover Cost 40
2.2.3.3 Average Throughput 43
2.3 Two-Tier Network Handover Skipping 43
Bibliography 51

Part II: Quantum Computing 55

3 Introduction to Quantum Computing 57
Shilpa Mehta and Celestine Iwendi
3.1 Introduction 57
3.1.1 Historical Background 58
3.1.2 Classical Computing vs Quantum Computing 59
3.1.3 Why Quantum Computers? 60
3.1.4 Bits versus Qubits 60
3.1.5 Quantum Registers 61
3.1.6 Key Principles of Quantum Computing 61
3.2 Quantum Gates 62
3.3 Quantum Algorithms 64
3.3.1 Fourier Transform-Based Algorithms 64
3.3.1.1 Overview of Discrete Fourier Transform 65
3.3.1.2 Quantum Fourier Transform 65
3.3.2 Amplitude Amplification-Based Algorithms 68
3.3.2.1 Grover's Algorithm 68
3.3.2.2 Quantum Counting 69
3.3.3 Quantum Walk Based Algorithms 69
3.3.3.1 Boson Sampling Problem 69

3.3.3.2 Element Distinctness Problem 70
3.3.3.3 Triangle Finding Problem 70
3.3.4 Bounded-Error Quantum Polynomial Time Problems 70
3.3.4.1 Quantum Simulation 71
3.3.5 Hybrid Algorithms 71
3.3.5.1 Quantum Approximate Optimization Algorithm 71
3.3.5.2 Variational Quantum Eigensolver Algorithm 71
3.3.5.3 Contracted Quantum Eigensolver Algorithm 72
3.4 Quantum Hardware and Software 72
3.4.1 Quantum Hardware 72
3.4.1.1 Types of Quantum Hardware 73
3.4.2 Quantum Software 74
3.5 Applications 75
3.6 Challenges of Quantum Computing 78
3.7 Current State-of-the-Art 79
3.8 Summary and Future Scope 85
References 85

4 Quantum-Secured Concealed Identifier for 6G Technology 89
Pratham Desai and Dipali Kasat
Introduction 89
4.1 Quantum Mechanical Properties for Security 90
4.1.1 Entanglement with Bell-State Example 90
4.1.2 Entanglement for Bipartite System 92
4.1.3 No Cloning Theorem 93
4.2 Quantum Key Distribution Technique (QKD) 96
4.3 BB84 Algorithm 96
4.4 Concept of Identifiers 97
4.5 Drawbacks of Classical Algorithms 99
4.6 Quantum Concealed Identifiers for 6G Technology 100
4.6.1 QKD Protocol with a Multiple Coding Basis 100
4.6.2 Parameters and Basic Equipment 102
4.6.3 Pseudo-Random Number Seed Key Construction Protocol for Security (PRNSKC) 104
4.7 A Post-Quantum SUCI for 6G 105
4.7.1 How SUCI is Vulnerable to Quantum Attacks 105
4.7.2 Post-Quantum Secure SUCI 106
4.7.3 Selecting the Perfect KEM for KEMSUCI 107

4.7.4 Understanding the Kyber Algorithm 109
4.8 Comparison Between the Existing Schemes 111
Conclusion 112
Bibliography 113

5 Quantum Cryptography: Present and Future 6G **117**
Dhananjay Manohar Dakhane, Vaibhav Eknath Narawade and Pallavi Sapkale
5.1 Introduction 117
5.2 Quantum Cryptography 119
5.3 Quantum Key Distribution 120
5.4 Post Quantum Cryptography 121
5.5 Conclusions 121
References 122

6 Network Intelligence with Quantum Computing for 6G **123**
H. Bhoomeeswaran, G. Joshva Raj, J. Mangaiyarkkarasi and J. Shanthalakshmi Revathy
6.1 Introduction 124
6.2 Quantum Computing 127
6.3 Spintronic QC 127
6.4 Literature Survey 129
6.5 SHSTNO 130
6.6 Photonic QC 133
6.7 Conclusion 137
6.8 Future Scope 138
References 139

Part III: Machine Learning **141**

7 Introduction to Machine Learning: Conceptualization, Implementation, and Research Perspective **143**
Snehasis Dey
7.1 Introduction to Machine Learning: Conceptualization Perspective 144
7.1.1 Basics of Machine Learning 144
7.1.2 Literature Survey 147
7.1.3 Problem Statement and Proposed Model 147
7.1.4 Evolution of Machine Learning 148
7.1.5 Machine Learning as a Powerful Tool for Future Advancement 150
7.2 A Dive Into Machine Learning: Implementation Perspective 151

7.2.1 Correlations and Differences Between Artificial Intelligence (AI), Machine Learning (ML), and Deep Learning (DL) 151
7.2.2 Learning Techniques in Machine Learning 153
7.2.3 Algorithms in Machine Learning 155
7.3 Recent Trends in Machine Learning: Research Perspective 156
7.3.1 Machine Learning in Fourth Industry Revolution or Industry 4.0 (4IR) 157
7.3.2 Machine Learning in Real-World Applications: ML for Everything, for Everywhere and for Everyone 157
7.3.3 Machine Learning in 5G Wireless Communications and Beyond 158
7.4 Conclusion 159
References 160

8 6G Wireless Networks: Pioneering with Machine Learning Technologies 161
Krupali Dhawale, Shraddha Jha, Mishri Gube, Shivraj Guduri and Khwaish Asati
8.1 Introduction 162
8.2 Introduction to 6G Wireless Networks and Machine Learning 162
8.2.1 6G Wireless Network and Its Significance 162
8.2.2 Challenges for 6G Networks 164
8.2.3 Goals for 6G Networks 166
8.2.4 Introduction to Machine Learning and Its Relevance in Wireless Networks 167
8.2.4.1 Importance of Machine Learning in Wireless Networks 168
8.2.5 Potential Benefits of Integrating Machine Learning in 6G Technology 169
8.3 Machine Learning Techniques for 6G Wireless Networks 171
8.3.1 Signal Processing and Optimization 171
8.3.2 Adaptive Beamforming and Spatial Processing Using Machine Learning 173
8.3.3 Benefits of Adaptive Rendering and Spatial Processing through Machine Learning 174
8.3.4 Signal Denoising, Interference Mitigation, and Resource Allocation 174
8.3.5 Spectrum Management and Allocation 176
8.4 Driven Network Management and Security 178

8.4.1 Self-Organizing Networks (SON) 178
8.4.2 Automatic Network Configuration and Optimization through AI 180
8.4.2.1 Network Management 180
8.4.2.2 Network Security 181
8.4.3 Fault Detection, Self-Healing, and Network Maintenance 181
8.5 Challenges and Future Directions 182
8.5.1 Data Privacy and Ethics Issues and Challenges 182
8.5.2 Future Directions in Data Privacy and Ethical Considerations 183
8.5.3 Balancing Data Usage and User Privacy in AI-Driven Networks 184
8.6 Conclusion 185
References 186

9 Machine Learning–Based Communication and Network Automation: Advancements, Challenges, and Prospects 187
J. Shanthalakshmi Revathy and J. Mangaiyarkkarasi
9.1 Introduction 188
9.2 Advancements in Machine Learning for Communication and Network Automation 189
9.2.1 Machine Learning Fundamentals 190
9.2.1.1 Supervised, Unsupervised, and Reinforcement Learning in Network Automation 190
9.2.2 Applications in Network Automation 192
9.2.2.1 Predictive Maintenance and Fault Detection 192
9.2.2.2 Quality of Service (QoS) Optimization 193
9.2.2.3 Traffic Engineering and Load Balancing 193
9.2.3 Data Sources and Preprocessing 194
9.2.3.1 Data Collection Methods in Network Environments 194
9.2.3.2 Data Preprocessing Techniques 195
9.2.3.3 Feature Selection and Engineering 195
9.2.4 Model Training and Deployment 196
9.3 Challenges in Implementing Machine Learning for Network Automation 199
9.3.1 Data Quality and Availability 199
9.3.2 Scalability and Resource Constraints 200
9.3.3 Interoperability and Standards 201

9.3.3.1 Need for Standardization 201
9.3.3.2 Compatibility with Existing Network Infrastructure 202
9.3.3.3 Vendor-Specific Challenges 202
9.3.4 Ethical and Regulatory Considerations 203
9.3.4.1 Bias and Fairness in Machine Learning Algorithms 203
9.3.4.2 Regulatory Compliance in Network Automation 204
9.3.4.3 Ethical Implications of Automation in Communication 205
9.4 Prospects and Future Directions 206
9.4.1 Emerging Technologies 206
9.4.2 AI-Driven Autonomous Networks 208
9.4.2.1 Toward Fully Autonomous Networks 208
9.4.2.2 Self-Healing and Self-Optimizing Networks 208
9.4.2.3 Human-Machine Collaboration in Network Management 208
9.5 Research and Development Trends 209
9.5.1 Current Research Trends in Machine Learning and Network Automation 209
9.5.2 Industry Collaborations and Academic Contributions 210
9.5.3 The Importance of Open-Source Projects 211
9.6 Conclusion 212
References 213

10 Empowering 6G Communication Systems: Harnessing Machine Learning for Advancements in Flexible and 3D-Printed Antennas 217
Duygu Nazan Gençoğlan and Shilpa Mehta
10.1 Introduction 218
10.2 Flexible and 3D-Printed Antennas 222
10.3 Challenges in 6G Antenna Design 224
10.4 Machine Learning for Antenna Design 225
10.5 Data-Driven Antenna Optimization 226
10.6 Topology Optimization with ML 227
10.7 Material Selection and Optimization 229
10.8 Simulation and Modeling with ML 230
10.9 Hardware-Software Co-Design for ML-Aided Antennas 231
10.10 Experimental Validation and Prototyping 232
10.11 Conclusion and Future Directions 232

10.12 Future Directions 233
References 233

11 Potential Communication in B5G Networks Through Hybrid Millimeter-Wave Beamforming and Machine Learning: Basics, Challenges, and Future Path 243
Snehasis Dey
11.1 Introduction 244
11.2 Literature Survey 245
11.3 HBF Open Challenges 251
11.4 Conclusion 258
Bibliography 258

12 Device-to-Device Communication in 6G Using Machine Learning 261
J. Shanthalakshmi Revathy, J. Mangaiyarkkarasi and J. Matcha Rani
12.1 Introduction 262
12.2 Fundamentals of Device-to-Device Communication 263
12.3 Evolution from Previous Generations 265
12.3.1 Early Foundations: Peer-to-Peer and Ad Hoc Networks 265
12.3.2 Device-to-Device Communications in Cellular Networks 266
12.3.3 The 5G Era 267
12.3.4 Enhancement in 6G 267
12.4 Role of Machine Learning in 6G D2D Communication 268
12.4.1 Supervised Learning 268
12.4.2 Unsupervised Learning 269
12.4.3 Reinforcement Learning 270
12.4.4 Integration of Machine Learning in 6G Networks 271
12.5 Applications of Machine Learning in D2D Communication Resource Allocation and Spectrum Management 273
12.6 Challenges and Solutions 275
12.7 Case Studies 277
12.7.1 Smart Cities and Urban IoT Networks 277
12.7.2 Autonomous Vehicles and Vehicular Communication 278
12.7.3 Healthcare and Wearable Devices 278
12.7.4 Augmented Reality (AR) and Immersive Media 279

12.8 Challenges and Future Scope 279
12.9 Conclusion 280
References 281

Part IV: Quantum Computing and Machine Learning 283

13 Integrating Quantum Computing and Machine Learning in 6G Networks 285
Ogobuchi D. Okey, Theodore T. Chiagunye, Henrietta U. Udeani, Ikechukwu Nicholas, Renata L. Rosa and Demóstenes R. Zegarra
13.1 Introduction 286
13.2 Background Study 288
13.2.1 Technology Evolutionary Trends Toward 6G Network 288
13.2.2 Unique Features of 6G Networks 289
13.2.3 The Principle of Quantum Computing 291
13.2.4 Machine Learning 292
13.3 Quantum Machine Learning Algorithms and Implementation Frameworks 294
13.4 Resource Allocation in QML-Enabled 6G Network 300
13.5 Security Challenges and Prospects in QML 6G 301
13.6 Limitations, Benefits, and Future Directions 303
13.7 Conclusion 305
References 305

14 A Quantum Computing Perspective in 6G Networks: The Challenge of Adaptive Network Intelligence 311
Pallavi Sapkale
14.1 Introduction 312
14.1.1 Quantum Computing in 6G 312
14.2 What is Network Intelligence in Quantum Computing? 313
14.2.1 Methods to Achieve the Network Intelligence in Quantum Computing 317
14.3 How to Accomplish Network Intelligence 319
14.4 Quantum Computing Opportunities with 6G 319
14.5 Challenges and Research Scope in Quantum Computing with 6G 320
14.5.1 Main Challenges in Quantum Computing with 6G 320

14.5.2 Research Scope in Quantum Computing 322
14.6 Conclusion 323
References 324

15 Role of QML in 6G Integrated Vehicular Networks 327
R. Palanivel, Muthulakshmi P., Snehasis Dey, Shilpa Mehta and Pallavi Sapkale
15.1 Introduction 328
15.2 Literature Survey 331
15.3 Methodology 332
15.3.1 Quantum Machine Learning for Traffic Prediction in 6G Networks 332
15.3.1.1 Environment Setup 333
15.3.1.2 Quantum Traffic Prediction Model 333
15.3.1.3 Quantum Circuit Representation 333
15.3.1.4 Safety Analysis 334
15.3.1.5 Interpretation 334
15.3.2 QML for Network Security in Vehicular Communication 336
15.3.2.1 Environment Setup 336
15.3.2.2 Quantum Key Distribution (QKD) 337
15.3.2.3 Node1's Side (Initialization) 337
15.3.2.4 Quantum Communication Channel (Simulated) 337
15.3.2.5 Node2's Measurement 338
15.3.2.6 Security and Key Sharing 338
15.3.2.7 Interpretation 338
15.3.3 6G Network Slicing and Resource Management by QML 339
15.3.3.1 Environment Setup 339
15.3.3.2 Implementation Process 340
15.3.3.3 Interpretation 341
15.3.4 Quality-of-Service (QoS) Optimization by QML 342
15.3.4.1 Environment Setup and Parameters 342
15.3.4.2 Implementation Process 342
15.3.4.3 Interpretation 343
15.4 Results and Discussion 344
15.5 Conclusion 346
References 346

Part V: Applications 349

16 Smart Irrigation Technique Using IoT Based on 5G 351
Jyoti B. Deone and Khan Rahat Afreen
16.1 Introduction 352
16.2 Related Work 353
16.3 5G Network on Smart Farming 357
16.3.1 The Following Decade Will See the Development of 5G and Smart Farming 358
16.4 Proposed Methodology 359
16.5 Working Modules of the System 360
16.5.1 Login and Registration Module 360
16.5.2 Change Number Module 360
16.5.3 Check Status Module 360
16.5.4 Start Water Pump Module 360
16.5.5 Stop Water Pump Module 361
16.5.6 Force Start Water Pump Module 361
16.5.7 Auto Stopped Module 361
16.6 Experimental Result Analysis and Working 361
16.7 Conclusion 364
References 364

17 Modeling and Development of Low-Cost Visible Light Communication System 367
Mrinmoyee Mukherjee, Kevin Noronha and Ravi Kumar Bandi
17.1 Learning Objectives 368
17.2 Introduction to VLC 368
17.3 VLC System Description 374
17.3.1 Key Parameters - Light-Emitting Diode 375
17.3.2 Key Parameters - Photodiode 378
17.3.3 Key Parameters - VLC Channel 379
17.4 Experimental Implementation of the VLC System 382
17.4.1 Block Diagram and Technical Specifications 382
17.4.2 Results and Discussions 390
17.5 Simulation and Modeling of the VLC System 392
References 418

Index 423

Preface

Despite the global implementation of 5G networks since 2022, their industrial applications have not fully met the evolving demands of wireless communication. This shortfall has propelled the development of 6G technologies, anticipated for deployment by 2030, promising nearly 100% coverage and enhanced cost-efficiency. 6G aims to address the increased performance needs with innovations like cell-free communications, visible light communications, and massive intelligent surfaces. This book highlights the role of real-time network learning and the integration of quantum computing (QC), machine learning (ML), and quantum ML (QML) to enhance service quality. It provides a deep dive into the interplay of these technologies within 6G networks, starting from 5G fundamentals.

The book elaborates on how these advanced technologies will underpin 6G's architecture to meet comprehensive service demands, including those for smart city applications requiring extensive coverage, ultra-low latency, and reliable connectivity. The book details how the synergy between QC, ML, and 6G technologies will transform communications, revolutionize markets, and enable groundbreaking applications globally.

The book is organized into five parts, each progressing the reader's understanding of advanced 6G technologies:

Part I: Introduction: Provides an overview of wireless communication's evolution from 1G to 6G, covering fundamental principles, global organizations involved in 6G standardization, and the current state-of-the-art in 6G technology.

Chapter 1 outlines the evolution of wireless communication from 1G to the projected 6G networks, spotlighting potential uses such as augmented reality and remote surgery, while covering the progress of 6G, including global standardization and research efforts. Chapter 2 delves into contemporary 6G technology, examining network handover management and advances via cloud computing and network virtualization through

SDN (Software-Defined Networking) and NFV (Network Functions Virtualization), and explains how SDN enhances scalability, flexibility, and service quality in 6G networks.

Part II: Quantum Computing: Introduces quantum mechanics principles and their applications in computing, detailing quantum computing's unique characteristics, cryptography, and its role in intelligent spectrum management.

Chapter 3 introduces the fundamentals of quantum computing, including qubits, quantum gates, and algorithms, contrasting them with classical computing. It examines the available hardware and software for quantum research and potential applications in complex engineering and interdisciplinary fields. Chapter 4 discusses how quantum computing enhances 6G network security, with a focus on quantum properties like entanglement and the no-cloning theorem, quantum key distribution (QKD), and the BB84 algorithm, highlighting the efficiency and security improvements quantum technologies can bring.

Chapter 5 provides an in-depth look at quantum cryptography in current and future networks, discussing the impact of Moore's Law on data security and introducing quantum mechanics-based cryptography. It advises organizations to stay updated with quantum advancements to improve security measures. Chapter 6 delves into how AI and quantum computing can optimize 6G networks, particularly for high-speed and low-latency performance. It discusses Standard Quantum Computing (SQC) and Post-Quantum Cryptography (PQC), suggesting innovative integration strategies. The chapter concludes with recommendations on material and technique choices for devices at THz frequencies, vital for 6G.

Part III: Machine Learning: Discusses machine learning's critical role in 6G networks, including its application in network optimization, integration with edge computing and IoT, and challenges in device-to-device communication.

Chapter 7 discusses the evolution and integration of machine learning (ML) in 6G contexts, tracing its development from 1950 and its application in sectors such as cybersecurity and healthcare, and emphasizing its importance in future wireless communications including 5G and beyond. Chapter 8 evaluates ML strategies for enhancing 6G remote networks, addressing robust network creation, spectrum, and management challenges, and identifying key research areas.

Chapter 9 examines ML in network automation and communication, focusing on integrating edge computing and IoT, and tackles challenges like algorithmic biases and data privacy while underlining ML's role in minimizing human error and optimizing network functions. Chapter 10 analyzes the interaction between ML and flexible 3D-printed antennas in 6G, covering design, monitoring, and optimization processes, and highlights the advantages of this synergy in improving antenna performance and adaptability.

Chapter 11 explores the combination of millimeter-wave technologies and ML in Beyond 5G networks, concentrating on beamforming and effective deployment of mm-wave technologies. Chapter 12 delves into ML applications in device-to-device (D2D) communication within 6G, addressing large data requirements and security issues, proposing federated learning for decentralized data processing, and projecting the future of D2D communications enhanced by ML to support advanced applications such as augmented reality and IoT.

Part IV: Quantum Computing and Machine Learning: Explores how quantum computing can enhance machine learning, focusing on scalable and fault-tolerant quantum architectures and the role of quantum machine learning in advancing 6G systems.

Chapter 13 explores the development of scalable, fault-tolerant quantum computing architectures and Quantum Machine Learning (QML) algorithms, emphasizing their optimization for 6G networks and role in advancing future research. Chapter 14 focuses on the strategic implementation of quantum computing in the cloud for 6G networks, discussing how quantum phenomena like superposition and entanglement can efficiently process large data volumes and solve complex network challenges, enhancing network intelligence beyond classical computing limits.

Chapter 15 discusses QML in vehicular networks, detailing how QML algorithms leverage quantum parallelism for optimizing resource allocation, spectrum management, and routing in 6G networks. It also introduces quantum-inspired reinforcement learning for autonomous network decision-making, highlighting significant improvements in latency reduction, throughput optimization, and overall network efficiency.

Part V: Applications: Presents practical use cases, such as IoT-based technology for 5G and the development of low-cost visible light communication systems, demonstrating these technologies' transformative potential in real-world scenarios.

Chapter 16 discusses the application of quantum computing and machine learning in 6G networks through smart irrigation systems, examining sustainable agriculture challenges in India and the use of IoT-based technology. It details the system's architecture, experimental setup, and algorithm implementation, concluding with results that demonstrate remote irrigation control advancements.

Chapter 17 provides an in-depth look at developing low-cost visible light communication (VLC) systems, tailored for real-world applications. It covers the principles of VLC, the construction of a hardware model supporting 1.2 Mbps data transmission over one meter using OOK-NRZ modulation, and the development of a MATLAB2023® software model to simulate VLC. The chapter concludes with results and future enhancements for system accuracy.

The Editors
November 2025

Acknowledgement

The editorial team extends heartfelt gratitude to our institution for fostering an encouraging research environment that laid the foundation for this proposal. We are deeply appreciative of the diverse group of contributors from various nations and offer special thanks to the reviewers worldwide who have diligently examined each chapter to maintain the book's high standards. Their insightful feedback has been invaluable. We sincerely thank all parties involved for their dedication and willingness to take on tasks that pushed them beyond their usual comfort zones. Finally, we are grateful to Martin Scrivener and the team at Scrivener Publishing for their help and publication of this volume.

Part I
INTRODUCTION

1

Introduction to Wireless Communication and Transition from 1G to 6G

Krupali Dhawale, Pranali Bhope*, Kunika Dhapodkar and Sejal Kumbhare

Department of Artificial Intelligence, G. H. Raisoni College of Engineering, Nagpur, India

Abstract

In the rapidly evolving landscape of communication technologies, the journey from the first generation (1G) to the sixth generation (6G) of wireless communication systems has been nothing short of revolutionary. This book chapter delves into the fundamental principles and evolutionary transitions that have shaped the development of wireless communication over the past few decades. The chapter commences by providing a comprehensive overview of wireless communication, explaining its historical roots as well as progressive growth from 1G to the cutting-edge 6G. The journey through the chapters unfolds with a historical perspective on the emergence of 1G, the first-generation wireless communication technology that revolutionized global communication. From its humble beginnings, we trace the rapid progression through 2G's digital capabilities, 3G's introduction of data services, the transformative impact of 4G's high-speed connectivity, and 5G's enormous potential. The heart of this book lies in the exploration of the impending 6G revolution. As the world hurtles toward an era of smart cities, autonomous vehicles, and the Internet of Things (IoT), 6G emerges as a sign of extraordinary speed, ultralow latency, and general connectivity. This chapter offers a glimpse into the potential applications and transformative possibilities that 6G presents, from immersive augmented reality to real-time remote surgery. Through a blend of historical context, technical insights, and futuristic hypotheses, this book chapter serves as a primer for anyone seeking to comprehend the evolution of wireless communication and the intricate path that leads to the forthcoming 6G revolution. With an eye on both the past and the future, readers are invited to embark on a journey that passes over the transformative landscape of

**Corresponding author*: pranali.bhope.ai@ghrce.raisoni.net

Pallavi Sapkale, Shilpa Mehta and S. Balamurugan (eds.) Quantum Computing and Machine Learning for 6G, (3–28) © 2026 Scrivener Publishing LLC

wireless communication, from its humble beginnings to the impending era of 6G innovation.

Keywords: Wireless communication, 6G communications, high-speed, low latency, 1G to 6G transition, data rates, LTE, networks

1.1 Introduction to Wireless Communication

1.1.1 Definition and Importance of Wireless Communication

Wireless communication refers to the transfer of information between two or more devices without the use of physical cables or wires. Instead, it utilizes electromagnetic waves, such as radio waves, microwaves, or infrared radiation to transmit data over varying distances. This technology enables devices to communicate and exchange data, voice, video, or other forms of information in a wireless manner, enhancing connectivity and convenience in various applications.

Importance of Wireless Communications

Wireless communication has become an integral part of modern society due to its numerous benefits and applications. Some key aspects highlighting its importance include:

Mobility and Flexibility: Wireless communication allows devices to communicate without being tethered by physical connections. This mobility and flexibility are crucial for devices such as smartphones, laptops, and wearable gadgets, enabling users to access information and communicate virtually anywhere.

Connectivity: Wireless communication ensures seamless connectivity. It enables devices to stay connected to the Internet, which is essential for accessing online resources, social media, email, and various online services.

Scalability: Wireless networks can be easily expanded and extended, making them suitable for various scenarios, from small-scale personal networks to large-scale deployments in urban areas or industrial settings.

Cost Efficiency: Wireless communication eliminates the need for extensive cabling infrastructure, reducing installation and maintenance costs, especially in areas where laying cables

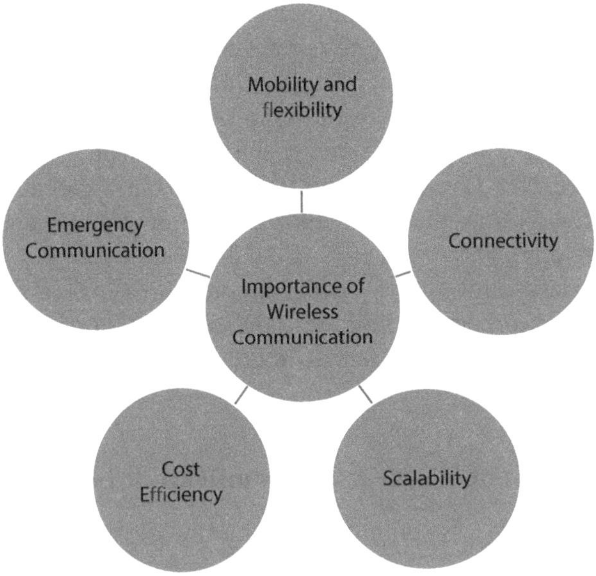

Figure 1.1 Importance of wireless communication.

might be challenging or expensive. Figure 1.1 depicts the importance of wireless communication.

Emergency Communication: Wireless networks are crucial during emergencies when traditional communication infrastructure might be compromised. They enable rapid dissemination of information to coordinate emergency response efforts [1].

1.1.2 Role of Wireless Communication in Connecting People and Devices Globally

Wireless communication plays a vital role in connecting people and devices on a global scale. Here's how it facilitates this connectivity:

- Wireless communication networks cover vast geographical areas, ensuring that even remote and underserved regions can access connectivity, bridging the digital divide.
- Wireless technology enables real-time communication through voice, text, and video, allowing individuals to interact instantly, regardless of their physical locations.

- Wireless communication tools like video conferencing and messaging apps facilitate remote collaboration among individuals and teams spread across different parts of the world, enhancing productivity and innovation.
- Wireless communication enables the swift sharing of information, news, and updates, fostering a globally connected society that stays informed about global events and developments.
- Wireless connectivity provides opportunities for e-commerce, remote work, and online education, empowering individuals and businesses to participate in the global economy irrespective of their physical location.

1.1.3 Evolution of Wireless Communication Technologies

The evolution of wireless communication technologies has been a remarkable journey, transforming the way we connect, communicate, and interact with information and each other as depicted in Figure 1.2. Here is a brief overview of the evolution of some key wireless communication technologies:

1. **Early wireless telegraphy:** It began with the pioneering work of individuals like Guglielmo Marconi in the late 19th century, who laid the foundation for wireless telegraphy, allowing messages to be transmitted over long distances *via* radio waves. This early form of wireless communication relied on Morse code for information exchange.

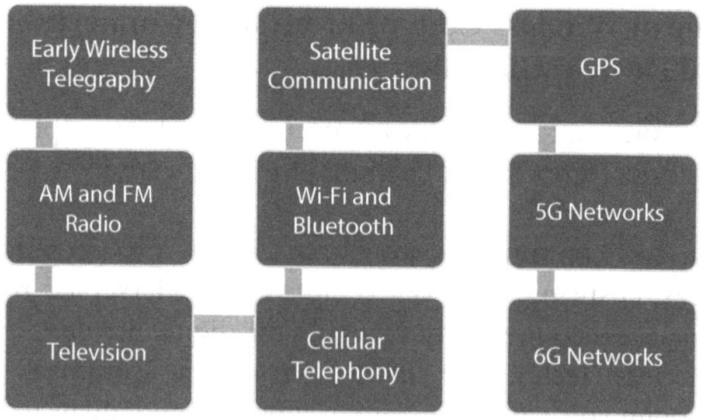

Figure 1.2 Evolution of wireless communication technologies.

2. **AM and FM Radio:** As the 20th century unfolded, so did wireless technology. AM (amplitude modulation) radio emerged, enabling the broadcast of audio signals, and ushering in an era of mass entertainment and news dissemination. However, the limitations of AM, such as susceptibility to interference, led to the development of FM (frequency modulation) radio in the 1930s, which offered superior sound quality and reduced static.
3. **Television:** Wireless communication reached new heights with the advent of television broadcasting, allowing the transmission of visual content to homes. This evolved further with the introduction of color television and high-definition TV (HDTV), offering viewers a more immersive experience.
4. **Cellular Telephony:** The telecommunications landscape underwent a seismic shift with the introduction of cellular networks in the 1980s. The first-generation (1G) cellular systems paved the way for mobile telephony, offering basic voice services. Subsequent generations (2G, 3G, and 4G) improved voice quality and introduced data capabilities, enabling mobile Internet access, video streaming, and app usage.
5. **Wi-Fi and Bluetooth:** Local wireless communication saw a revolution with the widespread adoption of Wi-Fi technology in homes, businesses, and public spaces. Meanwhile, Bluetooth technology enabled short-range wireless connections between devices, giving rise to wireless peripherals like headphones and keyboards.
6. **Satellite Communication:** Advances in satellite technology played a pivotal role in expanding global connectivity, providing Internet access in remote areas, and facilitating communication during disasters.
7. **GPS:** The development of GPS (Global Positioning System) revolutionized navigation and location-based services, impacting fields ranging from logistics to personal navigation.
8. **5G networks:** The ongoing deployment of 5G networks promises to take wireless communication to new heights, offering blazing-fast data speeds, ultralow latency, and support for emerging technologies like the Internet of Things (IoT) and augmented reality (AR).
9. **6G networks:** Research and development for 6G networks are already in progress, with goals of achieving even

faster speeds, near-instantaneous communication, and advanced applications like holographic communication and brain-computer interfaces [2].

1.2 Generations of Wireless Communication

1.2.1 1G (Analog Cellular)

1G, or "first generation," refers to the first generation of analog cellular telecommunications technology. It was the earliest form of mobile phone technology and was developed in the 1980s. 1G networks operated using analog signals to carry voice calls. These networks were characterized by their limited capacity, low call quality, and lack of advanced features that we associate with modern cellular networks.

Key features of 1G (analog cellular) technology include:

- Analog Signals: 1G networks use analog signals to transmit voice calls. This meant that the quality of calls could be susceptible to interference, static, and other forms of signal degradation.
- Low Capacity: The capacity of 1G networks was limited, which meant that only a certain number of users could be accommodated within a specific coverage area. This limitation led to congestion and difficulty in establishing connections during peak usage times.
- Limited Coverage: The coverage areas of 1G networks were relatively small compared to later generations. This meant that as users moved beyond the coverage area, they would lose their connection.
- No Data Services: 1G networks were primarily designed for voice communication, and they did not support data services like text messaging or Internet access.
- Large Handsets: The mobile phones used with 1G networks were often large and bulky, resembling cordless phones rather than the compact and portable devices we are familiar with today.

1.2.2 2G (Digital Cellular)

2G, or "second generation," refers to the second generation of cellular telecommunications technology. It marked a significant advancement over the earlier analog 1G networks. 2G networks were developed in the 1990s and introduced digital technology to mobile communication. This shift from analog to digital brought about improvements in call quality, capacity, and the introduction of various data services.

Key features of 2G (digital cellular) technology include:

- Digital Signals: 2G networks use digital signals instead of analog signals. This allowed for more efficient use of the available radio spectrum, resulting in clearer voice calls and better call quality.
- Improved Capacity: Digital technology allowed for more efficient use of available frequency bands, which increased the capacity of the networks. This meant that more users could be accommodated within a coverage area without the same level of congestion as in 1G networks.
- Introduction of Data Services: One of the significant advancements of 2G was the introduction of data services. Although data speeds were relatively low compared to modern standards, 2G networks enabled basic data services such as text messaging (SMS) and limited Internet access through technologies like WAP (Wireless Application Protocol).
- Encryption and Security: 2G introduced digital encryption, which enhanced the security of voice calls and data transmissions. This was a notable improvement over the lack of encryption in 1G analog networks.
- Global Roaming: 2G networks and devices were designed to support international roaming, allowing users to use their phones in different countries that had compatible 2G networks.
- Introduction of SIM Cards: Subscriber identity module (SIM) cards were introduced with 2G technology. These small cards contained subscriber information and allowed users to easily switch between different devices while retaining their phone numbers and personal data.
- Compact Handsets: With the transition to digital technology, mobile phones became smaller and more compact compared to the bulky devices used in 1G networks.

1.2.3 3G (Mobile Broadband)

3G, or "third generation," represents a significant advancement in cellular telecommunications technology beyond its predecessors, 2G and 1G. Introduced in the early 2000s, 3G brought about faster data speeds, improved voice quality, and the ability to support mobile broadband services. It marked a crucial step in enabling a wide range of data-intensive applications and services on mobile devices.

Key features of 3G (mobile broadband) technology include:

- Faster Data Speeds: 3G networks provided substantially faster data speeds compared to 2G, enabling data-intensive applications such as web browsing, email, and basic video streaming. While the speeds varied, typical 3G data rates were in the range of hundreds of kilobits per second (kbps) to several megabits per second (Mbps).
- Enhanced Voice Quality: 3G introduced improvements in voice quality by using advanced voice codecs and digital processing techniques. This led to clearer and more natural-sounding voice calls.
- Mobile Broadband Services: The most significant feature of 3G technology was its capability to provide mobile broadband services. Users could access the Internet on their mobile devices at reasonable speeds, opening up opportunities for various online activities beyond simple text-based services.
- Video Calling: 3G networks enabled video calling, allowing users to see the person they were speaking to in real time. This was a novel feature at the time and laid the groundwork for video communication on mobile devices.
- Advanced Data Applications: With the advent of 3G, various data applications became feasible, including multimedia messaging (MMS), online gaming, music streaming, and basic video streaming.
- Improved Roaming: 3G networks enhanced international roaming capabilities, allowing users to access high-speed data services in different countries that supported 3G technology.
- Wider Coverage: 3G networks aimed to provide broader coverage areas and better signal penetration compared to earlier technologies, thanks to advancements in network infrastructure.

- Transition to IP Networks: 3G networks laid the foundation for transitioning from circuit-switched networks to IP-based networks, which paved the way for more efficient data routing and the convergence of voice and data services.

1.2.4 4G (LTE and Beyond)

4G, short for "fourth generation," is a major advancement in cellular telecommunications technology that followed 3G. It introduced substantial improvements in data speeds, latency, and overall network performance. 4G technology enabled the rapid growth of data-intensive applications, streaming services, and more sophisticated communication on mobile devices.

Key features of 4G (LTE and beyond) technology include:

- High Data Speeds: 4G networks offer significantly faster data speeds compared to 3G. While the specific speeds can vary, typical 4G data rates can reach tens to hundreds of megabits per second (Mbps), making high-quality video streaming, online gaming, and other data-intensive applications possible.
- Low Latency: 4G technology brought lower latency, which is the time it takes for data to travel between devices and network servers. This reduction in latency enabled real-time applications like video conferencing and online gaming with minimal delay.
- IP-Based Network: 4G networks are based on Internet Protocol (IP), which facilitates the integration of voice and data services over a single network. This shift marked the convergence of traditional voice communication and data services.
- LTE (Long-Term Evolution): LTE is a common technology associated with 4G networks. It provides a roadmap for improving data speeds and network performance. LTE networks offer faster data rates, lower latency, and better overall efficiency compared to earlier technologies.
- VoLTE (Voice over LTE): With 4G, voice calls also transitioned to IP-based technology through VoLTE. This allowed for higher-quality voice calls and the ability to use data services simultaneously during a voice call.

- Improved Network Capacity: 4G networks have enhanced network capacity, enabling more users to connect to the network without causing congestion. This is crucial in densely populated areas with high user demand.
- Enhanced Coverage: 4G networks aimed to provide broader coverage areas and better indoor coverage through advancements in network infrastructure and signal propagation.
- Advanced Applications: The improved data speeds and low latency of 4G technology paved the way for a wide range of advanced applications, including high-definition video streaming, augmented reality (AR), virtual reality (VR), and IoT (Internet of Things) devices.
- Backward Compatibility: Many 4G networks are designed to be backward compatible with 3G technologies, allowing users with older devices to still connect to the network.
- Transition to 5G: While 4G brought substantial improvements, the demand for even faster speeds and lower latency led to the development of 5G technology. 5G builds upon the foundation laid by 4G and introduces even higher data speeds, lower latency, and the ability to support a massive number of connected devices [6].

1.2.5 5G (Next-Generation Connectivity)

5G, short for "fifth generation," is the latest generation of cellular telecommunications technology, succeeding 4G. It represents a significant leap forward in terms of data speeds, latency, capacity, and the ability to connect a massive number of devices simultaneously. 5G is designed to enable a wide range of applications and services that require ultrafast, low-latency connectivity.

Key features of 5G technology include:

- Faster Data Speeds: 5G networks offer exponentially faster data speeds compared to 4G. Peak data rates can reach multiple gigabits per second (Gbps), enabling incredibly fast downloads, high-quality 4K and 8K video streaming, and seamless virtual and augmented reality experiences.
- Ultralow Latency: 5G technology brings ultralow latency, reducing the time it takes for data to travel between devices and network servers. This low latency is essential

for applications that require real-time interactions, such as remote surgery, autonomous vehicles, and industrial automation.

- Massive Device Connectivity: 5G is designed to handle a massive number of connected devices simultaneously. This is crucial for the growth of the Internet of Things (IoT), where a wide range of devices, from sensors to smart appliances, can communicate and exchange data with minimal delay.
- Network Slicing: 5G introduces the concept of network slicing, which allows operators to create virtual, independent "slices" of the network optimized for specific use cases. This enables tailored connectivity for applications with varying requirements, from critical infrastructure to consumer entertainment.
- Improved Network Efficiency: 5G networks are designed to be more energy-efficient and capable of handling higher data loads while using less power per bit transmitted.
- Millimeter-Wave (mmWave) Frequencies: 5G utilizes higher frequency bands, including millimeter-wave frequencies, to achieve extremely high data speeds. However, these frequencies have shorter range and are more susceptible to signal blockages, requiring deployment of additional infrastructure.
- Diverse Spectrum Usage: 5G technology utilizes a broader spectrum range, including low, mid, and high-frequency bands, to balance coverage and capacity requirements.
- Enhanced Mobile Broadband: 5G significantly enhances mobile broadband capabilities, making it possible to deliver high-quality multimedia experiences on mobile devices.
- Smart Cities and Infrastructure: 5G is expected to play a critical role in enabling smart city initiatives, allowing for efficient management of resources, real-time data analysis, and improved public services.
- Remote Services: 5G's low latency and high bandwidth enable new possibilities for remote services such as telemedicine, remote industrial control, and virtual reality-based collaboration.
- Transitioning Industries: 5G has the potential to transform various industries, including healthcare, automotive, manufacturing, entertainment, and more, by enabling innovative applications and solutions [3].

1.2.6 Anticipating 6G (Future Evolution)

6G, or "sixth generation," is envisioned as the next evolution in cellular telecommunications technology beyond 5G. It is expected to build upon the capabilities of 5G while introducing new features and addressing challenges that were not fully addressed by previous generations. Some of the anticipated trends and possibilities for 6G include:

- Extreme Data Speeds: 6G is expected to push the boundaries of data speeds even further, potentially reaching terabit-per-second (Tbps) levels. This would enable unprecedented levels of data-intensive applications and services.
- Ultralow Latency: While 5G introduced low latency, 6G aims to reduce it even further, enabling real-time communication for applications that demand instantaneous responses, such as advanced robotics and remote surgery.
- AI Integration: 6G is expected to heavily integrate artificial intelligence (AI) and machine learning (ML) to optimize network performance, resource allocation, and intelligent data processing at the edge of the network.
- Holographic Communication: Holographic or immersive communication is envisioned for 6G, allowing users to interact with realistic holographic projections of remote individuals or objects.
- Advanced Spectrum Usage: 6G may utilize a broader spectrum range, including even higher frequencies, to support extreme data rates and capacities. This could involve the use of terahertz (THz) frequencies.
- Network Resilience: 6G is anticipated to introduce enhanced resilience to network disruptions, including the ability to quickly adapt to changing conditions and heal itself from failures.
- Global Coverage: 6G may strive for global coverage, including underserved and remote areas, using innovative satellite and airborne technologies.
- Sustainability and Energy Efficiency: 6G is likely to emphasize sustainability by focusing on energy-efficient network designs, contributing to a more environmentally friendly communication infrastructure.
- New Use Cases: 6G is expected to enable novel use cases, including brain-computer interfaces, advanced AI-powered

analytics, fully immersive extended reality experiences, and advanced connectivity for IoT devices.

- Security and Privacy: 6G is anticipated to address security and privacy concerns with advanced encryption techniques and enhanced user authentication methods [4].

1.3 1G to 4G: Evolution of Wireless Standards

1.3.1 Overview of 1G to 4G Transitions

An overview of the transitions from 1G to 4G in mobile communication technologies as depicted in Figure 1.3:

1G (First Generation): 1G refers to the first generation of mobile communication systems. It emerged in the 1980s and was primarily an analog system. The most notable technology within 1G was the advanced mobile phone system (AMPS), which allowed basic voice communication but had limited capacity and poor security.

2G (Second Generation): 2G marked a significant shift from analog to digital communication. This transition began in the early 1990s and introduced digital standards like GSM

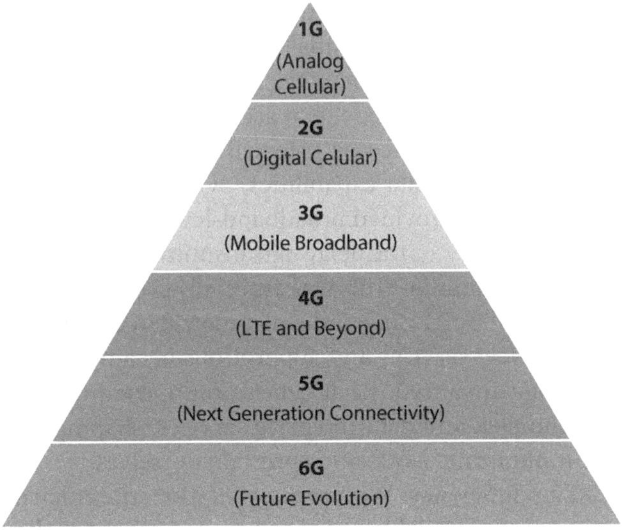

Figure 1.3 Transition from 1G to 6G.

(global system for mobile communications) and CDMA (code division multiple access). 2G brought improvements in voice quality, increased capacity, and the ability to send text messages (SMS).

3G (Third Generation): The 3G era began around the early 2000s and brought further advancements in mobile technology. It introduced faster data rates, enabling Internet browsing, video calling, and multimedia services on mobile devices. Technologies like UMTS (universal mobile telecommunications system) and CDMA2000 were prominent in the 3G era.

4G (Fourth Generation): 4G, which started around 2009, was a significant leap forward in mobile communication. It offered substantial increases in data rates, lower latency, and enhanced multimedia experiences. The key technologies in the 4G era included LTE (long-term evolution) and WiMAX (worldwide interoperability for microwave access). 4G enabled high-quality video streaming, online gaming, and other data-intensive applications [5].

The transitions between these generations were marked by advancements in multiple areas, including:

- Technology: Each new generation brought improvements in underlying technology, such as modulation techniques, encoding methods, and signal processing, leading to better performance and efficiency.
- Data Speeds: Data speeds increased dramatically with each generation. While 1G was primarily focused on voice, 2G introduced basic data capabilities, 3G improved data rates further, and 4G provided broadband-level speeds.
- Latency: Latency, or the delay in transmitting data, decreases with each generation. This was especially crucial for applications like online gaming and real-time video conferencing.
- Services: New services and applications became possible as technology advanced. Each generation opened the door to more complex and data-intensive services, shaping the way we communicate, work, and entertain ourselves.
- Spectrum Efficiency: With each generation, the efficient utilization of the available radio spectrum improved, allowing

more users to connect simultaneously and enjoy better coverage.

- Security: As generations progressed, mobile networks incorporated better security features to protect user data and communications [6, 7].
- Global Standardization: Standards like GSM and LTE were adopted globally, enabling interoperability and creating a more connected world.

1.3.2 Advancements in Digital Modulation and Compression

Advancements in digital modulation and compression have played a crucial role in improving the efficiency and performance of communication systems, particularly in the context of mobile and wireless technologies. Here's an overview of the key advancements in these areas:

Digital Modulation

- Amplitude Modulation (AM) and Frequency Modulation (FM): These were the earliest forms of analog modulation techniques. AM varied the amplitude of the carrier signal, while FM varied its frequency. These techniques were used in early radio broadcasting and communication systems.
- Phase Shift Keying (PSK): PSK modulates the carrier signal by changing its phase. Binary PSK (BPSK) and quadrature PSK (QPSK) are commonly used variations, with QPSK being capable of transmitting 2 bits per symbol.
- Quadrature Amplitude Modulation (QAM): QAM combines both amplitude and phase modulation. It is used to transmit multiple bits per symbol. Higher-order QAM, such as 16-QAM or 64-QAM, allows even more bits per symbol and increased data rates.
- Orthogonal Frequency Division Multiplexing (OFDM): OFDM divides the transmission bandwidth into multiple subcarriers, each using a form of modulation like QAM. It is highly resistant to frequency-selective fading and is a foundational technology in 4G and 5G systems.
- MIMO (Multiple-Input Multiple-Output): MIMO technology uses multiple antennas for both transmission and reception. It increases data rates and improves signal quality by exploiting spatial diversity and multipath propagation.

- Beamforming: This technique focuses the signal in a specific direction, improving signal strength and quality in that direction. It is especially important in millimeter-wave bands used in 5G.

Digital Compression

- Lossless Compression: Lossless compression algorithms reduce the size of data without losing any information. Techniques like run-length encoding (RLE), Huffman coding, and Lempel-Ziv-Welch (LZW) are commonly used in data storage and transmission.
- Lossy Compression: Lossy compression reduces the size of data by discarding some information, often imperceptible to human senses. This is widely used for multimedia applications.
- JPEG (Joint Photographic Experts Group): A widely used lossy compression algorithm for images.
- MP3 (MPEG Audio Layer III): A lossy compression algorithm for audio, known for its ability to significantly reduce file sizes while retaining reasonable audio quality.
- H.264 and H.265: Video compression standards, also known as AVC (advanced video coding) and HEVC (high-efficiency video coding), respectively. H.265 offers improved compression efficiency over H.264.
- Transform Coding: Techniques like discrete cosine transform (DCT) are used in image and video compression standards like JPEG and MPEG.
- Wavelet Compression: Wavelet-based compression is used in applications where preserving both frequency and time information is crucial, such as medical imaging.
- Vector Quantization: This technique groups similar data values and represents them with fewer bits, effectively reducing data size.

Advancements in both digital modulation and compression have led to increased data rates, improved spectral efficiency, better signal quality, and the ability to transmit multimedia content over communication channels efficiently. These advancements have been pivotal in shaping the capabilities of modern communication systems, from 2G to 4G and beyond.

1.3.3 Shift from Analog to Digital Transmission

The shift from analog to digital transmission has been a pivotal advancement in the field of communication technology, bringing numerous benefits and enabling a wide range of services as depicted in Figure 1.4. Here is an overview of the key aspects of this shift and its significance:

- **Improved Signal Quality:** Analog signals are susceptible to various types of interference and noise, which can degrade signal quality. Digital signals, on the other hand, can be reconstructed accurately at the receiver's end, even if they have been affected by noise during transmission. This improved robustness against noise leads to clearer and more reliable communication.
- **Efficient Use of Bandwidth:** Digital signals can be compressed, encoded, and modulated in ways that utilize the available bandwidth more efficiently. This allows for a higher density of information to be transmitted within the same frequency range, enabling more data to be sent simultaneously.
- **Error Detection and Correction:** Digital transmission employs error detection and correction techniques, such as checksums and forward error correction codes. These

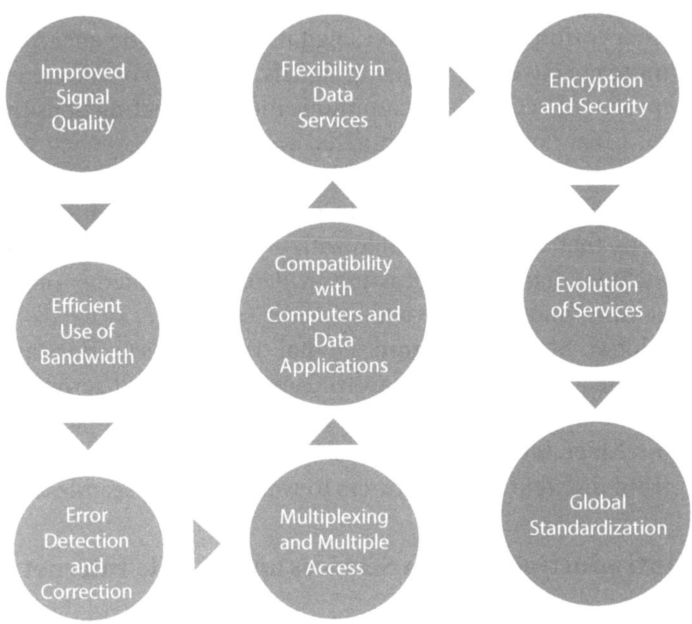

Figure 1.4 Shift from analog to digital transmission.

mechanisms enable the receiver to identify and correct errors that may occur during transmission, further enhancing the reliability of communication.

- **Multiplexing and Multiple Access:** Digital signals are easier to multiplex and manage. Multiple digital signals can be combined and transmitted over the same channel using techniques like time-division multiplexing (TDM) or frequency-division multiplexing (FDM). Digital systems also allow for more efficient management of multiple users accessing the network simultaneously (multiple access) through techniques like CDMA (code division multiple access).
- **Compatibility with Computers and Data Applications:** The digital nature of communication systems aligns well with the requirements of computers and data applications. This compatibility has driven the integration of telecommunications and computing technologies, leading to the convergence of services like voice, data, and multimedia.
- **Flexibility in Data Services:** Digital transmission enables a wide variety of data services, including text, images, audio, and video, to be transmitted over the same network infrastructure. This versatility has paved the way for services like Internet browsing, email, multimedia messaging, and video streaming.
- **Encryption and Security:** Digital signals can be encrypted more effectively than analog signals. This has contributed to improved security in communication, protecting sensitive information from unauthorized access [8].
- **Evolution of Services:** The shift to digital transmission has allowed for the development of new services and applications that were not feasible with analog systems. Examples include digital broadcasting, video conferencing, online gaming, and interactive multimedia content.
- **Global Standardization:** Digital transmission standards can be more easily standardized and harmonized across different regions and countries. This standardization facilitates interoperability, making it easier for devices and networks from different manufacturers to work together seamlessly.

1.3.4 Introduction of Data Services and Mobile Internet

The introduction of data services and mobile Internet has brought about a transformative revolution in the way we communicate, access information, and interact with the digital world. This evolution has empowered users with the ability to connect, share, and access information on the go, leading to the era of mobile communication and digital connectivity. Here is an introduction to the significance and impact of data services and mobile Internet:

- **Access to Information Anytime, Anywhere:** The advent of data services and mobile Internet has untethered communication from fixed locations. It has enabled people to access information, communicate with others, and perform various online activities from virtually anywhere with network coverage. This shift has facilitated real-time communication and information exchange.
- **Expansion of Communication Beyond Voice:** While traditional cellular networks primarily supported voice communication, the introduction of data services marked a pivotal expansion of capabilities. Users could now send text messages and multimedia messages and access a wide range of online services, transcending the limitations of voice-only communication.
- **Emergence of Mobile Applications**: The availability of mobile Internet opened the doors for the development of mobile applications, or "apps." These apps encompass an array of functionalities, from social networking and navigation to entertainment and productivity tools. Mobile app stores became hubs for users to discover and download apps tailored to their interests and needs.
- **Mobile Web Browsing:** Mobile Internet introduced the concept of web browsing on handheld devices. This meant that users could access websites, search for information, and consume online content on their mobile devices. Websites and services were subsequently optimized for mobile viewing, giving rise to responsive design and mobile-friendly interfaces.
- **Social Networking and Online Connectivity:** Data services facilitated the rise of social networking platforms, allowing users to connect with friends, share updates, and engage in online communities. Platforms like Facebook, Twitter, and later Instagram and TikTok became integral parts of people's digital lives.

- **Email and Messaging on the Go:** Mobile Internet enabled users to access their email accounts and exchange messages on their mobile devices. This was particularly beneficial for professionals who needed to stay connected to their work emails while being mobile.
- **Multimedia and Entertainment:** The availability of data services paved the way for multimedia experiences on mobile devices. Users could stream videos, listen to music, and enjoy other forms of entertainment while on the move. Services like YouTube, Netflix, and Spotify became popular choices.
- **E-Commerce and Online Transactions:** Mobile Internet played a significant role in the growth of e-commerce. Users could shop online, make transactions, and even use mobile payment solutions, turning their devices into digital wallets.
- **Impact on Societal Dynamics:** The accessibility of data services and mobile Internet has influenced societal dynamics. It has shaped how people receive news, participate in public discourse, and express their opinions online. The democratization of information and the rise of citizen journalism are some outcomes of this shift.

1.4 Industry and Research Initiatives for 6G

1.4.1 Involvement of Academia, Industry, and Standardization Bodies

The development of 6G wireless technology involves the active participation of academia, industry, and standardization bodies, much like in the case of previous generations of wireless technology. Here is how each of these entities is involved in shaping the future of 6G:

- **Academia:**

  - ☐ Research and Innovation: Academic institutions play a vital role in conducting advanced research in various domains related to 6G technology. They explore new concepts, technologies, and architectures that could potentially be part of the 6G ecosystem.

- ☐ Theoretical Foundations: Academia contributes by establishing the theoretical foundations of 6G, including the exploration of new waveforms, modulation techniques, signal processing algorithms, and network architectures.
- ☐ Testbeds and Prototyping: Academic research labs often develop testbeds and prototypes to experiment with novel 6G ideas, enabling practical validation of theoretical concepts.
- ☐ Collaboration: Collaboration between academia and industry fosters the exchange of ideas, leading to practical solutions that address real-world challenges.

- **Industry:**

  - ☐ Technology Development: Industries, including telecommunications companies and technology vendors, invest in the development of hardware, software, and infrastructure required for 6G networks. This involves creating innovative solutions that can handle the increased demands of future applications.
  - ☐ Use Case Exploration: Industries work on identifying potential use cases for 6G, such as enhanced augmented reality (AR), virtual reality (VR), Internet-of-Things (IoT) applications, and beyond.
  - ☐ Prototyping and Testing: Industry partners create prototypes and conduct extensive testing of 6G technologies to ensure their viability, efficiency, and compatibility with existing networks.
  - ☐ Commercialization: Industries take the lead in commercializing 6G technologies, bringing them to market and facilitating their adoption on a global scale.

- **Standardization Bodies:**

  - ☐ Defining Standards: International standardization bodies, such as the International Telecommunication Union (ITU) and the 3rd Generation Partnership Project (3GPP), play a crucial role in setting the technical standards for 6G. They define the specifications and requirements that ensure interoperability, compatibility, and performance.

- ☐ Collaborative Process: Standardization bodies bring together experts from academia, industry, and regulatory bodies to collaboratively develop and refine the standards. This process ensures that the standards reflect state-of-the-art technology and meet the needs of various stakeholders.
- ☐ Regulatory Alignment: Standardization bodies work to align 6G standards with regulatory frameworks to ensure that the technology adheres to legal and policy requirements while enabling global deployment.
- ☐ Global Consensus: The involvement of standardization bodies helps achieve a global consensus on 6G standards, enabling a consistent and unified approach to the technology's deployment.

1.4.2 Research Goals and Technological Roadmaps

Research goals and technological roadmaps for 6G are focused on pushing the boundaries of wireless communication technology to meet the evolving demands of society and industry. While specific research priorities may vary, here are some overarching goals and potential technological directions for 6G:

1) Extreme Data Rates and Capacity:

- ☐ Terabit Data Rates: Achieving data rates in the order of terabits per second to support applications like high-definition holographic communication, ultrahigh-definition video streaming, and massive data transfers.
- ☐ Spectrum Utilization: Exploring novel spectrum utilization techniques, including utilization of higher frequency bands, to accommodate the growing demand for bandwidth.

2) Ultralow Latency:

- ☐ Sub-Millisecond Latency: Reducing latency to sub-millisecond levels to enable real-time applications such as remote surgery, autonomous vehicles, and tactile Internet.
- ☐ Edge Computing: Integrating edge computing and distributed processing to minimize latency by processing data closer to the user or device.

3) Massive Connectivity:

- ☐ Millions of Devices per Square Kilometre: Enabling seamless connectivity for an unprecedented number of IoT devices, sensors, and wearables in urban and industrial environments.
- ☐ Device-to-Device (D2D) Communication: Investigating efficient D2D communication for improved local data exchange and network efficiency.

4) Energy Efficiency:

- ☐ Ultralow Power Consumption: Developing energy-efficient technologies to prolong the battery life of devices and reduce the environmental impact of wireless networks.
- ☐ Energy Harvesting: Exploring methods for harvesting energy from the environment to power low-energy devices and sensors.

5) Sustainable and Green Communication:

- ☐ Carbon-Neutral Networks: Designing networks and technologies with a focus on minimizing energy consumption and carbon emissions.
- ☐ Network Sharing: Investigating the sharing of infrastructure and resources to reduce the overall energy footprint of networks.

6) Enhanced Security and Privacy:

- ☐ Quantum-Safe Cryptography: Developing cryptographic methods that are resistant to quantum attacks to ensure the long-term security of communications.
- ☐ Privacy-Preserving Techniques: Enhancing privacy protection mechanisms to safeguard user data in an era of increased connectivity.

7) AI-Driven Communication:

- ☐ AI-Enhanced Network Management: Utilizing artificial intelligence and machine learning to optimize network

performance, predict failures, and dynamically allocate resources.
- ☐ Intelligent Beamforming: Using AI to optimize beamforming techniques for efficient and adaptive communication.

8) Terahertz Communication:

- ☐ Exploration of Terahertz Spectrum: Investigating the feasibility of utilizing terahertz frequencies for high-capacity, short-range communication, which could enable new applications.

9) New Antenna Technologies:

- ☐ Metamaterials and Smart Antennas: Developing advanced antenna technologies, including metamaterials and smart antennas, to enhance coverage, capacity, and energy efficiency.

10) Bio-Integrated Communication:

- ☐ Implantable Devices: Researching communication technologies that can be integrated into the human body to enable health monitoring and medical applications.

11) Global Collaboration and Regulatory Alignment:

- ☐ International Cooperation: Collaborating across borders to ensure harmonized standards, global spectrum allocation, and interoperability of 6G networks.
- ☐ Regulatory Flexibility: Advocating for regulatory frameworks that accommodate the unique requirements and technologies of 6G.

These research goals and technological directions form a roadmap for the development of 6G wireless technology. They reflect the aspirations to create a transformative communication ecosystem that supports a wide range of applications, drives innovation, and contributes to societal progress.

Conclusion

The journey of wireless communication, as explored in this chapter, is nothing short of remarkable. From its humble beginnings with 1G, which allowed us to make voice calls without cords, to the transformative power of 4G and 5G, which brought the Internet to our pockets and enabled a myriad of new applications, each generation has pushed the boundaries of what is possible in connecting people and devices. As we stand on the cusp of 6G, the horizon of wireless communication seems boundless. Terahertz frequencies promise data speeds that were once unimaginable, while AI-driven networks hold the potential to optimize performance and efficiency in ways that were science fiction just a few years ago. Integrated satellite-terrestrial communication opens doors to global connectivity that can bridge the digital divide and empower remote and underserved communities.

References

1. Islam, M. and Jin, S., An Overview Research on Wireless Communication Network. Advances in Wireless Communications and Networks. *Adv. Wireless Commun. Netw.*, 5, 19, 2019.
2. Chowdhury, M.Z., Shahjalal, M., *et al.*, 6G Wireless Communication Systems: Applications, Requirements, Technologies, Challenges, and Research Directions, 2019.
3. Vaigandla, K.K., Azmi, N., *et al.*, A Survey On Wireless Communications: 6G And 7G. *Int. J. Sci. Technol. Manage*, 2019.
4. Akhtar, M.W., Hassan, S.A., Ghaffar, R., *et al.*, The shift to 6G communications: vision and requirements. *Hum. Cent. Comput. Inf. Sci.*, 10, 53, 2020.
5. Malagi, K.B., Adarsh, K.M., *et al.*, A Study on Mobile Networks and Their Generations. *Int. J. Adv. Adv. Res. Sci. Commun. Technol. (IJARSCT)*, 11, 2021.
6. Shekhar, D.G.B., *et al.*, Analysis Of Wireless Communication Network From 0G To 5G With The Future Perspectives. *Antardrishti IUD J. Interdiscip. Res.*, 64, 1, 2021.
7. Kaushal, P., 6G Wireless Communications: Vision, Research Groups, and Future. *Int. Res. J. Eng. Technol. (IRJET)*, 08, 10, 1–5, 2021.
8. Tripathi, E.S., A Review Paper On Wireless Mobile Technology. *Int. J. Adv. Res. Innov. Ideas Educ.*, 16, 1, 663–666, 2020.

2

The State-of-the-Art and Future Visioning 6G Wireless Network

Payal Bansal

Poornima Institute of Engineering &Technology Jaipur, Rajasthan, India

Abstract

Because mobile devices are being used more and more, there is a growing need for dependable and fast wireless access, and sixth-generation (6G) networks have emerged as a promising solution. One of the critical challenges in 6G networks is the seamless handover of mobile devices between different network cells to ensure uninterrupted services. Software-defined networking (SDN) has gained considerable attention due to its ability to provide centralized network control and management, making it a suitable technology for addressing handover management in 6G networks. This abstract presents an overview of SDN-based handover management in 6G networks. Traditional handover mechanisms in cellular networks face limitations such as long latency, suboptimal network utilization, and complex network configurations. SDN offers an alternative approach by separating the control plane and data plane and providing a centralized controller to manage the network. In the proposed SDN-based handover management architecture, the controller acts as the central authority responsible for coordinating handover decisions and managing the necessary network resources. By leveraging real-time information from network elements, such as base stations and user devices, the controller can dynamically optimize handover decisions based on various factors, including signal quality, traffic load, and user preferences. The key advantages of SDN-based handover management in 6G networks include improved handover latency, enhanced network scalability, and efficient resource allocation. The centralized control and programmability of SDN enable dynamic adaptation to changing network conditions, resulting in faster handover completion times and reduced service disruptions. Moreover, the ability to optimize resource allocation based on real-time network information allows for better utilization of available network capacity, ensuring a seamless user experience. The abstract concludes by highlighting some ongoing research directions and

Email: payaljindalpayal@gmail.com

Pallavi Sapkale, Shilpa Mehta and S. Balamurugan (eds.) Quantum Computing and Machine Learning for 6G, (29–54) © 2026 Scrivener Publishing LLC

challenges in SDN-based handover management, including security considerations, mobility prediction algorithms, and interoperability with legacy network infrastructure. SDN-based technologies could greatly impact 6G networks as they continue to develop, enhance handover performance, and facilitate the seamless connectivity required for next-generation mobile services.

Keywords: 6G networks, handover management, software-defined networking (SDN), centralized control, network scalability, resource allocation, mobility prediction, seamless connectivity

2.1 Introduction

Due to their "always on" nature and asymmetric uplink/downlink requirements, mobile applications—like social networking and cloud services—have altered how consumers interact with the Internet and obtain information. The Internet of Things (IoT) and machine-type communication (MTC) are two instances of applications whose requirements for upstream and downstream bandwidth vary. As a result of the constantly changing nature of the data that MTC apps need to share or upload, many quality-of-experience (QoE) and quality-of-service (QoS) demand issues could arise simultaneously. The downlink requirements of MTC applications are quite consistent, but the uplink patterns are much more scattered.

More network resource flexibility is therefore necessary for these new mobile apps and services to properly meet a variety of QoS/QoE needs. The requirement for URLLC communication *via* Internet Protocol (IP) has grown with the emergence of Internet-of-Things (IoT) applications. This is especially true in areas where there must be as little latency from the sensor to the actuator as possible, including real-time vehicle control, traffic, and accident avoidance [location, vector, context, low round-trip time (RTT), etc.].

In addition, 6G networks' accelerated service testing and deployment capabilities will inspire novel ways to business. These objectives inform the whole process of migrating networks to 6G through the design of 6G network solutions. The UL/DL needs of developing heterogeneous services with various service level agreements (SLAs) might be met in part using 6G TDD. Two contemporary enabling technologies that are used are network virtualization and software-defined networking (SDN) because they offer multi-tenant capability. Resource flexibility is necessary since multi-tenancy can only be fully enabled with on-demand resource supply. The potential solutions offered by software-defined networks (SDN) and network programmability are receiving an increasing amount of study attention. Standardized interfaces are used by SDN to simplify connectivity between the infrastructure provider and other providers, including vertical markets and mobile virtual network operators (MVNOs). The service level agreements (SLAs) that the infrastructure provider has made with the service providers and vertical market players allow it to tailor the network resources to fulfill the QoS limitations.

Customizing operational network features and network resource-slicing restrictions to the demands of a certain tenant is what we mean when we speak about programmability in a network. In addition, mobile networks must simultaneously support many generations of mobile services (3G and 4G) and a wide range of user services (VoIP, streaming video, messaging, etc.), all of which contribute to highly variable traffic patterns. This help must be provided in the most effective manner feasible since the demand for more capacity is growing at a far quicker rate than revenue. It is crucial that budgets reflect these shifts. Continuity of service across technologies is another challenge faced by modern network operators. They need to put in place finer-grained controls to stop unwanted access and keep a firm rein on service handoffs. New mobile services must be introduced rapidly, and new technologies need to be embraced swiftly in order to be competitive in today's fast-paced corporate world.

2.1.1 Heterogeneous Wireless Networks

A wide variety of radio access technologies (RATs) are currently in use, including wireless local area networks (WLANs), worldwide interoperability for microwave access (WiMAX), Wi-Fi, LTE (long-term evolution), global system for mobile communication (UMTS), general packet radio service (GPRS), and GSM. Figure 2.1 depicts one such scenario in which a complex wireless ecosystem is created by the coexistence of fixed and mobile networks, access methods, applications, and multi-standard devices. Because each of these networks was created separately to satisfy the requirements of a certain service, they differ from one another in terms of the technologies, protocols, network architecture, and signaling processes that they permit.

Keeping up with the demands of mobile consumers and the proliferation of interdisciplinary multimedia services is crucial. From 1G, wireless technology has progressed to 6G. Wide area network architecture is the primary foundation of 3G networks like UMTS. They will not cut it when it comes to supporting cutting-edge applications like teleconferencing, live-streaming, and 3D animation. Furthermore, a lone RAT lacks the means to provide all possible service varieties with ubiquitous availability, vast transfer capacity, and low cost. One of the biggest challenges to implementing 3G is standardizing the technology needed to merge different

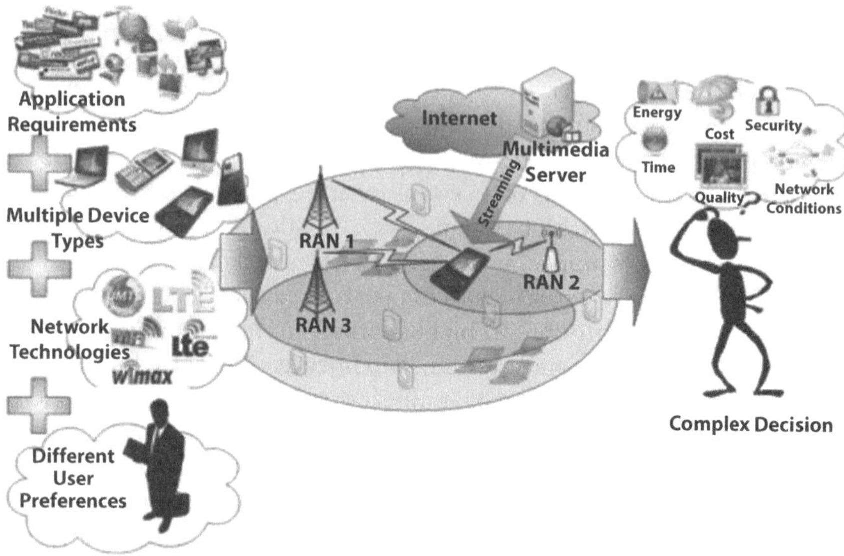

Figure 2.1 Heterogeneous wireless environment.

networks and frequencies into a single convergence platform. Therefore, innovative technology is required to improve the functionality of 3G networks, as well as an interworking mechanism to connect numerous technologies to effectively provide global roaming solutions.

2.1.2 Vertical Handover

Thanks to handover technology, users may move freely between networks with minimum interruption. A horizontal handoff occurs between nodes within the same network, while a vertical handoff occurs between networks. With the use of a method called "vertical handover," services utilizing multiple wireless network technologies will be available to customers of a next-generation wireless network. The three-step procedure used by mobility management to facilitate the vertical transfer between attachment points for mobile users, namely, network discovery (seeking out available networks), handover selection (deciding which point of attachment to utilize), and handover triggering (making a new connection and assigning network resources), is shown in Figure 2.2.

A dependable mobility management system is required to relocate the point of attachment without interrupting service. Figure 2.3 depicts the three steps that make up the process:

- Identifying available networks, deciding whether or not to do a handover, and actually performing the handover. Checking the availability and health of networks within a defined coverage area is a regular part of the network discovery process.

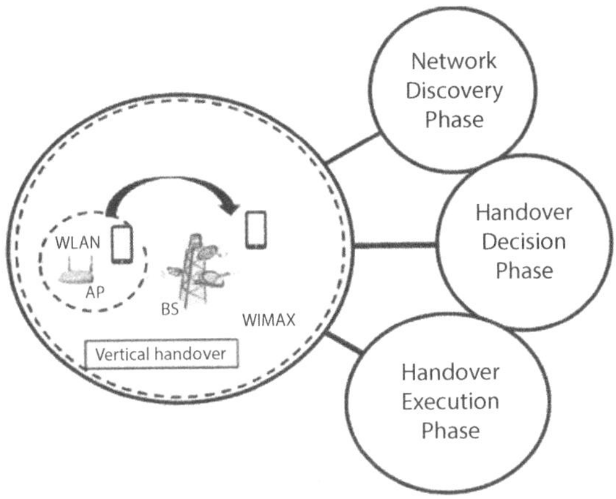

Figure 2.2 Phases representation of vertical handover.

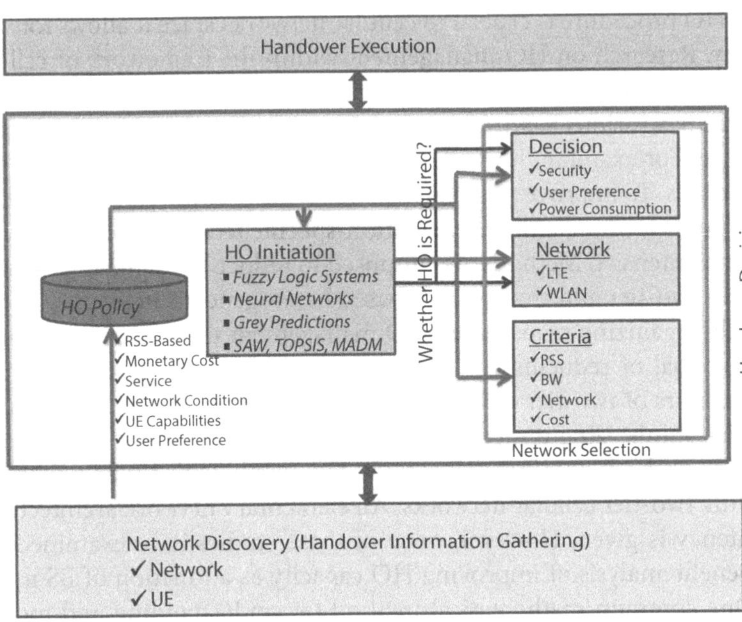

Figure 2.3 Vertical handover decision process.

2.2 Handover Management in 6G

2.2.1 History of Handover System

Global demand for transportation services has increased as the use of smartphones, tablets, and other portable electronic devices continues to surge in popularity. Micro, pico, and even nano base stations (BSs) have been deployed as cellular networks have shrunk in response to the ever-increasing need for data transmission capacity. For instance, 6G, the next generation of cellular networks, requires a capacity increase of a factor of a thousand. Evolutionary heterogeneous network densification is hypothesized to be the means through which this will be accomplished. It is advisable to install numerous BSs in the same region while minimizing the footprint of each BS in order to enhance spatial-spectral efficiency and offer extra capacity.

While increasing network density may increase capacity, it also increases the frequency with which handovers must occur. It is common practice to ignore the HO rate as a negative consequence of BS density. Because of the higher frequency of such unwelcome interruptions and the associated signaling expenditure, increasing the HO rate may limit or even erase the expected capacity increases from network densification. As a result, the HO price has to be included in any analysis of network density.

The HO procedure is crucial to cellular networks since it allows for user mobility. Research on HO management within the framework of cellular networks has, therefore, always been highly valued. The cellular network literature has various lectures on modeling and optimizing handover performance. For example, stay periods are specified for both hexagonal and circular cells. To improve the HOs that are vertical, we provide an analytical model predicated on an implementation-specific technique for modifying the signal intensity. Methods are proposed to reduce the signaling expense of HO in two-tier and cloud-RAN–based heterogeneous networks.

A self-organizing maps-based HO management technique is described with the goal of reducing the number of indoor HOs that are unnecessary for users of two-tier cellular networks. Research presented here indicates that minimizing unnecessary vertical HOs may have a considerable influence on both measures, especially for people with limited speed in downlink two-tier cellular networks. An elementary network architecture's HO latency is given. However, none of these studies have examined the cost-benefit analysis of improving HO capacity as a function of BS intensity. One common mathematical method for understanding and modeling cellular networks is stochastic geometry. It may be used to evaluate performance in terms of BS intensity and other physical layer metrics. It is researched how to increase throughput for stationary users in cellular networks modeled using PPP. Poisson cluster process (PCP) is added to the model as a special case.

The HO rate for PPP cellular networks is defined variously depending on whether the situation is single-tier or multi-tier. PCP is the subject of analysis. Recent hypotheses on phantom cells and their HO rate are discussed. None of these studies, however, examine the combined effect of network densification (intensity of BSs) on HO costs or throughput. We look at how much of a hit HO typically takes on throughput.

Of particular relevance are promoting the worst BS association to minimize handovers and avoiding particular HOs along the user's path at fast speeds. Although it compromises the best connection approach, it has been shown that skipping may boost user performance at high speeds. Modifications are made to the skipping approach to make it compatible with multi-level architectures. On the other hand, the topology-agnostic nature of the provided HO skipping algorithms may lead to less efficient skip selection. For example, if the cell size (coverage area) and/or the trajectory's orientation within the cell are both consistent, the user should be able to utilize a special HO skipping technique provided by your network to avoid attaching to every other BS along its route.

Because of this, a BS that can be skipped might potentially spend more time in its cell than a BS that cannot. By rerouting the user's route, it may become possible for the user to avoid crucial HOs in favor of BSs that handle a significant portion of the user's trip. Therefore, future cellular networks will need the encoding of more sophisticated HO skipping mechanisms. In this study, we present intelligent HO management techniques that leverage user trajectory predictions and topological awareness in single- and two-tier downlink cellular networks.

The recommended methods use the cell's dimensions and/or the trajectory's position inside the cells to determine whether or not to skip HOs. Stochastic geometry methods are used to evaluate the suggested systems' effectiveness. In particular, we examine two network situations where PPP is utilized to abstract cellular networks: one where macro BSs are layered over PCP tiny BSs and another where PPP is employed to abstract a cellular network that is single-tiered. We then analyze the effect of HO delay on user throughput in the two network setups using Monte Carlo simulations, highlighting the benefits and potency of the recommended techniques. These results highlight the HO conundrum of the best connection plan at high speeds in crowded cellular situations. When traveling at speeds of 30 km/h, the user throughput achieved by using the recommended skipping approaches is greater than that achieved by the always best-connected strategy. With regard to (w.r.t.) optimal connection, the suggested approaches demonstrate rate increases of up to 8%, and for a monorail operating at the typical downtown speed of 100 km/h, they demonstrate rate increases of up to 23%. It is believed that the benefits of BSs grow in proportion to their intensity.

2.2.2 Handover Process

The best-serving base station (BS) should always be selected by HO, regardless of the location of the user's equipment (UE). The received signal strength (RSS) guideline makes it easy and popular to find the best serving base station. The user equipment (UE) will switch its relationship to the new BS since it has a better RSS if the user moves from the current BS's coverage area into an area served by a different BS. To choose the best serving BS in today's increasingly varied cellular networks, several new metrics have been devised, such as load balancing, latency, and throughput. The UE's relationship to mobility will change regardless of the selection rule, and the BS density will cause the HO rate to rise. This suggests that a HO's price is directly related to the quantity of BSs that are in use. The three primary phases of HO are inception, planning, and actualization. The user provides the serving BS with measurements of reference signals from neighboring BSs during the activation phase. For example, the reference signal received power (RSRP) and reference signal received quality (RSRPQ) are two of the metrics included in the 4G LTE signal measurement report (RSRQ). The HO may also be activated by reports of downlink and/or uplink signal measurements. During this period, signals are used to communicate between the target BS, the admission controller, and the serving BS.

In light of the network's established criteria, the admittance controller will determine whether or not to start the HO. Following the fulfillment of the HO requirements, the user will try to use the random-access channel (RACH) to synchronize with and get access to the target BS, disconnecting the serving BS concurrently. A confirmation message will be sent to the network by the UE once it has synchronized with the targeted BS. This will show that the HO was performed successfully. Mobile user performance is negatively impacted by the aforementioned HO procedure owing to the signaling cost incurred by the user, the serving BS, the target BS, and the core network. These interruptions happen more often when the BS is stronger and the person is moving more faster. Each HO delay (the time it takes from the beginning of planning to the end of carrying out an action) might be rather lengthy.

HO skipping was created to reduce the impact of such HO disruptions in densely packed environments and/or at high velocities. Remembering that people with high levels of mobility may be moving in crowded areas, like crowded cities with elevated roads and monorails, is crucial. The HO technique is run fewer times when the optimal BS connections are skipped. As a result, the serving BSs may remain online for an extended period of time, hence decreasing the HO delay. For example, ideal signal-to-interference-plus-noise ratio (SINR) linkages lose their trajectory due to HO skipping in an RSS-based association scheme with universal frequency reuse. There is a potential that the SINR will drop considerably during the blackout (BK) time if the user chooses to forgo the BS with the weakest signal in favor of the BS with the strongest signal.

With non-coherent cooperative BS service, the signal-to-noise ratio (SNR) may be improved during power outages by means of coordinated multipoint (CoMP) transmission and interference cancellation (IC) at the nearest BS. It is important to note that the following skipping techniques all rely on having previously determined, either directly or *via* an iterative trajectory estimation procedure, the trajectory within the footprint of the target BS.

The first method is called location-aware HO skipping, and it works by figuring out which HOs on the way to the desired BS the user may safely bypass. As a result, the HO will not try to associate with the BS if the minimum distance between the user's trajectory and the BS is larger than some threshold L. The user may avoid BSs where the trajectory completely follows the cell border by selecting an appropriate threshold L.

The second technique is called "HO Skipping with Cell Size Information," which allows users to bypass HOs and connect straight to BSs whose service area, or footprint, is smaller than a predetermined threshold. A size-aware skipping technique modifies the cell stay length according to the size of the BS footprint in order to reduce crucial disruptions. Thus, it enables people to focus on the larger cells and overlook the smaller ones. Thanks to a number of network design tools used by cellular operators, like Mentum Planet and Aircom Asset, it is straightforward to presume that the network knows the coverage zones of all base stations (BSs). Because these techniques take into account several parameters such as antenna characteristics, BS configuration, location, and clutter, cell sizes are predictable.

Finally, because location-aware skipping and size-aware skipping are unable to accurately represent the amount of time spent in a particular cell, hybrid HO skipping is used. Therefore, combining the two methods offers a more precise estimate of the cell dwell time, which might result in better decisions and more efficiency from the HO. Thus, the hybrid HO skipping method considers the user's location and the cell's size to decide which BS to avoid. In other words, the HO call is made taking into account the user's position and the cell tower's service area.

2.2.3 Single-Tier Networks with Handover Skipping Process

In this work, we model the BS locations in a two-dimensional, intensity-homogeneous space PPP in order to analyze the downlink of a simplex cellular network. It is intended for all base stations (BSs) to have the same transmission power (P). In general, a route loss model assumes that the path loss exponent is greater than 2. Without compromising coverage, we concentrate on a single test mobile user and rank all BSs based on their instantaneous distances from that user. The Slivnyak-Mecke theorem shows that the test user's performance is equal to that of all other users in the PPP.

Infrared refers to the user's distance from the kth point; if the assumption is invalid, then the inequalities (R1, R2, R3, ...) must hold consistently. In particular, we assume that the channel gains follow a Rayleigh distribution with variance constant (h exp(1)). We examine the effectiveness of a solitary frequency channel while taking into account a strategy for universal frequency reuse. We examine the movement of users at a constant speed v along an arbitrary extended path, presuming that an HO is initiated upon the user's arrival at the destination BS's Voronoi cell. First, we determine the coverage probability for each HO skipping scenario using the simulation settings listed in Table 2.1. The average throughput and HO cost are then determined.

2.2.3.1 Coverage Probability

To be covered, there must be a larger than T threshold in the signal-to-noise ratio (SNR) experienced by the test users. Coverage is more likely to occur in the following case:

$$C_{BC} = \mathbb{P}\left\{ \frac{Ph_1R_1^{-\eta}}{\sum_{i\in\Phi\backslash b_1} Ph_iR_i^{-\eta} + \sigma^2} > T \right\}$$

Since serving BSs do not increase the overall interference, the closest BS (b1) is not included in the list of interfering BSs in (1). During the blackout scenario, the closest BS is not providing service to the testing user because of HO skipping. Since the serving BS is no longer the closest in this

Table 2.1 Parameter specifications for the PPP-based cellular network simulation.

Parameter	Value	Parameter	Value
Overall Bandwidth W:	10 MHz	Path loss exponent η:	4
BS Intensity λ:	50 BS/km^2	HO delay d:	1 s
Size Threshold s:	1.28/λ km^2	Location Threshold L:	2.3/λ m
Hybrid Threshold s, L:	0.38/λ km^2, 1.8/λ m	Tx Power P:	1 watt

scenario, the test user must choose whether to stay connected or move on to the next target BS. During the blackout time, the next target BS (bt) will be represented by Rs and Rt throughout the blackout time. The likelihood of coverage during a blackout using IC resources is then calculated, including scenarios with and without BS participation.

$$C_{BK(IC)}^{(1)^-} \text{ and } C_{BK(IC)}^{(2)},$$

respectively.

$$C_{BK(IC)}^{(1)} = \mathbb{P}\left\{\frac{Ph_x \min(R_s, R_t) - \eta}{\sum_{i\epsilon\Phi\backslash b_1, b_x} Ph_i R_i^{-\eta} + \sigma^2} > T\right\}$$

in which the subscript x = s if $R_s < R_t$ and x = t otherwise

$$C_{BK(IC)}^{(2)} = \mathbb{P}\left\{\frac{|\sqrt{P}g_x R_s^{-\eta/2} + \sqrt{P}g_t R_s^{-\eta/2}|^2}{\sum_{i\epsilon\Phi\backslash b_1, b_s, b_t} Ph_i R_i^{-\eta} + \sigma^2} > T\right\}$$

where the complex Gaussian channels gx and gt have unit variance and zero means, respectively, which aptly depicts the incoherent nature of CoMP transmission. Recall that the bypassed BS is represented by b1 and that the total interference was reduced by IC from its signal intensity. Using links, we give a mathematical interpretation of the coverage probability for the optimal case. We also present a mathematical characterization of the coverage likelihood for each of the HO skipping (i.e., blackout) situations that we offer. However, because of the Voronoi cell's unpredictable shape

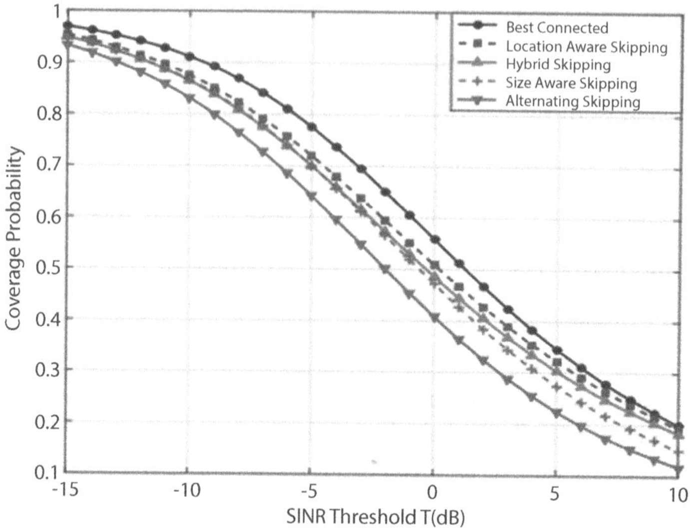

Figure 2.4 Coverage probability for both HO skipping and best-connected situations as a function of SINR threshold.

and the trajectory's unexpected location and orientation inside it, tractable analysis of the suggested HO skipping strategies is quite challenging. Using Monte Carlo simulations we can do it very easily & precisely.

The accuracy of these simulations is validated by the underlying mathematical analysis. Coverage probability diagrams which depicts in Figure 2.4, both with and without average coverage probability along the user's path, are presented as expected. This coverage probability drop, however, might be avoided with a cunning skipping strategy that takes the user's surroundings and the target item's size into account.

By comparing the results, we can quantify how much BS collaboration increases coverage probability. In particular, unlike location-aware and size-aware systems, the distance and size constraints used by the hybrid approach are more lenient. As a result, the coverage probability may be the same, but there may be more HO skips than in location- and size-aware algorithms. Remember that the coverage probability is the only indicator of the HO skipping's detrimental impact. The following part provides an objective assessment of HO skipping by taking the cost of HOs into account.

2.2.3.2 *Handover Cost*

We examine how the best-connected and HO skipping pricing differ from one another. Here, the normalized HO delay is used to explain the HO cost D as

$$D = \min(H_t \times d, 1)$$

The handoff delay, measured in seconds, is d. As a result, the cost of the switch time is lost along 1 as a result of the radio connection being moved from the serving BS to the destination BS during the changeover signaling procedure. The unitless number D indicates the user's trajectory. Remember that if Ht d 1, the handover delay is shorter than the cell dwell time. D is set to 1 since the entire time is spent on pointless handover signaling. In a PPP-based, single-tier network, the HO rate can be described using a conventional trajectory and mobility model.

$$H_t = \frac{4\upsilon}{\pi}\sqrt{\lambda}$$

By multiplying the user velocity by an HO density factor—HO density is the number of HOs per unit length—the HO rate is calculated through simulation. One can calculate the handoff rate per unit of journey distance by dividing the total number of handoffs by the whole trajectory length. Consequently, D may also be written as

$$D = H_l \times \upsilon \times d$$

Micrograms per square meter (Hl) is the HO density.

We give the HO cost of the best-linked and skipping HO algorithms. Due to the fact that HO costs increase with HO amount, the best connection link has a higher HO cost than HO skipping techniques. Figure 2.6 depicts the HO cost conventional and skipping, alternating HO skipping can complete the most skips since it shows the lowest feasible handover cost.

However, since it is not concerned with the underlying architecture, the alternative skipping may make inefficient skipping judgments. It is possible that knowing your location and network size may help you make better judgments, even if it means shelling out more money for your HO in return for wider coverage. You should emphasize the advantages of the tactics for skipping rather than the negatives. We then assess how each skipping strategy affects end-user throughput, both positively and negatively.

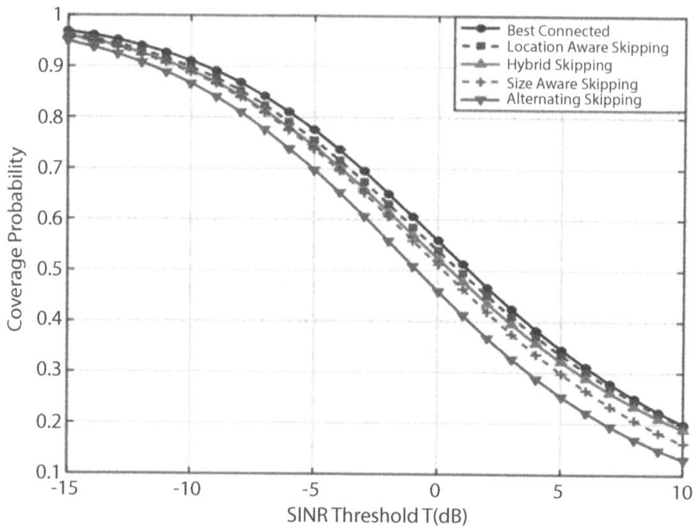

Figure 2.5 Coverage probability vs SINR threshold in best-connected CoMP transmission.

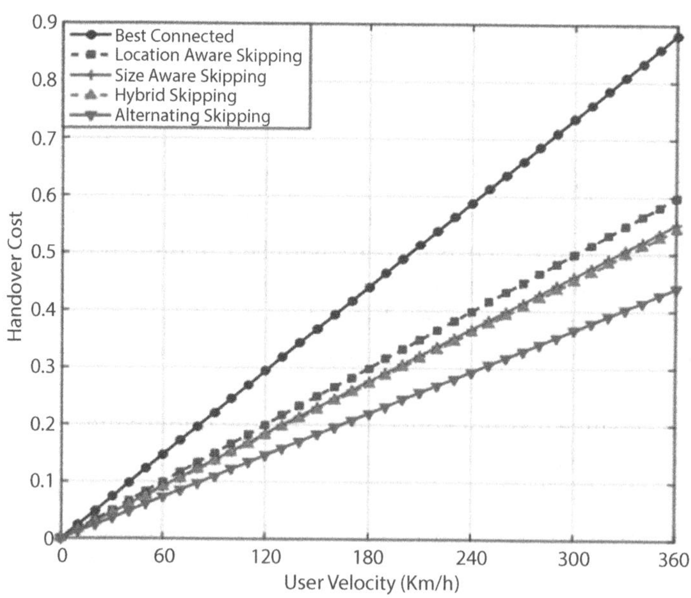

Figure 2.6 Handover cost for conventional and HO skipping cases.

2.2.3.3 Average Throughput

We are able to investigate the relationship between the cost of HOs and the capacity increase enforced by network densification by looking through the prism of the average throughput of telecom carriers. Here, we measure how different HO rates and HO skip counts affect the typical user's throughput through a range of techniques. The definition of "average throughput" T is defined as:

$$T = WR(1-D).$$

where W is the whole bandwidth and R is the ergodic spectral efficiency; the Shannon capacity formula reads

$$R = \mathbb{E}\left(\ln(1+\text{SINR})\right)$$

The definition is applied in simulations to determine the spectral efficiency with and without IC support under HO skipping and optimally connected conditions. Using the aforementioned spectral efficiencies, one may calculate throughput graphs. The cost of HO clearly changes as the velocity increases, as seen in the image.

Skipping systems, like the one seen below, may be used to reduce the negative effects of HO. In particular, HO skipping that considers location operates better than any other technique when traveling at slower speeds (less than 30 km/h). At its fastest, the hybrid skipping scheme is 135 km/h quicker than the location-aware scheme and 45 km/h faster than the best-connected association.

Changes to the minimum distance L and cell size s can alter the hybrid curve's steepness. The least effective of the three strategies is size-aware HO skipping, despite significant improvements over the topology-agnostic (i.e., alternating HO skipping) strategy.

2.3 Two-Tier Network Handover Skipping

Modern cellular networks are increasingly using a multi-tier architecture, with micro BSs positioned on top of the macro BSs, to offer coverage in densely populated areas. As hotspots typically gather in popular and social areas, a PCP offers a more accurate depiction of the minor BSs.

To produce the PCP, a large number of cluster points are substituted for the points in a parent PPP. The Figure 2.7 describes for PCP-based two-tier networks with P1 = 1 watt, P2 = 0.1 watts, λp = 4 BS/km2, λc = 12 BS/km2, d = 1 s, r = 0.6 km, η1 = η2 = 4, average throughput vs. user velocity. The PCP class is determined by the position of the cluster points with respect to the parents. A constant point process with intensity p generates the parent points. Points with parents indicate large tier-1 BSs, while points with children represent tiny tier-2 nodes.

The total network BS intensity reaches a new all-time high of '= pc + p. To be on the safe side, let us assume that the BSs on the ith and second levels of the tier both transmit with the same power.

A power-law with exponentiation is applied to model route losses for i>2i > 2i>2. Channel gains are assumed to follow a Rayleigh distribution, with a constant variance over time. To represent the coverage areas accurately, a weighted Voronoi tessellation is employed, accounting for the transmit power differences between macro and small base stations.

In order to evaluate the skipping solutions and determine the HO cost for the two-tiered network under examination, we employ the same technique to analyze user throughput. We conduct our study for a user traveling at v. We consider an RSS-based association where the user starts the HO by going into the target BS's Voronoi cell. This section focuses on location-aware skipping because of its better performance. In particular, we contrast the consistently best-linked technique and the location-aware skipping strategy at various distance constraints.

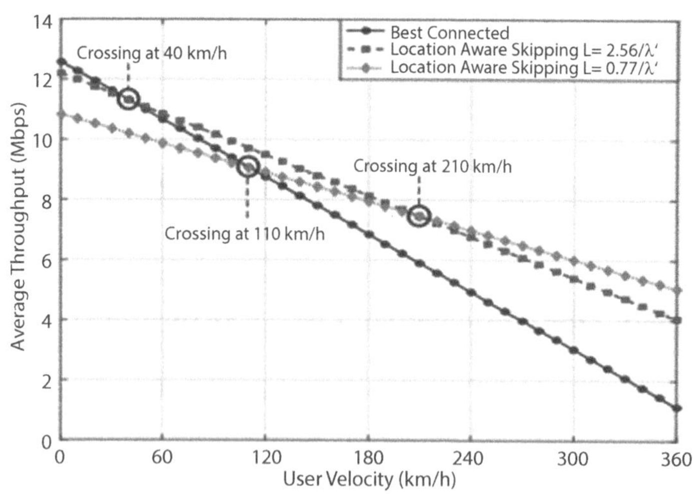

Figure 2.7 For PCP-based two-tier networks with P1 = 1 watt, P2 = 0.1 watts, λp = 4 BS/km^2, λc = 12 BS/km^2, d = 1 s, r = 0.6 km, η1 = η2 = 4, average throughput vs. user velocity.

Table 2.2 All situations in NATS/SEC/HZ have spectral efficiency.

Scenario	Non-IC	IC
Best connected (R_{BC})	1.49	-
Location Aware (R_{LA})	1.40	1.45
Hybrid (R_{HB})	1.36	1.42
Size Aware (R_{SA})	1.21	1.28
Alternating (R_{AL})	1.02	1.11

Refs. [2, 7, 13, 28, 29, 34]

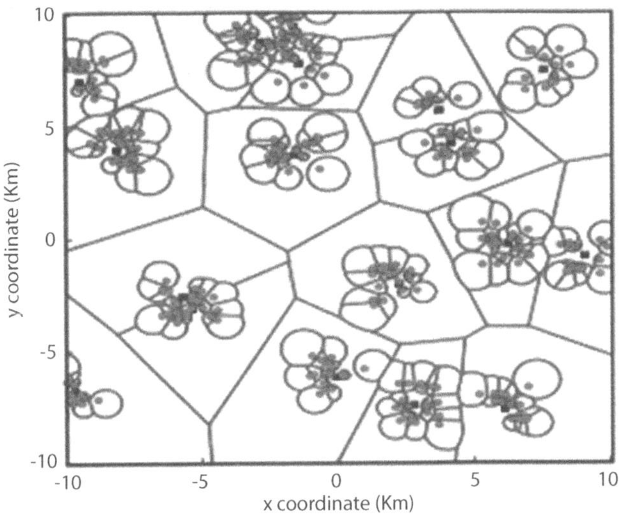

Figure 2.8 A two-tier PCP downlink cellular network with weighted Voronoi tessellation, where r = 2 km, λp = 0.04 BS/km², λc = 1 BS/km², P1 = 1 watt, and P2 = 0.5P1 watts. Femto BSs are shown as red circles and macro BSs are displayed as black squares.

We first compute the spectrum efficiency, HO costs, and coverage probabilities before assessing the user throughput. The findings suggest that the suggested smart handover technique may boost throughput by 47%. Figure 2.8 describe with a two-tier PCP downlink cellular network with weighted Voronoi tessellation, where r = 2 km, λp = 0.04 BS/km2, λc = 1 BS/km2, P1 = 1 watt, and P2 = 0.5P1 watts. Femto BSs are shown as red circles and macro BSs are displayed as black squares. It has been shown that at speeds more than 210 km/h, a smaller distance threshold for location awareness is more effective than

Table 2.3 Tabular settings for the network's spectral efficiency in NATS/SEC/HZ for PCP.

Scenario	Non-IC	IC
Best connected (R_{BC})	1.26	-
Location Aware $L = 2.56/\lambda'$ (R_{LA})	1.18	1.22
Location Aware $L = 0.77/\lambda'$ (R_{LA})	1.01	1.08

a bigger one. Table 2.2 and Table 2.3 shows the scenario for location aware and size aware in details. Due to the fact that the additional HO cost only appears at high mobility and can be made up for by raising the number of skips when the distance threshold L is reduced, high mobility is the optimal scenario. Keep in mind that the clustering approach used here is only an illustration; similar results and insights might be obtained using a different clustering strategy.

This chapter employs 6G technology to solve these problems in two significant ways. In this section, we dissected software-defined networking (SDN), the foundational technology for 6G networks. In addition, we explain the OpenFlow protocol, which was developed to improve communication between a network's control and data layers.

Our innovations in network functions virtualization, software-defined networking, and edge computing platforms may have a big influence on

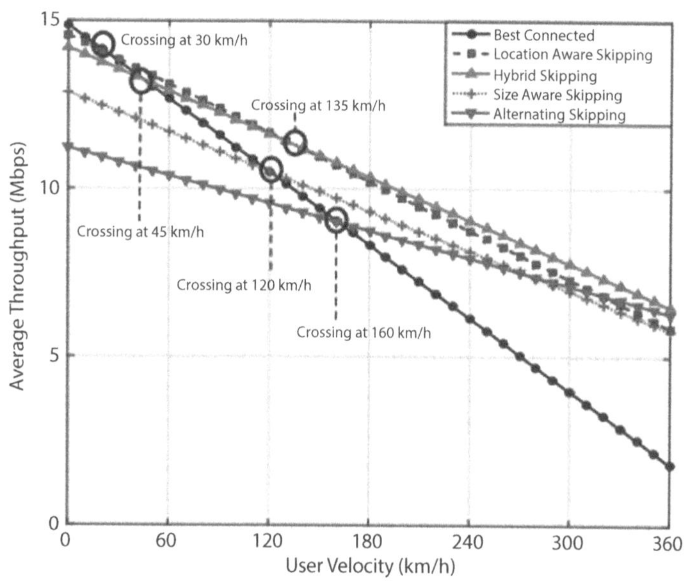

Figure 2.9 Average throughput vs. user velocity for conventional and HO skipping cases.

the next generation of 6G network architecture. 6G, sometimes known as the "nervous system" of the digital society and digital economy, may adopt the suggested design, functions, and procedures as the "de facto" answer. Through 6G's enabling of new service models like "fully immersive experience," "context information," and "anything as a service," the economy will grow more extensively and sustainably, and society as a whole will be better prepared to tackle its most pressing issues. Our proposed system appears to be both practically and technically realistic in order to achieve this goal, as it can deliver the necessary ultrahigh dependability and low latency. Let us conclude by emphasizing that the opinions shared here are solely those of the writers and do not reflect those of their employer or any other group.

Research on a quicker and more dependable foundation for 6G wireless networks has been demonstrated in numerous studies. The predominant technique for delivering virtualization in recent years has been software-defined networking, or SDN. This study analyzes a wide range of recent research in this area to determine the most effective methods for improving this system's many parts. Meanwhile, detailed explanations of the recommended architectures and rule sets from each study have been provided. Since the investigation into 6G is only getting started, new opportunities for creating such a system may emerge. The 6G network will consist of a wide variety of devices, programs, and hardware. Sharing limited LAN resources like radio waves and data transfer speeds across an ever-increasing user base is a problem. There has to be more study done in order to build a highly flexible network.

This research question cannot be answered without first understanding how network services are provisioned in SDN. Quality-of-service (QoS) delivery in SDN is the primary emphasis of this in-depth look at the software-defined networking (SDN) paradigm. Data plane resources are managed differently in SDN than in traditional networks. Creating QoS-aware services in SDN is simplified by well-developed QoS setup APIs.

In order to show how SDN may be utilized to simplify QoS provisioning *via* programmability, the concept of QoS slicing was introduced as an example application. In order to be useful in large networks, QoS provisioning through SDN requires an easily scalable architecture. It has been highlighted in the literature that although SDN has numerous benefits, it does have certain drawbacks when it comes to scalability. According to the author, the biggest problem on the data plane is the inability to store flow tables in forwarding devices. This severely restricts the scope of possible network configurations for SDN. Combining traffic flows is a tried and true method that may help us get around this problem. The author states that restricting controller performance is the key difficulty when it comes to achieving scalability in SDN at the control plane level. In Chapter 5, we offer a method for overcoming the performance limitations of the SDN controller by fine-tuning the control functions' operating parameters. Unlike traditional vertical or horizontal scaling methods, this breakthrough idea in SDN does not rely on external processes in the controller to provide scalability.

The proposed replacement may even coexist with current standards while being gradually brought in. By resolving the two key issues highlighted in the SDN design, the author thinks that an SDN-based QoS provisioning architecture can scale to the level of very large and complex networks. The difficulty involved in deploying and maintaining the various QoS approaches used in legacy networks has contributed to their failure. To address this shortcoming, researchers have been exploring methods to centralize QoS setting management inside network management. Thus, there arose a need for management based on policies. Because of its programmability, SDN is well-suited for the adoption of policy-based management, which in turn reduces the complexity of managing a network's infrastructure by demonstrating how an SDN deployment for policy-based management may completely remove the need for human intervention and further automate network administration.

The provides further support for this idea by outlining a policy framework based on models for managing networks across a whole ecosystem adopting the SDN paradigm may, therefore, enable automated frameworks for policy-based management, saving the state-of-the-art QoS approaches now in use shows that SDN may be used in a novel hybrid EPS/OCS network architecture to create smart algorithms for traffic planning with the ultimate objective of improving network resource efficiency. As an added bonus, the algorithms enable traffic categorization, which is crucial for establishing assured QoS. Last but not least, SDN's centralized control logic allows for and even promotes the adoption of global optimization methods, which in turn leads to better resource utilization and QoS for the network's services. This chapter includes research and conclusions that back up the author's hypothesis that SDN may significantly simplify QoS provisioning for very large and complex networks.

Consequently, there are strong reasons for network service providers to move away from overprovisioning network resources and toward quality-of-service solutions based on software-defined networking. Large, recognizable companies like Google are already using SDN to improve the scalability and efficiency of their networks and operations *via* the use of automation. Notable progress is being made in both commercial and academic SDN settings. This chapter discusses research that was undertaken at a time when it was difficult to provide recommendations that did not rely on out-of-date results or technology due to the ever-increasing number of standards (such as OF), open source projects (such as Floodlight), and publications. Therefore, NSPs should consider the pace of SDN advances when choosing which SDN technologies to use in their infrastructure.

Densifying the 6G network with small cells is how they plan to meet demand. However, because of the limited coverage areas of tiny cells, this method requires frequent handovers for the mobile nodes. The fast-moving mobile nodes suffer from the detrimental effects of frequent handover due to higher overhead and poorer average throughput. Figure 2.9 shows the average throughput graph. To lessen the load on the environment and the expense of switching between networks, this paper presents a method of allocating resources to mobile users in two-tier systems. The "association preference factor," a novel notion proposed here, is one of the two goals of the optimization model. Both carbon emissions and the network operator's electricity expenses have been decreased thanks to the approach. Results from a hypothetical setting using this method showed lower changeover costs, throughput, and power usage. According to the results, the suggested strategy has a good chance of outperforming the others. When compared to other possible solutions, this heuristic one performs better.

This paper illuminates the drawbacks of dense cellular networks that result from the high changeover rate that is required. This paper investigates the slowdown in average throughput that happens when a cellular network's user base grows. Consequently, topology-aware HO skipping is suggested by the study as a simple method of handling HOs. In order to eliminate pointless HOs along the route, the suggested techniques take the user's position and/or cell size into consideration. The proposed methods are tested in two types of cellular networks: a PCP two-tier and a PPP single-tier. According to the recommended skipping models, the average throughput for users traveling between 30 and 240 km/h at a BS intensity of 50 BS/km^2 is up to 47% higher than the best RSS-based connected approach. BS intensity is supposed to increase gains.

The authors of this paper detail the planning, implementation, and modeling of an ANN-FL handoff system. Fuzzy logic, artificial neural networks (ANN), and a hybrid of the two were all used in this protocol to determine the best course of action during handovers. There is some evidence to suggest that we may enhance efficiency in choosing the target eNB and decrease handover latencies if we combine fuzzy logic with an adaptive neuronetwork. There was reduced packet loss, fewer ping-pong handovers, and fewer handovers overall using the new protocol. However, the handover success rate was high and the failure rate was low using the proposed protocol. Using the planned protocol, the highest delay was 0.049 seconds and the lowest was 0.019 seconds.

As a result, both the mutual authentication and handover signaling handover latencies in the protocol were less than 200 ms, which is specified by the International Telecommunications Union. Its resilience to desynchronization and session hijacking ensures the safety of both signaling and user traffic. Not only do 6G and beyond networks have to cope with frequent handovers and the resulting need for quicker handovers but they also have to transfer sensitive data from a broad range of compatible devices, making security and low latency particularly crucial. A total of six input parameters were employed to construct the proposed protocol, which made deriving the membership function more challenging. Therefore, it is crucial for future studies in this area to look at techniques that may simplify the membership function derivation procedure.

To meet the requirements of 6G networks, the next generation of mobile network architecture will need to include cloud and virtualization *via* SDN and NFV. This will substantially aid the transition from 4G to 6G. We provide a high-level overview of the vision for future 6G networks based on SDN core concepts and present the basics of SDN, such as network programmability, SDN design components, and the OpenFlow protocol. We also discuss the benefits of deploying IPv6 through SDN in a 6G environment, including improved scalability, flexibility, and management. Then, we go through the many ways in which SDN might improve the 6G network's quality of service, and finally, we wrap up with a brief summary of where we are right now.

In this chapter, we investigated the possibility of using network slicing to implement a handoff that is driven by the network in the future generation of radio provides a variety of strategies for handoff in cellular networks of the future, each with an explanation of its potential use and a comparison to others. This dissertation took into consideration system components as well as user requirements. The continuation of the discussion began in the previous paragraph. FeMBMS was discussed as a potential mechanism for explaining the results of this research since it is responsible for physically separating the channels and giving them their own dedicated bandwidth. The strategy used and the functions that execute it are outlined, and spectrum consumption is examined with the use of the QoE performance indicator.

The findings revealed that 6G capabilities fall short of guaranteeing dependable service and stable networks. Therefore, in addition to network slicing and FeMBMS, we also need network-driven handoff. Since it was planned for 8,000 users and the global average QoE was 66.61%, the work accomplished is scalable. The number of contributors is also a significant element in deciding the quality of the final product. Depending on the state of the network and the ever-increasing demand for the service, a network-driven handover may not always be the best course of action. Increasing global QoE values necessitates planning for handover as well as adding the stream to the necessary cell. Pick the one that will give you the most satisfying experience.

Bibliography

1. Abdullah, R.M., Abdullah, A., Hamid, O.M., Subramanian, S., A network selection algorithm based on enhanced access router discovery in heterogeneous wireless networks. *Wireless Pers. Commun.*, 77, 3, 1733–1750, 2014.
2. Singhal, C. and De, S., Energy-efficient and QoE-aware TV broadcast in next-generation heterogeneous networks. *IEEE Commun. Mag.*, 54, 12, 142–150, 2016.
3. Tamijetchelvy, R. and Sivaradje, G., Analysis of IEEE 802.21 media independent handover with mobility management protocols for handover optimization. *Comput. Electr. Eng.*, 48, 119–134, 2015.
4. Vasu, K., Maheshwari, S., Mahapatra, S., Kumar, C.S., Energy and QoS aware fuzzy-top vertical handover decision algorithm for heterogeneous wireless' networks'. *IET Netw.*, 2, 3, 103–114, 2013b.
5. Vasudeva, K., Simsek, M., López-Pérez, D., Güvenç, I., Analysis of handover failures in heterogeneous networks with fading. *IEEE Trans. Veh. Technol.*, 66, 7, 6060–6074, 2017.
6. Trestian, R., Ormond, O., Muntean, G.M., Performance evaluation of MADM-based methods for network selection in a multimedia wireless environment. *J. Wireless Netw.*, 21, 5, 1745–1763, 2015, Springer.
7. Tariq, A., and Saquib, M., Analytical framework for WLANCellular Voice Handover Evaluation. *IEEE Trans. Mob. Comput.*, 12, 447–460, 2013.
8. Naeini, V.S., Performance analysis of WiMAX-based wireless mesh networks using an M/D/1 queuing model. *Int. J. Wireless Mobile Comput.*, 7, 1, 35–47, 2014.
9. Narayanan, V.A., Rajeswari, A., Sureshkumar, V., An intelligent vertical handover decision algorithm for wireless heterogeneous networks. *Am. J. Appl. Sci.*, 11, 5, 732, 2014.
10. Moscholios, I.D., Kallos, G.A., Vassilakis, V.G., Logothetis, M.D., Congestion probabilities in CDMA-based networks supporting batched Poisson input traffic. *Wireless Pers. Commun.*, 79, 2, 1163–1186, 2014.
11. Miyim, A.M., Ismai, L.M., Nordin, R., Vertical handover solutions over LTE-advanced wireless networks: An Overview. *Wireless Pers. Commun.*, 77, 4, 3051–3079, 2014.

12. Mehra, L. and Gupta, M.K., Fuzzy neural networks in vertical handover technology for next generation in wireless networks. *Int. J. Adv. Res. Comput. Sci.*, 4, 3, 145–150, 2013.
13. Mahardhika, G., Ismail, M., Nordin, R., Vertical handover decision algorithm using multicriteria metrics in heterogeneous wireless network. *J. Comput. Netw. Commun.*, 2015, 539750, 1–8, 2015.
14. Ma, D. and Ma, M., A QoS oriented vertical handoff scheme for WiMAX/wlan overlay networks. *IEEE Trans. Parallel Distrib. Syst.*, 23, 4, 598–606, 2012.
15. Louta, M. and Bellavista, P., Bringing always best connectivity vision a step closer: challenges and perspectives. *IEEE Commun. Mag.*, 51, 2, 158–166, 2013.
16. Lim, J.M.Y., Chow, C.O., Ishii, H., Intelligent handover across ubiquitous network. *Int. J. Innov. Manage. Technol.*, 4, 3, 341, 2013.
17. Li, X., Liu, F., Feng, Z., Xu, G., Fu, Z., A novel optimized vertical handover framework for seamless networking integration in cyber-enabled systems. *Future Gener. Comput. Syst.*, 79, 1, 417–430, 2018.
18. Kumar, A., Sengupta, J., Liu, Y.F., 3GPP LTE: the future of mobile broadband. *Wireless Pers. Commun.*, 62, 3, 671–686, 2012.
19. Kirsal, Y., Ever, E., Kocyigit, A., Gemikonakli, O., Mapp, G., Modelling and analysis of vertical handover in highly mobile environments. *J. Supercomputing*, 71, 12, 4352–4380, 2015.
20. Kim, Y., Pack, S., Kang, C.G., Park, S., An enhanced information server for seamless vertical handover in IEEE 802.21 MIH networks. *Comput. Netw.*, 55, 1, 147–158, 2011b.
21. Khattab, O. and Alani, O., IAM4 VHO:New approach to improve seamless vertical handover in heterogeneous wireless networks. *Int. J. Comput. Netw. Commun. (IJCNC)*, 5, 3, 53–63, 2013.
22. Khattab, O. and Alani, O., A survey on media independent handover (MIH) and IP multimedia subsystem (IMS) in heterogeneous wireless networks. *Int. J. Wireless Inf. Netw.*, 20, 2, 215–228, 2013.
23. Khan, M. and Han, K., A review of handover techniques in wireless Ad hoc networks based on IEEE 802.21 media independent handover standard. *IETE Tech. Rev.*, 31, 5, 353- 361, 2014.
24. Khalaf, G.A.F.M. and Badr, H.Z., A comprehensive approach to vertical handoff in heterogeneous wireless networks. *J. King Saud Univ. Comput. Inf. Sci.*, 25, 2, 197–205, 2013.
25. Kaleem, F., Mehbodniya, A., Islam, A., Yen, K.K., Adachi, F., Dynamic target wireless network selection technique using fuzzy linguistic variables. *China Commun.*, 10, 1, 1–16, 2013.
26. Jyotsna,Manisha, PG.N.N., SINR based vertical handoff algorithms: a survey. *Int. J. Comput. Sci. Netw.*, 1, 5, 1–5, 2012.
27. Jimaa, S., Chai, K.K., Chen, Y., Alfadhl, Y., LTE-A an overview and future research areas. In Wireless and Mobile Computing. *Networking and*

Communications (WiMob), IEEE 7th International Conference, pp. 395–399, 2011.
28. Hussain, R., Malik, S.A., Abrar, S., Riaz, R.A., Khan, S.A., Minimizing unnecessary handovers in a heterogeneous network environment. *PrzeglądElektrotechniczny (Electrical Review)*, 88, 6, 300–303, 2012b.
29. Huang, K.L., Chi, K.H., Wang, J.T., Tseng, C.C., A fast authentication scheme for WiMAX–WLAN vertical handover. *Springer Wireless Pers. Commun.*, 71, 1, 555-575, 2013.
30. Hindia, M.N., Reza, A.W., Noordin, K.A., Kausar, A.S.M.Z., Enhanced Seamless Handover Algorithm for WiMAX and LTE Roaming. *Adv. Electr. Comput. Eng.*, 14, 4, 9–14, 2014, doi:10.4316/AECE.2014.04002.
31. He, D., Chi, C., Chan, S., Chen, C., Bu, J., Yin, M., A simple and robust vertical handoff algorithm for heterogeneous wireless mobile networks. *Springer Wireless Pers. Commun.*, 59, 361–373, 2011.
32. Guohua, Z., Legg, P., Hui, G., A network controlled handover mechanism and its optimization in LTE heterogeneous networks, in: *Wireless Communications and Networking Conference (WCNC)*, IEEE, pp. 1915–1919, 20132013.
33. Goudarzi, S., Hassan, W.H., Anisi, M.H., Soleymani, A., Sookhak, M., Khan, M.K., Hashim, A.H.A., Zareei, M., ABC-PSO for vertical handover in heterogeneous wireless networks. *Neurocomputing*, 256, 1, 63–81, 2017.
34. Giacomini, D. and Agarwal, A., Optimizing end user QoS in heterogeneous network environments using reputation and prediction. *EURASIP J. Wireless Commun. Netw.*, 2013, 1, 256, 2013.
35. Gao, F. and Han, L., Implementing the Nelder-Mead simplex algorithm with adaptive parameters. *Comput. Optim. Appl.*, 51, 1, 259–277, 2012.
36. Fu, A., Zhang, G., Yu, Y., Zhu, Z., A privacy preserving vertical handover authentication scheme for WiMAX-WiFi Networks. *KSII Trans. Internet Inf. Syst.*, 8, 9, 3250–3265, 2014.
37. Fernandes, S. and Karmouch, A., Vertical mobility management architectures in wireless networks: a comprehensive survey and future directions. *IEEE Commun. Surv. Tutor.*, 14, 1, 45–63, 2012.
38. Fallon, E., Murphy, L., Murphy, J., Miro-Muntean, G., Frame - fixed route adapted media streaming enhanced handover algorithm. *IEEE Trans. Broadcast.*, 59, 1, 96–115, 2013.
39. Ernst, J.B., Kremer, S.C., Rodrigues, J.J., A survey of QoS/QoE mechanisms in heterogeneous wireless networks. *Phys. Commun.*, 13, 61–72, 2014.
40. Chinnappan, A. and Balasubramanian, R., Complexity–consistency trade-off in multi-attribute decision making for vertical handover in heterogeneous wireless networks. *IET Netw.*, 5, 1, 13–21, 2016.
41. Cheelu, D., Madda, R.B., Chen, C.Y., Venkata Krishna, P., Yenduri, S., Intelligent vertical handoff decision strategy based on network performance prediction and consumer surplus value for next generation wireless networks. *IET Netw.*, 6, 4, 69–74, 2017.

Part II
QUANTUM COMPUTING

3

Introduction to Quantum Computing

Shilpa Mehta[1]* and Celestine Iwendi[2]

[1]Department of Electrical and Electronic Engineering, Auckland University of Technology, Auckland, New Zealand
[2]School of Creative Technologies, University of Bolton, Bolton, Greater Manchester, UK

Abstract
Quantum computing is one of the emerging fields that combines the principles of quantum mechanics with computer science. The focus of this chapter is to provide readers with a detailed introduction to quantum computing by describing the fundamental concepts that differentiate quantum computing from classical computing. Moreover, the chapter provides an overview of quantum gates followed by quantum algorithms. Various hardware and software platforms are also explored in the chapter to provide readers with information on available quantum hardware and software platforms for exploration and research purposes. Some of the important applications are also covered in the chapter, and the current state-of-the-art section depicts problems that have been successfully resolved upon utilization of quantum computing approaches and what are the benefits and shortcomings of such approaches. The chapter concludes with a summary and provides a point of view on future directions.

***Keywords*:** Quantum computing, qubits, quantum gate, algorithms, quantum hardware, quantum software, artificial intelligence, machine learning

3.1 Introduction

Today, quantum computing is one of the most popular quantum mechanics–based technologies. It relies on physics, computer science, and mathematics to solve complex problems faster than classical computing. This technology

**Corresponding author*: shilpa.frnd1155@gmail.com

Pallavi Sapkale, Shilpa Mehta and S. Balamurugan (eds.) Quantum Computing and Machine Learning for 6G, (57–88) © 2026 Scrivener Publishing LLC

has significantly impacted various fields, such as machine learning, cryptography, optimization, etc., but it is not likely to replace classical computers. Instead, it will significantly influence how the world is managed in the upcoming years. This section will provide various concepts related to quantum computing including historical background, the necessity of quantum computers, how quantum computers are different from classical computers, the qubit concept, and key principles for quantum computing.

3.1.1 Historical Background

It has been found that it is possible to use quantum mechanics to solve complex computation problems, so it is interesting to know how it all started. Many researchers anticipated the idea of introducing this concept. However, Richard Feyman is often credited for introducing this notable technological concept. It was in 1979 when a physicist from Argonne National Labs named Paul Benioff theoretically demonstrated the idea of quantum computing, and it was possible to develop such a computer. Following this, in 1980, Yuri Manin introduced quantum computing in his book, originally written in Russian and translated into other languages a couple of years later. In 1981, Richard Feyman gave an expert talk where he argued that classical systems cannot represent quantum mechanical systems and set some features for the quantum computer (QC) in order to become useful. However, the physics community and Richard Feyman were not very clear on how such machines could be built. However, this paved the way for several other researchers who started researching QC after its introduction by these renowned researchers, namely, Richard Feyman, Paul Benioff, and Yuri Manin. Their main aim was to investigate the nature of algorithms that could be run on QCs. In 1985, David Deutsch, an Oxford physicist, provided a more promising and comprehensive framework where he claimed that it is feasible to build QC and what a quantum algorithm could look like. Later in collaboration with Richard Jozsa, he was able to provide a sample algorithm that could run faster on a QC. Following this, in 1993, Umesh Vazirani and Ethan Bernstein demonstrated an algorithm showing a clear separation between classical and quantum when small errors are allowed. Later, further upgradation was done by them where they demonstrated the quantum Fourier transform. In 1994, Daniel Simon followed the work proposed in 1993 and concluded that quantum computers can solve a problem in exponentially faster ways as compared to classical computers. Seth Lloyd was another researcher who demonstrated the process of developing a working model of the quantum computer which is one of the first practical approaches to demonstrate the use of quantum computers.

The previous works proposed by different researchers became a base for Peter Shor who proposed an algorithm for factorization of quantum numbers with two prime factors which was unmanageable on classical computers but was feasible and fast on QC. Later, Simon also solved other problems, being inspired by previous research. After these groundbreakings, it has been proved that quantum computers are powerful and can solve various challenging problems that were not possible by classical computers. This motivated emerging researchers to develop quantum algorithms for solving other real-life challenging problems that were not possible before the discovery of this groundbreaking innovation [1].

3.1.2 Classical Computing vs Quantum Computing

In the modern world of technology, computers are becoming smaller, more handy, cheaper, more efficient, and more powerful as compared to earlier computers. This became feasible due to the improved architecture, advanced software, and compact hardware facilities. Electronic circuits are the backbones of computers which are becoming smaller and smaller these days and are based on the use of transistors which are the tiny components that can easily fit in a compact area. Thus, it does not matter if the circuit is complex with multiple transistors but offers more advanced features as compared to its earlier version; it will easily embed on a single integrated circuit (IC). Moreover, the smaller the size, the less will be the cost of the overall IC. Thus, the IC industry is on the boom. However, according to Moore, every year, the number of transistors is increasing on a single IC, and the price of an IC is decreasing which is referred to as Moore's law. This led to the fact that computers and their computing power are getting less and faster with time [2]. It is possible to measure the time in billionths of seconds but with the advancements in the compact and fast circuits, we have reached a physical limit of materials and threshold for classical laws of physics to apply [3]. This is clearly demonstrated by quantum tunneling, a quantum mechanics phenomenon in which the circuit size of classical computers reaches a limit after 5–7 nanometers. Thus, quantum mechanics came into the picture, and it necessitates the need for new computing which is termed quantum computing. Quantum computing is well-known for solving complex problems which was not possible using classical computers. Storing and manipulating any information are possible using quantum bits, unlike classical computers that make use of binary bits 0 or 1. The computers using this computing are often referred to as quantum computers. Moreover, subatomic particles are used as bits for quantum computers, unlike circuits with transistors, logic gates, and ICs. Due to the ability of

QC to disobey the Turing thesis, quantum computers can provide exponentially faster performance as compared to classical computers [2]. Thus, this necessitates the need for QC.

3.1.3 Why Quantum Computers?

The main motivation behind the development and advancements in quantum computing is the successful implementation of Shor's algorithm on QC which was based on large numbers in an efficient and fast way which was not feasible with classical computers. However, to deeply view and understand QCs, it is necessary to understand that they provide exponentially fast performance only for limited problems especially those that are not solved by classical computers. Thus, various research studies are going on in this domain to understand which problems can be solved by them, and thus, algorithms can be developed to demonstrate and check the feasibility of the problems [4]. Some of the problems where quantum computers are found to be useful are quantum encryption, quantum system simulations, ab initio calculations, complex combinatorics problems, supply chain logistics, optimization, finance, drug development, data analysis, and weather forecasting [5]. These will be discussed in detail in the later sections.

In the next subsection, the focus will be on bits versus qubits.

3.1.4 Bits versus Qubits

Classical computers and QCs are different in terms of the way the information is stored by them. Classical computers make use of bits which can be of the value 0 or 1 in order to store information. However, QCs make use of quantum bits or qubits. A qubit $|\psi\rangle$ can be expressed in states $|0\rangle$ and $|1\rangle$ or any linear combination of 0 and 1 [6, 7]. Figure 3.1 depicts both classical bits and qubits along with the states in which bits or qubits can appear.

Moreover, qubit $|\psi\rangle$ is expressed as

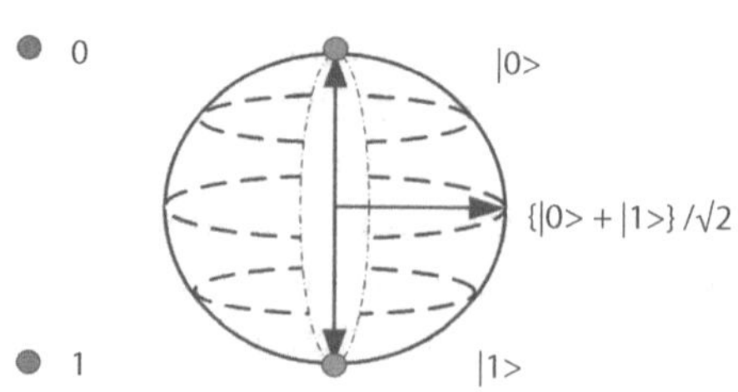

Figure 3.1 Classical bits versus quantum bits.

$$|\psi\rangle = a|0\rangle + b|1\rangle \tag{3.1}$$

where $|0\rangle$ and $|1\rangle$ represent quantum states and a and b refer to probability amplitudes which are complex numbers associated with each state subject to

$$|a|^2 + |b|^2 = 1 \tag{3.2}$$

3.1.5 Quantum Registers

In general, a quantum register refers to a physical system of more than one qubit. For a quantum register containing two qubits, $|q_1\rangle$ and $|q_0\rangle$, the state $|q_r\rangle$ is expressed as

$$|q_r\rangle = |q_1\rangle \otimes |q_0\rangle = |q_1\rangle|q_0\rangle = |q_1\, q_0\rangle \tag{3.3}$$

where $\otimes$ refers to the tensor product symbol which is used to perform the tensor product of qubit states.

Furthermore, the quantum register state with n-qubits is expressed as

$$|q_r\rangle = \sum_{i=0}^{2^n-1} c_i\,|i\rangle \tag{3.4}$$

where

$$\sum_{i=0}^{2^n-1} |c_i|^2 = 1 \tag{3.5}$$

3.1.6 Key Principles of Quantum Computing

QCs can store information in the objects primarily referred to as qubits and then perform transformation by utilizing specific properties such as superposition, interference, and entanglement from quantum mechanics which are responsible for performing computations by collecting different states of qubits. Starting with superposition, it refers to the ability of a quantum system where qubits can exist in multiple states simultaneously.

It can provide high-speed parallel processing and work differently than their classical computer counterparts which are dependent on bits. In classical computing, for 2 bits upon combination, we achieve 4 values and only 1 seems to be possible at any instant. However, in the case of quantum computing for 2 qubits, although the total possible values are 4, all are possible at the same time. Entanglement is another important concept of QC. It defines that there is always a strong correlation between two qubits if they get isolated by a large distance even if they are located at opposite ends of the universe. Thus, once entangled will always be correlated. In classical computers, when bits get doubled, the computational power also gets doubled. However, in the case of QC, if additional bits are added to a quantum computer, the computational power rises exponentially. Finally, the interference property in QC is like wave interference as per classical physics. Wave interference is a phenomenon when two waves interact with each other in the same medium and the resultant can be constructive and destructive interference. Thus, net waves can be bigger or smaller depending on whether it is constructive or destructive interference. This allows us to intentionally bias qubit content toward the desired state or it can also result in quantum computers where several computations can be combined into one to make them more error-prone [2].

A brief introduction to quantum computing is presented in this chapter. Section 3.1 discusses their background, key concepts, and principles. Section 3.2 is mainly focused on quantum gates and quantum algorithms are discussed in Section 3.3. Quantum hardware and software platforms are described in Section 3.4. Section 3.5 targets various quantum computing applications and challenges have been covered in Section 3.6. Section 3.7 focuses on the current state of the art, and finally, the chapter is summarized in Section 3.8.

3.2 Quantum Gates

Classical computers utilize bits to represent any information and normally bit manipulation is done using classical logic gates mainly AND, OR, NOT, and NAND. However, quantum computers typically use qubits to represent information, and manipulation is possible using quantum gates. These gates can function for one, two, or three qubits which are normally referred to as quantum registers. Moreover, the way gates act on qubits or quantum registers is described as

$$G|q_I\rangle = |q_R\rangle \tag{3.6}$$

where G refers to the quantum gate, $|q_I\rangle$ denotes the qubit or quantum register state before applying the gate, and $|q_R\rangle$ refers to the state obtained after applying the gate. Thus, depending on the selection of gates, qubits' state changes can be observed.

Some of the common quantum gates are described below:

- X Gate
  The X gate can also be termed Pauli-X gate which is like a classical NOT gate. It can flip the qubit state by changing $|0\rangle$ to $|1\rangle$ or $|1\rangle$ to $|0\rangle$.
- Y Gate
  The Y gate can also be termed the Pauli-Y gate which is quite similar to the X-gate with an extra feature of phase shifting. It mainly performs bit and phase flips on qubits.
- Z Gate
  The Z gate can also be termed the Pauli-Z gate. This gate can perform a phase flip without affecting the qubit state. Thus, it can change $|0\rangle$ to $|0\rangle$ and $|1\rangle$ to $-|1\rangle$.
- H Gate
  H gate is also termed the Hadamard gate. This gate is responsible for the rotation of qubit states which in turn leads to superposition. It can transform $|0\rangle$ to $\left(|0\rangle + |1\rangle\right)/\sqrt{2}$ and $|1\rangle$ to $\left(|0\rangle - |1\rangle\right)/\sqrt{2}$.
- CNOT Gate
  The CNOT gate is also termed the controlled-X gate. This gate is a two-qubit gate and it can invert the qubit only if the control qubit is in the $|1\rangle$ state.
- CCNOT Gate
  This gate is also termed the Toffoli gate, which is a three-qubit gate. The main purpose of this gate is to perform CCNOT operation on the third qubit when the first two qubits are in the $|1\rangle$ state.
- SWAP Gate
  This gate is responsible for exchanging states of two qubits.
- Rotation Gate
  This gate is responsible for performing rotation operations on the qubit state around the X, Y, and Z axes.

- S Gate
  This gate is also termed the phase gate, which is responsible for performing a 90-degree phase shift to the $|1\rangle$ state. This means that it converts $|0\rangle$ to $|0\rangle$ and $|1\rangle$ to $|1\rangle$, respectively.
- T Gate
  This gate is responsible for performing 45-degree phase shift to the $|1\rangle$ state. This means that it converts $|0\rangle$ to $|0\rangle$ and $|1\rangle$ to $(1+i)|1\rangle/\sqrt{2}$, respectively [9].

3.3 Quantum Algorithms

A quantum algorithm is implemented on a quantum computer using quantum circuits by following a step-by-step procedure, whereas a classical algorithm is implemented on a classical computer by following a similar procedure. Although classical algorithms can be implemented on quantum computers, quantum algorithms typically refer to utilizing certain common aspects of quantum computation. In addition, quantum algorithms are known to be fast at solving problems [8, 10]. Figure 3.2 depicts the classification of quantum algorithms and a detailed explanation of each algorithm is provided below:

3.3.1 Fourier Transform-Based Algorithms

A fundamental understanding of the discrete Fourier transform (DFT), which is the basis of classical algorithms, is required before we can fully

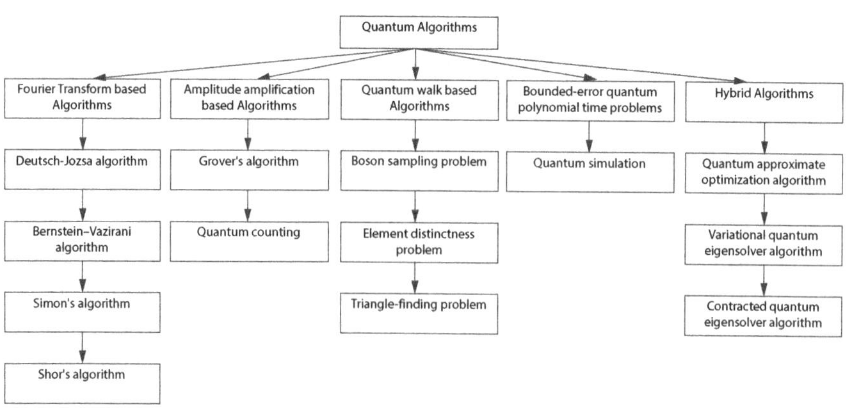

Figure 3.2 Quantum algorithms.

comprehend the quantum Fourier transform (QFT), which is analogous to DFT.

3.3.1.1 Overview of Discrete Fourier Transform

If there are two sequences x and y both with N complex numbers, then DFT is responsible for mapping these sequences where x and y can be expressed as

$$x = \{x_0, x_1, \ldots, x_{n-1}) \quad (3.7)$$

$$y = \{X_0, X_1, \ldots, X_{N-1}\} \quad (3.8)$$

This mapping is done in such a way that

$$y_k = \sum_{n=0}^{N-1} x_n . e^{\frac{i2\pi}{N}kn}, k = 0,1,2\ldots, N-1 \quad (3.9)$$

Thus, an N-point DFT is expressed as

$$y = Wx \quad (3.10)$$

where W corresponds to the DFT matrix

This operation is performed in the form of the algorithm using the fast Fourier transform (FFT), which lowers the number of basic arithmetic operations. This will further reduce the complexity by direct DFT computation which is $O(N \log N)$. Likewise, the time complexity in the case of QFT will be $O(log^2 N)$, whereas in the case of full output state, it will be $O(N\, log^2 N)$ [10].

3.3.1.2 Quantum Fourier Transform

QFT is basically a linear transformation of quantum bits. This transformation can be performed easily and efficiently on quantum computers. As compared to classical or discrete transform which acts on vector, QFT acts on quantum state vector or quantum register [11]. Each of these vectors is expressed as complex numbers. In quantum scenario, these are often referred to as eigenstates which is basically a sequence of probability amplitudes for all possible solutions when measurements are done which have length $N = 2^n$. Thus, just like DFT, QFT can act on quantum state $x\rangle = \sum_{i=0}^{N-1} x_i \,|i\rangle$ and map it with another quantum state $\sum_{i=0}^{N-1} y_i \,|i\rangle$ as per

$$yk = \frac{1}{\sqrt{N}} \sum_{n=0}^{N-1} x_n \omega_N^{nk}, k = 0,1,2,\ldots N-1 \tag{3.11}$$

where ω_N^n is a rotation [10].

Thus, after getting a brief overview of DFT and QFT, it is important to understand various commonly used QFT algorithms such as Deutsch-Jozsa, Bernstein-Vazirani, Simon, and Shor's algorithms, each of which is briefly explained below:

3.3.1.2.1 Deutsch-Jozsa Algorithm

This is one of the well-known quantum algorithms proposed by David Deutsch and Richard Jozsa in the year 1992. This algorithm is applicable to the Boolean function and can determine whether it is constant or balanced. The function is considered constant only if all outputs are 0 or all outputs are 1. Whereas when exactly half of the inputs are zeroes and exactly half of the inputs are ones, the function is termed balanced. This operation must be performed several times as per current error-prone quantum computers. However, future quantum computers might perform this accurately within the first attempt.

This algorithm follows five steps to implementation, which are listed below:

Step 1: Preparation of quantum registers and input states
Step 2: Organization of qubits into the Hadamard basis where each qubit has 50-50 chances of being either 0 or 1.
Step 3: Oracle which is basically a subroutine or a subcircuit whose main function is to encode the function that determines whether the outputs are constant or balanced *via* quantum entanglement.
Step 4: Return qubits to the measurement basis to find the solution.
Step 5: Qubit measurement is done to attain the solution [12].

3.3.1.2.2 Bernstein-Vazirani Algorithm

This is another quantum algorithm that was proposed by Ethan Bernstein and Umesh Vazirani in 1992. It is a restricted form of Deutsch- Jozsa algorithm. Thus, below are the steps followed to perform this algorithm.

> Step 1: Initially, for qubits, set the register to 0
> Step 2: Apply H gates
> Step 3: Enter the query to oracle and then perform a controlled negation operation of each state in the superposition which has been generated by the previous H transformation where it returned 1
> Step 4: Apply H gates, when the qubit is *s of i* = 1, then its negative state will be converted to 1, and when the qubit is *s of i = 0,* its positive state will be converted to 0
> Step 5: Then, to obtain *s, a* qubit measurement will be done [13].

3.3.1.2.3 Simon Algorithm

It is one of the important quantum algorithms proposed by Daniel Simon in 1994. This algorithm is well-known for determining the function periodicity at an exponentially faster rate as compared to the classical algorithms. For example, a function must be implemented while mapping an n-bit to m-bit string in such a way that.

$f : \{0,1\}^n \rightarrow \{0,1\}^m$, where f can be 1:1 or 2:1 function depending on the number of inputs and outputs. In the case of 1:1, both inputs and outputs are single, and each input provides a different output, whereas, in the case of 2:1, there are two inputs and a single output and both inputs provide the same output. Additionally, there is the non-zero time period, s, where $s \in \{0,1\}^n$ in such a way that for every x and x_0

$$f(x) = f(x_0) \tag{3.12}$$

The aim is to determine s, whether f is 2:1, which was successfully solved by Simon [1].

3.3.1.2.4 Shor's Algorithm

Peter Shor proposed an algorithm for the prime factorization of numbers and published this work in the year 1994. With the help of this algorithm, it is possible to find the factor of any number, n, by first determining the period of the proposed function, f, and utilizing that period to obtain the factor of that number [1].

3.3.2 Amplitude Amplification-Based Algorithms

Amplitude amplification refers to the technique of maximizing the probability of achieving the desired results of quantum algorithms. This is common in algorithms, such as Grover's algorithm for quantum search and quantum counting, respectively. This process utilizes two operations, namely, target state and average state reflections. By performing these operations, it became possible to boost the target state amplitude while minimizing the unwanted state amplitude which in turn leads to an efficient amplification mechanism. The whole process can be summarized into the below steps: initialization, oracle application, transformation, and iteration, respectively. The first step is initialization, which corresponds to quantum register initialization specifically to the superposition state. The second step is transformation, whose main purpose is to amplify target state amplitude and suppress other state amplitude. Finally, the iteration step corresponds to the repetition of previous steps for target state amplitude amplification. Thus, it can be concluded that amplitude amplification is one the most effective approaches that mainly utilizes interference and superposition principles of quantum theory to maximize the probability of attaining desired results [14].

3.3.2.1 Grover's Algorithm

Search problems are an important aspect of computing. As a result, searching through various databases becomes necessary to find information efficiently. Various algorithms have been used in classical computers to perform searches, such as linear or binary search, to find an item in a sorted or unsorted list. However, the time complexity of these search algorithms is dependent on dataset size, resulting in extended computations, especially when there is a need to search large amounts of data. This problem can be resolved by utilizing Grover's algorithm, which can perform searches at a much faster rate as compared to its classical counterparts.

Grover's algorithm is one of the most used quantum search algorithms developed to identify the target item within an unsorted database. In the classical analysis, to determine the item within an unsorted database, it is necessary to check half of the items on average. On the other hand, Grover's algorithm can easily obtain that within $\sqrt{N}$ steps, provided there are N items in the list. This is possible mainly due to the utilization of parallelism and interference concepts. This algorithm can be used for database search, cryptography, optimization, quantum simulation, and machine learning problems [15].

3.3.2.2 *Quantum Counting*

Quantum counting algorithms are responsible for efficiently counting the number of solutions for any search problem. Moreover, it is also possible to determine whether the solution will exist or not depending on the number of zero or non-zero solutions. This algorithm is considered as a special case of Grover's algorithm. Thus, it is possible to determine the number of solutions quickly and efficiently by combining the use of Grover's iteration with phase estimation which is based on quantum Fourier transformation as compared to classical approaches [16].

3.3.3 Quantum Walk Based Algorithms

Quantum walk is well-known for searching an unsorted database *via* quadratic speed-up. The first algorithm came into the picture because of Grover's algorithm which was introduced in 1996. The algorithm followed a different approach for achieving a similar quadratic speed-up. Thus, to identify the best among classical and quantum approaches, it is better to consider an example. Suppose there are N entries in an unsorted database, then classical search will go through all the entries present in the database, and, on average, at least half entries will be checked. However, in the case of quantum search, only make use of $\sqrt{N}$ queries. This algorithm follows the superposition principle over the whole database and converges toward the solution [17].

3.3.3.1 *Boson Sampling Problem*

Following Lidror Troyansky and Naftali Tishby's original work that explored the possibility of using boson scattering to estimate the expectation values of permanents of matrices, Scott Aaronson and Alex Arkhipov introduced the boson sampling model of nonuniversal quantum computation. Interferometers perform scattering using identical bosons taken from probability distributions. Despite being known for bosonic particles, the photonic form offers the most promise for the scalability of the boson sampling process. Additionally, the boson sampling scheme may not be universal, but it can accomplish computing tasks that are impractical for classical computers. Thus, it is a good candidate for demonstrating quantum computation's near-term capabilities due to its low resource usage [18].

3.3.3.2 *Element Distinctness Problem*

The element distinctness problem can be best explained by considering the below example where numbers refer to

$$x_1, \ldots\ldots, x_N \in [M]$$

Quantum and classical computing have different approaches to deciding whether all the numbers are distinct. Sorting is the most common approach which is classically followed to solve such problems that require $\Omega(N)$ queries. However, in the quantum environment, different algorithms have been proposed by researchers that can effectively solve such problems such as Buhrman's algorithm that uses $O(N^{\frac{3}{4}})$ queries. Likewise, Aaronson and Shi proposed that $\Omega\left(N^{\frac{2}{3}}\right)$ queries are necessary to solve such problems. An improved version of Buhrman's algorithm is proposed in [19], which is a combination of quantum walk and quantum graph search approach with $O\left(N^{\frac{2}{3}}\right)$ queries. Additionally, the $O\left(N^{\frac{k}{k+1}}\right)$ query-based quantum algorithm was also proposed for the element distinctness generalization to determine k equal items among N items.

3.3.3.3 *Triangle Finding Problem*

The triangle finding problem is a graph-based theoretical problem. In general, for a graph with n vertices, triangle finding is possible within $O\left(n^{\omega+\varepsilon}\right)$ time for any constant $\varepsilon > 0$, where ω refers to the square matrix multiplication exponent. This is a well-known classical time complexity triangle finding approach for unweighted graphs. However, the approach and time to determine a triangle vary for weighted graphs, where $\Omega\left(n^{3-\delta}\right)$ refers to the time for all $\delta > 0$ where 3 corresponds to the vertices of a graph [20].

3.3.4 Bounded-Error Quantum Polynomial Time Problems

Bounded-error quantum polynomial time corresponds to decision problems that can be solved by a quantum computer in polynomial time. The distinguishing characteristic of this problem is that it allows for an error probability of at most 1/3 across all instances [21].

3.3.4.1 Quantum Simulation

Quantum simulation is the best approach to solve bounded-error polynomial time problems as compared to the classical simulation approach. Such problems can be solved using probabilistic algorithms having polynomial time complexity and minimal error probability. Quantum parallelism is useful in solving such problems in a rapid and efficient manner. Authors in [22] focused on discussing the benefits of quantum simulation of bounded error problems while incorporating quantum parallelism.

3.3.5 Hybrid Algorithms

Hybrid algorithms combine classical and quantum computing techniques to solve complex problems, allowing researchers to take advantage of the benefits of both forms of computing. These algorithms not only provide accurate results but are also efficient. Another advantage of such algorithms is that large datasets can be divided into smaller parts so that they can be analyzed simultaneously on different computers [23].

3.3.5.1 Quantum Approximate Optimization Algorithm

The quantum approximate optimization algorithm (QAOA) refers to a hybrid classical-hybrid algorithm suitable for handling combinatorial optimization problems. In this algorithm, the main role of the quantum processor is to prepare the quantum state as per the set of variational parameters. Furthermore, parametric optimization must be done using classical computers and provided back to the quantum machine. This algorithm is one of the best candidates for quantum speed-up explorations, especially on near-term quantum machines due to its high performance as compared to classical computers [24].

3.3.5.2 Variational Quantum Eigensolver Algorithm

Quantum computers containing hundreds of qubits are normally referred to as near-term quantum computers. The number of qubit counts is directly proportional to the number of problems that can be solved. Thus, the lower the qubit counts, the lesser the number of problems that can be solved. Moreover, for noise intermediate scale quantum devices (NISQ) the circuit depth can be limited due to decoherence and gate infidelity. To overcome these limitations, variational quantum algorithms are used. These algorithms utilize a classical quantum optimization loop for training quantum circuit parameters. The role of classical optimizers is to allow quantum circuit depth to remain shallow. Thus, these algorithms become powerful tools for NISQ devices. One of the most common forms of variational quantum algorithms is the variational quantum eigensolver algorithm that is responsible for finding energies, as well as ground and excited states, of the provided Hamiltonian matrix [25].

3.3.5.3 Contracted Quantum Eigensolver Algorithm

The contracted quantum eigensolver algorithm is another hybrid algorithm. The main aim of this algorithm is to determine the solution of the Schrödinger equation by performing its integration on a quantum computer. The solution to an equation can be accurately obtained by optimizing the wave function [26].

This concludes the brief explanation of some of the most important quantum algorithms that can be used in various applications.

3.4 Quantum Hardware and Software

This section briefly describes quantum hardware and software.

3.4.1 Quantum Hardware

Quantum hardware can be categorized into different abstract layers such as quantum data plane, control and measurement plane, control processor plane, and host processor, respectively. The quantum data plane is the home for qubits. Furthermore, the control and measurement planes' main purpose is to perform various operations and measurements on qubits. Moreover, control processor planes can estimate the operation sequence and measurements required for an algorithm based on the measurement results. Finally, the host processor is one of the classical computers that can facilitate user interactions by running a traditional system or user interface and is connected to the control processor. The host processor has access to networks, storage arrays, and user interfaces, respectively [27].

3.4.1.1 Types of Quantum Hardware

Quantum hardware can be classified into superconducting qubits, trapped ion qubits, and photonic qubits.

3.4.1.1.1 Superconducting Qubits

Superconductors are one of the important materials which can be useful for qubits within quantum computing environments. These materials can switch from a normal state when cooled to a superconducting state. Superconducting electrical circuit-based qubits are common among initial quantum computers.

Benefits

- Fast computation rate as compared to other qubits.
- These qubits can make use of highly efficient and available printable circuit processes.
- Simple and straightforward quantum computer development approaches.

Shortcomings

- Short life and requires error correction techniques to overcome problems.
- They can only operate in cold environments.
- Reconfigurable but limited size and depth of the circuit which can run when different qubits are connected.

3.4.1.1.2 Trapped Ion Qubits

When atoms or ions get trapped by lasers, they start behaving like qubits. If we consider a nucleus, then the outermost particle which orbits about it, i.e., electron follows the superposition principle which in turn can be utilized as qubit. These qubits are responsible for encoding quantum data in ions energy level within vacuum.

Benefits

- Higher stability as compared to superconducting qubits.
- They can operate both at room temperature and they perform better in cold environments as compared to superconducting qubits.
- Reconfigurable ion trap quantum computers.

Shortcomings

- Immature technology as compared to superconducting qubits.

3.4.1.1.3 Photonic Qubits

Photonic qubits utilize light particles to transfer or process any information.

Benefits

- These qubits can operate at room temperature.
- They are less sensitive to the environment.
- They can be easily integrated into optical infrastructures.

Shortcomings

- They are emerging qubits in the quantum market [28].

3.4.2 Quantum Software

Software components are one of the important parts of functional quantum computers. This is quite like classical computers' operations; however, there is a difference between the tools that are required to perform quantum operations. These tools may not only include programming languages but also compilers. Both languages and compilers perform important tasks that convert provided information to implementation which is executed on a computer. Largely, languages provide syntax to express concepts followed by operations, and different languages are required at different levels of abstraction. These languages vary for both classical and quantum computers as concepts and operations are different. Thus, there is a need for distinct tools and new languages while working with quantum computers.

High-level language features

- There should be a perfect balance between abstracting level and description.
- These languages must be able to perfectly express quantum algorithms and applications for which they are developed.
- Software programmers must be able to provide sufficient algorithmic information that can be easily mapped to hardware operations.

Low-level language features

- The languages should be more hardware-specific as compared to classical computer languages.

Compilers

The compiler translates the language of higher-level programming languages into the language of computers, in classical computing. In quantum computing, the role of the compiler is to translate commands from the Quantum Assembly Language into instructions for quantum computers. Each of these instructions determines what state and entanglement a certain set of qubits must assume to carry out these orders [29].

3.5 Applications

The advent of quantum computers opens a world of opportunities to solve complex problems that are hard for classical computers to solve. Figure 3.3 illustrates some common applications for quantum computing.

- **Artificial Intelligence and Machine learning**
  Almost every facet of humanity has been impacted by artificial intelligence (AI) and machine learning (ML) in recent years. There are several common applications, such as voice recognition, image recognition, and handwriting recognition. However, as the number of applications increases, traditional computers find it increasingly difficult to cope with accuracy and speed. In that case, quantum computing can be used to solve complex problems very efficiently, compared to traditional computers taking thousands of years to solve.

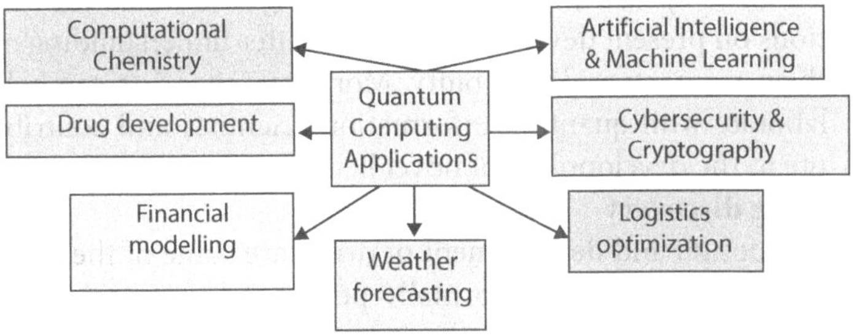

Figure 3.3 Quantum computing applications.

In general, quantum computing and AI are similar in many ways. With quantum computing, AI and ML algorithms will have an advantage in terms of speed and computational power [30]. Examples of where quantum computing concepts were incorporated within AI include semantic analysis, word entanglement in natural languages, quantum Bayesian networks, quantum states and operations identification, and learning [31]. AI, on the other hand, can provide quantum computers with necessary error correction algorithms [30]. In [32], the authors discussed examples of support vector machines and principal component analysis that have been implemented successfully. Thus, it can be concluded that while incorporating quantum algorithms with AI approaches, it is possible to enhance machine learning abilities. Likewise, if quantum computing is incorporated with ML, algorithms' training time can be further improved.

- **Computational Chemistry**
  In a single molecule, there are millions of quantum states, and conventional computing memory cannot process them all. Thus, quantum computers have the potential to provide immense power to pharmaceutical research in the future as they can map molecules based on both 1 and 0 states simultaneously. By applying quantum computing, some critical problems could be solved, such as improving nitrogen fixation for fertilizers, developing room-temperature superconductors, removing carbon dioxide to improve the climate, and last but not least, making solid-state batteries. In [33], the authors discussed the role and benefits of quantum computing for chemists. Based on the literature survey, the authors proposed that chemists can introduce a variety of chemical systems, which will enable algorithm demonstrations on present devices, as well as a better understanding of their accuracy and scalability. Moreover, chemists can collaborate with quantum information scientists and contribute to the development of novel heuristics.
- **Drug discovery**
  The design and development of drugs are some of the most critical tasks that are normally performed using trial and error. However, due to its limitations, such as being expensive, risky, and challenging, it is better to find an alternative that is not only cost-effective but also more time-saving and

can solve the problem effectively. Thus, quantum computing is considered the best approach to introducing new and advanced medical treatments to the pharmaceutical sector [30]. Based on the literature survey on recent advancements in one of the popular drug discovery algorithms, i.e., quantum phase estimation algorithms (QPE), it has been found that fewer quantum resources are required for performing quantum computations in active space with large numbers of electrons and orbitals within less duration with the help of the sparse qubitization approach instead of the Trotterization approach [36].

- **Financial modelling**
  In the finance sector, Monte Carlo simulations are commonly used to perform complex calculations on traditional computers. However, companies can improve the quality of their solutions and cut down on the time it takes to develop them by using quantum technology [30]. In [37], as per the study, it has been found that quantum computing is highly beneficial for solving various challenging financial sector problems. For example, quantum algorithms and quantum annealing can support portfolio optimization, credit scoring, risk analysis, derivative prices, etc. Moreover, this work also focuses on the integration of quantum machine learning with deep learning to upgrade the existing approaches. Besides, quantum amplitude estimation is found to be one of the best candidates for quantum speed-ups, especially for Monte Carlo sampling.
- **Weather forecasting**
  The traditional computer can help predict weather conditions; however, it might take longer than usual; therefore, quantum computing is the best alternative to provide accurate predictions in a matter of seconds [30]. One such study has validated this point that it is possible to obtain promising predictions with the help of quantum computing, especially in the case of processing large datasets. Moreover, the integration of nonlinear systems on QC is highly beneficial for weather predictions [38].
- **Logistics optimization**
  Improved data analysis and robust modeling will facilitate logistics optimization. While traditional computers are useful for tasks such as optimal route calculation for traffic

management or air traffic control, quantum computers are useful in cases where traditional computers are unable to solve complex problems [30]. Various top multinational firms are utilizing QC approaches in this sector or cases like fleet management, vehicle feature testing, transportation coverage, truck loading, and vehicle routing purposes [34].

- **Cybersecurity and Cryptography**
  Due to the large number of cyber-attacks around the world, virtual security space is quite vulnerable. Various companies are working in this domain to develop highly secured virtual space while utilizing traditional digital computers. However, it becomes impractical and difficult to resolve such issues with the help of traditional computers. Thus, quantum computing can propose various approaches that can help overcome these threats and define quantum cryptography methods [30]. Based on this, the authors in [35] discussed cybersecurity and the schemes that they use to mitigate vulnerability caused by quantum computers. With a quantum computer, it can be significantly faster to break modern cryptographic schemes since they are based on mathematical problems that can be addressed with ease. This work concluded that post-quantum cryptographic schemes are one of the most important schemes that must be adopted by industries since quantum computers cannot easily exploit them.

3.6 Challenges of Quantum Computing

Quantum computing is one of the important advancements that can revolutionize different sectors due to its ability to solve complex problems that cannot be solved using classical computing approaches. However, there still exist some major challenges that hinder its integration in different sectors, sometimes out of which quantum decoherence, error correction, and scalability are the critical ones. The summary of each of these is presented below:

> **Quantum decoherence** refers to quantum behavior loss due to system interaction with its own environment leading to change in state from quantum to classical state which in turn leads to quantum errors. Thus, increasing qubit coherence time is one of the possibilities to overcome this problem.

Supercomputing qubits can help enhance coherence time or longer coherence time materials can be used for qubits to get rid of this problem. Besides, error correction codes can help in this regard, performing decoherence error detection and correction before computation gets affected.

Error correction

Quantum error correction is another common challenge in quantum computing. For error and correction within the quantum systems, the first basic rule is to follow the quantum no-cloning theorem, which defines that it is impractical to develop an identical copy of an arbitrarily unspecified quantum state. However, it opposes classical error correction where it is possible to duplicate any information to identify errors. The second rule is that it is possible for quantum errors to be available in different variants, which demand complex and advanced correction codes. Shor and Steane codes were proposed to correct errors within individual qubits; however, they are inefficient for practical purposes due to requirements of large numbers of physical qubits just for solving a single qubit. Moreover, topological quantum error correction and surface codes are due to their simple implementation, fewer physical qubit requirements, and high error thresholds.

Scalability

It is well-known that within QCs, proper interaction between two qubits is important for maximizing computational power. With the increasing number of qubits, it is quite challenging, leading to errors. Thus, it leads to scalability issues. Thus, novel qubits impervious to errors can help for easy scale [39].

3.7 Current State-of-the-Art

The current state of the art in quantum computing can be easily determined by progress, especially with the hardware, software, and algorithmic advancements. This section covers the state of the art in terms of all of them in a tabulated form.

a) Hardware advancements

Quantum hardware and its classification are already covered in Section 3.4. This section covers practical examples of quantum hardware in a tabulated form. Table 3.1 depicts the selection of different hardware based on the problems, their benefits, and shortcomings.

b) Software advancements
Quantum software and its classification are already covered in Section 3.4. This section covers practical examples of quantum software in a tabulated form. Table 3.2 depicts the selection of different open-source software based on the problems, their benefits, and shortcomings.

c) Algorithmic implementation
Quantum algorithmic research and its classification are already covered in Section 3.3. This section covers some of the practical examples of quantum algorithm implementation in a tabulated form. Table 3.3 depicts the selection of different algorithms based on the problems, their benefits, and shortcomings.

Table 3.1 Hardware advancements.

References	Problem	Hardware	Benefits	Shortcomings
[40]	Introduction of quantum digital signal processing framework and arbitrary pulse sequence for superconducting qubit readouts and control purposes.	Raytheon BBN Technologies hardware	FPGA-based readout and control platforms are suitable for qubit control systems for reconfigurable fabric.	For system synchronization purposes, future hardware systems may include time distribution protocols like White Rabbit which is not the case in this study.
[41]	Performance determination of neutral atom hardware	Neutral atom hardware	High scalability, connectivity, and tunability in terms of qubit arrangements and computing modes.	Long preparation times.

Table 3.2 Software advancements.

References	Problem	Software	Benefits	Shortcomings
[42]	Role of open-source software in quantum computing and how they help benefit the quantum community.	Qrack Quirk Python-based simulator Other commonly used open-source simulators	Qrack is beneficial for parallelization support for multi-CPU or GPU cores. Quirk is a user-friendly and drag-and-drop simulator that makes it easier to develop quantum circuits. Python-based simulators support quick quantum circuit development. A commonly used open-source simulator develops and tests algorithms before implementation on quantum chips for error determination at early stages.	There is no fixed field standardization where competing software platforms have been proposed by various people. No standalone compilers are available.
[43]	Introduction to the new open-source software framework	Open-source software platform	Ability to quickly develop novel quantum algorithms within high-level language. Better compilation, optimization, gate synthesis, and layout modules. Flexible for executing quantum algorithms with switching testbeds or prototypes.	Improved compilers will be required for advanced layouts which in turn will be useful for processing complex circuits on advanced hardware and gaining resource usage information before the actual availability of quantum computers.

Table 3.3 Recent advancements as per algorithms implementation.

References	Problem	Algorithm	Benefits	Shortcomings
[44]	Deutsch-Jozsa problem	Machine learning–assisted quantum algorithm	Suitable for oracle-based problems such as the Deutsch-Jozsa problem Learning speed-up as compared to their counterparts.	Improved behavior in algorithm design with quantum feedback rather than classical feedback.
[45]	Modified adiabatic computation for solving Bernstein-Vazirani problem	Bernstein-Vazirani algorithm	Efficient	Desired practical implementation to check the applicability and feasibility
[46]	Lightweight cryptographic algorithm for IoT applications	Simon cryptographic algorithm	Good trade-offs among security, performance, and memory costs.	A speck algorithm is required for future developments and performance comparison with developed algorithms to check suitability with IoT applications.

(Continued)

Table 3.3 Recent advancements as per algorithms implementation. (*Continued*)

References	Problem	Algorithm	Benefits	Shortcomings
[47]	Performance evaluation of Shor's algorithm for numbers that are not within the scope of current quantum hardware.	Shor's factorization algorithm	The main aim is to perform direct permutation-based multiplications without additional qubits. Shor's algorithm is well-known for solving factorization problems but is not suitable for solving problems on gate-based quantum computers. Using the shorgpu implementation in the study, two full-state vector buffers can be maintained, which decreases the simulation time. However, the amount of memory-imposed limits the size of simulatable factoring problems, since it sets a limit on how many qubits can be simulated.	The proposed approach is suitable for determining initialization errors and measurement errors after the multiplication process is completed. Thus, general multiplication circuits can be proposed utilizing standardized quantum gates and extra workspace qubits. Ekerå-Håstad factoring approach is most suitable for solving problems on gate-based quantum computers. To push the boundary of factoring problems, a single state vector buffer must be used as a substitute for contiguous memory transfers.

(*Continued*)

Table 3.3 Recent advancements as per algorithms implementation. (*Continued*)

References	Problem	Algorithm	Benefits	Shortcomings
[48]	Grover's algorithm for solving transcendental logarithm problem	Grover's algorithm	Grover's algorithm can enhance the security of current cryptosystems.	High time consumption to solve such problems.
[49]	Role of boson sampling and its applications	Boson sampling	Boson sampling is beneficial for generating random numbers and cryptography applications.	–

3.8 Summary and Future Scope

This chapter presents a detailed overview of quantum computing, which includes foundational principles, algorithms, hardware/software, and potential applications. Moreover, this study also depicts the current state of the art in quantum computing based on hardware, software, and algorithmic research. The studies presented in this chapter show that quantum computing can be utilized to solve complex problems which are not possible with the classical computational approaches in less time and efficient manner. This chapter acts as a solid foundation for further exploration of quantum computing and its revolutionary impact in various domains. The study explored a few applications of quantum computing in these areas, as well as their advantages, shortcomings, and future directions. However, quantum computing can be used to solve complex engineering problems or industry problems related to specific disciplines or that are interdisciplinary but have not yet been solved or are being solved using classical computing approaches which are inefficient, inaccurate, or time-consuming.

References

1. Hidari, J.D., *Quantum Computing: An Applied Approach*, pp. 1–422, Springer, USA, 2019.
2. Marella, S.T. and Parisa, H.S.K., Introduction to Quantum Computing, in: *Quantum Computing and Communications*, Y. Zhao (Ed.), pp. 1–21, IntechOpen, London, United Kingdom, 2022.
3. Banafa, A., *Introduction to Quantum Computing*, pp. 1–52, River Rapids, Denmark, 2023.
4. Gamble, S., Quantum Computing: What Is It, Why We Want It, and How We're Trying to Get It. *Frontiers of Engineering: Reports on Leading-Edge Engineering from the 2018 Symposium*, 2018, https://www.ncbi.nlm.nih.gov/books/NBK538701/.
5. Bellapu, A., 10 Difficult Problems Quantum Computers can Solve Easily, 2022, https://www.analyticsinsight.net/10-difficult-problems-quantum-computers-can-solve-easily/.
6. Akyildiz, I.F., Kak, A., Nie, S., 6G and beyond: The future of wireless communications systems. *IEEE Access*, 8, 133995–134030, 2020.
7. Hagouel, P., II and Karafyllidis, I.G., Quantum computers: Registers, gates and algorithms. *2012 28th International Conference on Microelectronics Proceedings*, pp. 15–21, 2012.
8. Hughes, C., Issacson, J., Perry, A., Sun, R.F., Turner, J., *Quantum Computing for the Quantum Curious*, p. 159, Springer Cham, Switzerland, 2021.

9. Williams, C.P., Texts in Computer Science, in: *Explorations in Quantum Computing*, pp. 1–717, Springer-Verlag, Germany, 2011.
10. Wikipedia, Quantum algorithm, 2023, https://en.wikipedia.org/wiki/Quantum_algorithm.
11. Musk, D.R., A Comparison of Quantum and Traditional Fourier Transform Computations. *Comput. Sci. Eng.*, 22, 103–110, 1 Nov.-Dec. 2020.
12. Classiciq, The Deutsch-Jozsa Algorithm Explained, 2023, https://www.classiq.io/insights/the-deutsch-jozsa-algorithm-explained.
13. Jadhav, N., Introduction to the Bernstein-Vazirani Algorithm, 2020, https://nidhivjadhav.medium.com/introduction-to-the-bernstein-vazirani-algorithm-12c8a03d545a.
14. Gaurikhard, Amplitude amplification Algo in Quantum Computing, 2023, https://gaurikhard.medium.com/amplitude-amplification-algo-in-quantum-computing-f77c443d3fc4.
15. Murshed, S.K., Grover's Algorithm: Quantum Leap in Search Efficiency, 2023, https://murshedsk135.medium.com/grovers-algorithm-quantum-leap-in-search-efficiency-996023862769.
16. UOW, 6 Quantum search algorithms, https://homes.cs.washington.edu/~jrl/teaching/cse599Q/notes/qex1.pdf.
17. Kendon, V.M., A Random Walk Approach to Quantum Algorithms. *Philos. Transactions Mathematical Phys. Eng. Sci.*, 364, 1849, 3407-3422, 2006.
18. Wikipedia, Boson Sampling, 2024, https://en.wikipedia.org/wiki/Boson_sampling.
19. Ambainis, A., Quantum walk algorithm for element distinctness, https://arxiv.org/abs/quant-ph/0311001.
20. Gall, F.L., Improved Quantum Algorithm for Triangle Finding *via* Combinatorial Arguments, 2014, https://arxiv.org/abs/1407.0085.
21. Mishra, B.K. (Ed.), Technology Road Mapping for Quantum Computing and Engineering, IGI Global, USA, 2022.
22. Smolin, J.A. and Smith, G., Quantum Simulation of Bounded Error Classical Algorithms. *Phys. Rev. Lett.*, 98, 1–10, 2007.
23. QuAIL Technologies, Hybrid Quantum-Classical Algorithms, 2023, https://medium.com/quail-technologies/day-7-hybrid-quantum-classical-algorithms-c3b533fa4217.
24. Zhou, L., Wang, S.-T., Choi, S., Pichler, H., Lukin, M.D., Quantum, Approximate Optimization Algorithm: Performance, Mechanism, and Implementation on Near-Term Devices, in: *Physical Review X*, vol. 2, American Physical Society, USA, 2020.
25. Cerezo, M., Sharma, K., Arrasmith, A., Coles, P.J., Variational quantum state eigen solver. *npj Quantum Inf.*, 8, 113, 2022.
26. Smart, S.E. and Mazziotti, D.A., Accelerated Convergence of Contracted Quantum Eigensolvers through a Quasi-Second-Order, Locally Parameterized Optimization. *J. Chem. Theory Comput.*, 18, 9, 5286–5296, 2022.

27. Grumbling, E. and Horowitz, M., Quantum Computing: Progress and Prospects, in: *National Academies of Sciences, Engineering, and Medicine*, The National Academies Press, Washington, DC., 2019.
28. Brown, R., The Many Faces of a Qubit, QCI Innovative Quantum Solutions Company, 2023, https://www.quantumcomputinginc.com/blog/the-many-faces-of-a-qubit/.
29. Leibniz Supercomputing Centre of the Bavarian Academy of Sciences and Humanities, A compiler of quantum computing, 2022, https://www.quantum.lrz.de/bits-of-qubits/detail/a-compiler-for-quantum-computing.
30. Das, S., Top Applications Of Quantum Computing Everyone Should Know About, 2024, https://analyticsindiamag.com/top-applications-of-quantum-computing-everyone-should-know-about/.
31. Ying, M., Quantum Computation, quantum theory and AI. *Artif. Intell.*, 174, 2, 162–176, 2010.
32. Abdelgaber, N. and Nikolopoulos, C., Overview of Quantum Computing and its Applications in Artificial Intelligence. *2020 IEEE Third International Conference on Artificial Intelligence and Knowledge Engineering*, pp. 198–199, 2020.
33. Motta, M. and Ric, J.E., Emerging quantum computing algorithms for quantum chemistry. *WIREs Comput. Mol. Sci.*, 12, 3, 2022.
34. Quantum Technology and Application Consortium – QUTAC, *et al.*, Industry quantum computing applications. *EPJ Quantum Technol.*, 8, 1–17, 2021.
35. Brijwani, G.N., Ajmire, P.E., Thawani, P.V., Future of Quantum Computing in Cyber Security, in: *Handbook of Research on Quantum Computing for Smart Environments*, A.K. Tyagi (Ed.), pp. 267–298, IGI Global, USA, 2023.
36. Blunt, N.S., Camps, J., *et al.*, Perspective on the Current State-of-the-Art of Quantum Computing for Drug Discovery Applications. *J. Chem. Theory Comput.*, 18, 12, 7001–7023, 2022.
37. Orus, R., Mugel, S., Lizaso, E., Quantum computing for finance: overview and prospects. *Rev. Phys.*, 4, 100028, 2019.
38. Tennie, F. and Palmer, T.N., Quantum Computers for Weather and Climate Prediction: The Good, the Bad, and the Noisy. *Bull. Am. Meteorol. Soc.*, 104, 2, E488–E500, 2023.
39. Tarraf, G., The quantum conundrum: Challenges to getting quantum computing on deck, 2023, https://atelier.net/insights/quantum-conundrum-challenges-quantum-computing.
40. Ryan, C.A., Johnson, B.R., Riste, D., *et al.*, Hardware for dynamic quantum computing. *Rev. Sci. Instrum.*, 88, 10, 1–27, 2017.
41. Wintersperger, K., Dommert, F., *et al.*, Neutral atom quantum computing hardware: performance and end-user perspective. *EPJ Quantum Technol.*, 10, 1–26, 2023.
42. Fingerhuth, M., Babej, T., *et al.*, Open source software in quantum computing. *PLoS One*, 13, 12, 1–28, 2018.

43. Steiger, D.S., Haner, T., *et al.*, ProjectQ: an open source software framework for quantum computing. *Quantum Open J. Quantum Sci.*, 2, 49, 2018.
44. Bang, J., Junghee, R., *et al.*, A strategy for quantum algorithm design assisted by machine learning. *New J. Phys.*, 16, 1–15, 2014.
45. Nakayama, S., Gang, P., *et al.*, Study on Quantum Parallel Processing by Adiabatic Quantum Computation in Bernstein-Vazirani Problem. *2012 13th International Conference on Parallel and Distributed Computing, Applications and Technologies*, pp. 678–682, 2012.
46. Alassaf, N., Gutub, A., *et al.*, Enhancing speed of SIMON: A light-weight-cryptographic algorithm for IoT applications. *Multimed. Tools Appl.*, 78, 32633–32657, 2019.
47. Willsch, D., Willsch, M., *et al.*, Large-Scale Simulation of Shor's Quantum Factoring Algorithm. *Mathematics*, 11, 19, 1–38, 2023.
48. Tang, Y., Su, S., *et al.*, Application of Grover's Quantum Search Algorithm to Solve the Transcendental Logarithm Problem. *2014 Tenth International Conference on Computational Intelligence and Security*, pp. 445–449, 2014.
49. Yeh, M., Boson-Sampling: progress, Challenges, and Opportunities Beyond Quantum Supremacy, pp. 1–8, 2020, https://mudyeh.github.io/files/Physics130_FinalPaper_MatthewYeh_2020.pdf.

4

Quantum-Secured Concealed Identifier for 6G Technology

Pratham Desai* **and Dipali Kasat**

Sarvajanik College of Engg. & Tech., Surat, India

Abstract
The abstract encapsulates the salient insights derived from comprehensive deliberations on quantum computing, 6G technology, and post-quantum secure communication protocols. It accentuates the paradigm-shifting potential inherent in quantum technologies to redefine the landscape of information security, juxtaposed against the imminent challenges posed by quantum adversaries. Central to its discourse is the imperative of devising post-quantum secure solutions to fortify communication networks amidst the epochal advent of quantum computing. The abstract underscores the pivotal role of concerted efforts in research, collaboration, and innovation to mitigate emergent threats and uphold the integrity and robustness of digital infrastructure frameworks.

Keywords: Quantum computing, 6G, identifiers, cryptography, post quantum

Introduction

In the era of technology, we are heading toward more and more development, and we are becoming more advanced than yesterday. In the 1973s, an innovator named Martin Copper demonstrated the first ever handheld mobile phone in the city of NY, which changed the whole scenario of wireless technology. Similar to that, the discovery of transistors made another revolutionary change by changing the size of computers. Today, humans are in a position where we are going to witness another revolution, in which computers will get more advanced and we will use the quantum

**Corresponding author*: prathamdesai071204@gmail.com

Pallavi Sapkale, Shilpa Mehta and S. Balamurugan (eds.) Quantum Computing and Machine Learning for 6G, (89–116) © 2026 Scrivener Publishing LLC

mechanical property of atoms to calculate one of the most complex problems which could take years to be computed on the fastest supercomputer made by the human race. As the technology gets more advanced, it also unlocks potential threats to the security of users, quantum computing is a perfect example of that kind of technology. It takes only 10 Qubits to solve the integer factorization problem for a 48-bit string, making the security specialist think again about discovering post-quantum cryptography and protocols. In this chapter, we are going to discuss three different kinds of protocols that ensure post-quantum security.

4.1 Quantum Mechanical Properties for Security

Quantum computing is a field that uses the principles of quantum mechanics and some of the mathematical formulas to leverage quantum supremacy over the known classical devices. QCs can do this with certain types of quantum mechanical properties. Some of those properties which will be useful in further chapter are entanglement and no-cloning theorems. While we talk about both of these theorems, we can refer to our two candidates Alice and Bob to give insights into both of these principles.

4.1.1 Entanglement with Bell-State Example

The theory of entanglement dates was originated by EPR. They conducted a thought experiment, which talked about "Spooky action at a distance" [2]. It says that if we connect 2 atoms, if we measure a property of one particle, then it will also be able to calculate the other properties of that atom, regardless of their distance. It says that information is being transferred at a speed greater than the speed of light. However, this idea clashes with the theory of relativity proposed by Herr Einstein [relativity]. Also, we can include the name of Erwin Schrodinger for perplexing the given concept of entanglement.

A general example while we discuss the concept of entanglement is Bell states. Bell states can form between at least two qubits. Consider that in this project, two parties Alice and Bob are involved having one qubit to each. Quantum entanglement is like as we discussed in the above paragraph, we can share two bits of data while having one qubit, in the context of Bell states. Suppose that we create a Bell state by applying superposition to one qubit and making a C-NOT to the other bit with control to the first qubit. It will invert the output if the first qubit is in one state.

We have two Hilbert spaces, H_A and H_B, of two arbitrary quantum systems, A and B, given to Alice and Bob. As we combine the Hilbert space of both quantum systems with the help of the tensor product, we will get $H_A \otimes H_B$. The combined state of both systems could be represented by the tensor product of both systems, called the separable states, but not all of the states are represented by it. The most general state in said Hilbert space H is given by

$$|\psi\rangle_{AB} = \sum_{i,j} V_{ij} \, |i\rangle_A \otimes |j\rangle_B, \tag{4.1}$$

The state is called entangled if there exist vectors $[V_i^A]$ and $[V_j^B]$ such that $\left[V_{ij}\right] \neq \left[V_i^A\right]\left[V_j^B\right]$, which are also called inseparable states. If the composite system is in this state, it is impossible to attribute either system *A* or system *B* to a definite pure state. Another way to say this is that while the von Neumann entropy of the whole state is zero (as it is for any pure state), the entropy of the subsystems is greater than zero. In this sense, the systems are "entangled".

Let's say that Alice wants to send information to Bob by using her Qubit part, as they both have entangled states, they can send-receive the two-bit data for the said Bell state. Bob can receive two-bit data as Alice sends him an acquisition of her part of the qubit and he performs the POVM measurements. As Bell states are orthogonal to basis, he will have the full information of two bits. Bell states that are formed are as said below.

$$|\varphi^+\rangle = \frac{\left(|00\rangle AB + |11\rangle AB\right)}{\sqrt{2}}, \tag{4.2}$$

$$|\varphi^-\rangle = \frac{\left(|00\rangle AB - |11\rangle AB\right)}{\sqrt{2}}, \tag{4.3}$$

$$|\psi^+\rangle = \frac{\left(|01\rangle AB + |10\rangle AB\right)}{\sqrt{2}}, \tag{4.4}$$

$$|\psi^-\rangle \frac{(|01\rangle AB - |10\rangle AB)}{\sqrt{2}}. \tag{4.5}$$

In general, we can write this superposition as below.

$$|\beta_{(x,y)}\rangle = \frac{(|0, y\rangle AB + (-1x)|1, y'\rangle AB)}{\sqrt{2}}. \tag{4.6}$$

4.1.2 Entanglement for Bipartite System

Entanglement, in practicality, could be understood by the concept of entanglement for bipartite systems given to Alice and Bob. Quantum mechanics and maths are like tea and sugar; they both blend very well. Entanglement and majorization both are connected [1]. We can explain entanglement with the help of majorization. Let's say we have two vectors x and y having $x = (x_1, x_2, \ldots, x_d)$ and $y = (y_1, y_2, \ldots, y_d)$, then we can say that x is majorized by y if and only if we have $\sum_{i=1}^{k} x_i \downarrow \leq \sum_{i=1}^{k} y_i \downarrow$, written by $x \preceq y$ for k = (1, 2, …, d) and this inequality goes to equality when k = d.

To prove that a bipartite pure state $|\psi\rangle$ can be transformed to another pure state $|\varphi\rangle$ by LOCC if and only if $\lambda\psi \preceq \lambda\varphi$, we first assume that $|\psi\rangle$ can be transformed to $|\varphi\rangle$ by LOCC. We can assume that Alice performs a measurement with measurement operator M_j and then sends the result to Bob, who performs a unitary transformation U_j. Regardless of the measurement outcome, Alice starts with state $\rho\psi$ and ends with state $\rho\varphi$, implying:

$$M_j \rho_\psi M_j^\dagger = p_j \rho_\varphi \tag{4.7}$$

where P_j is the probability of outcome j. Using the polar decomposition of $M_j\sqrt{\rho_\psi}$, we find a unitary V_j such that:

$$M_j\sqrt{\rho_\psi} = M_j \rho_\psi M_j^\dagger V_j = \sqrt{p_j \rho_\varphi} V_j \tag{4.8}$$

Pre-multiplying this equation by its adjoint gives:

$$\sqrt{\rho_\psi} M_j M_j^\dagger \sqrt{\rho_\psi} = p_j V_j^\dagger \rho_\varphi V_j \quad (4.9)$$

Summing over j and using the completeness relation $\sum_j M_j M_j^\dagger = I$ gives:

$$\rho_\psi = \sum_j p_j V_j^\dagger \rho_\varphi V_j \quad (4.10)$$

which implies $\lambda\psi \preceq \lambda\varphi$ by majoring.

For the converse, suppose $\lambda\psi \preceq \lambda\varphi$, implying $\rho\psi \preceq \rho\varphi$. By Theorem 12.13, there exist probabilities P_j and unitary operators U_j such that $\rho_\psi = \sum_j p_j U_j \rho_\varphi U_j^\dagger$. Assuming that ρ_ψ is invertible, define operator M_j for Alice's system by:

$$M_j \sqrt{\rho_\psi} = \sqrt{p_j \rho_\varphi} U_j^\dagger \quad (4.11)$$

These operators form a measurement due to the completeness relation:

$$\sum_j M_j M_j^\dagger = I \quad (4.12)$$

If Alice obtains outcome j, her reduced density matrix ρ_j satisfies $\rho_j = \rho_\varphi$, Bob can convert $|\psi_j\rangle$ into $|\varphi_j\rangle$ by a suitable unitary transformation V_j. However, this is still a good area of research and further development is still under process ([1, 8]).

4.1.3 No Cloning Theorem

Imagine a scene where Alice is sending some secret messages to Bob, and there is an eavesdropper who is trying to steal the information or trying to manipulate that information. In classical communication, we can do that by interfering with the channel, but in the meantime, we are doing that communication with the help of quantum states, and at that time, Alice can send any arbitrary state to Bob in a secure way. If there is any eavesdropper trying to access that data, then s/he will be caught or cannot access that data as per the no-cloning theorem.

To prove this theorem, we have to make some assumptions such as the following:

1. =Alice is sending pure states to Bob.
2. Eavesdropper is coping with the help of unitary evolution.

If the state is a mixed state, then this theorem will be said as the "No-Broadcast Theorem" [7]. Let two subsystems have a common Hilbert space $H=H_A$(for Alice) and $H=H_E$ (for Eve). Let's say Alice has prepared a state $|\psi\rangle_A$ and Eve wants to copy that state. To clarify, it is impossible for Eve to make an exact copy $|\varphi\rangle_E$ of Alice's state $|\psi\rangle_A$, and it is also impossible for both subsystems to have $|\psi\rangle_A$ as their final state. This theorem says that perfect is unattainable in the realm of quantum mechanics as long as the states are orthogonal, otherwise one has to face a finite loss over the said states. In this case, you cannot achieve your desired outcome due to the no-cloning theorem

$$|\psi\rangle_A \otimes |\varphi\rangle_B \rightarrow U(|\psi\rangle_A \otimes |\varphi\rangle_B) \tag{4.13}$$

$$\rightarrow |\psi\rangle_A \otimes |\psi\rangle_B, \text{(said result)} \tag{4.14}$$

It is essential to understand that the unitary evolution operator, $U = e^{\frac{-itH}{\hbar}}$, is a fundamental concept for manipulating quantum states. However, it is important to note that for bipartite systems ($H_A \otimes H_B$), there does not exist an operator that could clone an unknown quantum state from one subsystem to another state while preserving all its properties. This limitation is a direct consequence of the no-cloning theorem, which asserts that it is impossible to create an identical copy of an unknown quantum state through unitary operations, especially in the context of bipartite systems.

$$U(|\varphi\rangle A|e\rangle B) = e^{i\alpha(\phi,e)}|\varphi\rangle A|\varphi\rangle_B \tag{4.15}$$

where α is a real number depending upon φ, and e.

$$\langle\varphi|\psi\rangle\langle e|e\rangle = \langle\varphi|_A \langle e|_B|\psi\rangle_A|e\rangle_B$$

$$= \langle \varphi |_A \langle e |_B U^{\dagger} U | \psi \rangle_A | e \rangle_B$$

$$= e^{-i(\alpha(\phi,e)-\alpha(\psi,e))} \langle \varphi |_A \langle \varphi |_B | \psi \rangle_A | \psi \rangle_B$$
$$= e^{-i(\alpha(\phi,e)-\alpha(\psi,e))} \langle \varphi | \psi \rangle \quad (4.16)$$

Thus,

$$| \langle \varphi | \psi \rangle |^2 = | \langle \varphi | \psi \rangle | \quad (4.17)$$

suggests that the inner product $\langle \varphi | \psi \rangle$ is either 1 or 0. According to the Cauchy-Schwarz inequality, this result implies that either φ is proportional to ψ, i.e., $|\varphi\rangle = e^i \beta |\psi\rangle$ (where β is a phase factor), or the states φ and ψ are orthogonal, meaning that they are perpendicular in the Hilbert space [1].

Certainly, quantum computing introduces a paradigm shift in information security. It capitalizes on fundamental quantum mechanical properties that can potentially render current security systems, such as ECDH and RSA, more susceptible. Elliptic curve encryption relies on logarithmic encryption, and RSA employs prime factorization for encryption [5]. Classical algorithms, while effective to a degree, face computational limitations when attempting to break these encryption technologies, a feat that current supercomputers find immensely challenging due to their computational complexity, ensuring their viability for the time being [5].

In contrast, Shor's and Grover's algorithms offer significant speed-up compared to their classical counterparts. To solve the integer factorization problem, we can use Shor's algorithm (crucial for RSA) and the discrete logarithm problem (central to elliptic curve–based encryption). Quantum computing has the potential to revolutionize the landscape of information security by exploiting these quantum mechanical properties and significantly accelerating cryptographic attacks ([11, 12]).

In this age of rapid modernization, our progress is nothing short of exponential, ushering in a multitude of advantages for humanity. However, this technological advancement has simultaneously opened doors for potential eavesdroppers, jeopardizing the security of our most sensitive information and our very identities. As we approach the realization of the full potential of 6G technology, we must confront the looming challenges concerning privacy and security brought about by the advent of quantum computers. This necessitates a reassessment by security agencies, as they confront the urgent need to develop encryption solutions capable of withstanding the disruptive potential of quantum computing.

4.2 Quantum Key Distribution Technique (QKD)

QKD is a protocol that basically has the implementation of basic principles of quantum mechanics and quantum computing. It is said to be secured over the said eavesdropping. However, in order to create a private key between two parties, they can use a public channel having an error less than a certain threshold, thus the security of this kind of key distribution is guaranteed by the laws of quantum mechanics until and unless steps are followed perfectly.

Let's consider that Alice has created a state $|\psi\rangle_A$ for Bob; here, there is Eve between the communication channels, and she wants to decode that message or steal that information. Here, as we earlier discussed, Eve cannot copy or duplicate the exact $|\psi\rangle_A$ unless they both are orthogonal states. Also, Eve cannot gain the information of $|\psi\rangle_A$ without creating any disturbance in the state. We can derive that proposition by following the steps.

Let's say that $|\psi\rangle$ and $|\varphi\rangle$ are two non-orthogonal states, and Alice wants to gain information about that state with the help of the ancilla state $|u\rangle$, which is then converted to the states $|v\rangle$ and $|v'\rangle$ *via* a unitary transformation. As per the definition of unitary, the inner product is preserved; thus, $\langle v|v'\rangle = \langle u|u\rangle = 1$, thus both v and v' must be identical. With the help of these algorithms, Alice and Bob send and receive the information without any possible eavesdropping, and Bob receives information with fewer errors.

4.3 BB84 Algorithm

In this section, we will go through the most basic QKD algorithm which we will use with some modifications in the set of measurements, proposed by Charles Bennett and Gilles Brassard, leveraging the quantum mechanical properties and quantum computing advantages in the cryptography field.

Alice and Bob engage in a quantum communication protocol where Alice encodes two strings, a and b, consisting of classical bits into a quantum state using qubits. The encoding is such that b determines the basis (either X or Z) in which a is encoded. Alice then sends the resulting quantum state to Bob over a public quantum channel. Upon receiving the state, Bob applies a quantum operation ξ, which encompasses both channel noise and potential eavesdropping by Eve. Bob then publicly announces receiving the state.

At this stage, neither Bob nor Eve has the knowledge of the basis b used by Alice for encoding. Thus, Eve's attempts to eavesdrop by guessing the basis are ineffective, as any incorrect guess would disturb the state received by Bob. Bob, unaware of b, proceeds to measure each qubit on a randomly generated basis, obtaining measurement results a'.

Subsequently, Alice publicly discloses the basis b, and Bob and Alice discard bits from b and b' that are unequal. The remaining bits, denoted as a = a', are considered to be measured on the same basis as prepared by Alice. To assess the integrity of their communication, Alice and Bob perform a subset of their shared bits. If the number of discrepancies exceeds a threshold t, indicating potential interference or eavesdropping, they abort the protocol and retry. Otherwise, they proceed with information reconciliation and privacy amplification algorithms to extract a shared secret key from the remaining bits.

In summary, Alice and Bob establish a secure communication channel by encoding classical bits into a quantum state, ensuring security against eavesdropping attempts through a series of verification steps.

4.4 Concept of Identifiers

Identifiers are very helpful in a way to check whether the user is legitimate or not. There are multiple ways for identifiers for identification and authentication. In 6G technology, there will be some parameters providing security to the end user with some features. Some of them are listed below [9].

1. **Device identifiers**: We are transmitting our data in a wireless manner; however, to enable this feature in one's device, he or she needs to verify the device with the help of several parameters such as IMEI, IMSI, and MAC address for the Wi-Fi system.
2. **User Identification**: Identifiers that are helpful in the process of authentication to the user are email, name, phone number, and address, which are some of the most crucial and sensitive data to be handled. Also, 6G may introduce some new methods in order to handle a large set of data with such ease. Making 6G more secure, however, those technologies might not be quantum-proof.

3. **Location-Based Identifiers**: In 6G, precision and accuracy will play a crucial role in order to identify a user. To achieve this accuracy and precision, we might take the help of geospatial coordinates.
4. **Virtual Identifiers**: As networks become more virtualized, identifiers might include software-defined networking (SDN) identifiers, virtual network function identifiers, or other similar digital markers for network components.
5. **Network Identifiers**: Networks themselves may have unique identifiers. For instance, in 5G, you have PLMN (public land mobile network) identities that help in identifying different mobile networks.

There are many more identifiers that work on the basis of the various parameters to achieve a high level of accuracy and precision. Technologies and knowledge of previous generations can help, to build this generation more secure from previous ones. Here are some of the flaws described below.

In 5G, there were a lot of possible attacks which makes 5G even more vulnerable such as [10] the following:

- Denial-of-service (DoS) or resource-based attacks
- Concealment of active and passive eavesdropping through large multiple-input multiple-output (MIMO) systems
- Threats to software-defined networking (SDN) and infiltration of rogue applications
- Security challenges in network functions virtualization (NFV) services
- Vulnerabilities and attacks on the 5G authentication and key agreement (5G-AKA) protocol
- IMSI-catcher attacks compromising mobile network security
- Voice over IP (VoIP) attack vectors
- Traceability threats targeting network anonymity
- Exploitation of failure message data for information disclosure

In B5G technology, we are working to overcome this kind of attack in order to make communication between two parties even more secure. Apart from classical attacks, researchers are working on making 6G technology quantum-secure, and this could take a lot of brainstorming and hard work. Beyond addressing these known vulnerabilities, there is a strong focus on making 6G networks quantum-secure. Achieving quantum security will necessitate innovative solutions and significant collaboration among experts, as quantum computing poses both a threat and an opportunity for securing future communication networks.

4.5 Drawbacks of Classical Algorithms

Classical algorithms exhibit certain limitations that quantum computers have the capability to exploit, thereby compromising security measures. One such vulnerability lies in the realm of factorization and discrete logarithm problems. Quantum algorithms like Shor's algorithm have demonstrated the ability to efficiently factor large numbers and solve discrete logarithm problems, posing a threat to classical encryption methods such as RSA and certain ECC implementations. These encryption schemes rely on the complexity of factoring large numbers or solving discrete logarithm problems for their security [11].

However, it is important to note that Shor's algorithm requires a significant number of qubits to effectively break standard RSA-2048 encryption. While recent advancements in quantum computing have shown promising results in reducing qubit requirements, the current technology still faces limitations.

Furthermore, hash functions, crucial components of classical identifiers, are also vulnerable to attacks from quantum computers. Grover's algorithm, for example, enables quantum computers to search unsorted databases quadratically faster than classical algorithms, thereby posing a threat to hash-based identifiers and verification systems. This jeopardizes data integrity and identity management systems reliant on hash functions for security.

Additionally, quantum computers have the potential to weaken classical cryptographic techniques such as symmetric-key encryption and digital signatures. While not all classical identifiers rely on these methods, some do, and their security could be compromised in a quantum computing environment [5].

In essence, the drawbacks of classical algorithms underscore the pressing need for security agencies to reassess encryption solutions in light of the evolving capabilities of quantum computing. This calls for a reevaluation by security agencies, as they confront the urgent need to develop encryption solutions capable of withstanding the disruptive potential of quantum computing.

4.6 Quantum Concealed Identifiers for 6G Technology

In this section, we will explore some of the newest quantum key distribution (QKD) protocols that offer top-notch security, making them ideal for integration into 6G technologies' security systems. Additionally, we will delve into a QKD method featuring two-way authentication. This system relies on a central authentication mechanism supported by symmetric encryption principles. This method combines pseudo-random functions, various sets of quantum conjugate bases, and measurement-device-independent technology (MDIT) to facilitate simultaneous two-way authentication.

4.6.1 QKD Protocol with a Multiple Coding Basis

In the realm of secure communication, BB84 plays a pivotal role in ensuring the confidentiality of messages exchanged between authenticated parties. These protocols leverage the no-cloning theorem, making it incredibly challenging for eavesdroppers to intercept information without detection. Should an unauthorized party attempt to breach the security, they face either the futility of cracking the encryption key or the imminent risk of being exposed, leading to the immediate termination of the communication. Now, let's delve into the workings of the BB84 QKD protocol, which is widely regarded for its effectiveness [15]:

- Encoding with Conjugate Bases: Alice initiates the process by selecting two sets of conjugate bases. To determine which set of bases to use, she assigns each bit of one of her random strings.
- Bit Encoding: Subsequently, Alice employs the chosen set of bases to encode the bits of her other random string.
- Quantum State Transmission: Alice sends this quantum-encoded information to Bob in the form of a single optical quantum state.
- Random Basis Selection: Bob receives the state prepared by Alice and he chooses one of the states as bases for measurement which will be randomly chosen.
- Public Comparison: To ensure the security of their communication, both Alice and Bob publicly share the information about their chosen coding bases and measurement bases over a public channel.

The BB84 protocol is a sophisticated quantum key distribution (QKD) scheme renowned for its ability to ensure secure communication by leveraging the principles of quantum mechanics. At its core, BB84 involves a meticulously orchestrated interplay of encoding, transmission, and measurement, augmented by the public comparison of bases. This dance serves as the bedrock of the protocol, rendering it highly resilient against eavesdropping and potential breaches of sensitive information.

One of the distinguishing features of BB84 is the utilization of multiple sets of coding bases by Alice, the sender. Rather than restricting herself to a binary choice of bases, Alice typically opts for 2^n sets of bases for enhanced security, convenience, and efficiency. Consequently, the size of the reserved message becomes proportional to 1/2^n of the original message size, ensuring a compact representation while preserving the integrity of the communication.

Central to BB84's security architecture is the shared secret key generated by Alice and Bob, the recipient, through the utilization of pseudo-random numbers. These keys serve as the cornerstone for determining the quantum encoding and measurement bases for both parties. Unlike conventional methods, BB84 dispenses with the need for a protracted sifting process by employing multiple sets of orthogonal bases evenly distributed across the Bloch sphere. This strategic distribution not only bolsters security but also substantially elevates the rate of key generation, thereby enhancing the efficiency of the protocol.

To elucidate the concept of multiple sets of orthogonal bases, let's denote the total number of bases as M. By taking the logarithm base 2 of M and rounding up to the nearest integer using the ceiling function, denoted as m = $\lceil \log 2(M) \rceil$, we can ascertain the requisite number of sets to achieve the desired level of security and performance within the BB84 framework [21].

$$\psi(k) \in \left\{ \frac{\pi j}{2M} \right\}, j \in \{0,\ldots,M-i\}, i \in \{1,\ldots,N\} \tag{4.18}$$

Also, $|\psi_i(k)\rangle = cos(|\psi_i(k)\rangle)|0\rangle + sin(|\psi_i(k)\rangle)|1\rangle$, thus one pair of the basis will be

$$\left\{ |\psi_i(k)\rangle, |\psi_i(k) + \frac{\pi}{2}\rangle \right\} \tag{4.19}$$

To address the challenge of low key generation rates in the MDI protocol, researchers have introduced the concept of high-dimensional MDI (as seen in the work by Dellantonio *et al.* in 2018). This advancement enables the encoding of quantum states with more information, leading to a significant boost in the key generation rate. In the standard MDI protocol, which is built upon the principles of the BB84 protocol, both Alice and Bob assume the role of senders. They randomly send quantum states, adhering to the BB84 protocol guidelines. After a sequence of instrumental transformations, these quantum states eventually pass through a beam splitter. In the central part of the setup, detectors are employed to perform Bell state measurements. In this process, successfully measured Bell state involves a concept known as "phase encoding I." This entails encoding information into the quantum states in a particular way, leading to successful measurement outcomes. This innovative approach to quantum key distribution, as exemplified in high-dimensional MDI, contributes to the enhancement of key generation rates. "Phase encoding I" is ([15, 19])

$$\psi^{+} = \frac{1}{\sqrt{2}}(|\psi_i(k)\rangle_A \psi_i(k)\rangle_B - |\psi_i(k)+\frac{\pi}{2}\rangle_A |\psi_i(k)+\frac{\pi}{2}\rangle_B) \quad (4.20)$$

When the quantum states of Alice and Bob are the same.

$$\psi^{-} = \frac{1}{\sqrt{2}}(|\psi_i(k)\rangle_A |\psi_i(k)+\frac{\pi}{2}\rangle_B - |\psi_i(k)+\frac{\pi}{2}\rangle_A \psi_i(k)\rangle_B) \quad (4.21)$$

In this method, there will be a center to identify and authenticate whether the party is a legitimate user or not. If it is a legitimate user, that communication will be moved further, and if it is not, then communication will be terminated. Here, the center assigns a key bound with identity to a legitimate user. For each time, Alice and Bob have to send that key in order to start the communication process.

4.6.2 Parameters and Basic Equipment

Here, in the whole communication process, there are three parties, Alice, Bob, and the center [21]. Also, the communication is done with the help of any quantum; here, we are going to talk about light quanta mainly. Also, there are mainly two channels: the classical channel and the quantum channel. If parties want to prevent DoS, then authentication is required, and for the quantum channel, it is not necessary to perform pre-certification as it is secured due to properties. For the authentication, Alice and Bob send their authentication information *via* the coding bases to the center. Here, we can achieve the key generation rate of

$$R = Q^{\varphi}\left(1 - f_e\left(E^{\varphi}\right)H_2\left(E^{\varphi}\right)\right), \tag{4.22}$$

Q^{φ} (Raw Key Rate): This indicates the frequency at which the center verifies a positive outcome when both Alice and Bob transmit photons using one of three predetermined bases. E^{φ} (QBER): It assesses the error rate during data transmission from Alice and Bob to the center, utilizing a particular encoding method (WCPS) under specific intensity conditions. $f_e()$ This function describes the inefficiency in error correction, capturing how efficiently errors are corrected during the process. $H_2()$: It is the binary entropy function used to measure the information content of the data. The relationship between these factors is derived from a specific scheme called "phase encoding scheme I" [19]. This scheme is used to encode and transmit quantum information, and the mentioned metrics help assess the quality and efficiency of the transmission and error correction process.

However, the probability of Eve to guess the correct bases,

$$P(k \mid eve) = P(\varphi_i \mid eve) = \frac{P(eve \mid \varphi_i)P\left(\varphi_i\right)}{P\left(eve\right)}, \tag{4.23}$$

$$P(eve \mid \varphi_i) = P(eve \mid \varphi_i, k=0)p\left(k=0\right) + P(eve \mid \varphi_i, k=1)p\left(k=1\right),$$
$$= \frac{1}{2}\left(\langle eve|\varphi_i\rangle^2 + \langle eve|\varphi_i + \frac{\pi}{2}\rangle^2\right), = \frac{1}{2}\left(cos\left(eve - \varphi_i\right)^2 + sin\left(eve - \varphi_i\right)^2\right), = \frac{1}{2}.$$

$$P\left(eve\right) = \sum_{i=0}^{M-1} P(eve \mid \varphi_i)P\left(\varphi_i\right), = \frac{1}{2}\sum_{i=0}^{M-1} P\left(\varphi_i\right), = \frac{1}{2}.$$

$$\text{So, } P(k \mid eve) = P\left(\varphi_i\right) = P\left(k\right). \tag{4.24}$$

4.6.3 Pseudo-Random Number Seed Key Construction Protocol for Security (PRNSKC)

The reliability of identity certification reflects our confidence in the legitimacy of a verified identity following the authentication process. This reliability encompasses two key aspects: firstly, the accuracy of the verified identity information in representing the individual and, secondly, the absence of tampering or falsification in the provided information.

In our earlier discussion, we explored methods to bolster the security of identity authentication through the utilization of quantum key distribution (QKD) protocols. These protocols facilitate the extraction of specific identity information from a larger dataset, aided by pseudo-random number seed key creation pseudo-random number seed key construction (PRNSKC).

Within this protocol, the security of selecting registration information is heightened by simultaneously adjusting its location and length. This strategy complicates the task of potential eavesdroppers attempting to guess the registration details. Even if an eavesdropper gains access to Alice's identity information, their ability to impersonate Bob is restricted. In this scenario, the eavesdropper can only measure Bob's quantum states and endeavor to deduce his identity details, presenting a substantially more challenging task compared to compromising Alice's identity. Consequently, we can assess the level of difficulty that eavesdropper Eve encounters when intercepting and deciphering Alice's registration information within the center using a defined equation

$$R \xrightarrow{PRNSKC} \rangle K_a \xrightarrow{P()} \rangle l \xrightarrow{1/m} \rangle \varphi(\mathrm{N}) \tag{4.25}$$

Within this framework, "R" symbolizes Alice's registration data housed within the central system. "PRNSKC" denotes the previously mentioned protocol for pseudo-random number seed key creation. "k_a" represents the seed of Alice's pseudo-random number, which is also retained by the central system (referred to as the center). The function "P()" signifies a pseudo-random function, while "l" denotes the length of the pseudo-random number dictating the quantum base. "(N)" signifies the ultimate quantum state dispatched during the communication procedure ([14]).

Eve, an eavesdropper, is limited to measuring the quantum states of "φ(N)." Due to the dynamic nature of the communication process, where all the information changes with each interaction between Alice and the center, it becomes computationally infeasible for Eve to deduce Alice's registration information through the quantum states alone. In this scenario, acquiring a sufficient number of correct bases is necessary to make educated guesses about the pseudo-random numbers. This can be further substantiated by rigorous proofs demonstrating that the probability of successfully guessing pseudo-random numbers in unexplored situations is extremely low [15].

4.7 A Post-Quantum SUCI for 6G

In the preceding method, we explored a communication process involving three parties: Alice, Bob, and a central entity responsible for authentication and establishing measurement and coding bases. However, this approach, although effective for secure communication, entails numerous instruments, rendering it less suitable for mobile communication environments. To address this limitation, we introduce a post-quantum secure scheme for the Subscriber Concealed Identifiers (SUCI) protocol, aimed at enhancing the security of mobile communications in the forthcoming era of 6G technology.

To achieve key-based encryption, we adopt the key encapsulation mechanism subscriber concealed identifiers (KEMSUCI). Notably, in the transition from 5G to 6G, researchers have introduced the SUPI (subscription permanent identifier) as a superset of the IMSI (international mobile subscriber identity) to mitigate its vulnerabilities.

In the SUCI calculation process, the subscriber's device encrypts the SUPI through ECDH (elliptic curve Diffie-Hellman) key exchange, a computation typically executed within the SIM card or the mobile device itself. However, these conventional methods lack quantum security, rendering them susceptible to vulnerabilities. Recognizing the pressing need for quantum-secure identifiers in 6G technologies, standardization bodies such as ETSI (European Telecommunications Standards Institute) and NIST (National Institute of Standards and Technology) are actively engaged in addressing this imperative through ongoing research and standardization efforts.

4.7.1 How SUCI is Vulnerable to Quantum Attacks

In the current realm of network security within 5G technology, asymmetric cryptography plays a pivotal role in encrypting the subscription permanent identifier (SUPI) into the subscriber concealed identifier (SUCI). However, with advancements in technology and ongoing research, encryption schemes for SUPI to SUCI conversion are now primarily based on the elliptic curve integrated encryption scheme (ECIES). The key distinction between these methods lies in the choice of elliptic curve utilized.

The proposed ECIES method operates as follows: Initially, the home network (HN) and subscribers' devices establish a shared secret through the elliptic curve Diffie-Hellman (ECDH) using the key derivation function (KDF). Subsequently, they derive an ephemeral encryption key from this shared secret and employ it to encrypt the SUPI *via* a symmetric cipher. Only the encrypted results are transmitted over the network. Both encryption methods for SUCI utilize Curve25519 and Secp256r1.

In ensuring secure encryption and decryption of data, both schemes employ AES-128 in counter mode. Additionally, they utilize ANSI-X9.63 as the key derivation function (KDF), allowing variable-length output from a shared secret value. The message authentication code (MAC) employed is HMAC-SHA-256 with a key length of 256 bits.

However, the security of the SUCI protocol is contingent upon the resilience against quantum attacks. A successful quantum computer would need to execute Shor's algorithm to obtain the private key of the home operator. Recent research indicates that breaking the discrete logarithm of a point on Curve25519 requires only 2330 qubits. Consequently, this protocol may not provide state-of-the-art security.

Mathematically, given an operator's public key $H_A = d_A.P$, where P is the base point of the chosen curve, eavesdroppers need to solve this equation once to obtain the private key d_A. This underscores the importance of continually advancing security measures to mitigate quantum vulnerabilities in network protocols.

4.7.2 Post-Quantum Secure SUCI

To make the cellular devices secure against the quantum networks, we should use some aspects which would be tough even for a successful quantum computer and a feasible solution which can be implemented in the SIM card technology. Also, we have to make sure that there is a limited space and there are other constraints which make it even more difficult to select the appropriate method to upgrade SUCI.

KEM: To bolster the security of the key encapsulation mechanism (KEM), implementing the IND-CCA2 (indistinguishability under adaptive chosen-ciphertext Attack) scheme could be considered. This ensures robustness against chosen-ciphertext attacks, further fortifying the encryption process.

Moreover, it is imperative to ensure that the security level of KEMSUCI matches that of ECIES in a quantum channel. Ideally, KEMSUCI should require approximately 2^{128} quantum iterations to thwart potential attacks, mirroring the resilience provided by ECIES in a classical channel. This level of security ensures that the encryption scheme remains robust and resistant to quantum threats, thereby safeguarding sensitive information exchanged over quantum communication channels.
Symmetric Cipher: To protect against attacks using Grover's algorithm, which requires $O\sqrt{N}$ iterations to find a secret key, it's recommended to use AES-256 instead of AES-128 to maintain a 128-bit security level.
KDF/MAC: KDF/MAC will remain the same as it was in ECIES.

4.7.3 Selecting the Perfect KEM for KEMSUCI

KEM should be able to provide full-fledged security along with following some constraints. Due to the constraint of limited capacity, KEM should be made such that it is useful for low latency. Also, there are some standard thresholds to replace the current security system, such as none of the KEMSUCI protocols should use flash storage greater than 256 kilobytes and 10 kilobytes of RAM usage. Those are the upper bound of storage in the SLC14MCO256 controller, which we are going to use as the reference. Also, there is another SIM with high configurations ([17, 18]). We have enlisted some of the pre-requisite and most essential constraints to be followed for KEMSUCI protocols [21]:

Less Ciphertext Size (Essential): Depending upon the various KEM structures, the size of ciphertext varies which is an essential component to secretly share k. As we will be sharing those ciphertexts while we are establishing the network, that will be done through the over-the-air channel. The size of those ciphertexts should be less, and the upper bound of that size is set by 3GPP, which is about 3000 bytes, making and directing the researcher to think about the quantum-resistant protection scheme as a reason.
Few cycles required for encapsulation of the KEM (Important): In order to maintain efficient performance within computational constraints, it is essential to employ faster and lighter encapsulation techniques during key encapsulation mechanism (KEM) operations. Solutions like Kyber or FrodoKEM are crucial for ensuring a smooth and satisfactory user experience in this regard.
Low memory usage of encapsulation (Important): Given the constrained nature of random access memory (RAM) on smart cards, and considering

that KEM encapsulation occurs on the SIM card, typically once per connection attempt, it is imperative to prioritize low memory usage during encapsulation. This is critical for enabling the seamless execution of schemes on SIM cards. Notably, the Infineon SLC 14MCO imposes a limitation, allowing only KEM schemes that utilize a maximum of 10 kilobytes of RAM during encapsulation.

The small size of the public key (Nice-To-Have): While discussing this metric, we are considering the standard flash memory of SLC-14MCO256, having a flash memory of 256 kilobytes. Earlier, we discussed that smart cards not only store the codes but also store the public key in the flash memory. Most of the KEMs prefer the smaller size of the public key, but currently, state-of-the-art SIM cards provide ample amount of storage.

Few cycles are required for decapsulation of the KEM (Nice-to-Have): The decapsulation is also a necessary work while we talk about security purposes; here, as we discussed above, there should be an upper bound to the public key, thus it will eventually have the less computation time and cost for this task which is done at the network level.

Energy consumption of encapsulation (Nice-To-Have): The encapsulation process, occurring either on the phone or the SIM card, confronts the challenge of limited battery capacity inherent to these devices. While acknowledging this constraint, it is essential to note that encapsulation operations are not anticipated to be frequent occurrences on the device. Therefore, any incremental power consumption resulting from encapsulation, when juxtaposed against the overall energy consumption of the smartphone, is presumed to wield minimal significance.

Small size of the private key (Negligible): The private key, a critical component of security, is securely stored within the operator's infrastructure, specifically within the Authentication Center (AuC) or Home Location Register (HLR). These systems are designed to provide robust storage solutions, ensuring the confidentiality and integrity of the private key.

Low storage size of the code (Negligible): In the market, we have such efficient SIM cards which have large read-only memory making the storage and execution process of codes easy.

Few cycles required for key generation (Negligible): Key generation occurs once per home operator, after which the resulting public key is distributed to all SIM cards. Therefore, there is no need to prioritize speed in the key generation process.

Low memory usage of key generation (Negligible): Given the singular occurrence of key generation per operator, the impact of this metric is deemed insignificant within the broader context of system operations and optimization.

Low memory usage of decapsulation (Negligible): As we already assumed that the network side is having sufficient computation power, we can neglect this aspect.

Moreover, the protocol in question should adhere to predefined thresholds and benchmarks, encompassing various parameters such as computational efficiency, security robustness, and adherence to resource constraints. This necessitates a meticulous approach to protocol design, where each aspect is intricately balanced to ensure optimal performance within the specified thresholds.

- Size of ciphertext $\leq 3000\,bytes$
- Size of public key $\leq 256\,kBytes$
- Memory usage of encryption $\leq 10\,kBytes$

Kyber and Saber protocols excel in adhering to these stringent constraints and requirements, making them standout candidates for KEMSUCI, providing both security and efficiency in the realm of key encapsulation mechanisms. Their ability to meet the outlined thresholds showcases their suitability for securing communication in resource-constrained environments while balancing the demands of real-time, low-latency communication. However, there are still some differences between those protocols which are displayed in the following table for easy comparison.

4.7.4 Understanding the Kyber Algorithm

Introducing "Infant Kyber," a distilled version of the Kyber public key encryption system, crafted to provide a clearer grasp of its mechanics. In this simplified iteration, we will opt for reduced security parameters to bolster comprehension. Additionally, we will forgo ciphertext compression, as it is not central to the fundamental concepts we aim to convey [22].

At the core of Infant Kyber lies a modulus q, crucial for ensuring all computations remain within defined limits. For this simplified rendition, we will set q=11. Furthermore, extensive work with polynomials necessitates another modulus, $f = x^2 + 1$, to effectively manage polynomial degrees. While the precise structure of f may seem arbitrary, its function is pivotal in restricting polynomial degrees to less than 2 when taken modulo f ([20, 22]). Table 4.1 shows the list of essential parameters and differences in those parameters making Kyber and Saber the most eligible protocols to be used.

Table 4.1 List of essential Params and Differences in those parameters making Kyber and Saber the most eligible protocols to be used [20].

Metrics	Kyber	Saber
Parameter Configuration	Kyber-512	LightSaber
Implementation	m4	m4fspeed
Ciphertext size (Bytes)	768	736
Speed of Kem.Enc (Cycles)	551,681	481,006
Memory Usage of Kem.Enc (Bytes)	2,300	6,284
Storage Size of the Code (Bytes)	10,700	18,900
Public Key Size (Bytes)	800	672
Energy Usage (μj)	533,953	559,310
Speed of Kem,Dec on Haswell (Cycles)	34,572	61,000
Scheme Output Size (Bytes)	847	815
Public Key Size (Bytes)	800	672
Cycle count until secrete Establishment	551,681	481,006

Key Generation: In Infant Kyber, the private key consists of two polynomials with diminutive coefficients, denoted as s. For instance, a sample private key might be represented as s = (x^2 - x + 1, -2x^2 + 3x), with coefficients randomly selected within defined parameters.

Generating the public key involves constructing a random polynomial matrix A and a polynomial vector t through matrix multiplication and addition with an error vector e. For example, A could be A = (3x^2 + 2x + 1, 4x^2 - 2x + 3, x^2 + x + 2), while t = (x^2 - 2x + 3, -2x^2 + x + 1).

Encryption: To encrypt a message, it must first be converted into polynomial form. For instance, if the message is 5, with a binary representation of $(101)_2$, we create the binary polynomial m_b = x^2 + 1. This polynomial is then scaled to ensure that its coefficients are sufficiently large for the encryption process.

Once scaled, the polynomial is encrypted using the public key (A, t), yielding two values, u and v, which form the ciphertext (t, u, v).

Decryption: Given the private key s and the ciphertext (t, u, v), decryption involves computing a noisy result m_n. This is achieved by subtracting $s^T.u$ from v. The resulting polynomial m_n is then analyzed to recover the original scaled message polynomial m_b.
Scaling Up: While Infant Kyber offers a simplified view, the full Kyber system operates with larger parameters and incorporates compression mechanisms. Key parameters for standard Kyber parameter sets include the maximum polynomial degree n, the number of polynomials per vector k, modulus q, parameters controlling polynomial coefficient sizes, and compression factors for ciphertext components. These parameters collectively determine the security and efficiency of the encryption scheme.

By progressing from Infant Kyber, we gain a comprehensive understanding of the Kyber encryption system and its broader applications in real-world scenarios [22].

4.8 Comparison Between the Existing Schemes

We can calculate the output in a simple way such as Size of KEMSUCI Output=Encapsulating Ciphertext size + 64-bit MAC + length of SUPI.

For LightSaber, it is: 736+64+15=815.

For Kyber-512, it is: 768+64+15=847.

As we delve into the intricacies of post-quantum secure protocols poised to shape the landscape of 6G networks, a critical examination of leading contenders becomes imperative. In this chapter, we embark on a comparative journey between Kyber-512 and LightSaber, two prominent protocols that epitomize the quest for security and efficiency in the quantum era.

Kyber-512, nestled within the esteemed Kyber family, represents a pinnacle of cryptographic engineering, meticulously crafted to withstand the onslaught of quantum adversaries while maintaining commendable performance metrics. Conversely, LightSaber emerges as a beacon of innovation, optimized for lightweight implementations and minimal resource usage, catering to the demands of resource-constrained environments inherent in mobile communication systems.

At the heart of our comparison lies the examination of fundamental metrics essential for evaluating the efficacy of these protocols in real-world scenarios. We begin by scrutinizing the ciphertext size, a pivotal determinant of communication efficiency. Here, LightSaber shines with its smaller ciphertext size, offering a compelling advantage for applications prioritizing data transmission optimization.

Moving beyond mere size considerations, we delve into the realm of performance, dissecting key encapsulation speed measured in cycles. LightSaber's superiority in this domain is unmistakable, boasting faster key encapsulation rates that translate to reduced latency and heightened responsiveness in communication systems.

Memory usage during key encapsulation emerges as another critical battleground, where Kyber-512 showcases its prowess with lower memory requirements compared to LightSaber. This advantage underscores Kyber-512's suitability for environments where memory constraints dictate implementation choices.

Yet, the narrative is not solely defined by efficiency metrics; considerations of storage size and energy consumption further shape our understanding of these protocols' real-world applicability. Kyber-512's leaner storage footprint positions it favorably in scenarios where code size optimization is paramount, while both protocols exhibit comparable energy consumption profiles suitable for mobile devices and communication infrastructure.

As we navigate the nuanced landscape of post-quantum secure protocols, the choice between Kyber-512 and LightSaber becomes a delicate balancing act, contingent upon the specific requirements and constraints of the envisioned application scenarios. While LightSaber's compact footprint and swift performance appeal to resource-conscious deployments, Kyber-512's robust security guarantees and efficient memory utilization offer resilience in diverse operational contexts.

In conclusion, the comparative analysis of Kyber-512 and LightSaber underscores the multifaceted nature of protocol selection in the 6G era. By juxtaposing their strengths and weaknesses, we gain valuable insights into the trade-offs inherent in securing communication networks against quantum threats, paving the way for informed decision-making in the pursuit of quantum-safe communication protocols.

Conclusion

In conclusion, the emergence of quantum computing heralds both unparalleled opportunities and profound challenges for information security, particularly in the context of advancing communication technologies toward 6G networks. Traditional cryptographic methods are increasingly vulnerable to the potent algorithms of quantum mechanics, such as Shor's and Grover's, necessitating a paradigm shift in security protocols.

To address these challenges, the development of post-quantum secure protocols like quantum key distribution (QKD), quantum concealed identifiers, and key encapsulation mechanisms (KEMs) for subscriber concealed identifiers (SUCIs) is paramount. These protocols leverage quantum mechanics to establish secure communication channels and authenticate identities, offering resilience against quantum attacks. Innovative approaches like measurement-device-independent technology (MDIT) and pseudo-random number seed key construction protocols (PRNSKC) further enhance the security and efficiency of quantum communication. Kyber and Saber exemplify the balance between security, efficiency, and compatibility with existing infrastructure, making them promising choices for securing communication in resource-constrained environments.

In essence, proactive collaboration and innovation are critical in navigating the complexities of the digital age and ensuring the integrity and resilience of communication networks against emerging threats. By embracing the transformative potential of quantum technologies and prioritizing advancements in quantum-safe encryption, we can forge a future where communication networks are not only faster and more efficient but also inherently secure and robust.

Bibliography

1. Nielsen, M.A. and Chuang, I.L., *Quantum Computation and Quantum Information, 10th Anniversary Edition*, Cambridge University Press, ISBN 9781107002173, 2010.
2. Einstein, A., Podolsky, B., Rosen, N., Can Quantum-Mechanical Description of Physical Reality Be Considered Complete? *Phys. Rev.*, *47*, 777–780, 1935.
3. Bell, J.S., On the Einstein Podolsky Rosen paradox. *Physics Physique Fizika*, 1, 3, 195–200, Nov. 1964, doi: 10.1103/PhysicsPhysiqueFizika.1.195.
4. https://doi.org/10.48550/arXiv.0902.3827.
5. Arute, F., Arya, K., Babbush, R., *et al.*, Quantum supremacy using a programmable superconducting processor. *Nature*, 574, 505–510, 2019. https://doi.org/10.1038/s41586-019-1666-5.
6. Wootters, W. and Zurek, W., A Single Quantum Cannot be Cloned. *Nature*, 299, 5886, 802–803, 1982, Bibcode:1982Natur.299.802W, doi:10.1038/299802a0. S2CID 4339227.

7. Abramsky, S., No-Cloning in Categorical Quantum Mechanics, *arXiv preprint arXiv:0910.2401*, 2012. [Online]. Available: https://arxiv.org/abs/0910.2401.
8. Gour, G. and Scandolo, C.M., Entanglement of a bipartite channel. *Phys. Rev. A*, *103*, 6, 2021.
9. Garzon, S.R., Yildiz, H., Küpper, A., Decentralized Identifiers and Self-Sovereign Identity in 6G. *IEEE Netw.*, 36, 4, 142–148, July/August 2022, doi: 10.1109/MNET.009.2100736.
10. Trevlakis, S.E., Boulogeorgos, A.-A.A., Pliatsios, D., Ntontin, K., Sarigiannidis, P., Chatzinotas, S., Di Renzo, M., 6G wireless systems: A comprehensive survey and an outlook.
11. Xiao, L., *et al.*, Distributed Shor's algorithm, 2022, arXiv [quant-ph], Available at: http://arxiv.org/abs/2207.05976.
12. Grover, L.K., A fast quantum mechanical algorithm for database search, 1996, arXiv [quant-ph], Available at: http://arxiv.org/abs/quant-ph/9605043.
13. Bennett, C.H. and Brassard, G., Quantum cryptography: public key distribution and coin tossing, in: *Proceeding of the IEEE International.*
14. Khan, M.M., High error-rate quantum key distribution for long-distance communication, 2009, arxiv:0901.3909v4,26.
15. Trushechkin, A.S., *et al.*, Quantum-key-distribution protocol with pseudorandom bases. *Phys. Rev. A. Am. Phys. Soc. (APS)*, 97, 1, 2018, doi: 10.1103/physreva.97.012311.
16. J. ur Rehman, Jeong, Y., Shin, H., Quantum key distribution with a control key. *2017 International Symposium on Wireless Communication Systems (ISWCS)*, pp. 112–116, 2017, doi: 10.1109/ISWCS.2017.8108093.
17. Kannwischer, M., Rijneveld, J., Schwabe, P., Stoffelen, K., *pqm4: Testing and Benchmarking NIST PQC on ARM Cortex-M4*, 2019.
18. Fujii, H. and Aranha, D.F., Curve25519 for the Cortex-M4 and beyond, in: *International Conference on Cryptology and Information Security in Latin America*, Springer, pp. 109–127, 2017.
19. Zheng, X. and Zhao, Z., Quantum key distribution with two-way authentication. *Opt Quant Electron*, 53, 304, 2021. https://doi.org/10.1007/s11082-021-02845-8.
20. Ulitzsch, V., Park, S., Marzougui, S., Seifert, J.P., A Post-Quantum Secure Subscription Concealed Identifier for 6G, in: *Proceedings of the 15th ACM Conference on Security and Privacy in Wireless and Mobile Networks*, Association for Computing Machinery, pp. 157–168, 2022.

21. Beaudry, N.J., Lucamarini, M., Mancini, S., Renner, R., Security of two-way quantum key distribution. *Phys. Rev. A*, 88, 6, 2013.
22. Pathum, U., CRYSTALS Kyber: The Key to Post-Quantum Encryption. *Medium*, 7 Feb. 2024, medium.com/@hwupathum/crystals-kyber-the-key-to-post-quantum-encryption-3154b305e7bd#:~:text=Kyber%2C%20one%20of%20these%20selected,path%20in%20quantum%2Dresistant%20encryption.

5

Quantum Cryptography: Present and Future 6G

Dhananjay Manohar Dakhane[1]*, Vaibhav Eknath Narawade[2] and Pallavi Sapkale[1]

[1]*Department of Computer Science and Engineering, Ramrao Adik Institute of Technology, Nerul, Navi Mumbai, India*
[2]*Department of Computer Engineering, D. Y. Patil Deemed to be University, Navi Mumbai, India*

Abstract
Quantum cryptography is a field that investigates how quantum mechanics can be utilized to make secure communication frameworks. Quantum cryptography utilizes the laws of quantum physical science to send private data, which makes undetected snooping unimaginable. Quantum cryptography depends on photons for information transmission. A photon, in basic terms, is a solitary molecule of light. Photons address paired bits that are sent by means of fiber optic links. One quantum key requires a solitary photon laser shaft signal through a fiber optic link. Just a single photon goes through at a time, making this interaction slower than current specialized strategies. Also, quantum key circulation (QKD) requires a committed fiber optic link between the source and the beneficiary, which confounds things further.

Keywords: Cryptography, quantum key distribution (QKD), security, 6G, photon, optics, physics, fiber optic communication

5.1 Introduction

The high-velocity present-day PC is generally the same as its enormous 30-ton predecessors, who were furnished with approximately 18,000 vacuum cylinders and 500 miles of wiring. Even though computers are now

**Corresponding author*: dhananjay.dakhane@dypatil.edu

Pallavi Sapkale, Shilpa Mehta and S. Balamurugan (eds.) Quantum Computing and Machine Learning for 6G, (117–122) © 2026 Scrivener Publishing LLC

much smaller and can complete their tasks much more quickly, the task still remains the equivalent: to control and decipher an encoding of two-fold pieces into a helpful computational outcome. Gordon Moore's 1965 observation laid the basis for what became known as "Moore's law," which expresses that PC handling power duplicates at regular intervals. Assuming that Moore's regulation is extrapolated guiltlessly to the future, it is found that at some point, each piece of information should be encoded by a real game plan of subatomic size. With the size of parts in old-style PCs contracting to where the behavior of the parts is essentially overwhelmed by a quantum hypothesis rather than a traditional hypothesis, scientists have started exploring the capability of these quantum ways of behaving for calculation. A computer whose components are all designed to function in a quantum manner appears to be more powerful than any classical computer. The quantum computer has the potential to perform certain useful tasks more quickly than any classical computer's physical limitations. This is the motivation to study quantum computing.

In spite of the multitude of advantages and benefits of the web, it is seen as the greatest unregulated and uncontrolled field in humankind's arrangement of encounters. Thus, the issue of information security is fundamental to the web. From one perspective, information development and industry have entered a remarkable period of flourishing. Then again, the method for a wide range of attacks arises in a perpetual stream. Attacks and malicious code, like viruses, worms, and Trojans, create problems for organizations in terms of data security. Besides, the advancement of science and technology also presents new hardships for web security. On account of the properties of quantum computers, many available public key crypto-algorithms (RSA [1, 2], and ElGamal [3], elliptic cryptography (ECC) [4], etc.) will not be protected in quantum computing. RSA algorithm is generally used as a popular encryption technique that depends on the trouble of factoring very large prime numbers. Quantum computers can factor these very large prime numbers a lot quicker than conventional digital computers, so they might actually break RSA encryption very easily. Researcher Ed Gerck, PhD, claims that they just cracked RSA 2048 with the help of quantum computers. If it is true, then there will be serious security issues for sensitive data, including man-in-the-middle attacks and DoS attacks. It is vital to take note that the case RSA-2048 encryption that has been broken has not been autonomously checked. Notwithstanding, the potential security suggestions are serious, so associations ought to begin pondering how to alleviate the dangers.

5.2 Quantum Cryptography

Cryptography is the method involved with encoding information or changing plain text into mixed text so that just somebody who has the right "key" can understand it. Quantum cryptography, likewise, just purposes the standards of quantum mechanics to scramble information and send it in a manner that cannot be hacked. It means that quantum cryptography utilizes the standards of quantum mechanics to send secure messages and, in contrast to numerical encryption, is really un-hackable. The quantum computing definition looks simple; however, the intricacy lies in the standards of quantum mechanics behind quantum cryptography, for example,

1. You can clone some quantum properties of a molecule, yet not the entire molecule.
2. The particles that make up the universe are intrinsically unsure and can all the while exist in more than one spot or more than one condition.
3. The quantum property cannot be computed or estimated without changing or upsetting it.
4. Photons are created arbitrarily in one of two quantum states, i.e., in digital terms, it can be 0, 1, or both.

Quantum cryptography, also called quantum encryption. Basically is a technique that uses the principles of quantum mechanics to secure communication. It provides encryption and key-sharing methods that are nearly impossible to hack. Quantum encryption enables the generation and sharing of secret key sequences (bits) between two communicating parties. These keys are then used for both encryption and decryption of messages. Quantum cryptography can secure messages against decryption attempts, whether the encryption was done using quantum methods or traditional (classical) cryptographic techniques.

A key feature of quantum cryptography is its ability to detect the presence of a third party attempting to intercept the key. This is based on a fundamental principle of quantum physics: the act of measuring a quantum system disturbs it. If an eavesdropper tries to secretly observe the key, they must measure the quantum states (such as photons), which introduces anomalies or disturbances in the system. These disruptions make it impossible to establish a secure key, and communication is immediately halted.

Importantly, the main goal of quantum cryptography is not to transmit the actual data, but to securely generate and distribute the encryption key. Once this key is safely exchanged, it can then be used with classical cryptographic methods to encrypt and decrypt messages.

Let us consider the classical example of Alice and Bob, who want to communicate a message securely. Initially, Alice sends the message by sending a sequence of bits as a key. Actually, this key is a one-directional stream of photons which can represent 0 or 1. These protons vibrate and oscillate in a certain manner. In this way, before Alice starts the message, the photons travel through a polarizer. The polarizer is a channel that empowers specific photons to go through it with similar vibrations and permits others to go through a changed state of vibration. The energized states could be upward (1 bit), even (0 bit), 45 degrees right (1 digit), or 45 degrees left (0 bit). The transmission has one of two polarizations addressing a solitary piece, either 0 or 1, in either plot she utilizes. The photons presently traverse optical fiber from the polarizer toward the beneficiary, Bob. This cycle utilizes a beam splitter that peruses the polarization of every photon. While getting the photon key, Bob did not have any idea about the right polarization of the photons, so he chose one random polarization. Now, Alice compares what Bob used to polarize the key, and afterward, Alice tells which polarizer she used to send every photon. Bob then, at that point, affirms if he utilized the right polarizer. The photons read with some unacceptable splitter are then disposed of, and the excess arrangement is viewed as the key.

How about we guess that there is a man in the middle named Eve? Eve endeavors to tune in and has similar devices as Bob. However, Bob can confirm which polarizer type was used for each photon with Alice, but Eve does not. Eve winds up delivering the last key incorrectly.

Alice and Bob would similarly know that Eve was snooping around on them. Eve, seeing the movement of photons, would then change the photon so that Alice and Sway are mindful of it.

5.3 Quantum Key Distribution

It is a secure, specialized technique that executes an encryption/decryption algorithm, including parts of quantum mechanics. It empowers two parties to deliver a common randomized secret key known exclusively to them, which, at that point, can be utilized to scramble and decode messages. The course of quantum key distribution is not to be mistaken for quantum cryptography, as it is the most popular illustration of a quantum cryptographic errand.

A significant and remarkable property of quantum key distribution is the capacity of the two parties to distinguish the presence of any outsider attempting to acquire information on the key. The outcome from a basic part of quantum mechanics: the most common way of estimating a quantum framework overall upsets the framework. On the off chance that the degree of snooping is under a threshold, a key can be created that is destined to be secure. In any case, no secure key is conceivable, and correspondence is cut off. The security of encryption that utilizes quantum key circulation depends on the underpinnings of quantum mechanics, rather than conventional public key cryptography, which depends on the computational difficulty of specific numerical capabilities. The QKD has provable security in view of information theory and forward secrecy.

The primary downside of quantum key distribution typically depends on having a validated classical channel of communications.

5.4 Post Quantum Cryptography

On the other hand, post-quantum cryptography considers modern classical encryption techniques for converting plaintext into ciphertext that is believed to be secure against attacks by quantum computers. These complex numerical equations take digital computers months or even a long time to break. As quantum computers use Shor's algorithms, they will actually be able to break math-based frameworks in minutes.

Starting around 2023, quantum computing will miss the mark on handling the ability to break generally utilized crypto-algorithms [5]. Cryptographers are planning new calculations to get ready for Q-Day, the day when current algorithms will be defenseless against quantum computing–type attacks. Their work has acquired attention from academics and industry through the PQCrypto meeting series facilitated since 2006, and a few workshops on Quantum Safe Cryptography facilitated by the European Broadcast Communications Guidelines Organization (ETSI) and the Foundation for Quantum Computing [6–8]. The supposed presence of boundless reap now, unscramble later projects has likewise been viewed as an inspiration for early consideration of post-quantum algorithms, as information recorded now might, in any case, stay delicate numerous years into the future [9–11].

5.5 Conclusions

Quantum computing is still in its beginning phases of advancement, yet it can possibly change the universe of cryptography. Organizations ought to begin pondering how to alleviate the dangers of quantum computing and safeguard their information and frameworks for the future. Organizations ought to screen for improvements in quantum computing and be ready to refresh their safety efforts, depending on the situation.

References

1. Rivest, R.L., Shamir, A., Adleman, L., A method for obtaining digital signatures and public-key cryptosystems. *Commun. ACM*, 21, 2, 120–126, 1978.
2. Shen, J., Zhou, T., Chen, X., Li, J., Susilo, W., Anonymous and Traceable Group Data Sharing in Cloud Computing. *IEEE Trans. Inf. Forensics Secur.*, 13, 4, 912–925, 2018.
3. ElGamal, T., A public key cryptosystem and a signature scheme based on discrete logarithms. *IEEE Trans. Inf. Theory*, 31, 4, 469–472, 1985.
4. Tseng, Y.-M., An efficient two-party identity-based key exchange protocol. *Informatica*, 18, 1, 125–136, 2007.
5. Hatridge, M., Shankar, S., Mirrahimi, M., *et al.*, Quantum feedback control of a superconducting qubit: Persistent Rabi oscillations. *Science*, 339, 6116, 178–181, Jan. 2013. DOI: 10.1126/science.1226897.
6. Seitz, N., Cryptographers take on quantum computers. *IEEE Spectrum*, 46, 1, 30–35, Jan. 2009. DOI: 10.1109/MSPEC.2009.4734299.
7. Q&A With Post-Quantum Computing Cryptography Researcher Jintai Ding. *IEEE Spectr.*, 2008-11-01.
8. ETSI Quantum Safe Cryptography Workshop. ETSI Quantum Safe Cryptography Workshop. ETSI, October 2014, Archived from the original on 17 August 2016, Retrieved 24 February 2015.
9. Gasser, L., Post-quantum Cryptography, in: *Trends in Data Protection and Encryption Technologies*, V. Mulder, A. Mermoud, V. Lenders, B. Tellenbach, (Eds.), pp. 47–52, Springer Nature Switzerland, Cham, 2023, ISBN 978-3-031-33386-6, doi: 10.1007/978-3-031-33386-6_10.
10. Townsend, K., Solving the Quantum Decryption 'Harvest Now, Decrypt Later' Problem. *SecurityWeek*, 2022-02-16, Retrieved 2023-04-09.
11. Quantum-Safe Secure Communications. UK National Quantum Technologies Programme, October 2021, Retrieved 2023-04-09.

6

Network Intelligence with Quantum Computing for 6G

H. Bhoomeeswaran[1]*, G. Joshva Raj[2], J. Mangaiyarkkarasi[3] and J. Shanthalakshmi Revathy[4]

[1]*Department of Physics, SRM Madurai College for Engineering & Technology, Pottapalayam, Tamil Nadu, India*
[2]*Department of Physics, Lovely Professional University, Phagwara, Punjab, India*
[3]*PG and Research Department of Physics, Nadar Mahajana Sangam S. Vellaichamy Nadar College, Nagamalai, Madurai, India*
[4]*Department of Computer Science and Engineering, Velammal College of Engineering and Technology, Viraganoor, Tamil Nadu, India*

Abstract

In this chapter, the author shares his viewpoint on a way to enhance the better output functionalities for the 6G applications. We are in an era of digital communication, where the network remains the backbone. It is our key duty to protect the networks. The notion of network intelligence (NI) has evolved in a rapid swiftly, but it is growing only with the help of quantum computing (QC). To run the high-end programs for NI, we need a QC with high specifications. The core objectives of the high-end NI program include autonomous network operation, real-time decision-making, enhanced security, scalability, and flexibility. QC is touted as a revolutionary approach to the field of computation. It leverages the principles of quantum mechanics (QM) and deals with quantum phenomena at atomic and subatomic levels. QC uses quantum bits, or Qubits based on unique properties that allow for better powerful computational abilities. Here, QC and NI are two advanced fields that go hand in hand in multiple ways. It creates synergies that act as a crucial element for driving next-generation computing and network management. The overlapping of the above technologies such as NI and QC harness the revolutions in a way that how networks are managed, secured, and optimized. This collaboration leads to more powerful, efficient, and intelligent systems for the 6G applications.

**Corresponding author*: eswarhbk05@gmail.com

Pallavi Sapkale, Shilpa Mehta and S. Balamurugan (eds.) Quantum Computing and Machine Learning for 6G, (123–140) © 2026 Scrivener Publishing LLC

Finally, the author discussed how to model a better QC with the help of novel fields such as spintronics and photonics or better output for the 6G applications.

***Keywords*:** Quantum computing, machine learning, 6G, network intelligence, spintronics, photonics, quantum networks, artificial intelligence

6.1 Introduction

Evolving the digital landscape, the concept is considered the heart due to its advancements. As compared to the initial days, both networks and computers are developed drastically. In this section, we are going to have a short look at how it evolved during the various stages. In terms of NI, 1G deals with mobile networks, introduced in the 1980s. Analog signals are used for voice communications. But it had poor voice quality low security along with limited capacity. It only supports fundamental voice calls, with zero data services like messaging or browsing. The analog nature of this era made it highly susceptible to eavesdropping as well as interference. 2G is introduced in the 1990s. It is a stage where analog communications are transformed into digital communications. It has some features like SMS and Internet access. This 2G improves the voice quality and security, offering data rates (up to 144 kbps). It was not designed in a fashion to handle heavy data applications such as video streaming and social media. In the early 2000, 3G is launched with broadband in the mobile, leading to high-speed Internet at 2 Mbps. It supports multimedia messages, video calls, and high-speed browsing. 3G networks struggled with higher data rates needed for upcoming applications like mobile video streaming and large-scale Internet usage. Moreover, 3G had relatively high latency. To overcome this issue, 4G came up in the late 2000s with a speed of 1 Gbps. Also, it is to be noted that the latency is reduced drastically. It enabled the widespread usage of video streaming and high-definition video calls. At this juncture, mobile gaming started to evolve because of the advancements in technology. User can feel the adventure at their fingertips anywhere, any time. Despite its advancements, 4G experiences congestion in densely populated areas, and it lacks the ultralow latency required for real-time applications like autonomous vehicles and remote surgery. The ultimate cons are the coverage and penetration indoors in rural areas that need to be addressed. 5G technology offers faster data rates of up to 10 Gbps with lower latency and the ability to connect billions of devices [24]. It supports niche applications like IoT, smart cities, and enhanced mobile broadband. While 5G represents a significant leap forward, it still has many limitations.

The ultrahigh-frequency bands are used for 5G. However, it has limited range and penetration, requiring a dense network of small cells to provide consistent coverage. Additionally, as the number of connected devices continues to grow, even 5G may struggle to meet future demands, in terms of latency and energy efficiency. We need 6G and it is envisioned to address the challenges by providing even faster speeds, lower latency, greater connectivity, and the ability to support a wide range of advanced applications. In short, 6G is not just an upgrade of 5G; it is about anticipating the needs of the future digital world and creating a network infrastructure that can support the next wave of technological innovation. To process the NI, we need a computer with high performance.

A computer is an electronic device that processes data and performs tasks according to a set of instructions, called programs. It can perform a wide range of operations, including calculations, data storage, communication, and more. In other words, a computer is an essential tool in modern life, helping us perform tasks more efficiently and effectively. But, the traditional computer has certain drawbacks. Initially, computers started to grow called the nascent stage from 1946 to 1955. The devices were made of vacuum tubes, magnetic drums, etc. that seemed to be so big and clumsy. These computers were made of 4000 bits and required high electric consumption, where high-end hardwires were programmed in the computers from 1956 to 1965. To overcome this issue, second-generation computers came with a bit of improvements which were made of transistors. Therefore, in terms of size, there is a considerable reduction. Also, it required lower electricity consumption. It worked on the principle of core memory with magnetic cores. Bit levels were increased to 32,000 with punch cards. Then, a modified third generation arose with silicon chips along with the high-level languages from 1966 to 1975 where the cores and ICs were used. Also, the bits were expanded to 128,000. At this point, the keyboard emerged. In 1976-1985, fourth-generation computers with smaller ICs for faster operation became popular. IBM and Apple started to grow at this time. Also, slowly, portable computers surge into the market. Also, the data communication was developed. Finally, fifth-generation computers arrived in 1986, which are more reliable, work faster, and easily portable; different-sized computers came up with multiple features for an affordable cost. Extra high processing speed is the key thing, with the parallel processing works as wireless, and this type of computer continues to grow to date with some sort of modifications to match the modern demands. So far, we have discussed how both the evolution of 5G from 1G networking and the first to fifth generation of computers in a brief manner. To put it simply, the next generation of computers with the 6G network is the future.

Therefore, QC is designed to process the NI that represents the integration of advanced algorithms, including artificial intelligence (AI) and machine learning (ML), into network management and operations. As of today, due to the evolving digital landscape, where connectivity is ubiquitous and the number of devices and users is skyrocketing, NI is becoming increasingly essential. In Figure 6.1, it is depicted that as the years pass by, the need for connected devices also increases exponentially because of the demands created nowadays due to the advent of multiple devices. It is expected that in the next half-decade, the surge of connected devices will double as compared to today. The plot is drawn by taking the data from ergoit.net. Although it is an approximated plot, the trend seems true. The surge is due to the growth of AI [23], ML [18], IoT [3], cloud servers [2], and edge intelligence servers [4]. Therefore, NI is considered as the need of the hour and many researchers started to work on it due to its enticing applications in many fields. Looking ahead, 6G networks are expected to fully integrate AI-driven management systems. These networks will feature self-healing capabilities, extreme automation, and the ability to adapt to user needs in real time. The future of network intelligence will likely involve even more advanced forms of AI, including QC-based intelligence for solving complex optimization problems. QC is the upgrade of fifth-generation computers. In this chapter, with the help of QM, we try to model a QC with different two novel fields called spintronics and photonics and we hope that if we model a QC using Sand P, it enhances the user experience.

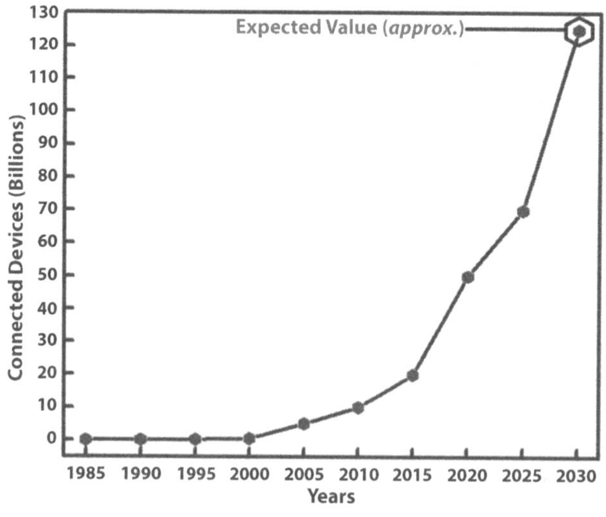

Figure 6.1 A graph plotted for the connected devices in billions against the years.

6.2 Quantum Computing

QC is an extending technology that leverages the principles of QM to process information. Unlike classical computers, which use bits as the basic unit of information by 0 or 1 [10], QC uses quantum bits, or qubits [12]. It can exist in multiple states simultaneously due to the superposition phenomena. They may be entangled with each other, leading to strong correlations. The key ingredients for the QM are superposition, entanglement, quantum gates, and circuits. However, some factors need to be addressed as early as possible for the betterment of the future due to the growing demands which include qubit stability, scalability, and quantum software development. Presently, there are many QCs available in the market from IBM, INTEL, GOOG, HON, IONQ, etc. But, due to the advancement of NI, we are in need of a QC on par with NI, so that they can easily solve the complex problems.

6.3 Spintronic QC

Researchers started to work on spintronic technology where the field got additional intrinsic properties called spin along with the charge. So, to the best of our knowledge, we have proposed the theory of designing a new QC called spintronic QC aka SQC. It combines principles of spintronics and QC to create a new type of quantum processor. Therefore, one can perform many calculations at once due to quantum parallelism, making it theoretically capable of solving certain problems much faster than traditional computers where the previous one sequentially performs calculations, processing one operation at a time. In QC, the processing and the storage of data are mentioned as 0 and 1 [10], whereas in the SQC, it is done by the up (+1/2) and down spin (-1/2) states of the electrons [11]. Therefore, one can potentially store more data in smaller spaces and process with higher energy efficiency. Electrons have angular momentum, which is the tendency of something to keep rotating; eventually, it leads to 360 degrees of freedom in spin states to store and process the information [1]. By utilizing and incorporating the above phenomena, one can make use of all the 360 degrees, for storing the data allowing for the encoding of much richer information. This is described by the spin vector's orientation on the surface of a Bloch sphere in Figure 6.2 [8]. The Bloch sphere is a geometrical representation of a qubit's state. Any point on the sphere corresponds to a unique quantum state, with the poles representing the

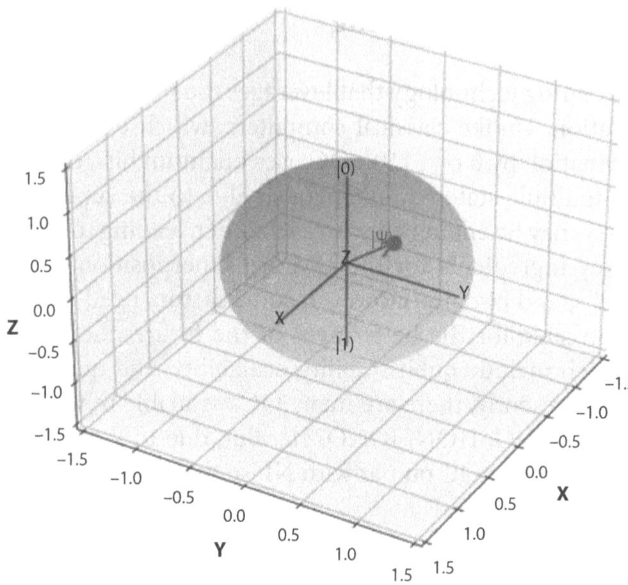

Figure 6.2 The schematic representation of the Bloch sphere drawn in Python.

traditional "up" and "down" states. The 360 degrees of freedom allow a qubit to exist in a superposition of "up" and "down" states. The qubit's state can be described by two angles, namely, θ (latitude) and φ (longitude), which determine the exact point on the sphere. By leveraging the full 360 degrees of spin freedom, more complex quantum states can be encoded, which could theoretically increase the information density and processing power of quantum systems. In principle, each spin could store more than just binary information. By controlling the spin's orientation precisely, it might be possible to store multiple levels of information within a single spin system, significantly increasing data storage capacity. It is achievable but not in an easy manner because it has some bottlenecking issues which include the fine manipulation of magnetic fields, electric fields, or other external controls. Measuring the exact spin state without collapsing the quantum state is another challenge. Because quantum states are fragile, and interactions with the environment can lead to decoherence, where the qubit loses its quantum properties. Advanced spintronic materials, such as topological insulators and spin-orbit–coupled systems, are being explored for this purpose. Among those, spin-orbit coupling (SOC) can be achieved with the help of spin Hall spin torque nano-oscillators (SHSTNO) [6]. Therefore, our aim is to model an SHNO that emits a high-frequency, high-power, and high-quality factor with low line-width for the 6G applications in the future.

6.4 Literature Survey

In this section, literature surveys on NI and QC are presented separately. This literature survey not only helps us to know the results of what happened in the past but also gives a clear insight into what direction we need to move further in order to achieve the best possible solutions for the 6G applications. Initially, as far as the NI is concerned [20], carried out their work in AI techniques. In particular, they worked more on deep learning (DL) to manage the traffic signals of 5G. The study reveals how AI predicts traffic accurately and optimizes the allocation of resources in a dynamic manner. They concluded that the role of DL is influential in terms of enhancing its efficiency and traffic response in an effective way. Micheal Zhang *et al.* discussed the use of reinforcement learning (RL) for the autonomous management network slices in 6G. Their aim is to achieve real-time, adapting slicing that meets the diverse quality of services (QoS). Their results show how they obtained a 30% improvement as compared to other methods using RL. Sarah Thompson *et al.* investigated AI for the detection and mitigation of security threats in modern communication networks, and they incorporated ML. Their results are fascinating because of their 95% accuracy in terms of detection, with a 2% false positive rate. Robert Kim *et al.* oriented their works toward federated learning (FL) for optimizing network performance for the privacy of individual users. Through the FL model, by keeping the privacy of users without transferring any data to the server, they have significantly reduced the risk of data breaches. John Williams *et al.* focused their work on cognitive radio networks (CRN) and proved that the technique is very helpful in enhancing the dynamics of spectrum management. Also, they achieved a 40% improvement by utilizing the spectrum efficiency properly. The above survey throws some insights, and by keeping all this in mind, we did a brief literature survey for QC, which is discussed as follows: Elena Roberts *et al.* reported the advancements in quantum error correction (QEC) codes. Their work is devoted to improving fault tolerance in QC. They concluded that by incorporating the surface codes, they can be able to achieve their agenda as compared to the color codes and concatenated codes. Aisha Patel *et al.* wrote a review on quantum machine learning algorithms and their pros over classical algorithms. They identified that QML algorithms outperform the classical algorithms especially when it comes to quantum hardware.

Michael Li *et al.* analyzed the quantum circuits which are more resilient to noise by nature leads to a critical issue during commercialization. Their reports show that they have successfully reduced the noise by up to 20% by gate reduction technique. Robert Kim *et al.* evaluate the attacks pertaining to QC. They came to the conclusion that the lattice-based and code-based protocols are promising candidates with which we can optimize security further. Finally, Emily Harris *et al.* examine quantum supremacy (QS), focusing on solving complex problems over QC. Their study reveals that QC can perform tasks on its own. For instance, using random circuit sampling, QC performs at a very swift speed, holding a promising future for QS. Based on the literature survey, we identified that it is our duty to address the research gap mentioned above. For that, we have modeled a device that works under the principle of both spintronics and photonics. The spintronics part is very essential for the speed of the device which is very efficient when it comes to the traffic response because of its high-quality factor. On the other hand, the photonics part is very influential in quantum circuits and enhances qubits. SHSTNO, a hybrid device, works on the underlying principle of spintronics and photonics and poses the solution for the abovementioned research problems, and the detailed depiction of the device shall be discussed in the next section.

6.5 SHSTNO

As far as electronics are concerned, the entire microelectronic devices work by accounting for the charge of an electron alone, and the spin degree of freedom of an electron has been neglected in traditional electronics. Most recently, electron spin is taken into account in addition to its charge. Thereafter, a field called spintronics burst out into the limelight with many potential applications in everyday life. Spin-based electronics is an interdisciplinary research field in magnetism that encompasses the brief study of electronic devices that require a nano-platform for both design and fabrication for cutter-breaking commercialization. Particularly, spintronics serves as another edging area in the speedy spread of microelectronic devices [9]. Spintronics aims at marrying the science of spin, the fundamental rotational degree of freedom of an electron, with microelectronics technology subjected to huge interest to produce devices with new functionality. In spintronics, electron spins must be conserved in both the time and spatial manner. So, the diminutive device dimension must be smaller than the spin relaxation time as well as the spin diffusion length. In hindsight, [i] information is stored (written) into spins as a particular spin orientation (up or down), [ii] the spins attached to mobile electrons carry the information along the wire, and [iii] the information is read at the terminal. The conduction electrons' spin orientation exists for lesser nanoseconds which turn out to be very effective for memory storage, QC, and magnetic sensor application. These devices are primarily proposed for applications in the magnetic sensor in reading heads and NV MRAM. The eventual aim of this field is to notably exploit the spin of an electron in addition to the charge of an electron to transport the information and data. Not only in the magnetization switching but also it emits high frequency which explores spin torque nano-oscillator [STNO], a new class of nanoscopic oscillator. It has an ultra-wide frequency window with huge modulation rates, and the manufacturing process is highly compatible with RF CMOS processing. STNOs use several spintronic and nanomagnetic phenomena for their operation, such as spin polarization, spin transfer torque (STT), and spin-orbit torque (STT) [5]. Here, an SOT-based spintronic device called SHSTNO acts as an ideal candidate for remitting high frequency and power poses as the solution for the 6G applications. SHSTNO device is a combination of STNO and SHNO device, the previous one works on the principle of STT, and the latter one works on the principle of SOT [19]. The main difference between STT and SOT resides in the current injection geometry used for the writing process. In STT, the current is injected perpendicularly into the device, whereas in SOT, the current is injected in-plane, through an adjacent SOT layer—typically a heavy metal such as tungsten (W). In this regard, we modeled an SHSTNO device. SHSTNO [13] is a bilayer device with current-in-plane (CIP) geometry, as shown in Figure 6.3, composed of heavy metal along with an FM material. In Figure 6.3, top FFL material such as CoFeB is taken. This device works under the principle called SHE, which originates from spin-orbit scattering that paves the way for the deflection of conduction electrons with opposite signs oriented in the opposite direction. The thickness of the Pt is taken as 5 nm and all other FM in FFL as 3 nm. It is well-known that the Hall effect (HE) in nonmagnetic metals or semiconductors refers to the buildup of a so-called Hall voltage across an electrical conductor, transverse to both the electric current in the conductor and to an external magnetic field perpendicular to the current. Edwin Hall found that the SHE [17] in FM results was ten times greater than HE in nonmagnetic materials. The SHE is then a limiting case of this phenomenon in materials without any spontaneous magnetization but with substantial spin-orbit coupling. As there is no spin imbalance in a nonmagnetic material, the asymmetric spin-dependent scattering does not result in any Hall voltage. What it results in, however, is a net spin current transverse to the charge current and, in a steady state, the

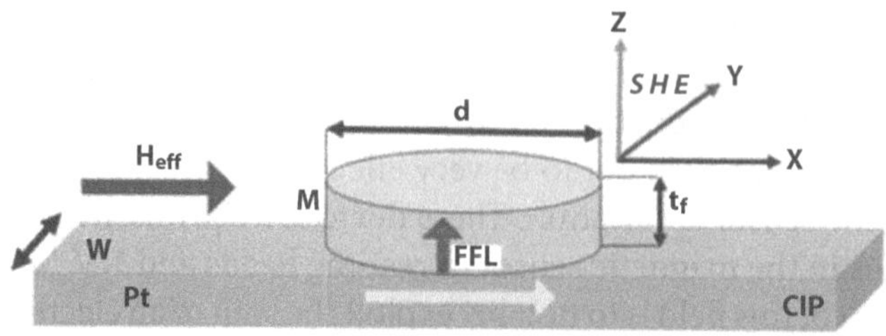

Figure 6.3 SHSTNO device.

buildup of spin accumulation zones at the edges of the conductor, which can be directly observed by optical means and which is used in spin-current driven devices. Thus, the generated spin current injected into reaches the free layer, STT will occur. It is due to the transformation of conduction electrons from one layer to another made the FFL magnetization process. Eventually, it ends up generating the frequency, which will be in the order of the microwave regime. The governing LLGS [15] equation, including SHE and STT effect, may be written as:

$$\frac{d\vec{M}}{dt} = -\gamma\left[\vec{M}\times\vec{H}_{eff}\right] - \frac{\alpha\gamma}{M_s}\vec{M}\times\left[\vec{M}\times\vec{H}_{eff}\right] - a_{j1}\left[\vec{M}\times\left(\vec{M}\times\vec{Y}\right)\right] + a_{j2}\left[\left(\vec{M}\times\vec{Y}\right)\right]$$

The first term of the LLGS equation is the precession term that conserves magnetic energy and regulates magnetization dynamics' precessional frequency. The second term is the damping term that depletes the energy during magnetization dynamics. The third term is the spin transfer term. It either amplifies or attenuates the precessional motion so that purely relies on the current flow direction. The fourth term renders the field-like spin torque which is due to effectively pinned layer magnetization and produces a precessional motion about the free layer magnetization. The effective magnetic field ($\vec{H}_{eff}$) that acts on the free layer is composed of anisotropy and demagnetization which may be written as $\vec{H}_{eff} = \vec{H}_{ani} + \vec{H}_{demag}$, i.e., $\vec{H}_{eff} = K\vec{M}_x\vec{e}_x - 4\pi N_z\vec{M}_z\vec{e}_z$. Here, $\vec{e}_x$ and, $\vec{e}_z$ are the unit vectors along the x and z directions. $aj_1 = \left[\frac{2\mu j\theta}{\left(1+\alpha^2\right)edM_s^2 m_s} g\left(\vec{M}.\vec{Y}\right)\right]$ and $aj_2 = \left[\frac{2\mu j\alpha\theta}{\left(1+\alpha^2\right)edM_s m_s} g\left(\vec{M}.\vec{Y}\right)\right]$ are the coefficients of STT.

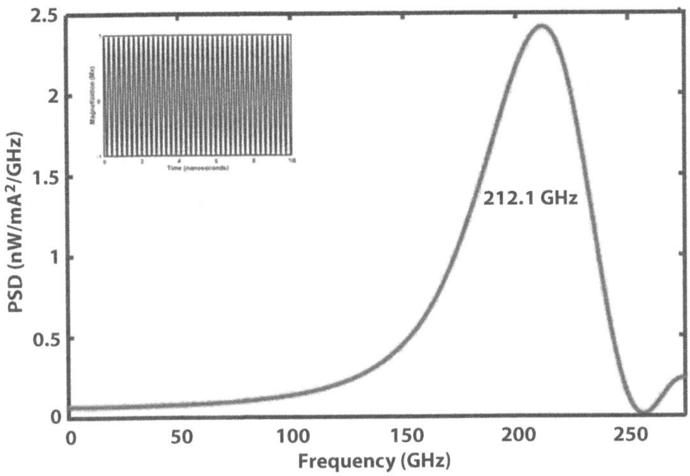

Figure 6.4 A graph plotted for the frequency vs. PSD. Inset plot, time vs. magnetization.

This type of device will be able to generate the frequency close to terahertz. If we try to make this device emit terahertz, it can be easily applicable to the 6G applications since it requires high frequency. It can be achieved by incorporating certain techniques, called synchronization or coupling schemes, which are nothing but connecting two devices to deliver a better output. Apart from getting better results, we can also model this type of device by carefully choosing novel materials. Therefore, the author suggests that by incorporating the above techniques or methods into the QC, eventually, we are a step ahead of marching toward the high-tech 6G technology. In Figure 6.4, it is evident that the device would be able to emit a frequency of about 212 GHz [7]. The inset plot shows, time (ns) vs. magnetization. To bolster the QC further, we are also giving the guidelines on how to model a QC with the help of photonics called photonics QC aka PQC in the next section.

6.6 Photonic QC

In this section, we discuss the significant role of photonics in the field of QC-based NI. Photonics is a subject that deals with the exploration of light for various applications, such as communication, networking, computing, and other optical systems (Michael R. *et al.*, 2007). Photonics is advantageous over other platforms in various aspects. For instance, in communication, the speed of light is incredibly high compared to other communication carriers, and it also offers enormous bandwidth for accommodating more channels. Other benefits of light in communication include low loss, high security, and compatibility with other devices.

The discussion for this section is to explore the role of photonics in QC-based NI. This section was motivated by two factors: networks themselves benefit from photonics and QC is essentially implemented using the concepts of photonics. Nowadays, photonics plays a crucial role in the field of networks and communication because of its aforementioned advantages. Photonics-based communication technology has matured as various macro- and micro-photonic components have been studied and developed. The immense presence of photonics and its continuous influence in networking call for research into its role in NI. This implies that the future development of NI must focus on photonics aspects. Although QC is a separate domain on its own, its influences in other areas such as networks are significant. QC too gets benefits from photonics [14] as the implementation of QC largely depends on photonics systems and phenomena.

As detailed in the previous sections, NI has become an unavoidable development in the field of communication. There are multiple aspects of NI, from hardware to algorithms which need to be addressed. The focus on the integration of photonics and NI should primarily be on the hardware aspect. The reason for this is that networks are based on photonics, so NI should also necessarily depend on photonics. In particular, the focus will be on how photonics can be used for enhancing NI. Photonics also plays a pivotal role in implementing neural networks [20].

NI may have different motivations, such as improved performance, security enhancement, and traffic management. Based on the application, the implementation strategy will differ. For instance, the hardware part of a traffic management system includes routers and switches. Routers direct data packets toward different networks. They use routing tables to find the optimal path to direct data and avoid congestion. Photonic routers have started to replace conventional routers. The advantages of using optical routers over conventional routers include compatibility with other optical communication components, efficient detection of data for optimization, etc. The usage of photonic routers and components such as beam splitters in a networking system calls for a new research area as they have to be configured for performing the task of intelligence. A schematic diagram for an NI system for traffic management is shown in Figure 6.5. Photonic systems are advantageous in performing the task of intelligence as they are compatible with carrier signals and are faster and more efficient. Of those algorithms which are available, photonic systems can use Dijkstra's algorithm. This algorithm is given as follows.

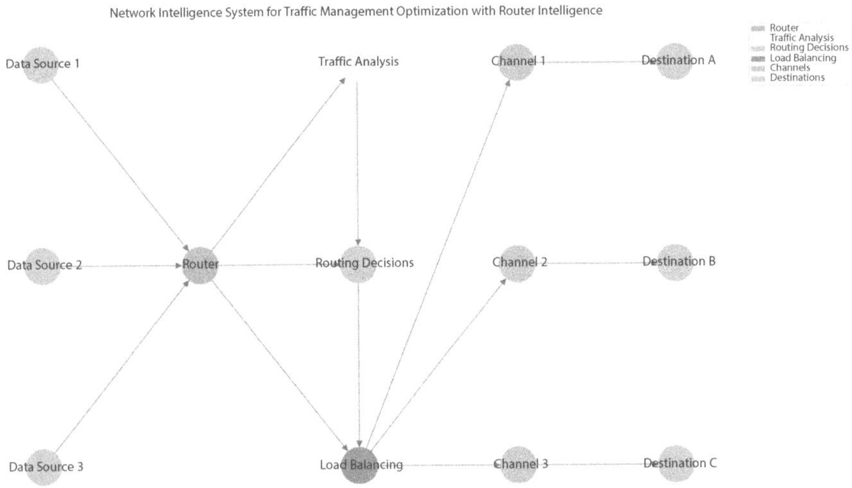

Figure 6.5 The diagram illustrates the flow of data from multiple sources to a router which analyze the data to take a decision to send the information through an available channel.

Decision-making processes of networks by themselves are very crucial nowadays as the amount of data handled by the network is increasing. This will be helpful for the optimization of available hardware components for efficient performance. Various strategies have been proposed and demonstrated for implementing NI. In this section, we explore photonics-based QC-assisted NI. Research on quantum NI has already started. The role of photonics in a QC-based intelligence system is crucial, as the implementation of QC itself is based on photonics. Quantum networks are based on quantum gates, which manipulate qubits. Qubit is a superposition state of the binary states of a system. It means that the two states of a binary system exist in a single state at the same time, as shown in Figure 6.6.

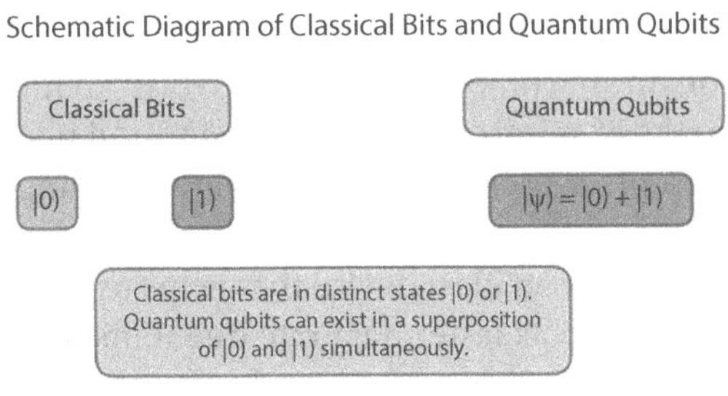

Figure 6.6 Schematic diagram of classical and quantum bits.

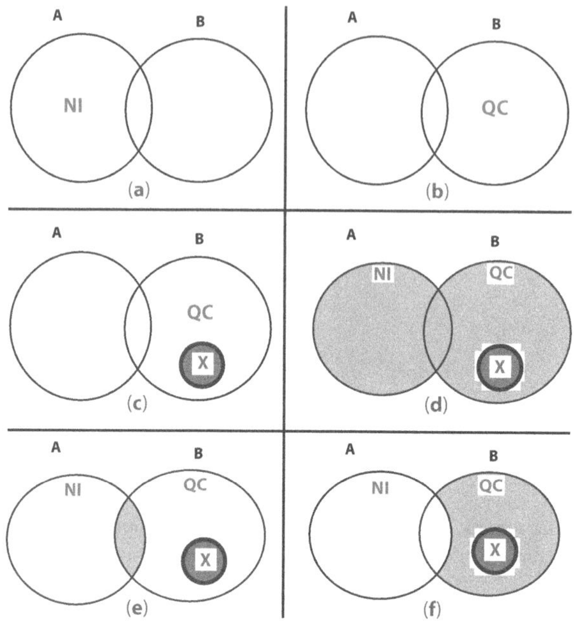

Figure 6.7 Illustration of Venn diagram for the modeling of NI and QC using X.

The present work can be illustrated with the aid of the above Venn diagram with which the logical relationships between the NI and QC are discussed in Figure 6.7. The above Venn diagram consists of two circles A and B. A denotes NI and B denotes QC. In circle B, there is an inner circle called X, i.e., $X \subset B$. It means that X is directly proportional to B. The performance of B can be enhanced with respect to X. Here, $X = S + P$, where S denotes spintronics and P denotes photonics. The performance of QC depends on S and P: QC α X or QC α S & P.

Modeling a better QC using S and P involves leveraging advanced architectures that combine the strengths of both fields to improve computational power, scalability, and error resilience. The goal is to develop hybrid systems that utilize novel qubits and interconnects to achieve superior performance in quantum computations. This hybrid architecture, utilizing the distinct strengths of spintronics for processing and photonics for communication, represents a promising path toward building more efficient, scalable, and powerful QC.

The SHSTNO device is an ideal device that helps us to achieve 6G based on the performance, such as faster data rate due to its high QF over 1000, with low latency. Here, the network latency deals with the delay in network communication, i.e., the time taken to transfer the network. More delay or lag paves the way for high latency and vice versa. The connections are reliable between the nodes, which helps for a stable connection. Moreover, terahertz [21] is the frequency spectrum required for 6G and this device is capable of emitting such frequency. Also, the coverage is good due to the densification of the network. On the other hand, photonics also offers some benefits for the betterment of QC in terms of its quantum processors for faster operations. Also, scalability is high because more optical components can be scaled up easily. They are operable at room temperature. Photons have a superposition state, meaning they can be at 1 and 0 simultaneously. Finally, the fault tolerance is very low, meaning they are less susceptible to noise. Mathematically, it can be represented as X subset of B. Hereafter, X is the subset in all the remaining Venn diagrams within B. Our motto can be easily achieved with the help of A∪B, put together all three including the subset helps to achieve the 6G application. NI + QC + X = 6G. Meanwhile, A∩B renders the quantum enhancer or quantum networks and specifies the common points between the NI and QC. At last, B-A or B difference A is the theme of this research article. Simply speaking, one can model the QC by accounting S and P in a simultaneous manner, and the output is extremely higher which can be applicable for real-time data processing, decision-making, etc.

In 6G, NI and QC will likely work in tandem. For instance, AI models running on QC could dynamically optimize spectrum allocation in real time, based on data collected from millions of connected devices, ensuring efficient use of the limited wireless spectrum. In a smart healthcare system, 6G with NI and QC can be used to enable real-time, secure remote surgeries. NI can ensure network reliability, while QC can process vast amounts of patient data and provide high-speed data encryption, ensuring both speed and security during the operation.

6.7 Conclusion

In this chapter, we have suggested how to model a QC called SQC and PQC. If we combine both the SQC and PQC together, it is expected that we will be closer to achieving the dream of designing a novel QC with the help of fundamental quantum physics. Also, the NI of any complex structure can be easily solved in the above proposed QC. Although it is not an easy process, SHSTNO is the ideal device that emits high frequency, PSD, and QF. By carefully choosing the material and technique, this device is highly capable of emitting terahertz frequency which is the fundamental frequency spectrum with which the 6G technology can able to work.

The anticipated timeline for 6G deployment is around 2030, with ongoing research and development shaping what it will eventually become. 6G is expected to deliver data rates up to 100 times faster than 5G [22], potentially reaching speeds of 1 terabit per second (Tbps) enabling instantaneous downloads and seamless streaming of ultrahigh-definition content. Latency in 6G networks could be reduced to sub-millisecond levels, making real-time interactions like augmented reality (AR), virtual reality (VR), and autonomous driving more responsive and precise. 6G will likely utilize the terahertz (THz) frequency spectrum, which offers much higher bandwidth than the millimeter-wave spectrum used by 5G. This will not only enable faster data transmission but also present new challenges in terms of signal propagation and infrastructure requirements.

6.8 Future Scope

The synergy between QC and NI will be essential for the success of 6G networks. QC provides the computational power needed for solving complex optimization and cryptographic problems, while NI ensures real-time decision-making and automation across the network. Together, they create a more secure, efficient, and intelligent network capable of supporting the massive demands of 6G applications, from autonomous systems to hyper-connected smart cities. The aforementioned device called SHSTNO is an ideal candidate for 6G applications due to its rich functionalities and promising frontiers. As research advances, with the aid of Neuromorphic Computing (NC), an advanced form of QC, SHSTNO coupled with NC can mimic neural structures and functions for applications like speech recognition and sensory data interpretation. It works with like the network of neurons and synapses for computation as well as the memory storage. The proposed NC-based SHSTNO device helps to solve many problems such as speech recognition and sensory data interpretation. This type of work is devoted to the hot topic of science as of today where Neuralink founded by Elon Musk *et al.* tries to restore personal control over limbs, prosthetics, or communication devices by fabricating a brain chip [16]. The integration of QC and NI in future networks offers a rich area for research and development. Quantum Computing can empower Network Intelligence by providing computational power for complex tasks like optimization, security, and resource management, while NI can leverage this power to enhance real-time decision-making and autonomy. Research directions like Quantum-enhanced AI, quantum-secured AI, quantum federated learning, and quantum-based digital twins hold the potential to transform how future network technologies like 6G operate, providing both increased efficiency and security.

References

1. Ahn, E.C., 2D materials for spintronic devices. *npj 2D Mater. Appl.*, 4, 17, 2020, https://doi.org/10.1038/s41699-020-0152-0.
2. Aldahwan, N.S. and Ramzan, M.S., Descriptive Literature Review and Classification of Community Cloud Computing Research. *Sci. Program.*, 2022, 1–12, 2022, https://doi.org/10.1155/2022/8194140.
3. Arányi, G. and Szücs, V., IoT related security issues and black-box testing experiences in a smart lighting system, vol. 64, pp. 61–64, 2023.
4. Barbuto, V., Savaglio, C., Chen, M., Fortino, G., Disclosing Edge Intelligence: A Systematic Meta-Survey. *Big Data Cognit. Comput.*, 7, 44, 2023, https://doi.org/10.3390/bdcc7010044.
5. Barla, P., Joshi, V.K., Bhat, S., Spintronic devices: a promising alternative to CMOS devices. *J. Comput. Electron.*, 20, 805–837, 2021, https://doi.org/10.1007/s10825-020-01648-6.
6. Bhoomeeswaran, H., Bakyalakshmi, R., Vivek, T., Sabareesan, P., Tunability of output frequency using Spin Hall Angle in Spin Hall Spin Torque Nano Oscillator, p. 020086, 2019, https://doi.org/10.1063/1.5130296.
7. Bhoomeeswaran, H. and Sabareesan, P., Enhancing Frequency and Reducing the Power of Spin-Torque Nanooscillator By The Generated Oersted Field. *SPIN*, 10, 2050012, 2020, https://doi.org/10.1142/S2010324720500125.
8. Filatov, S. and Auzinsh, M., Towards Two Bloch Sphere Representation of Pure Two-Qubit States and Unitaries. *Entropy*, 26, 280, 2024, https://doi.org/10.3390/e26040280.
9. Hirohata, A., Yamada, K., Nakatani, Y., Prejbeanu, I.-L., Diény, B., Pirro, P., Hillebrands, B., Review on spintronics: Principles and device applications. *J. Magn. Magn. Mater.*, 509, 166711, 2020, https://doi.org/10.1016/j.jmmm.2020.166711.
10. Joshi, V.K., Spintronics: A contemporary review of emerging electronics devices. *Eng. Sci. Technol. Int. J.*, 19, 1503–1513, 2016, https://doi.org/10.1016/j.jestch.2016.05.002.
11. Klümper, A., Free energy and correlation lengths of quantum chains related to restricted solid-on-solid lattice models. *Ann. Phys.*, 504, 540–553, 1992, https://doi.org/10.1002/andp.19925040707.

12. Leuenberger, M.N. and Loss, D., Spintronics and quantum computing: switching mechanisms for qubits. *Physica E*, 10, 452–457, 2001, https://doi.org/10.1016/S1386-9477(01)00136-9.
13. Li, X., Zheng, Y., Khan, W.U., Zeng, M., Li, D., Ragesh, G.K., Li, L., Physical Layer Security of Cognitive Ambient Backscatter Communications for Green Internet-of-Things. *IEEE Trans. Green Commun. Netw.*, 5, 1066–1076, 2021, https://doi.org/10.1109/TGCN.2021.3062060.
14. Lu, Y., Sigov, A., Ratkin, L., Ivanov, L.A., Zuo, M., Quantum computing and industrial information integration: A review. *J. Ind. Inf. Integr.*, 35, 100511, 2023, https://doi.org/10.1016/j.jii.2023.100511.
15. Meo, A., Cronshaw, C.E., Jenkins, S., Lees, A., Evans, R.F.L., Spin-transfer and spin-orbit torques in the Landau–Lifshitz–Gilbert equation. *J. Phys.: Condens. Matter*, 35, 025801, 2023, https://doi.org/10.1088/1361-648X/ac9c80.
16. Musk, E., An Integrated Brain-Machine Interface Platform With Thousands of Channels. *J. Med. Internet Res.*, 21, e16194, 2019, https://doi.org/10.2196/16194.
17. Puebla, J., Kim, J., Kondou, K., Otani, Y., Spintronic devices for energy-efficient data storage and energy harvesting. *Commun. Mater.*, 1, 24, 2020, https://doi.org/10.1038/s43246-020-0022-5.
18. Sarker, I.H., Machine Learning: Algorithms, Real-World Applications and Research Directions. *SN Comput. Sci.*, 2, 160, 2021, https://doi.org/10.1007/s42979-021-00592-x.
19. Shao, Q., *et al.*, Roadmap of Spin–Orbit Torques. *IEEE Trans. Magn.*, 57, 1–39, 2021, https://doi.org/10.1109/TMAG.2021.3078583.
20. Shastri, B.J., *et al.*, Photonics for artificial intelligence and neuromorphic computing. *Nat. Photonics*, 15, 102–114, 2021, https://doi.org/10.1038/s41566-020-00754-y.
21. Wang, M., *et al.*, Spintronics Based Terahertz Sources. *Crystals*, 12, 11, 1661, 2022, https://doi.org/10.3390/cryst12111661.
22. Wang, Z., *et al.*, Vision, application scenarios, and key technology trends for 6G mobile communications. *Sci. China Inf. Sci.*, 65, 151301, 2022, https://doi.org/10.1007/s11432-021-3351-5.
23. Yu, B., Wang, B., Zhang, Y., Application of artificial intelligence in coal mine ultra-deep roadway engineering—a review. *Artif. Intell. Rev.*, 57, 262, 2024, https://doi.org/10.1007/s10462-024-10898-w.
24. Zikria, Y.B., *et al.*, Next-Generation Internet of Things (IoT): Opportunities, Challenges, and Solutions. *Sensors*, 21, 1174, 2021, https://doi.org/10.3390/s21041174.

Part III

MACHINE LEARNING

7

Introduction to Machine Learning: Conceptualization, Implementation, and Research Perspective

Snehasis Dey

College of Engineering, Bhubaneswar (BPUT University), Odisha, India

Abstract

Machine learning (ML) has become a commodity in every sphere of routine life today. It is a subfield of artificial intelligence, broadly defined as the ability of a machine to imitate intelligent human behavior. It has become a standard tool in every field of science, research, technology, and engineering. Many ML applications are changing people's lives at unprecedented speed and scale. Both AI and ML have become popular subjects of research interest in the current era as they are the building blocks of data science. Like humans, machines can make intelligent decisions by learning from their past experiences. Evolved way back from 1950 to the current age of the Fourth Industrial Revolution (4IR), ML has progressed like a giant in the field of data science. ML intelligently prioritizes the analysis of the wealth of data, processes them to build models, and develops the corresponding smart and automated applications. Various learning algorithms, like supervised, unsupervised, semi-supervised, and reinforcement learning, are key methods in ML technology for data analysis. Deep learning is a part of machine learning which can also intelligently analyze the wealth of data on a large scale. This chapter describes the basics of ML, its evolution, and subsequent implementation in different research fields like cybersecurity, healthcare, agriculture, and communication. But more specifically, it dives into the 5G and beyond wireless communication field.

***Keywords*:** ML, artificial intelligence, data analysis, supervised learning, unsupervised learning, 5G

Email: Snehasis9dey@gmail.com

Pallavi Sapkale, Shilpa Mehta and S. Balamurugan (eds.) Quantum Computing and Machine Learning for 6G, (143–160) © 2026 Scrivener Publishing LLC

7.1 Introduction to Machine Learning: Conceptualization Perspective

Machine learning is a set of algorithms skilled from a wealth of data or experiences rather than being explicitly programmed. Basically, machine learning (ML) is a concept based on two important interrelated questions: First, "How can we construct a machine that automatically improves itself through past experience?" Second, "What are the set of rules or algorithms that govern these machines to practically execute their learning experience into reality?" The true phenomenon of machine learning is vital in addressing these two basic scientific questions. Without being in our knowledge, we use daily machine learning concepts just like Google searching for an eBook to read or identifying inbox-worthy emails and discarding the spam that needs less attention. In the simplest way, we can say "Machine learning is everything and for everyone nowadays".

Machine learning caters to a wide set of learning tasks, from learning to classify the modules that are of higher importance in a scientific research article, to learning to recognize the important pixels in images, to learning to control driverless automobiles, etc. Each machine learning concept is unique and one of its kind here. But, it is basically based on three main attributes: some measure of performance (P), some specific task (T), and accomplishing through some training experience (E). When these three attributes are described properly, then the learning problem is well modeled and defined.

Definition: *"Machine learning is the phenomenon of educating machines to learn concepts and techniques, precisely skill on them, and perform intelligently the way humans do."*

7.1.1 Basics of Machine Learning

Machine learning and artificial intelligence are perhaps the biggest achievements that science can make and are probably the core of all technological advancements in recent times. ML, being a subset of AI techniques, caters mostly to algorithms to extract patterns by using mathematics, statistics, optimization, and knowledge invention methods. Finding specific patterns in data is the building block of machine learning [1]. It is all about the intelligent system and its advancement that learns and adapts without following generic explicit instructions. It is a systematic procedure of data analysis that results in creating an automated analytical model building. Alan Turing, in 1950, first conceived the terminology "Computing machinery and intelligence" by publishing a paper in the "Mind". The terminology "Turing test" then came to light. That approach is then referred to as "Learning Machine" [2]. Recently, the field of powerful ML techniques has been conceived and inspired by nature and is hence called the field of natural computation. Here, ML is basically a set of computer algorithms that learn from examples instead of being programmed to execute a certain task. More like human learning, the machine becomes more intelligent from its acquired knowledge. Previously, machines would only be able to think in Boolean logic—having a stringent yes (1) or no (0) answer to a question. In fact, this limited the options of a machine answering a question. An intelligent system, however, can now answer some offbeat questions like, for example, "Will it be sufficient for a graduate to get a job easily?" The answer may vary from a "definite yes" to a "definite no", such as definitely, very likely, probably, or not likely, depending upon the probability of the occurrence of the system function. That is the advancement and beauty of machine learning that could answer today.

Let us define the learning procedure of a machine in a more specific way. It is said that a machine learns from experience (E) respectively to some set of tasks (T) and performance measure (P) if and only if "P at T improves with E".

For example:

Learning Problem: Handwriting recognition from a bulk image learning problem.

- Task T: Recognizing and classifying handwritten words within the bulk image.
- Performance P: Percentage of words correctly classified within the bulk image.
- Training experience E: A dataset of handwritten words with proper classifications.

A machine program that learns from previous experiences and executes specific tasks by taking performance measures into consideration is called a "machine learning program". It is, many times, also referred to as a "learner".

Learning by a machine is a process that comprises some well-defined components like data storage, abstraction, generalization, and evaluation.

- Data storage: storing and retrieving of data.
- Abstraction: extracting knowledge from stored data.
- Generalization: turning the knowledge about stored data into a form that can be utilized for future action.

- Evaluation: giving feedback to the user to measure the utility of the learned knowledge.

Figure 7.1 gives a detailed idea of the different components of the learning process by a machine. Starting from storing and retrieving data in the data storage section to data extraction by classification procedure, the learning process behaves like a training and testing model. After generalizing the data into a form that can be utilized in the future so that the machine can run on experiences, the final accomplishment section comes, i.e., evaluation, which measures the utility of the learned knowledge. A general way to model a machine learning–based structure is to define a set of trained and tested data from a wealth of data. This structure of modeling a machine learning system is called a predictive model. The predictive-based ML model is trained from historical data, and the result or outcome is fetched from the new test data. It can be easily visualized in Figure 7.2.

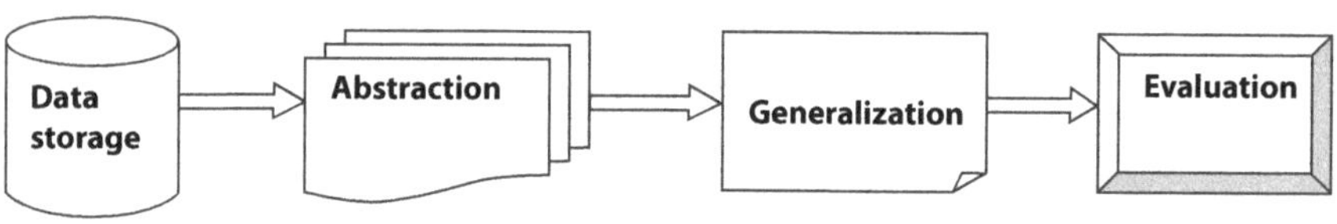

Figure 7.1 Learning process by machine.

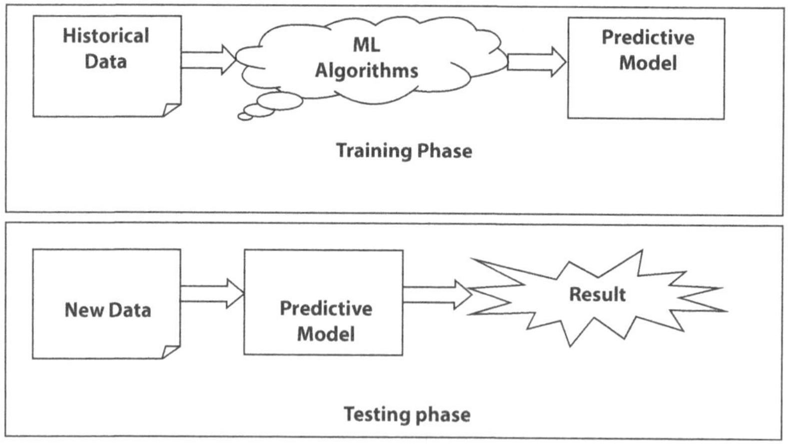

Figure 7.2 Predictive model of ML for training and testing.

7.1.2 Literature Survey

There are several types of research in the area of systematic study of the basics of machine learning, and its evolution has been done. Some authors focused on basics and evolution in a technological advancement way year-wise.

Boutaba *et al.* [2] presented a comprehensive study of machine learning and its evolution. He discussed machine learning basics and its different applications in the real world. The study also directed toward future research opportunities.

O. Simeone [3] proposed a brief idea of introduction of machine learning with application to different communication fields. He focused on the acquisition of domain knowledge and data-driven machine learning techniques.

I. H. Sarker [4] studied the machine learning basics and their respective application in the current industry (4IR) along with its future advancement in the research field. He verified and modeled the real popularity of the ML algorithm that increases very rapidly from 2015 onward. He further discussed about the ML algorithm and its future in problem solving.

J. Kaur *et al.* [5] reviewed the basics of machine learning and its future in communication. He systematically studied ML algorithms and their real application to mainly wireless communication. Research directions are proposed to carry out ML-based applications in communications.

S. Dey *et al.* [6] quantified the real distinction between AI and ML in general. He modeled and designed a communication system that emphasized an AI/ML-based massive MIMO system and its real application. This paper also studied the growth of machine learning algorithms in recent times.

F. Tariq *et al.* [8] studied completely different ML technologies and their respective applications in futuristic research. It basically emphasized on present communication system as an area of ML applications.

S. Dey *et al.* [7] again proposed the potential solution to next-generation communication and AI/ML evolution in relation to technological solutions in real communication. They further stressed different algorithms, like supervised, unsupervised, and reinforcement.

7.1.3 Problem Statement and Proposed Model

The literature review gives a clear idea about each and every research that is done to study about basics of machine learning but no study has defined it in a systematic way starting from conceptualization to implementation and application in the real field. A clear dive into concept building starting from the evolution of machine learning to the present trend in machine learning after COVID-19 is missing. A detailed study of key learning algorithms and their present research scope is also an area to build up post-COVID. This chapter has been proposed and designed in three main categories. These are "Introduction to Machine Learning", conceptualization perspective, implementation perspective, and research perspective. It mainly dives into concept building as well as gives direction about future research areas. A proposed model is designed here for the same.

- *Introduction to machine learning: Conceptualization perspective.*
- *Introduction to machine learning: Implementation perspective.*
- *Introduction to machine learning: Research perspective.*

7.1.4 Evolution of Machine Learning

The machine learning concept was first conceived in the year 1950, and then gradually, it advanced like a booming technological invention for the researcher, academician, and technocrats. Machine learning (ML) has gained unprecedented growth in different applications that solve problems and enable automation across industries. It is only for the basic reason that a wealth of data is easily available and the systematic advancement in computing capabilities. In this section, the evolution of machine learning techniques is briefly discussed. Figure 7.3 shows the evidence of evolution of machine learning.

1950: The Turing Test
Alan Turing first invented and performed the magic "T TEST" or Turing Test to accomplish the knowledge that a computer has intelligence. This test has the criteria of a unique thing that the computer had to fool another human to set a belief that it was also human.

1952: The First Learning Program
Arthur Samuel discovered the first proper implementation of machine learning in 1952 by the game of checkers. The computer improved its game by playing more and more and defining the winning strategies.

1957: The First Neural Networks
Frank Rosenblatt designed the first neural networks for computing. It was designated to simulate the thought process of a human brain with ease.

1967: The Nearest Neighbor Algorithm
Thomas Cover and Peter Hart extended the work of Evelyn Fix and Joseph Hodges to design the nearest neighbor algorithm that allowed computers to recognize basic patterns. It is basically used for classification and regression.

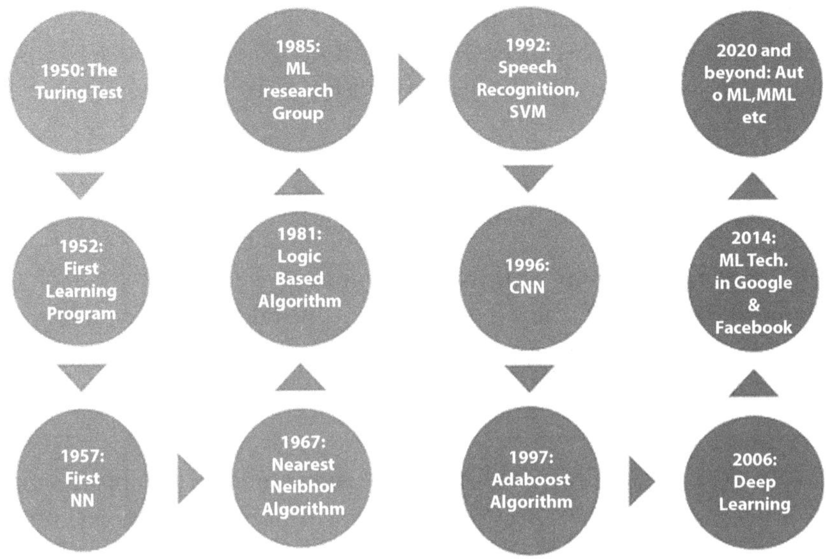

Figure 7.3 Evolution of machine learning.

1981: Logic- or Explanation-Based Learning

Gerald Dejong conceived the logic-based learning concept which allowed a computer to properly analyze the training data and set a generic rule by discarding the less important data.

1985: Machine Learning Research Group

Researchers from AT&T created the first research group for machine learning that started to conduct some initial meetings on machine learning which further converted to the leading conference on machine learning, called Neural Information Processing Systems or NIPS.

1992: Speech Recognition

Jay Wilpon and his team deployed the hidden Markov model which used automated speech recognition techniques. The model was developed with the exclusive concepts of machine learning.

1992: Support Vector Machines

Researchers at AT&T discovered the SVM technique that performs large-scale classification.

1996: Convolutional Neural Network

Patrick Haffner invented the first CNN to check large-scale recognition. It is now considered as the most influential technology.

1997: The AdaBoost Algorithm

A researcher from AT&T invented the AdaBoost algorithm which handled unstructured datasets with the help of decision trees.

2006: Deep Learning

Geoffrey Hinton is called the father of DL. Image, text, and video recognition can be successfully done using a deep learning algorithm.

2014: Machine Learning as Pivotal Technology

Google and Facebook utilized ML as their pivotal tool of technology in their business standards. Google Brain and DeepFace of respective companies are revolutionizing the concept of ML now.

2020: and to date

Automated machine learning (AutoML), multi-modal learning (MML), and cybersecurity are some key advances in ML to date. These technologies are based with the basics of artificial intelligence and machine learning. They are the top priority concepts of researchers nowadays.

7.1.5 Machine Learning as a Powerful Tool for Future Advancement

As discussed in the previous section of the history of machine learning evolution, it can be précised that technology is evolving like a technological revolution among all fields of science, technology, and research. To every decade, ML serves as a powerful tool. Now, it is a must for future advancement of our civilization. Technology has touched every possible field it could have done, and now, day by day, it is applied to fields like agriculture, medicine, disease control, and prediction. Let us see the application of machine learning algorithms in a broader way as a powerful tool for future advancement.

Application of Machine Learning as a Powerful Tool for Future Advancement:

- Product recommendation for customer
- Predictive analytics and intelligent decision-making capabilities
- Image, speech, and pattern recognition
- Sentiment analysis
- Automatic employee access control
- Marine wildlife preservation
- Machine learning in regulating the healthcare sector
- Machine learning in the banking sector

- Machine learning in wireless communication system design
- Machine learning in language translation
- Industry automation
- Robotics manipulation
- Self-driving car technology
- Machine learning in algorithmic trading
- Machine learning in stock market pricing
- Machine learning in traffic control and transportation
- Agricultural advancement
- Bioinformatics, etc.

Apart from all these applications, machine learning is mainly used in network optimization, signal detection, intelligent communication system design, channel modeling in communication, computer networking, DNA sequence classification, advanced engineering, etc. Researchers are keen on applying machine learning techniques to every possible field in order to get sufficient output and results.

7.2 A Dive Into Machine Learning: Implementation Perspective

This section describes the basic relationship between artificial intelligence, machine learning, and deep learning. These three terms are very closely related to each other and they make data science so colorful and advanced that their basic knowledge is a must for every individual.

7.2.1 Correlations and Differences Between Artificial Intelligence (AI), Machine Learning (ML), and Deep Learning (DL)

Deep learning is a subset of machine learning and, in turn, machine learning is a subset of artificial intelligence. Figure 7.4 shows the relationship between AI, ML and DL. Figure 7.5 shows details regarding AI, ML and DL. They all together form data science.

Artificial Intelligence: As the name suggests, it is the intelligence shown by a computer-like human being. A very popular definition proposed by Francois Chollet, creator of Keras. He defined it as "the effort to automate intellectual tasks normally performed by humans". In the very simplest way, we can say that in AI, computers possess and process the characteristics of humans like reasoning, interacting, and thinking. AI is basically a broader field of data science where the main focus is to create intelligent machines.

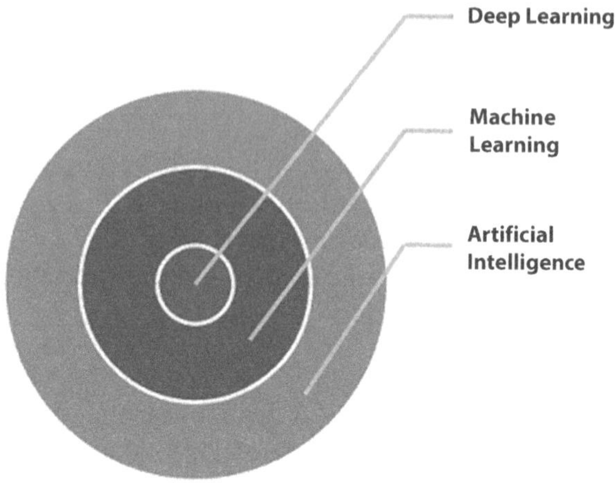

Figure 7.4 Artificial intelligence, machine learning and deep learning relationship.

Machine Learning: It is a subset of artificial intelligence and probably the most searched and learned field of data science. This technology enables machine to learn from experience and past data and makes prediction accordingly.

Deep Learning: A subset of machine learning employs neural networks to learn the complex patterns and relationships within data. It is used to solve complex problems without being explicitly programmed and totally based on artificial neural networks and deep neural networks.

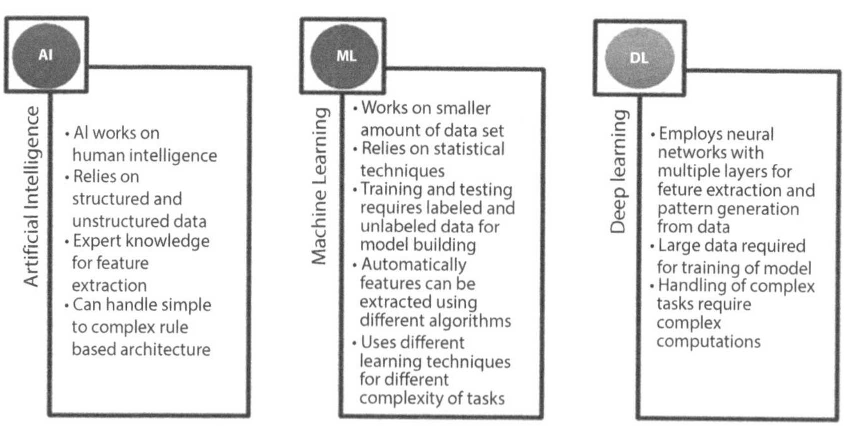

Figure 7.5 AI vs ML vs DL.

7.2.2 Learning Techniques in Machine Learning

Basically, there are four types of learning techniques in machine learning. These are supervised, unsupervised, semi-supervised, and reinforcement.

Supervised learning:
Supervised learning is a machine learning technique where the machine is getting smarter and more intelligent by examples. Here, the user provides labeled data points to the ML algorithm. A dataset is labeled means its label value is known. The inputs and outputs are predefined or pre-known to the user. Only the algorithm finds a way to achieve these values of inputs and outputs by making correct predictions which in turn are guided or supervised by the user or operator. This is a continuous process until satisfactory higher accuracy prediction values are achieved. Supervised learning includes different concepts like classification, regression, and forecasting. Classification is a way of representing data into different classes based on different parameters. It is used for classifying spam or nonspam mail, the attitude of customers to repay loans, etc. Regression is the correlation between the dependent and independent variables or simply the relationship between the variables. Regression may be like a decision tree, random forest, simple linear, super vector, polynomial, and principal components type. Forecasting is the predictions for the future based on the present and past datasets. Physicians implement their study into reality when predicting whether a person will have a heart attack within a year or not by analyzing the previous records of age, weight, height, and blood pressure of patients, etc. This is a problem of designing a model that will predict the heart attack of a new patient by observing the records of the previous one by supervised learning methods.

Supervised learning algorithms are generally used for solving classification and regression problems.

Application of supervised learning includes:

- Spam detection
- Object recognition
- Speech recognition etc.

Unsupervised learning:
In this type of learning technique, there is the provision of studying the set of data without the help of human interference or any human assistance. Unsupervised learning determines the basic correlation and relationship by analyzing the dataset which is large in nature. Structuring these data into a specific format is the main priority of unsupervised learning.

Grouping and clustering of datasets in specific ways so as to arrange the wealth of data to look more organized are the main characteristics of this type of learning. Here, the input dataset is more valuable, unlike supervised learning with no target output. That is why there is no specific guide required to correct the model.

Application of unsupervised learning includes:

- Customer segmentation
- Pattern recognition
- Anomaly detection, etc.

Semi-supervised learning:

It is a type of machine learning algorithm that combines the features of supervised and unsupervised learning into itself. It is an intermediate of these two learning algorithms. It uses labeled as well as unlabeled datasets during the training period. The semi-supervised algorithm comes into the picture in order to overcome the disadvantages of supervised and unsupervised learning. In supervised learning, hand labeling by ML specialists is required, and in unsupervised learning, there is a limited spectrum for its application. So, to avoid these limitations, the semi-supervised concept comes into the picture.

Firstly, it trains the model with a smaller or lesser amount of training data, similar to supervised learning models. Training continues until the model produces satisfactory results. Algorithms use an unnamed dataset with pseudo-labels in the next step, and hence, the result may not be as accurate as required. Labeled training data and pseudo-labels are now linked. The input data for labeled training data and unlabeled training data are also linked. Finally, train the model again with the new combined input as in the first step. This reduces errors and improves model accuracy. Figure 7.6 shows reinforcement learning process cycle.

Applications of semi-supervised learning include:

- Text document classifier
- Speech analysis
- Web content classifier
- Protein sequence classifier etc.

Reinforcement learning:

It is a feedback-based learning technique where an agent is trained to learn and behave in an environment by performing the actions and seeing through them. For good action, the agent gets positive feedback, and for

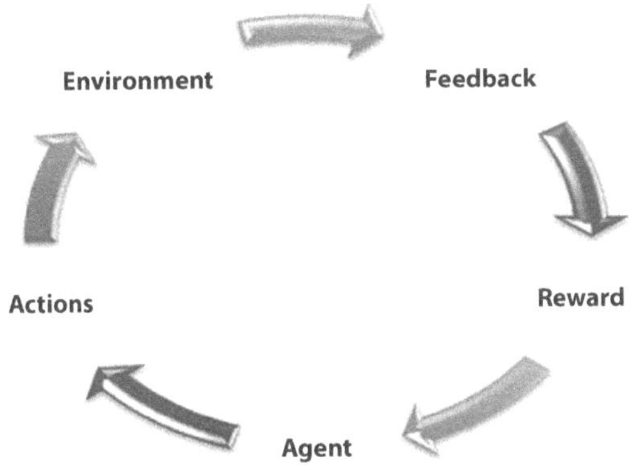

Figure 7.6 Reinforcement learning process cycle.

bad action, it gets negative feedback. In RL, the agent learns from experience and feedback. There is no labeled data here. So, RL is an ML algorithm where an intelligent agent or computer program interacts with the environment and learns to act accordingly within its scope of interest. It is the core technology of AI because, in AI, the main concept is to act intelligently without much human intervention and the system learns from experiences. RL concept is also called a reward-based concept.

Applications of reinforcement learning include:

- Robotics
- Image processing
- Natural language processing
- Advertising, etc.

7.2.3 Algorithms in Machine Learning

In this section, some algorithms respective to different learning techniques are briefly discussed.

This is presented in a tabular format as described below. Algorithms like support vector machine (SVM), random forest (RF), naïve Bayes (NB), k-means, frequent pattern growth, and Q-learning are more frequently used in solving different problems in machine learning technologies.

Table 7.1 below demonstrates a brief idea of learning techniques in machine learning along with its different algorithms.

Table 7.1 Algorithms in ML.

Properties	Supervised	Unsupervised	Semi-supervised	Reinforcement
Definition	ML algorithm that requires human supervision	ML algorithm that happens without human supervision and interventions	ML algorithm that conceives the advantages of both supervised and unsupervised	ML algorithm that learns from the environment with feedback and reward options
Input	Labeled	Unlabeled	Both	Data is accumulated from ML systems that use a trial and error method. No pre defined data
Algorithms	• Support vector • Decision tree • Random forest • Naive Bayes	• K-Means • Frequent pattern growth • Gaussian mixture model • Principal Component Analysis	Both	• Q-learning • SARSA
Applications	• Spam detection • Object recognition • Speech recognition	• Customer segmentation • Pattern recognition • Anomaly detection etc	• Speech analysis • Text document classifier	• Robotics • Image processing • Natural language processing • Advertising etc

7.3 Recent Trends in Machine Learning: Research Perspective

This section describes the machine learning application and its research perspectives. As it is a recent technological revolution in every field, so we look at its different perspective here.

7.3.1 Machine Learning in Fourth Industry Revolution or Industry 4.0 (4IR)

The current industrial growth promises a rebirth of technological discoveries. Industry 4.0 or the Fourth Industry Revolution (4IR) reboots different technologies like the Internet of Things (IoT), machine learning, artificial intelligence, deep learning, blockchain, and cloud computing [4]. Roots being surrounded by AI, the recent data science has emerged like anything. Machine learning also shares the bulk percentage in 4IR growth. Companies like Google and Facebook conceive ML technology as their core in key technological advancement. Different start-ups also build their firms with ML as a profound technology. As more research is going into ML from government and nongovernment agencies, it is now a time-bound and must-dive sector of the science field to reach numerous undisclosed inventions. At least Industry 4.0 has taught mankind like that. Researchers are spending years and every hour on possible ways of implementing ML techniques in different spheres of science.

7.3.2 Machine Learning in Real-World Applications: ML for Everything, for Everywhere and for Everyone

ML is considered to be a powerful tool for technological advancement today. The key areas where ML is being applied successfully today range from banking to the automobile industry, mills to marine, customer care to the health sector, and agriculture automation to the healthcare sector. So, ML can be considered a technology that is for everyone, for everything, and for everywhere. A list of real-world applications with key research areas is given below:

Research area: Health care sector

- Drug discovery and manufacturing
- Disease diagnosis
- Medical image diagnosis
- Smart health records
- Clinical trial and research
- Crowd-sourced data collection
- Outbreak prediction, etc.

Research area: Banking sector and Automation

- Fraud detection
- Cybersecurity

- ❖ Customer satisfaction
- ❖ Sentiment analysis
- ❖ Product recommendation
- ❖ Data storing and billing automation
- ❖ Employee access control
- ❖ Intelligent process automation, etc.

Research area: Wireless communication

- ❖ Channel estimation
- ❖ Beamforming
- ❖ Data processing and detection
- ❖ Signal performance analysis and monitoring
- ❖ Channel modeling, etc.

Research area: Agriculture sector

- ❖ Crop management
- ❖ Precision spraying
- ❖ Insect detection
- ❖ Field condition management
- ❖ Yield mapping
- ❖ Price forecasting
- ❖ Automatic harvesting robot

Apart from these areas, other current research topics are computer vision, speech recognition, signal processing, message extraction, artificial neural networks, machine learning–based communication in 5G and beyond, etc.

7.3.3 Machine Learning in 5G Wireless Communications and Beyond

Researchers are embarking recently on 5G wireless communication and beyond [5]. In fact, the 5G and beyond wireless communication is designed with the core technology being AI and ML [6, 7]. Each and every component of wireless communication relies on AI/ML techniques–based design. It may be the physical layer, the network layer, or the application layer. Machine learning is playing an integral part in 5G wireless communication and beyond [3, 9]. Data handling, efficient energy consumption, latency, and more accurate localization are some key improvement factors in wireless communication using AI and ML techniques [8]. Some basic areas where ML gives the 5G and beyond (6G) communication robust networks

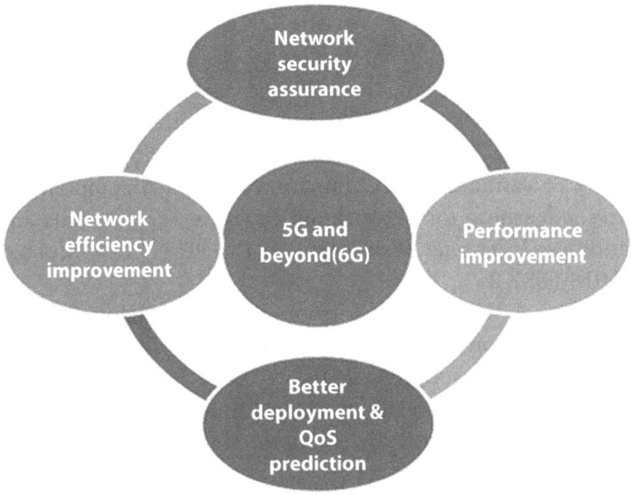

Figure 7.7 ML as key technology in 5G and beyond network.

are network security assurance, network performance improvement, network efficiency improvement, better deployment, QoS prediction, etc. Figure 7.7 describes ML as a key technology in 5G and beyond network.

Analyzing massive data; user behavior localization, like network security assurance; congestion control and monitoring; and admission control, like network efficiency improvement, are performed by AI/ML algorithms. ML-based mobility and traffic control, like performance improvement factors, are also done by ML algorithms. Signal-to-noise ratio control and quality-of-service improvement are some of the best deployment techniques that can also be performed by ML techniques.

7.4 Conclusion

Machine learning has become a day-to-day affair today. As previously cited, ML is really a technology that is for everything, for everyone, and for everywhere. Now, a lot of academician and researchers keep their research pivotally into ML. Different learning techniques of ML are also best suited for further research to come. This chapter provides a detailed study of the basics of machine learning from a conceptualization perspective to implementation perspective and a research perspective. Future studies may aim toward the broader area of ML application in specific fields like 6G wireless communication and cybersecurity with efficient data processing and data handling in different scoped and required fields.

References

1. Taye, M.M., Understanding of Machine Learning with Deep Learning: Architectures, Workflow, Applications and Future Directions. *Computers*, 12, 91, 2023, https://doi.org/10.3390/computers12050091.
2. Boutaba, R., Salahuddin, M.A., Limam, N., *et al.*, A comprehensive survey on machine learning for networking: evolution, applications and research opportunities. *J. Internet Serv. Appl.*, 9, 16, 2018, https://doi.org/10.1186/s13174-018-0087-2.
3. Simeone, O., A Very Brief Introduction to Machine Learning With Applications to Communication Systems. *IEEE Trans. Cognit. Commun. Netw.*, 4, 4, 648–664, December 2018.
4. Sarker, I., Machine Learning: Algorithms, Real-World Applications and Research Directions. *SN Comput. Sci.*, 2, 1–21, 2021, 10.1007/s42979-021-00592-x.
5. Kaur, J., Khan, M.A., Iftikhar, M., Imran, M., Emad Ul Haq, Q., Machine Learning Techniques for 5G and Beyond. *IEEE Access*, 9, 23472–23488, 2021, doi: 10.1109/ACCESS.2021.3051557.
6. Dey, S., *et al.*, Study of future generation communication system and quantifying the AI based massive mimo system. *J. Interdiscip. Cyclic Res.*, xiii, iv, 1807–1817, April 2021, doi: 18.0002.JICR.2021.V13I4.008301.3171228720, issn:0022-1945.
7. Dey, S., *et al.*, The potential solutions to next generation wireless communication: AI and Massive MIMO technology design and development. *Int. J. Emerging Technol. Innov. Res.*, 9, 4, 980–g87, April-2022, (www.jetir.org), issn:2349-5162.
8. Tariq, F., Khandaker, M.R.A., Wong, K.-K., Imran, M.A., Bennis, M., Debbah, M., A speculative study on 6G. *IEEE Wireless Commun.*, 27, 4, 118–125, Aug. 2020.
9. Wang, H., Ma, C., Zhou, L., A Brief Review of Machine Learning and Its Application. *2009 International Conference on Information Engineering and Computer Science*, pp. 1–4, 2009, doi: 10.1109/ICIECS.2009.5362936.

8

6G Wireless Networks: Pioneering with Machine Learning Technologies

Krupali Dhawale, Shraddha Jha, Mishri Gube*, Shivraj Guduri and Khwaish Asati

Department of Artificial Intelligence, G. H. Raisoni College of Engineering, Nagpur, India

Abstract

Within the changing environment of remote communication, the sending of 6G systems has brought phenomenal challenges and openings. The time of 6G remote systems will be characterized by uncommon network, speed, and proficiency. The combination of counterfeit insights and communication opens up better approaches to enhance execution strategies and meet future needs. This chapter investigates machine learning calculations such as deep learning, reinforcement learning, and neural learning, pointing at making strides in planning, operation, and support of 6G remote systems. The main reasons for machine learning (ML) integration in wireless networks are to diminish budget, make strides, organize execution, and produce modern income. This article centers on optimizing range utilization, effective asset assignment, smart beamforming, adaptive tuning, and advanced commotion administration. This consideration focuses on making strides in organizing execution and optimizing inactivity in energetic and thick 6G situations. Here, we will evaluate machine learning strategies for 6G wireless networks and highlight the significance of explaining artificial insights and strengths in the implementation of solid and vigorous 6G networks. We will also record open research issues that have to be settled promptly to facilitate the planning and optimization of 6G remote systems, paving the way for improved user experiences and modern communication standards.

Keywords: 6G wireless networks, machine learning algorithms, artificial intelligence, network optimization, deep learning, reinforcement learning, federated learning, budget optimization

**Corresponding author*: mishri.gube.ai@ghrce.raisoni.net

Pallavi Sapkale, Shilpa Mehta and S. Balamurugan (eds.) Quantum Computing and Machine Learning for 6G, (161–186) © 2026 Scrivener Publishing LLC

8.1 Introduction

6G wireless networks revolutionize telecommunications and connectivity by combining state-of-the-art technology with artificial intelligence. This comprehensive discussion explores the essence of 6G wireless networks, their importance in lightning-fast data transmission and unparalleled reliability, and the transformative role of machine learning in their development. [1] 6G wireless communication, which follows 5G, offers increased capacity, higher throughput, and reduced latency. It unites AI, ML, and AR/VR technologies for immersive user experiences. This book explores 6G use cases, requirements, technologies, spectrum challenges, privacy preservation, aerial infrastructure, and economic challenges. Machine learning techniques revolutionize signal processing, adaptive beamforming, interference mitigation, resource allocation, and spectrum management. [2] The 6G wireless network, which is scheduled to be operational in 2030, requires a combination of existing solutions and innovative technologies. AI and machine learning will be crucial for human-centric networks. AI-powered network management and security are also woven into the narrative, focusing on self-managing networks, autonomous network configuration, fault detection, self-healing mechanisms, and network maintenance. However, this journey also presents challenges, such as data privacy and ethical considerations. The focus for AI-powered networks is on striking a delicate balance between the use of personal data while respecting user privacy. Scalability and the management of the complexities of these advanced systems are also on the radar. Ultimately, the research will culminate in an in-depth examination of the synergy between AI and 6G wireless networks, with an emphasis on how machine learning is fueling the evolution of 6G networks, setting the stage for an interconnected future marked by significant breakthroughs and the constant pursuit of excellence in amid the challenges that lie ahead.

8.2 Introduction to 6G Wireless Networks and Machine Learning

8.2.1 6G Wireless Network and Its Significance

6G, short for "sixth-generation wireless," is the hypothetical successor to the emerging 5G wireless technology. While 5G is still in the process of global deployment, researchers and experts have begun to think about the capabilities and potential features of 6G. The potential importance of 6G is in the further development of wireless communication and technology as depicted in Figure 8.1.

Expected Features and Benefits of 6G:

1. Higher data rates: 6G can provide faster data rates than 5G, reaching speeds of terabits per second. This will enable high-definition streaming, real-time remote operations, and data-intensive applications.
2. Ultralow latency: 6G aims to significantly reduce latency compared to 5G, enabling real-time communication for applications that require fast response. This can be important for scenarios such as autonomous vehicles, industrial automation, and augmented reality (AR) experiences.
3. Expanded connectivity 6G can provide better connectivity in remote and underserved areas, further bridging the digital divide and giving more people around the world access to secure Internet.
4. Increasing use of spectrum: 6G is expected to use a wide range of frequencies, including terahertz frequencies. This can provide greater throughput and capacity, as well as better performance in congested urban areas.

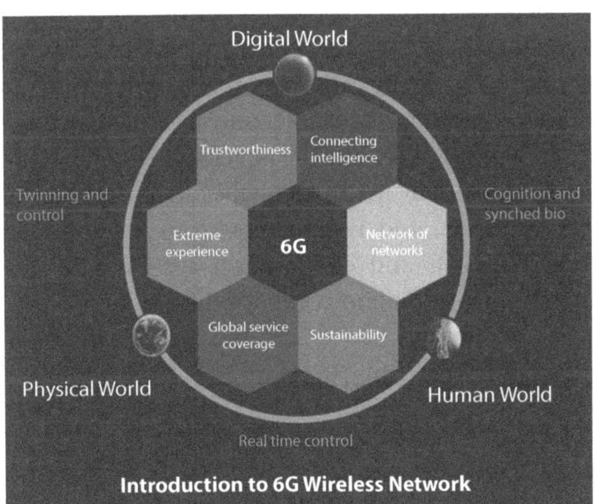

Figure 8.1 6G networks introduction.

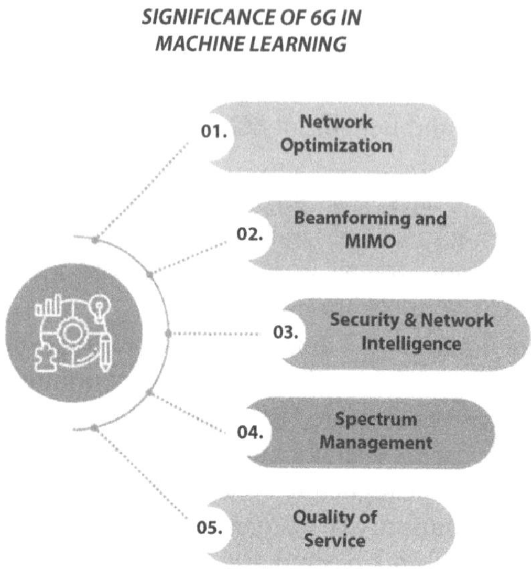

Figure 8.2 Significance of 6G networks.

5. AI integration: Artificial intelligence (AI) will play an increasingly important role in 6G networks, helping to optimize network resources, manage congestion, and create intelligent network features. Figure 8.2 shows the significance of 6G.
6. Sustainable and green technology: 6G is expected to place more emphasis on energy efficiency and environmental sustainability. This could include developing energy-efficient communication protocols, reducing the carbon footprint of network infrastructure, and promoting environmentally friendly practices.
7. Global collaboration: Like the development of 5G, the development of 6G will involve collaboration between governments, industry, and researchers from around the world. Global standards and cooperation are essential to ensure seamless integration and compatibility.

8.2.2 Challenges for 6G Networks

Since the 6G network is still in the conceptual and development stage, there are several challenges and objectives related to the integration with machine learning (ML). [3] AI techniques, especially machine learning, have gained popularity in various fields, leading to the belief that AI will play a crucial role in future wireless communications. This article presents six challenges to be addressed in the interdisciplinary fields of wireless communications with a focus on sixth-generation (6G) networks as mentioned in Figure 8.3. These challenges must be overcome in order to fully exploit the potential of ML in improving the capabilities of 6G networks. Here are some challenges and goals:

1. Massive Data Processing: 6G networks are expected to generate and process massive data due to the increasing number of connected devices and advanced applications. ML algorithms must efficiently process and analyze these large amounts of data.
2. Complex network management: 6G networks will be very heterogeneous and dynamic, consisting of different types of devices, frequencies, and technologies. Managing such complexity requires ML algorithms capable of real-time adaptation and optimization.
3. Energy efficiency: While 6G aims to increase data speed and connectivity, energy efficiency must also be considered to ensure stable operation. ML can be used to optimize energy consumption and resource allocation.
4. Latency Optimization: Achieving ultralow latency is a key goal of 6G. ML algorithms can help optimize network

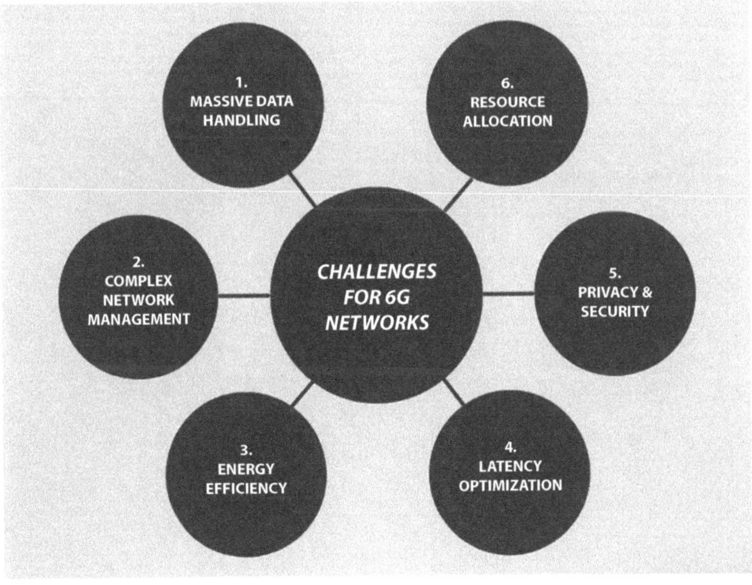

Figure 8.3 Challenges for 6G networks.

architecture and traffic management to reduce latency, which is important for real-time applications.

5. Privacy and Security: Since 6G networks are interconnected and devices generate sensitive data, privacy and security are top priorities. ML can help develop advanced encryption, recognition, and anomaly detection mechanisms.
6. Resource Allocation: Efficient allocation of system resources, including bandwidth and computing power, is essential to meet various application demands. ML can provide a dynamic resource allocation strategy.

8.2.3 Goals for 6G Networks

Goals for 6G networks are mentioned and depicted in Figure 8.4 and explained below:

1. Smart network management: The goal is to create ML-driven solutions that can independently manage, optimize, and adapt 6G networks based on real-time data and changing conditions.

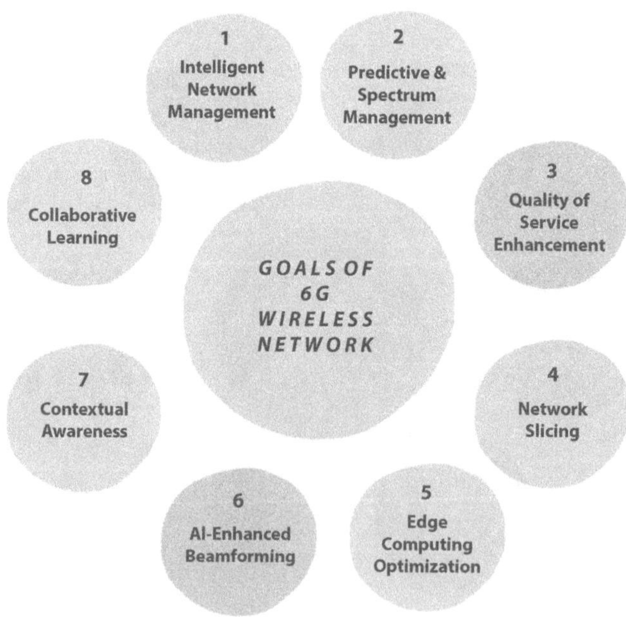

Figure 8.4 Goals of 6G networks.

2. Efficient service: ML can be used to predict and prevent system failures and outages, reduce downtime and improve 6G network reliability.
3. Spectrum management: The development of ML algorithms for dynamic and efficient spectrum allocation is needed to use the available frequency bands more efficiently to solve the problem of spectrum shortage.
4. Improve service quality: ML can help maintain and improve service quality across various applications by dynamically adjusting parameters such as data rates, latency, and bandwidth.
5. Network slicing: Network slicing allows you to create virtualized networks based on specific application needs. ML can play a role in optimizing the creation and management of these slices.
6. Edge Computing Optimization: 6G networks are expected to use edge computing to reduce latency. ML algorithms can help efficiently allocate computing resources to support applications that require low latency.
7. AI-Powered Reflection: Reflection technology is essential for high data rates. ML can develop reflective algorithms, adapt to different situations, and optimize signal transmission.
8. Context Awareness: ML algorithms can analyze contextual information from devices and applications to provide personalized and context-aware services.
9. Collaborative learning: 6G networks can facilitate collaborative learning between devices while maintaining data privacy, allowing devices to learn and improve performance collectively.

8.2.4 Introduction to Machine Learning and Its Relevance in Wireless Networks

Introduction to Machine Learning:
Machine learning (ML), a subset of artificial intelligence (AI), focuses on developing algorithms and models that allow computers to learn data and make predictions or decisions without being explicitly programmed. Instead of relying on implicit instructions, ML algorithms learn patterns and relationships in the data and use that knowledge to make informed decisions or predictions. This process involves developing an algorithm in the database that allows us to generalize the data and make accurate

predictions about new, unseen data. Machine learning includes a variety of techniques, including supervised learning (algorithms that learn from labeled data), unsupervised learning (algorithms that find patterns in unlabeled data), and reinforcement learning (algorithms that learn by interacting with the environment).

8.2.4.1 Importance of Machine Learning in Wireless Networks

Machine learning supports the development and optimization of wireless networks, improving efficiency, performance, and adaptability. [4] 6G networks demand enhanced E2E connectivity and AI advancements, requiring advanced machine learning (ML) models and computational power. Intelligent resource management is crucial for energy efficiency and computational capacity in 6G networks. This article reviews ML algorithms applied in emerging networks, focusing on resource allocation, task offloading, and handover management. Important areas in machine learning in the context of wireless networks are the following:

1. Spectrum management: Machine learning can optimize spectrum allocation by analyzing historical usage patterns and adapting to demand in real time. This helps in the efficient use of frequency bands and reduces spectrum congestion.
2. Resource allocation: ML algorithms can dynamically allocate resources such as bandwidth, power, and computing resources to different users and applications, optimizing network performance and QoS.
3. Interference management: Machine learning techniques can identify sources of interference and reduce their effects by adjusting transmission parameters or adjusting resource allocation.
4. Beamforming and MIMO: ML algorithms can optimize beamforming and multiple-input–multiple-output (MIMO) systems to improve signal quality, reduce interference, and improve coverage.
5. Sufficient maintenance: ML can predict system failures and equipment failures based on historical data, enabling proactive maintenance and reducing downtime.
6. Network optimization: Machine learning can optimize network architecture, topology, and routing, improving overall efficiency and performance.

7. Dynamic channel selection: ML algorithms can determine the best channel to reduce packet loss and improve reliability based on real-time channel conditions.
8. Delivery and traffic management: ML can predict user movement patterns and optimize delivery decisions to ensure seamless connectivity on the move.
9. Quality of Service (QoS) Management: ML algorithms can monitor network conditions and user behavior to adjust (QoS) parameters dynamically, ensuring a comfortable user experience.
10. Security and Anomaly Detection: Machine learning can improve security by identifying unusual behaviors that indicate security threats or anomalies.
11. Energy efficiency: ML algorithms can contribute to the stability of wireless networks and optimize energy consumption in wireless devices and infrastructure.
12. Edge Computing: Machine learning and local processing can be applied to edge devices to reduce latency and improve responsiveness for real-world applications.
13. Network slicing: ML can help create and manage virtualized network slices according to the requirements of different applications.

8.2.5 Potential Benefits of Integrating Machine Learning in 6G Technology

The integration of machine learning (ML) into 6G technology offers many benefits that will transform the capabilities of wireless networks, allowing them to operate smarter and more efficiently. The key benefits of incorporating ML into 6G technology are the following:

1. Dynamic resource allocation: ML algorithms can optimize the allocation of network resources such as bandwidth, computing power, and energy in real time. This dynamic allocation ensures efficient allocation of resources to meet the varying requirements of different applications and users.
2. Intelligent network management: ML can predict historical congestion, device failures, and performance degradation based on historical and real-time data. This allows proactive business management, reduced downtime, and consistently

high-quality service. [5] Wireless research is moving toward 6G with a focus on creating a digital twin world that integrates the physical, biological, and digital worlds. 6G system requirements include new man-machine interfaces, ubiquitous universal computing, multi-sensory data fusion, and precision sensing. Advances in artificial intelligence could lay the foundation for 6G air interfaces and networks.

3. Ultralow latency optimization: ML techniques can optimize network architecture and traffic management to reduce latency, a critical requirement for real-time applications such as augmented reality (AR), virtual reality (VR), and remote sensing.
4. Mass connectivity management: As 6G aims to support a large number of connected devices, ML can help manage and orchestrate communication between these devices, ensure efficient data exchange, and reduce network overhead.
5. Intelligent mirroring: ML algorithms can optimize reflection patterns and strategies, adjusting to environmental conditions and the user's location. This leads to improved signal quality, reduced interference, and better coverage.
6. Improve energy efficiency: ML can intelligently manage sleep schedules, bandwidth levels, and resource usage, contributing to stability and optimizing energy consumption in wireless devices and network infrastructure.
7. Network slice optimization: ML can help create and manage configured network segments and virtual networks tailored to specific application requirements. This ensures that various applications receive the resources and QoS guarantees they require.
8. Security and Anomaly Detection: ML can identify unusual behavior patterns and potential security threats by analyzing network traffic and user behavior. This improves network security and helps mitigate cyber threats in time.
9. Context-aware services: ML algorithms can analyze contextual information from devices, applications, and users to provide personalized and context-aware services, improving user experience.
10. Collaborative learning: ML can enable devices on a network to learn together with one another while maintaining

data privacy. This improves decision-making and network optimization.

11. Efficient use of spectrum: ML algorithms can analyze spectrum usage patterns and dynamically allocate frequencies for optimal use, reducing congestion and improving overall system efficiency.
12. Adaptive network planning: ML can help design network architectures and coverage patterns based on user density, mobility, and operational requirements.

8.3 Machine Learning Techniques for 6G Wireless Networks

8.3.1 Signal Processing and Optimization

The integration of machine learning (ML) into 6G technology offers many benefits that will transform the capabilities of wireless networks, allowing them to operate smarter and more efficiently. The key benefits of incorporating ML into 6G technology are the following:

- Dynamic resource allocation: ML algorithms can optimize the allocation of network resources such as bandwidth, computing power, and energy in real time. This dynamic allocation ensures efficient allocation of resources to meet the varying requirements of different applications and users.
- Intelligent network management: ML can predict historical congestion, device failures, and performance degradation based on historical and real-time data. This allows active system management, reduces downtime, and ensures consistent, high-quality service. [6] Emerging wireless services demand 6G networks with target sensing, intelligent computing, and information communication. This paper presents a unified framework for optimizing limited system resources and revealing the effects of key parameters.
- Ultralow latency optimization: ML techniques can optimize network architecture and traffic management to reduce latency, a critical requirement for real-time applications such as augmented reality (AR), virtual reality (VR), and remote sensing.

- Mass connectivity management: As 6G aims to support a large number of connected devices, ML can help manage and orchestrate communication between these devices, ensure efficient data exchange, and reduce network overhead.
- Intelligent mirroring: ML algorithms can optimize reflection patterns and strategies, adjusting to environmental conditions and the user's location. This leads to improved signal quality, reduced interference, and better coverage.
- Improve energy efficiency: ML can intelligently manage sleep schedules, bandwidth levels, and resource usage, contributing to stability and optimizing energy consumption in wireless devices and network infrastructure.
- Network slice optimization: ML can help create and manage configured network segments and virtual networks tailored to specific application requirements. This ensures that various applications receive the resources and QoS guarantees they require.
- Security and Anomaly Detection: ML can identify unusual behavior patterns and potential security threats by analyzing network traffic and user behavior. This improves network security and helps mitigate cyber threats in time.
- Context-aware services: ML algorithms can analyze contextual information from devices, applications, and users to provide personalized and context-aware services, improving user experience.
- Collaborative learning: ML can enable devices on a network to learn from each other while maintaining data privacy. This improves decision-making and network optimization.
- Efficient use of spectrum: ML algorithms can analyze spectrum usage patterns and dynamically allocate frequencies for optimal use, reducing congestion and improving overall system efficiency.
- Edge Intelligence: ML at the edge of the network enables local processing and decision-making, reducing latency and enabling applications in real time without relying on centralized cloud resources.
- Adaptive network planning: ML can help design network architectures and coverage patterns based on user density, mobility, and operational requirements.

[7] Machine learning-based data rate estimation is crucial for anticipatory mobile networking, but limited accuracy is achieved due to the ignorance of UEs about the network load. A cooperative approach reduces prediction error by up to 30%, promoting extensive machine learning and UE-based network optimization.

8.3.2 Adaptive Beamforming and Spatial Processing Using Machine Learning

Adaptive reflection and spatial processing through machine learning is a method that uses machine learning algorithms to improve the efficiency and performance of reflection and spatial processing in wireless communication networks. Beamforming refers to the process of directing the transmission or reception of signals, while spatial processing involves the manipulation of signals from several antennas to improve signal quality, reduce interference, and improve overall communication reliability. Conventional reflectance and spatial processing methods often rely on predefined algorithms and heuristics based on antenna geometry and the environment. However, this method may not be optimal in complex and dynamic wireless environments. This is where machine learning comes into play.

This is reflective and spatial adaptive processing using machine learning:

- Data Collection: In adaptive reflectivity and spatial processing systems, data are collected from multiple antennas and their surroundings. This information includes signal strength, phase difference, noise level, and other relevant information.
- Feature Extraction: Machine learning involves extracting relevant features from the collected data. These features can include spatial correlation, channel characteristics, interference patterns, and more.
- Training Phase: During the training phase, the machine learning algorithm is provided with specific training data, where the best reflection or spatial processing results are known. The algorithm learns the feature map extracted for the desired result.
- Learning Algorithms: Commonly used machine learning algorithms for this purpose include neural networks, deep learning architectures, vector machines, decision trees, and

others. This algorithm explores the complex relationship between the extracted features and the optimal reflection weights or spatial processing coefficients.

- Adaptation and optimization: Once a machine learning model is trained, it can adapt to changing environmental conditions and changes in the wireless channel. Using real-time data from the antenna to adjust the reflected weight or spatial processing coefficient optimizes signal quality, reduces interference, and improves overall communication efficiency.

8.3.3 Benefits of Adaptive Rendering and Spatial Processing through Machine Learning

1. Dynamic adaptation: ML-driven adaptation techniques can adapt to environmental changes, user movements, and interference patterns, resulting in improved signal quality and reliability.
2. Optimized performance: Machine learning can discover complex patterns and relationships that may be difficult to capture with traditional analytics, leading to better performance in challenging environments.
3. Reduce interference: ML algorithms can effectively identify and minimize sources of interference, thereby improving overall communication quality.
4. Real-time optimization: The adaptive nature of machine learning enables real-time tuning, ensuring optimal performance even in rapidly changing scenarios.
5. Energy efficiency: ML-driven adaptive methods will optimize energy allocation and lead to energy-efficient communication.
6. Adaptation for different scenarios: Machine learning can adapt reflective and comprehensive processing strategies for different applications, such as open environments or high-density versus low-density user scenario.

8.3.4 Signal Denoising, Interference Mitigation, and Resource Allocation

Signal detection, interference mitigation, and resource allocation are critical to the development of advanced wireless networks such as 6G. This technique plays an important role in improving the overall performance, reliability, and efficiency of wireless communication systems. Here is a brief overview of each of these concepts in the context of 6G wireless networks, depicted in Figure 8.5:

• Signal Denoising:
Signal Denoising involves removing unwanted noise and interference from the received signal, improving the quality of received data. In 6G networks, which are expected to operate in higher frequency bands and support mass device connectivity, the risk of signal degradation due to noise becomes more significant. Advanced denoising techniques, often powered by machine learning and AI algorithms, can extract valuable information from noisy signals. Deep learning models such as Convolutional Neural Networks (CNN) and Recurrent Neural Networks (RNN) can lead to increased data accuracy and reliability to identify and extract noise patterns from received signals.

• Interference Mitigation:
Interference mitigation involves reducing or managing interference caused by overlapping signals from different communication sources. This is especially important in dense urban environments where many devices and networks operate in close proximity. Interference mitigation techniques in 6G networks may include beamforming, spatial filtering, and advanced spectrum management. Machine learning algorithms can help dynamically

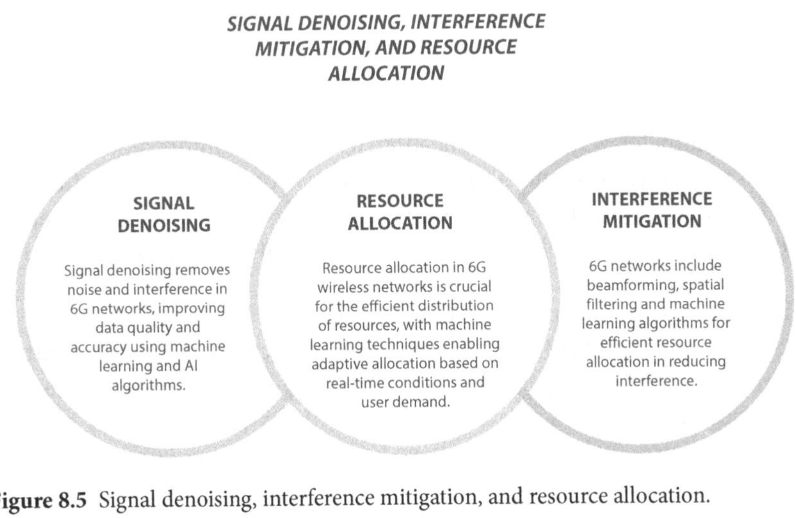

Figure 8.5 Signal denoising, interference mitigation, and resource allocation.

adjust transmission parameters to avoid outages, as well as predict outage patterns to optimize resource allocation.

• Resource Allocation:
Resource allocation refers to the efficient allocation of network resources such as frequency bands, time slots, and power among different users and services to improve overall network performance. Dynamic resource allocation becomes more important in 6G wireless networks, which are expected to support a variety of applications and different requirements (e.g., high-speed data, low-latency communication, and IoT devices). Machine learning techniques, including reinforcement learning and optimization algorithms, can be used to adaptively allocate resources based on real-time network conditions and user preferences. This ensures that resources are used efficiently and that the network can provide the desired quality of service for various applications.

8.3.5 Spectrum Management and Allocation

Spectrum management and allocation are critical aspects of wireless communication systems and have become more complex and important in the context of advanced technologies such as 6G networks. Here is an overview of how Machine Learning (ML) relates to spectrum management and allocation in 6G wireless networks, depicted in Figure 8.6:

• Spectrum management in 6G network:
6G is the next generation of wireless communication technology and aims to deliver unprecedented levels of performance, connectivity, and capabilities. Massgirt envisages a sophisticated and dynamic network environment that includes various technologies such as MIMO (multiple-input–multiple-output), millimeter-wave communication, terahertz communication, and others. Spectrum management in the 6G network is very important to efficiently use the frequency band as a result of increasing device density, various applications, and the need for highly reliable and low-latency communication.

• Machine learning in spectrum management:
Machine learning (ML) techniques have attracted considerable attention in spectrum management due to their ability to optimize complex and dynamic network scenarios. ML algorithms can adaptively allocate frequency, power, and resources based on real-time network conditions, traffic patterns, interference levels, and user requirements. Reinforcement learning, deep learning, and other ML approaches can learn patterns from

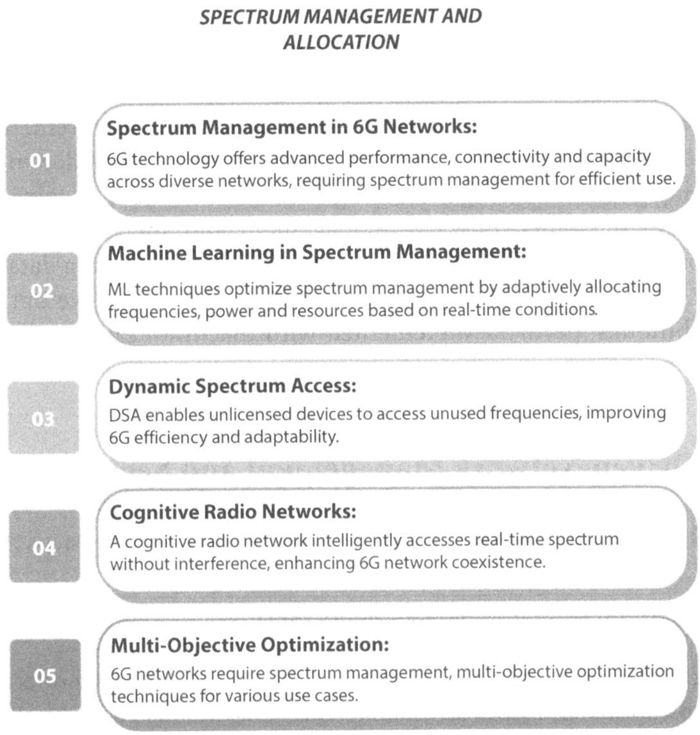

Figure 8.6 Spectrum management & allocation.

historical data and make intelligent decisions to improve spectrum efficiency and overall network performance.

• Introduction to dynamic spectrum:
Dynamic spectrum access (DSA) is a spectrum management approach that allows unauthorized devices to access temporarily unused frequency bands while avoiding interference from unauthorized users. The DSA technique, combined with the ML algorithm, allows the 6G network to dynamically allocate spectrum resources according to real-time demand. This increases spectrum efficiency and enables more flexible and adaptive system operation.

• Cognitive Radio System:
Cognitive radio systems are an extension of dynamic spectrum access, where devices can access available spectrum bands and are available in real time. Cognitive radio uses ML algorithms to identify and exploit spectrum opportunities without causing harmful interference to end users. This approach can be particularly useful in 6G networks to ensure the efficient coexistence of different services and applications.

• Multi-objective optimization:
6G networks will enable advanced mobile broadband, large-scale IoT applications, mission-critical communications, and more. These networks will serve various use cases, each with distinct requirements like effective management and spectrum allocation must consider multiple conflicting goals, including increasing data speed while maintaining low latency and reliability. Effective management and spectrum allocation must consider multiple conflicting goals, including increasing data speed while maintaining low latency and reliability. Many objective optimization techniques, perhaps implemented with machine learning, can help balance these goals.

8.4 Driven Network Management and Security

Figure 8.7 depicts important network management and security steps for 6G.

8.4.1 Self-Organizing Networks (SON)

Self-organizing networks (SON) play an important role in modern telecommunications and network management, as well as security. [8] Self-organizing networks (SON) aim to provide high-quality services while

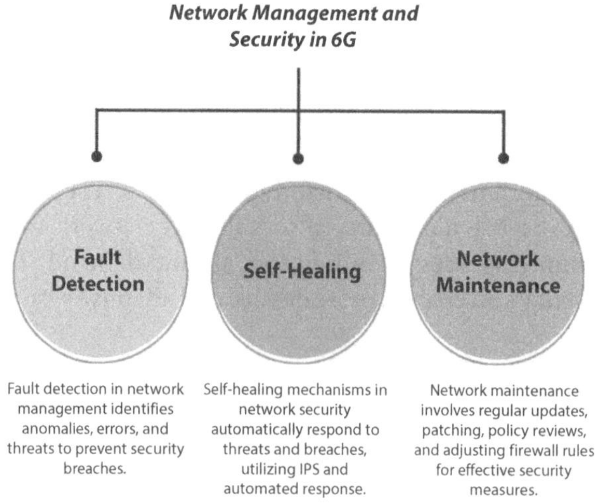

Figure 8.7 Network management and security in 6G.

reducing capital and operational costs by enabling three key functions: self-configuration, self-optimization, and self-healing. Although only a few studies have emerged on self-healing, it plays an important role in intelligent network maintenance. Here is how SON can affect these areas:

1. Automatic Configuration: SON provides automatic configuration of network elements, ensuring correct configuration during network expansion or upgrades and reducing human error.
2. Optimized Resource Allocation: The SON algorithm monitors network traffic and dynamically allocates resources to avoid congestion and ensure the use of available capacity.
3. Load Balancing: SON can distribute traffic to cells or access points to prevent the overloading of certain network elements, leading to better user experience and optimal performance.
4. Interference Management: SON techniques help detect and mitigate interference problems, especially in wireless networks, improving signal quality and reducing dropped calls or data loss.
5. Handover Optimization: SON can improve handover operations between different cells or access points and ensure a seamless transition for users while maintaining connection quality.
6. Energy Efficiency: SON technology can optimize the energy consumption of grid elements based on demand, which will lead to lower energy costs and a smaller environmental footprint.
7. Network Security: Although SON's primary focus is network optimization and management, it also has implications for network security.
8. Automated Threat Detection: By continuously monitoring network behavior and performance, SON can identify unusual patterns that may indicate a security breach or attack.
9. Intrusion Detection and Prevention: SON algorithms can learn to recognize patterns associated with various attacks, helping to detect and prevent attacks early on.
10. Rapid response: In the event of a security incident, SON can trigger an automatic response to isolate the affected area in the network, preventing the spread of threats.

11. Vulnerability Management: SON can help identify network vulnerabilities and reduce the attack surface and potential risks.
12. Access control: SON's automated management process can enforce access control policies, ensuring that only authorized devices and users can access the network.

8.4.2 Automatic Network Configuration and Optimization through AI

Automatic network configuration and optimization through AI can have a significant impact on network management and security aspects. How AI-driven automation can benefit these industries:

8.4.2.1 Network Management

1. Dynamic resource allocation: AI can analyze traffic patterns in real time and dynamically allocate resources such as bandwidth, processing power, and memory to different parts of the network to optimize performance as demand changes.
2. Traffic Optimization: AI algorithms can predict peak traffic times and adjust network parameters to manage increased load, avoid congestion, and provide a smooth user experience.
3. Load balancing: Autonomous load balancing ensures the even distribution of network resources, prevents bottlenecks, and improves overall network performance.
4. Efficient service: AI can predict hardware failure and network damage, thus reducing the downtime of active operations.
5. Network scaling: AI-driven insights can help network managers plan for capacity expansion by identifying where additional resources are needed.
6. Automatic Provisioning: AI can facilitate the provisioning of new network services or resources, reducing the time and effort required for manual configuration.
7. Real-time monitoring: AI-Powered monitoring can determine anomalies and performance problems in real time, enabling quick response and resolution.

8.4.2.2 *Network Security*

1. Threat Detection: AI can detect unusual behavior and analyze network traffic patterns to identify potential security threats, such as malware or unauthorized access attempts.
2. Intrusion Detection and Prevention: AI algorithms can recognize specific types of attacks and anomalies that reveal new attack vectors, creating automated responses to mitigate threats.
3. Behavioral Analysis: By studying common user and device behaviors, AI can spot errors that could indicate a compromised system or unauthorized access.
4. Automated Incident Response: When security breaches are detected, AI-driven systems can independently isolate affected segments, block malicious traffic, and take other protective measures.
5. Vulnerability Management: AI configuration can identify network vulnerabilities by analyzing software versions and other factors, prompting administrators to apply patches and updates.

8.4.3 Fault Detection, Self-Healing, and Network Maintenance

In terms of network management and security, fault detection, self-healing, and network maintenance play an important role in ensuring the reliability, availability, and security of technical systems. These concepts are specific to network management and security:

1. Fault detection: fault detection in network management involves identifying anomalies, errors, or omissions that may cause system disruptions or security breaches. These include hardware failures, software errors, configuration errors, and security vulnerabilities. Rapid detection of errors helps prevent service interruptions and security breaches. Intrusion detection systems (ids), network monitoring tools, and routine analysis are often used to detect vulnerabilities in system security.
2. Self-healing: self-healing mechanisms are required in system security to automatically respond to identified threats or violations. When a security incident, such as a distributed denial-of-service (DDoS) attack, is detected, the self-healing system can redirect traffic, enable security protocols, and adjust firewall rules to mitigate the impact of the attack.

Intrusion prevention systems (IPS) and automated incident response play an important role in self-healing by blocking malicious traffic and isolating compromised systems.

3. Network maintenance: from a security perspective, network maintenance includes ongoing efforts to maintain network infrastructure and security measures. Regular software development, software updates, and security policy reviews are essential to address known vulnerabilities and adapt to evolving threats. Maintenance also includes reviewing and adjusting firewall rules, access controls, and user rights to ensure security measures are effective and meet organizational needs.

8.5 Challenges and Future Directions

8.5.1 Data Privacy and Ethics Issues and Challenges

[9] The role of AI in 6G can be a double-edged sword, as it can protect security and privacy. Proactive threat detection, mitigation techniques, and self-sustaining networks are critical to 6G automation.

Challenges in Data Privacy and Ethical Considerations:

1. Data Breaches and Privacy: Increasing digitization of data has led to data breaches and privacy. Cyberattacks targeting sensitive data can cause significant financial losses and reputational damage to individuals and organizations.
2. User Consent and Control: Balancing the need to collect data with user consent and control over their personal information is a challenge. Many users are unaware of how their data are collected and used, leading to the issue of informed consent.
3. Monetization and data processing: Organizations often collect and monetize user data for advertising and profiling purposes. This can lead to ethical problems if the data are used without the user's knowledge or consent.
4. Algorithm Inconsistencies and Discrimination: Algorithm-driven data can maintain inconsistencies in their learning data and produce discriminatory results. Ensuring fairness

Figure 8.8 Challenges in privacy and ethical consideration.

and addressing bias in algorithmic decision-making is a complex issue.

5. Global regulatory landscape: Data privacy regulations such as GDPR and CCPA have set stricter requirements for data processing and user rights. When operating in a digital ecosystem, it can be difficult for organizations to comply with various global regulations.
6. Emerging technologies: Technological advances such as artificial intelligence (AI), machine learning, and the Internet of Things (IoT) present new privacy and ethical challenges. For example, AI systems can process personal data without knowing the personal data. Figure 8.8 gives the challenges in privacy.

8.5.2 Future Directions in Data Privacy and Ethical Considerations

- Privacy by Design: Incorporating privacy considerations into the design phase of products and services ensures that privacy is a central aspect of the architecture. This approach aims to reduce the collection of sensitive data and increase user control.

- Ethical AI and algorithmic transparency: It is essential to develop AI systems that are open, transparent, and free from bias. Research and development in AI ethics focuses on ways to reduce bias, ensure fairness, and provide explanations for AI decisions.
- Decentralized identity and data ownership: Concepts such as decentralized identity and decentralized data storage give people more control over their personal data. Blockchain technology is explored to create a secure and user-driven data ecosystem.
- Increased Data Protection Regulations: More regions and countries will adopt data protection regulations such as GDPR, increasing the responsibility of organizations to protect user data and respect their rights.
- Ethical data use framework: Developing a framework that guides organizations in collecting, using, and sharing ethical data can help reduce risk and ensure responsible data practices.
- Public awareness and education: Educating individuals about their data rights, the importance of data privacy, and the potential risks of sharing personal data can allow users to make informed choices.
- Collaborative efforts: Government, industry, and academia must collaborate to establish standards and best practices for data privacy and ethics. Joint efforts can lead to more effective solutions.
- Ongoing monitoring and accountability: Organizations must actively monitor data operations, regularly assess privacy, and be accountable for any breaches or breaches.

8.5.3 Balancing Data Usage and User Privacy in AI-Driven Networks

[10] 6G is based on AI for data-driven machine learning solutions in heterogeneous networks. Traditional ML techniques require centralized data collection and processing, leading to privacy concerns. Federated learning, an emerging distributed AI approach, is attractive for wireless applications in 6G. This article introduces the integration of 6G and federated learning, addressing technical challenges, methods, and open problems for future

research in 6G communication. Challenges in balancing data usage and user privacy in AI-driven networks are the following:

- Data sensitivity: AI models require large amounts of data to function effectively. However, some of this information may be sensitive, including personal, financial, or medical information. Balancing data needs with user privacy concerns is a challenge.
- Informed Consent: Obtaining informed consent from users to use their data for AI training can be difficult. Users do not fully understand how their data will be used, resulting in privacy violations.
- Data ownership: Determining who owns the data and how it can be used is complex, especially when multiple parties contribute data to the AI model. Clear instructions are needed to resolve ownership and control.
- Algorithmic Bias: AI models trained on biased data can harbor inherent biases that lead to discriminatory results. It is important to balance the need for different types of information while maintaining privacy.
- Privacy Protection Techniques: Using data while protecting user privacy requires advanced techniques such as differential encryption, federated learning, and homomorphic encryption. This technique can be difficult to implement effectively.
- Third-party sharing: AI models can be trained on data collected by third-party organizations, ensuring the safe and ethical sharing of user data.

8.6 Conclusion

The convergence of 6G wireless networks and machine learning presents a promising avenue for revolutionizing the telecommunications landscape. With ultrahigh data rates, low latency, and massive device connectivity, 6G networks are poised to redefine communication paradigms. Machine learning techniques, such as adaptive beamforming and spectrum management, can enhance network performance and efficiency. However, ethical considerations surrounding data privacy, scalability, and complexity management are crucial. As networks become more intricate and data-intensive, managing these complexities is a pressing issue. The synergy of AI and 6G wireless networks is poised to usher in a new era of connectivity and innovation.

References

1. Prasad, R., Mihovska, A., Prasad, A.R., Nidhi, Introduction, in: *6G Enabling Technologies: New Dimensions to Wireless Communication*, pp. 1–8, River Publishers, 2023. ISBN: 9788770227742.
2. Henrique, P.S.R. and Prasad, R., Introduction, in: *6G: The Road to the Future Wireless Technologies 2030*, pp. 1–8, River Publishers, 2021. ISBN: 9788770224390.
3. Tong, W. and Li, G.Y., Nine Challenges in Artificial Intelligence and Wireless Communications for 6G. *IEEE Wireless Commun.*, 29, 4, 140–145, August 2022, doi: 10.1109/MWC.006.2100543.
4. Noman, H.M.F., *et al.*, Machine Learning Empowered Emerging Wireless Networks in 6G: Recent Advancements, Challenges and Future Trends. *IEEE Access*, 11, 83017–83051, 2023, doi: 10.1109/ACCESS.2023.3302250.
5. Viswanathan, H. and Mogensen, P.E., Communications in the 6G Era. *IEEE Access*, 8, 57063–57074, 2020, doi: 10.1109/ACCESS.2020.2981745.
6. Qi, Q., Chen, X., Khalili, A., Zhong, C., Zhang, Z., Ng, D.W.K., Integrating Sensing, Computing, and Communication in 6G Wireless Networks: Design and Optimization. *IEEE Trans. Commun.*, 70, 9, 6212–6227, Sept. 2022, doi: 10.1109/TCOMM.2022.3190363.
7. Sliwa, B., Falkenberg, R., Wietfeld, C., Towards Cooperative Data Rate Prediction for Future Mobile and Vehicular 6G Networks. *2020 2nd 6G Wireless Summit (6G SUMMIT)*, pp. 1–5, 2020, doi: 10.1109/6GSUMMIT49458.2020.9083767.
8. Wang, Y., Zhu, K., Sun, M., Deng, Y., An Ensemble Learning Approach for Fault Diagnosis in Self-Organizing Heterogeneous Networks. *IEEE Access*, 7, 125662–125675, 2019, doi: 10.1109/ACCESS.2019.2925566.
9. Siriwardhana, Y., Porambage, P., Liyanage, M., Ylianttila, M., AI and 6G Security: Opportunities and Challenges. *2021 Joint European Conference on Networks and Communications & 6G Summit (EuCNC/6G Summit)*, pp. 616–621, 2021, doi: 10.1109/EuCNC/6GSummit51104.2021.9482503.
10. Liu, Y., Yuan, X., Xiong, Z., Kang, J., Wang, X., Niyato, D., Federated learning for 6G communications: Challenges, methods, and future directions. *China Commun.*, 17, 9, 105–118, Sept. 2020, doi: 10.23919/JCC.2020.09.009.

9

Machine Learning–Based Communication and Network Automation: Advancements, Challenges, and Prospects

J. Shanthalakshmi Revathy[1]* and J. Mangaiyarkkarasi[2]

[1]Department of Computer Science and Engineering, Velammal College of Engineering and Technology, Viraganoor, Madurai, India
[2]PG and Research Department of Physics, Nadar Mahajana Sangam S. Vellaichamy Nadar College, Nagamalai, Madurai, India

Abstract

Machine learning (ML) has become a disruptive force in network automation and communication in an era of rapid technological innovation. This chapter examines the various ways that machine learning has affected different fields, looking into methods including natural language processing, reinforcement learning, and neural networks. These approaches have transformed spectrum management, wireless channel modeling, interference mitigation, resource allocation, decision-making procedures, and interference reduction, which has improved connectivity and maximized the use of communication resources.

The chapter also explores machine learning's application to network automation, where algorithms reduce manual involvement and minimize the possibility of human mistakes by streamlining operations like configuration management, problem detection, and network optimization. Despite these developments, algorithmic biases, data privacy issues, and ethical issues continue to be major obstacles to the implementation of ML-based systems. This has inspired discussions on methods to guarantee the impartial and responsible use of ML technology.

The chapter explores the potential applications of ML in network automation and communication, with a view to integrating these technologies with upcoming innovations such as edge computing, 6G, and the Internet of Things (IoT). It is projected that this integration would create a highly flexible and effective network ecosystem, changing the way we interact and oversee networked devices and opening the door to a more intelligent and connected future.

**Corresponding author*: jslr@vcet.ac.in

Pallavi Sapkale, Shilpa Mehta and S. Balamurugan (eds.) Quantum Computing and Machine Learning for 6G, (187–216) © 2026 Scrivener Publishing LLC

Keywords: Machine learning, communication systems, network automation, spectrum management, ethical considerations, edge computing, interconnected systems

9.1 Introduction

ML has emerged as a transformative force in the fields of communication and network automation, accompanied by a new era of efficiency, reliability, and adaptability. In today's interconnected world, where data flows seamlessly across vast networks, the need for intelligent, self-adjusting systems has never been more crucial. Machine learning, a subset of artificial intelligence, has risen to this challenge by offering the promise of automating complex tasks, optimizing network performance, and enhancing communication services [1]. One of the primary reasons for the growing significance of ML in communication and network automation is its ability to process and analyze massive datasets at unprecedented speeds. ML algorithms can uncover patterns, anomalies, and insights within these data, allowing networks to adapt in real time to changing conditions. For instance, predictive maintenance models can forecast network failures before they occur, preventing costly downtime. ML also plays a pivotal role in enhancing communication services. Natural language processing (NLP) algorithms enable more efficient customer support through chatbots and virtual assistants, while recommendation systems personalize content and services for users [2]. Despite its immense potential, ML in communication and network automation also presents challenges, including data security, scalability, and ethical considerations. This chapter explores these advancements and challenges, providing insights into the prospects of this transformative technology in shaping the future of networked communication systems.

Automation has become the cornerstone of modern networks, driving efficiency, reliability, and agility to unprecedented levels. In the ever-evolving landscape of information technology, automation plays a pivotal role in ensuring that networks can keep up with the demands of the digital age. Automation in modern networks offers numerous advantages. It enhances efficiency by streamlining tasks, such as provisioning and troubleshooting, reducing the need for manual intervention and saving time while minimizing human errors [3]. Additionally, automation bolsters reliability through consistent application of configurations and policies, mitigating misconfigurations and deviations from best practices, while automated monitoring and alerting swiftly detect and respond to anomalies or security threats. Moreover, automation fosters agility, enabling networks to swiftly adapt to evolving demands, allocate resources efficiently, and implement changes in real time, which is particularly crucial in cloud-based and software-defined network environments [4]. Lastly, it contributes to cost reduction by diminishing manual labor requirements and minimizing downtime, enabling network administrators to concentrate on strategic initiatives rather than routine maintenance. These combined benefits make automation an indispensable tool in modern network management [5]. Automation is the backbone of modern networks, empowering organizations to deliver more reliable and responsive services while simultaneously optimizing resource utilization and reducing operational costs. It is an essential tool for navigating the complexities of contemporary network management. Existing work in machine learning–based communication and network automation faces challenges such as data quality, scalability, and interpretability. Data heterogeneity and inconsistency impede model accuracy and generalization. Scaling models to large networks demands substantial computational resources and may introduce latency. Moreover, opaque model decision-making hinders trust and interpretability, which are critical for network operations. Robustness to dynamic network conditions and adversarial attacks remains a concern. Addressing these issues requires interdisciplinary collaboration, emphasizing data management, model scalability, interpretability techniques, and robustness validation methods. Enhancing existing work in these areas holds promise for more effective and reliable machine learning–driven communication and network automation systems.

The chapter begins by highlighting the significance of machine learning in communication and network automation. It then delves into advancements in ML, challenges faced in its implementation, and prospects for the future. Throughout, it examines the role of automation in modern networks, emphasizing efficiency, reliability, agility, and cost reduction.

9.2 Advancements in Machine Learning for Communication and Network Automation

In this section, the core advancements in machine learning as applied to communication and network automation are explored.

Topics include fundamental ML concepts, practical applications, data sources, preprocessing, model training, and real-time deployment, shedding light on the transformative capabilities of ML in optimizing network

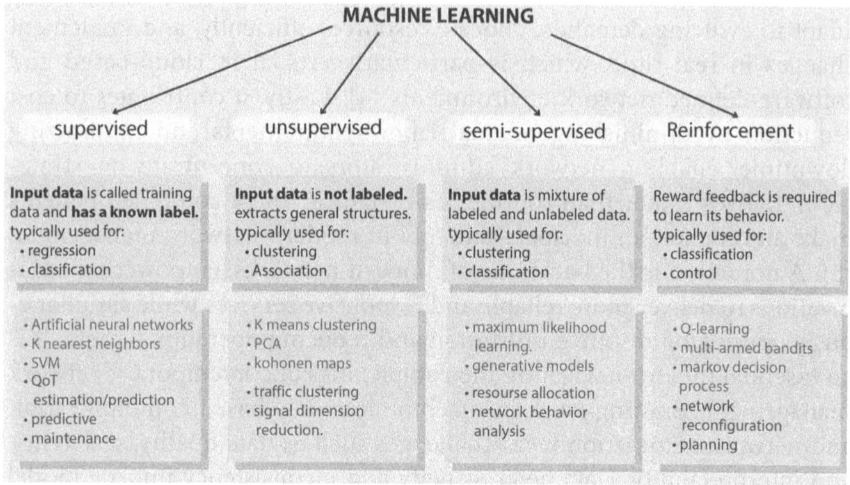

Figure 9.1 Machine learning for communication and network automation.

operations and communication services. Figure 9.1 depicts the concept of "Machine Learning Algorithms for Communication and Network Automation."

9.2.1 Machine Learning Fundamentals

ML is a subset of artificial intelligence [AI] that empowers systems to learn and make decisions based on data rather than explicit programming. At its core, ML revolves around the idea of training algorithms to recognize patterns, make predictions, or optimize processes by feeding those vast datasets. It encompasses various techniques and paradigms, including supervised, unsupervised, and reinforcement learning, as well as deep learning.

9.2.1.1 Supervised, Unsupervised, and Reinforcement Learning in Network Automation

In network automation, supervised learning involves training models with labeled data [6]. For instance, it can predict network failures by learning from historical data where failure instances are labeled. This approach enables predictive maintenance, traffic optimization, and intrusion detection. Unsupervised learning does not require labeled data. It discovers hidden patterns or structures within network data [7].

Table 9.1 Machine learning algorithms for communication and network automation use cases.

Use case	Algorithm(s)
Classification of network traffic	Random forest, support vector machines (SVM), neural networks (e.g., convolutional neural networks for deep packet inspection)
Regression for network performance prediction	Linear regression, decision trees, gradient boosting (e.g., XGBoost)
Predictive maintenance for network equipment	Decision trees, random forest, support vector machines (SVM), recurrent neural networks (RNN)
Anomaly detection for network security	Isolation forest, one-class SVM, autoencoders (deep learning)
Clustering network nodes for resource optimization	K-Means clustering, DBSCAN (density-based spatial clustering of applications with noise)
Network fault detection	Bayesian networks, hidden Markov models (HMM), Long Short-Term Memory (LSTM) networks
Network routing and optimization	Q Learning, deep Q networks (DQN), proximal policy optimization (PPO)
Dynamic network resource allocation	Reinforcement learning (RL) with custom reward functions
Self-healing network systems	Reinforcement learning (RL), genetic algorithms, fuzzy logic systems
Natural language processing for network log analysis	Recurrent neural networks (RNN), long short-term memory (LSTM) networks, transformer models (e.g., BERT)
Image recognition for network infrastructure monitoring	Convolutional neural networks (CNN), YOLO (You Only Look Once) for real-time object detection
Time-series forecasting for network traffic prediction	Recurrent neural networks (RNN), long short-term memory (LSTM) networks, Prophet (for seasonal time series)

Table 9.1 presents a concise overview of machine learning algorithms tailored for communication and network automation, highlighting their specific use cases. Clustering algorithms, for example, can group similar network elements together, aiding in network segmentation or anomaly detection. Reinforcement learning operates based on an agent interacting with an environment to achieve specific goals. In network automation, this can optimize routing decisions, adapt to changing network conditions, or enhance quality of service (QoS) by learning from the consequences of its actions.

Deep learning is a subset of ML that focuses on neural networks with multiple layers (deep neural networks). These networks can automatically learn hierarchical representations of data, making them highly effective for tasks like image recognition, natural language processing, and even certain aspects of network automation. Convolutional neural networks (CNNs) and recurrent neural networks (RNNs) are examples of deep learning architectures used in network anomaly detection, traffic prediction, and security [8]. Machine learning concepts are foundational in modern network automation, with supervised, unsupervised, reinforcement learning, and deep learning techniques offering powerful tools for optimizing network performance, enhancing security, and automating various aspects of communication and networking. These methodologies enable networks to become more adaptive, efficient, and responsive to the ever-evolving demands of the digital landscape.

9.2.2 Applications in Network Automation

Machine learning is revolutionizing network automation by enabling intelligent decision-making and automation of complex tasks.

9.2.2.1 Predictive Maintenance and Fault Detection

ML models can analyze historical network data to predict potential failures or anomalies. By identifying issues before they cause service disruptions, network operators can perform maintenance proactively, reducing downtime and improving overall reliability [9]. Figure 9.2 depicts a predictive maintenance system, utilizing data analysis and machine learning to forecast equipment failures and optimize maintenance strategies.

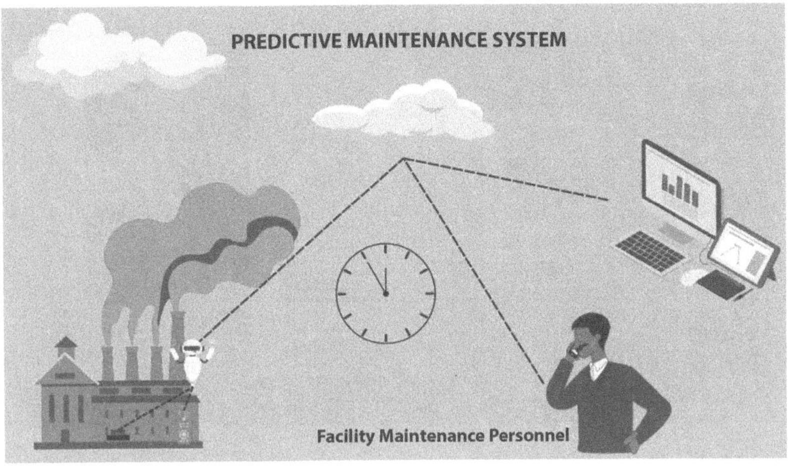

Figure 9.2 Predictive maintenance system.

9.2.2.2 *Quality of Service (QoS) Optimization*

ML algorithms can monitor network performance in real time and make dynamic adjustments to ensure consistent QoS. This is particularly crucial in video streaming, online gaming, and voice-over-IP (VoIP) applications, where even minor disruptions can result in a poor user experience.

9.2.2.3 *Traffic Engineering and Load Balancing*

ML-powered traffic engineering optimizes network routing to distribute traffic efficiently. Load balancing ensures that network resources are utilized effectively, preventing congestion and bottlenecks, which is essential in data centers and content delivery networks (CDNs). Figure 9.3 illustrates the combined concept of traffic engineering and load balancing, optimizing network routes and distributing workloads for improved efficiency.

Predictive maintenance is a vital application of ML in network automation [10]. By analyzing historical network data, ML models can detect patterns indicative of impending failures or performance degradation. For example, fluctuations in traffic, device temperatures, or error rates can be early indicators of network issues. ML algorithms can not only identify these issues but also predict when they are likely to occur. This proactive approach to maintenance allows network administrators to schedule repairs or replacements during planned maintenance windows,

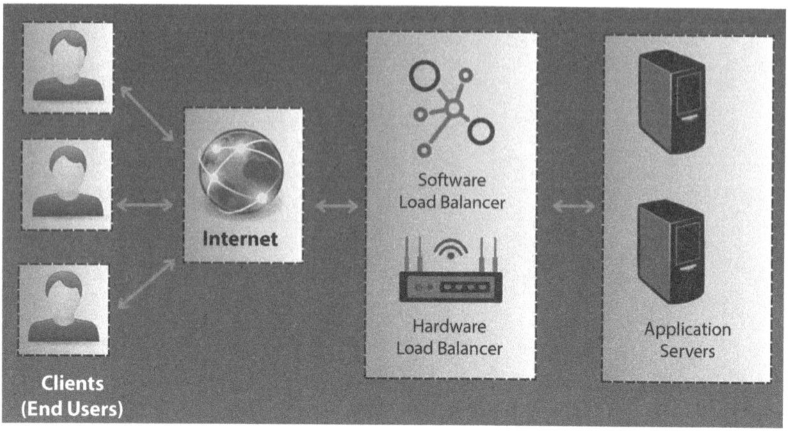

Figure 9.3 Load balancing.

minimizing service disruptions and avoiding costly emergency repairs. By reducing downtime and improving network reliability, predictive maintenance not only enhances user satisfaction but also results in significant cost savings for network operators.

9.2.3 Data Sources and Preprocessing

Data play a pivotal role in the success of machine learning applications in network automation. This section focuses on data sources, collection methods, preprocessing techniques, and the importance of feature selection and engineering.

9.2.3.1 Data Collection Methods in Network Environments

Network monitoring is a critical aspect of managing and maintaining computer networks. Network administrators employ various methods and tools to monitor network performance, security, and overall health. One fundamental approach involves the use of specialized network monitoring tools, such as SNMP (Simple Network Management Protocol) or packet analyzers. These tools collect data on network performance, device status, traffic patterns, and more, providing real-time and historical insights into the network's operation. Logs and event data generated by network devices also play a pivotal role in network monitoring. These logs contain valuable information about the operational status of devices, errors, and warnings. Centralized log management systems, such as syslog servers, are employed to collect and analyze these logs, helping administrators troubleshoot issues and monitor network performance effectively.

Flow data technologies like NetFlow and sFlow capture information about communication between devices on the network. This flow data offers valuable insights into traffic patterns, including the source and destination of traffic and the protocols used. Network administrators utilize flow data for tasks like capacity planning, security monitoring, and optimizing traffic routing [11]. For in-depth network diagnostics and security analysis, packet-level data capture tools, such as Wireshark, are employed. These tools capture and analyze individual network packets, allowing administrators to inspect packet content, identify issues like congestion or packet loss, and investigate security incidents.

In practice, network administrators often combine these monitoring methods and tools to gain a comprehensive understanding of their network's behavior [12]. Integrated network monitoring solutions bring together data from various sources to provide a unified view of network health, enabling quick responses to issues, optimizing performance, and ensuring network security and reliability.

9.2.3.2 *Data Preprocessing Techniques*

In the process of preparing data for machine learning, several crucial steps are undertaken to ensure its quality and suitability for model training. Initially, data cleaning techniques are applied to handle issues like missing values, outliers, and errors, guaranteeing that the dataset is reliable. Next, normalization and scaling are performed to standardize data attributes, eliminating the potential bias caused by varying scales or units. Feature extraction, including dimensionality reduction methods such as principal components analysis (PCA), may be employed to derive new relevant features from raw data, thus improving model performance. Additionally, data transformation techniques, such as logarithmic scaling or one-hot encoding, are applied to categorical data, rendering it compatible with machine learning algorithms [13]. These preparatory steps collectively enhance the quality and usability of the data for effective machine learning model training.

9.2.3.3 *Feature Selection and Engineering*

In the field of machine learning, two critical strategies, namely, feature selection and feature engineering, contribute considerably to model performance optimization. Feature selection methods, like recursive feature elimination or leveraging feature importance from tree-based models, aid in the identification of the most pertinent attributes within the dataset, streamlining the model's focus on the most relevant information. On the other hand, feature engineering entails the creation of new attributes or modification of existing ones, often guided by domain knowledge and insights, to capture crucial data relationships. For instance, in network data analysis, engineers may craft features like bandwidth utilization ratios or the detection of traffic spikes during specific time intervals, ultimately enhancing model accuracy by incorporating domain-specific expertise into the dataset's representation. These two techniques collectively empower machine learning models to make more informed and precise predictions by optimizing the selection and creation of relevant features.

Data sources and preprocessing are fundamental in network automation, as high-quality data and effective preprocessing are essential for training accurate and reliable machine learning models. Properly collected and processed data can enable ML algorithms to make informed decisions, leading to improved network performance, security, and automation capabilities.

9.2.4 Model Training and Deployment

Model training and deployment are critical phases in the application of machine learning (ML) to network automation. This section explores the processes involved, considerations for algorithm selection, and challenges related to real-time deployment:

Model training is a fundamental step in harnessing the power of machine learning for network automation. It involves a series of processes designed to transform raw data into a trained model capable of making informed predictions or classifications. Data preparation is the initial phase, where the quality and readiness of the data are assessed. High-quality and properly preprocessed data are crucial as they form the foundation upon which the model will be built. This includes data cleaning to remove inconsistencies and errors, data transformation to make it suitable for analysis, and feature selection to identify relevant attributes for the specific task. Algorithm selection is the next critical step. Different network automation tasks may demand various machine learning algorithms, ranging from regression and classification to clustering. The choice of algorithm hinges on the nature of the task and the characteristics of the data at hand. Once the data are ready, it is typically divided into three subsets: the training set, the validation set, and the test set. Figure 9.4 represents the integration of data sources, preprocessing, training, testing, and model deployment in a network environment, highlighting the end-to-end data lifecycle and AI model deployment.

The training set serves as the basis for the model's learning process, while the validation set aids in fine-tuning hyperparameters to optimize performance. The test set, consisting of unseen data, evaluates the model's ability to generalize to new scenarios. The heart of model training lies in iterative learning. Machine learning algorithms learn from the training data by making predictions and adjusting their internal parameters to minimize errors between their predictions and actual outcomes. This process continues until the model reaches a satisfactory level of accuracy. Hyperparameter tuning further refines the model's performance. Hyperparameters, such as learning rates or tree depths, influence the model's behavior and effectiveness [14]. Hyperparameter tuning involves finding the optimal combination of hyperparameters for the specific network automation task. Cross-validation techniques, such as k-fold cross-validation, provide an additional layer of assurance regarding the model's generalization capabilities. By repeatedly splitting the data into subsets for training and testing, cross-validation assesses the model's consistency and robustness.

Choosing the right machine learning algorithm is a critical decision in network automation, and it largely hinges on the specific task at hand and the characteristics of the available data.

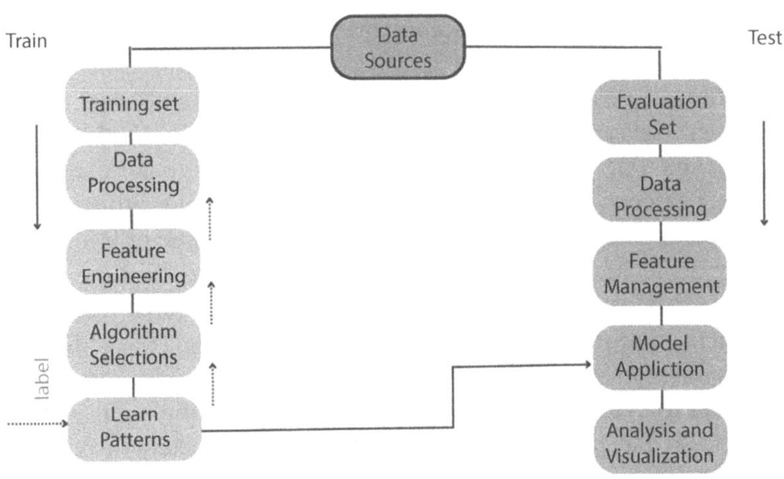

Figure 9.4 Data sources and preprocessing in network environment.

Supervised learning is an excellent choice when dealing with labeled data, making it well-suited for tasks such as classification and regression in network automation. Algorithms like decision trees, random forests, support vector machines (SVMs), and neural networks can be deployed to solve these tasks effectively. Decision trees and random forests are known for their interpretability and versatility, while SVMs excel in handling complex data patterns. Neural networks, especially deep neural networks, are valuable for tasks that involve processing large volumes of data, such as image recognition in network security.

Unsupervised learning, on the other hand, is valuable for tasks that involve discovering patterns or structures within data without labeled examples. Clustering algorithms like k-means or hierarchical clustering can group similar network elements together, aiding in network segmentation or anomaly detection. Dimensionality reduction techniques like principal components analysis (PCA) are instrumental in managing high-dimensional data, reducing complexity while retaining important information. For dynamic network optimization tasks where actions must adapt to changing conditions, reinforcement learning algorithms come into play. Algorithms such as Q-learning and deep reinforcement learning enable networks to make decisions that maximize certain objectives while adapting to evolving network states [15]. These algorithms are particularly valuable in scenarios where network conditions fluctuate, requiring continuous adjustments for optimal performance. In essence, the choice of a machine learning algorithm in network automation should align with the specific objectives and data characteristics of the task. Each type of algorithm offers unique capabilities that can be harnessed to improve network efficiency, security, and overall automation, depending on the nature of the network automation problem.

Real-time deployment of machine learning models in network automation presents several key challenges. Firstly, the scalability challenge arises when dealing with large-scale networks. The computational demands of processing extensive data in real time require efficient algorithms and distributed computing resources to handle the sheer volume of information. Secondly, achieving low-latency responses is crucial for real-time network decisions. This necessitates the optimization of model architectures and deployment environments to ensure rapid ML inference [16]. Additionally, model maintenance is an ongoing requirement. ML models must continuously adapt to evolving network conditions, necessitating regular retraining with fresh data to maintain accuracy. Lastly, data privacy and regulatory compliance are paramount. Real-time ML deployments must implement robust measures to securely handle sensitive network data while adhering to privacy regulations to protect user information and maintain trust.

9.3 Challenges in Implementing Machine Learning for Network Automation

Implementing machine learning for network automation presents a spectrum of challenges. From data quality and scalability issues to interoperability concerns and ethical considerations, these obstacles demand innovative solutions to harness the full potential of artificial intelligence in managing modern networks effectively. Figure 9.5 explores the hurdles encountered while implementing machine learning for network automation, addressing the complexities in deploying this technology.

9.3.1 Data Quality and Availability

One of the foremost challenges in implementing machine learning for network automation is dealing with noisy and incomplete data. In network environments, data can be riddled with errors, missing values, and inconsistencies due to various factors like hardware malfunctions, network congestion, or data transmission issues. Noise in the data can mislead ML models, leading to inaccurate predictions or automation decisions. Robust data preprocessing techniques, including data cleaning and imputation, are crucial to mitigate these challenges and ensure the quality of input data [5].

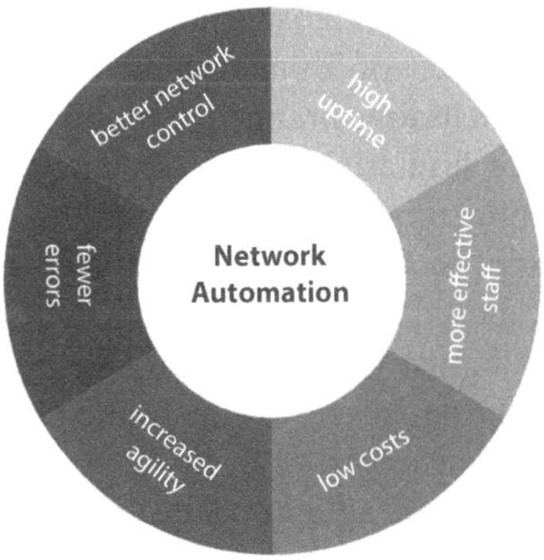

Figure 9.5 Challenges in network automation.

Data privacy and security are paramount concerns in network automation, especially when dealing with sensitive network data. ML algorithms often require access to network traffic and configuration data, which can include confidential information. Ensuring the confidentiality and integrity of these data is crucial to prevent unauthorized access or data breaches. Implementation of encryption, access controls, and compliance with data protection regulations are essential steps in addressing these concerns while still harnessing the benefits of ML. In network automation, data often arrives in real time, in the form of streaming data. This poses unique challenges as ML models must make rapid decisions based on constantly changing information. Efficiently handling streaming data requires the development of real-time data processing pipelines and algorithms capable of ingesting, processing, and making predictions or automation swiftly. Latency considerations become critical in this context, as delays in decision-making can have significant implications for network performance and security.

9.3.2 Scalability and Resource Constraints

Scalability is a paramount concern when applying machine learning to large-scale networks. As network infrastructures expand, the volume of data generated and the complexity of tasks also increase. Traditional machine learning models may struggle to handle the sheer scale of these networks. To address this challenge, it is essential to develop and implement scalable machine learning algorithms and frameworks. Distributed computing resources and techniques, such as parallel processing and distributed machine learning, can be employed to train and deploy models that can efficiently operate on extensive network data.

Edge and IoT (Internet-of-Things) networks often operate under resource constraints, including limited computing power, memory, and energy. These resource limitations pose challenges for deploying traditional machine learning models that may require significant computational resources. To address this, lightweight and energy-efficient machine learning algorithms tailored for edge and IoT environments are essential. Edge computing paradigms, where data processing occurs closer to the data source, can also alleviate resource constraints by reducing the need for data transfer to centralized servers [17].

Distributed machine learning approaches are increasingly valuable in addressing scalability and resource constraints in network automation. By distributing the training and inference processes across multiple nodes or devices, these approaches leverage parallelism to handle large datasets and resource-constrained environments effectively. Techniques like federated learning, where models are trained collaboratively on decentralized devices, enable privacy-preserving and resource-efficient machine learning in networks with diverse constraints.

The challenges of scalability and resource constraints in network automation necessitate innovative approaches [18]. Scalable machine learning algorithms, lightweight models for edge and IoT networks, and distributed machine learning techniques are pivotal in ensuring that machine learning can operate effectively in diverse network environments while maximizing resource utilization and performance.

9.3.3 Interoperability and Standards

Interoperability and standards play a crucial role in the realm of network automation, ensuring that networks can function efficiently, securely, and reliably. Here are some key points related to the need for standardization, compatibility with existing infrastructure, and challenges posed by vendor-specific solutions:

9.3.3.1 Need for Standardization

Standardization plays a pivotal role in the world of networking, offering a range of significant benefits that contribute to the efficiency and reliability of network environments. First and foremost, it fosters consistency by establishing a common set of rules and practices. This consistency is essential, as it ensures that devices and components from various manufacturers can seamlessly work together within the network, promoting interoperability. In multi-vendor environments, where a variety of equipment is used, standardization becomes paramount, facilitating the smooth communication and interaction of disparate systems.

Furthermore, standardized protocols and interfaces support scalability, allowing network infrastructure to grow and adapt easily to evolving needs. Network administrators can confidently expand their networks without worrying about compatibility issues or the need for extensive reconfiguration. Reduced complexity is another key advantage of standardization. It simplifies network management and troubleshooting by providing a well-established framework for network operators to follow. This simplification not only saves time and resources but also enhances the overall reliability of the network [19].

Moreover, standardization contributes significantly to network security. By adhering to standardized security protocols and practices, networks can fortify their defenses against potential threats and vulnerabilities. This consistency in security measures ensures that networks are less susceptible to risks that might arise from proprietary or ad-hoc solutions, bolstering overall network resilience. In essence, standardization is the cornerstone upon which modern networks are built, underpinning their efficiency, reliability, and security.

9.3.3.2 Compatibility with Existing Network Infrastructure

The adoption of standardized automation solutions in network management offers several significant advantages for organizations. Firstly, it facilitates the harmonious integration of automation with legacy systems, ensuring compatibility and efficiency without requiring a costly and extensive network infrastructure overhaul. Secondly, standardized automation allows for incremental deployment, enabling organizations to introduce automation gradually, reducing disruptions, and mitigating risks commonly associated with large-scale changes [20]. Additionally, the vendor-agnostic nature of standardized protocols and interfaces provides organizations with greater flexibility when it comes to upgrading or expanding their network infrastructure, as they are not locked into proprietary solutions, fostering adaptability and future-proofing network management practices. These benefits collectively support the efficient and strategic implementation of automation in network operations.

9.3.3.3 Vendor-Specific Challenges

While network automation can streamline operations, several challenges exist, including the potential for vendor lock-in. Some automation solutions are tightly integrated with specific vendors, making it challenging to switch to alternative providers or technologies, incurring substantial effort and costs. Proprietary protocols and APIs can limit interoperability, fostering vendor-dependent silos and hindering network flexibility. Furthermore, even when standards exist, vendors may implement them differently, leading to interoperability issues and necessitating additional work to ensure compatibility. Despite these challenges, it is essential to note that vendor-specific solutions might offer unique features, creating complications when migrating to different vendors or technology stacks, highlighting the need for careful consideration and strategic planning in the adoption of network automation [21].

Standardization in network automation is essential for ensuring that networks are efficient, secure, and adaptable. It enables compatibility with existing infrastructure, promotes interoperability across vendors, and helps address the challenges associated with vendor-specific solutions. Organizations must carefully consider these factors when planning and implementing network automation strategies to achieve a balance between innovation and compatibility.

9.3.4 Ethical and Regulatory Considerations

Ethical and regulatory considerations are increasingly important in the development and deployment of machine learning algorithms, network automation, and communication technologies. Here are some key points related to these considerations:

9.3.4.1 Bias and Fairness in Machine Learning Algorithms

Algorithmic bias is a pressing concern in the development and deployment of machine learning systems. These algorithms have the potential to inadvertently perpetuate or even exacerbate biases present in the training data they rely on, which can lead to unfair or discriminatory outcomes.

Figure 9.6 visualizes various sources of bias during the training phase of machine learning models, highlighting potential sources of data imbalance. Addressing bias at its roots is of paramount importance, involving careful algorithm design and the selection of training data that are representative and unbiased. Fairness metrics play a pivotal role in this process,

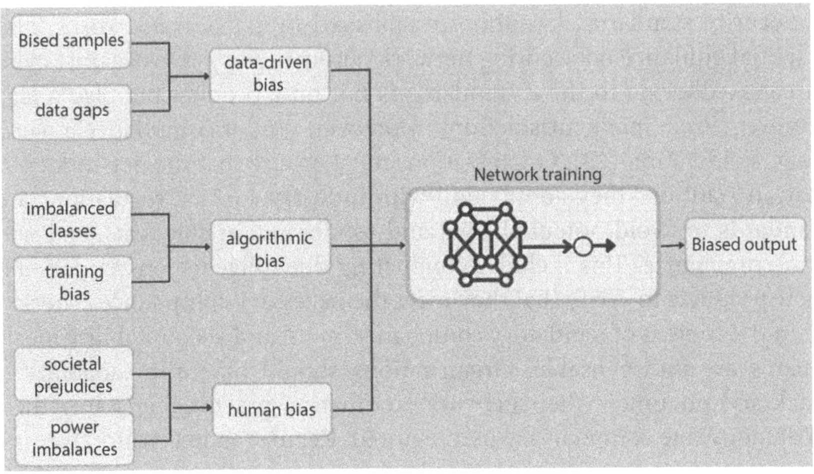

Figure 9.6 Bias sources in training machine learning models.

allowing developers to assess and audit algorithms for any bias they may exhibit. The goal is to ensure equitable outcomes for all demographic groups, mitigating disparities and discrimination. Transparency is another critical aspect of combating algorithmic bias [22]. Making machine learning algorithms transparent involves open-sourcing them and providing clear explanations of how they operate. This transparency not only helps stakeholders understand the algorithms but also aids in identifying and rectifying any unintended biases that may emerge during their use.

Ethical considerations extend beyond algorithm design to data collection practices. Responsible data handling, including obtaining informed consent, anonymizing data, and safeguarding privacy, is essential to avoid ethical violations and potential harm to individuals. By addressing algorithmic bias and adhering to ethical data practices, the development and deployment of machine learning systems can progress toward more equitable, responsible, and transparent applications that benefit society as a whole.

9.3.4.2 Regulatory Compliance in Network Automation

The regulatory landscape surrounding network automation and data privacy is increasingly complex, requiring organizations to be diligent and proactive in their compliance efforts. Data privacy regulations such as GDPR and CCPA have set stringent requirements for handling and safeguarding sensitive data. Any network automation solutions must, by necessity, handle data in strict accordance with these laws to protect individual privacy rights.

Security standards, like those established by NIST frameworks, offer essential guidance on securing network automation systems against cyber threats. Adhering to these standards is not only prudent but also a legal requirement in many jurisdictions. Moreover, vendor compliance is a crucial consideration [23]. Organizations must ensure that the network automation solutions they adopt align with industry-specific regulations and standards to avoid potential legal and reputational risks associated with non-compliance. This includes conducting due diligence on vendors and their products to verify that they meet the necessary compliance criteria.

In the context of regulatory compliance, audit and accountability mechanisms are indispensable. Organizations should have the capability to track and document their network automation practices, enabling them to demonstrate compliance when required. Regular audits ensure that processes remain in line with relevant regulations, providing transparency and reassurance to both regulators and stakeholders. In essence, navigating the complex regulatory landscape in network automation necessitates a comprehensive approach that encompasses data privacy, cybersecurity, vendor scrutiny, and rigorous auditing to mitigate risks and ensure compliance with the law.

9.3.4.3 Ethical Implications of Automation in Communication

The automation of communication processes, exemplified by the adoption of customer support chatbots, presents ethical considerations that need careful attention. One significant concern is job displacement, where human workers may find their roles automated, potentially leading to unemployment and economic disruption. Ethical practices in this context necessitate a commitment to supporting and retraining affected workers, ensuring that they can transition to new roles or industries as automation advances. Another ethical concern revolves around privacy and surveillance in automated communication. Transparent data collection, secure storage, and responsible data usage are imperative to maintain individuals' privacy rights. Consent mechanisms should be explicit and clear, allowing users to make informed decisions about how their data are utilized.

Misuse of technology is another ethical dilemma, where automated communication tools might be exploited for malicious purposes such as spreading misinformation or conducting cyberattacks. Ethical guidelines must strongly discourage such misuse, emphasizing responsible and ethical usage of automated communication technologies.

Finally, accessibility is a core ethical imperative in automation. Ensuring that these technologies are accessible to all, including individuals with disabilities, involves designing inclusive interfaces and ensuring compatibility with assistive technologies. Ethical considerations, therefore, encompass not only the technology itself but also the accessibility and inclusivity of its use, reflecting a commitment to fairness and equity in the adoption of automated communication processes [24].

Addressing bias in machine learning algorithms, complying with regulatory requirements in network automation, and considering the ethical implications of automation in communication are essential components of responsible and ethical technology development and deployment. Organizations and developers must prioritize fairness, transparency, data privacy, and accessibility to create technologies that benefit society while minimizing harm.

9.4 Prospects and Future Directions

9.4.1 Emerging Technologies

Emerging technologies are rapidly transforming the landscape of various industries, and three notable trends are shaping the future. Figure 9.7 showcases the latest developments and emerging trends within the realms of AI and machine learning, illustrating evolving technologies and methodologies.

Firstly, 5G and beyond are playing a pivotal role in network automation. These high-speed, low-latency networks enable the seamless connectivity of devices and machines, laying the foundation for the Internet of Things (IoT) and enabling real-time data exchange. With network automation, tasks that were once manual are now being orchestrated and managed through software, making networks more efficient and reliable. These trends encompass edge computing integration, 5G network optimization, self-healing networks, autonomous operations, and federated learning for enhanced privacy, collectively shaping the future of network management and efficiency.

Secondly, edge computing and machine learning at the edge are revolutionizing data processing. Instead of relying solely on centralized data centers, edge computing brings computation closer to where data are generated. This approach reduces latency and enhances responsiveness, which is crucial for applications like autonomous vehicles and smart cities.

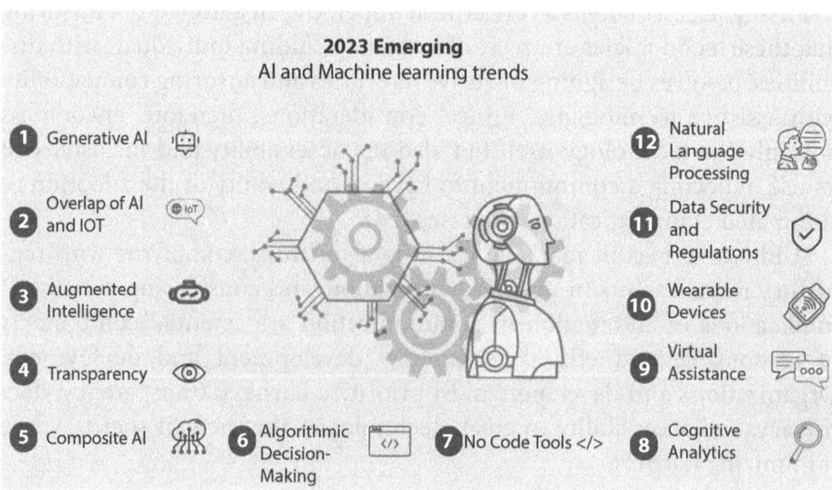

Figure 9.7 Emerging trends in AI and machine learning.

Machine learning algorithms deployed at the edge can analyze data locally, offering quicker insights and enabling more efficient decision-making. Table 9.2 highlights the promising future trends in communication and network automation, where machine learning technologies play a pivotal role.

Lastly, quantum computing is on the horizon, with the potential to disrupt numerous industries. Quantum computers use the principles of quantum mechanics to process information in ways that classical computers cannot. While still in its infancy, quantum computing holds the promise of solving complex problems in fields like cryptography, drug discovery, and optimization that were previously insurmountable for classical computers. Its impact could be transformative, revolutionizing entire industries and changing the way we approach computation.

In [25], 5G and beyond are driving network automation, enhancing connectivity, and paving the way for IoT. Edge computing and machine learning at the edge are transforming data processing by bringing computation closer to the source and improving response times. Quantum computing, although in its early stages, has the potential to revolutionize various industries by solving complex problems that were once out of

Table 9.2 Emerging trends in machine learning–driven network automation.

Future trends	Description
Edge computing integration	Integration of machine learning into edge devices to enable real-time data analysis and decision-making at the network's edge.
5G network optimization	Leveraging machine learning to optimize 5G network resource allocation, reduce latency, and enhance overall network performance.
Self-healing networks	Implementation of autonomous systems that can detect and rectify network issues without human intervention, improving network reliability.
Autonomous network operations	The development of self-operating network systems that can manage configurations, adapt to changing conditions, and optimize performance autonomously.
Federated learning for privacy	Utilizing federated learning techniques to train machine learning models across decentralized network nodes while preserving data privacy.

reach. These emerging technologies are poised to reshape the future and have far-reaching implications across multiple sectors.

9.4.2 AI-Driven Autonomous Networks

AI-driven autonomous networks represent a significant evolution in the field of networking and telecommunications, with several key trends and concepts shaping their development.

9.4.2.1 Toward Fully Autonomous Networks

The goal of AI-driven autonomous networks is to achieve a level of automation where networks can operate independently with minimal human intervention. Through the use of machine learning algorithms and AI-driven analytics, networks can continuously monitor their performance, detect issues, and make real-time adjustments. This includes tasks such as load balancing, routing optimization, and resource allocation. The ultimate aim is to create networks that can adapt to changing conditions and demands without the need for human intervention.

9.4.2.2 Self-Healing and Self-Optimizing Networks

One of the core principles of AI-driven autonomous networks is self-healing and self-optimization. These networks have the ability to identify and mitigate problems on their own, such as network congestion, hardware failures, or security breaches. They can also optimize their performance based on traffic patterns and user behavior. For example, a self-optimizing network can dynamically allocate resources to meet the demands of high-traffic areas, improving overall user experience without manual configuration.

9.4.2.3 Human-Machine Collaboration in Network Management

While the goal is full autonomy, human network administrators and operators will still play a role. Human-machine collaboration is essential for the design, oversight, and policy setting of autonomous networks. Network professionals will work alongside AI systems to define objectives, establish policies, and handle exceptional or unforeseen situations that AI may not have encountered before. This collaboration ensures that the network's behavior aligns with business goals and regulatory requirements while benefiting from AI's real-time capabilities.

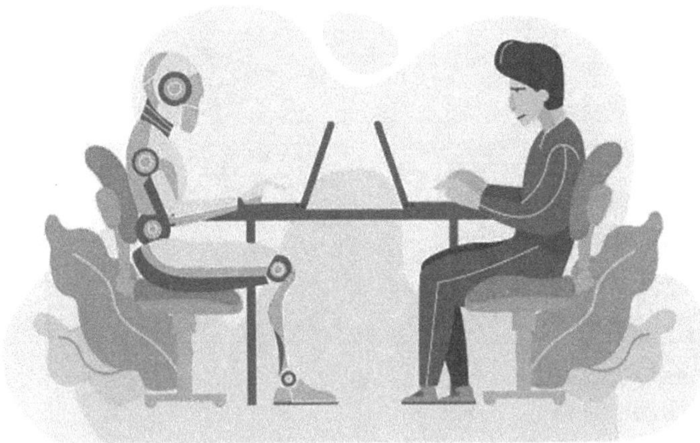

Figure 9.8 Human-machine collaboration in network management.

Figure 9.8 illustrates the collaboration between humans and machines in network management, emphasizing their combined roles and interactions for efficient operations. AI-driven autonomous networks are advancing toward a future where networks can operate independently, self-heal, and optimize their performance [26]. However, human expertise will continue to play a crucial role in guiding and overseeing these networks, ensuring that they align with broader business objectives and adapt to new challenges and opportunities in the ever-evolving landscape of network management and telecommunications.

9.5 Research and Development Trends

Research and development in machine learning and network automation are at the forefront of technological advancements, and several notable trends are shaping these fields.

9.5.1 Current Research Trends in Machine Learning and Network Automation

In the realm of machine learning, ongoing research is focusing on improving model robustness, interpretability, and fairness. Federated learning, which enables training machine learning models across decentralized

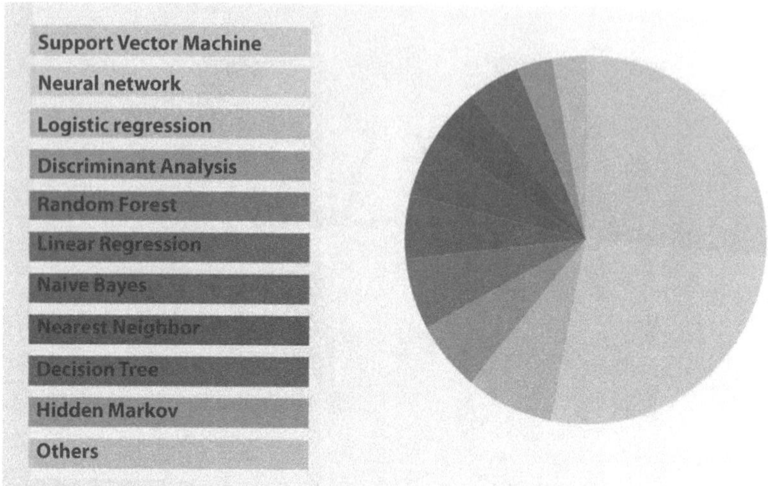

Figure 9.9 Current research trends in machine learning.

devices while preserving data privacy, is gaining traction [27]. Figure 9.9 presents the current research trends in machine learning algorithms, with a focus on those predominantly utilized in network automation.

Additionally, research is directed toward reinforcement learning for more autonomous decision-making in network management. In network automation, trends involve intent-based networking, which uses AI and automation to align network behavior with business goals, and the development of self-healing networks through AI-driven analytics and predictive maintenance.

9.5.2 Industry Collaborations and Academic Contributions

Collaboration between industry and academia is crucial for advancing research in machine learning and network automation. Industry players often provide real-world data and use cases, while academic institutions contribute innovative algorithms and methodologies. These partnerships foster a dynamic ecosystem where research findings can be applied in practical scenarios [28]. Notable collaborations include technology companies working with universities to develop cutting-edge solutions for network optimization and security.

9.5.3 The Importance of Open-Source Projects

Open-source projects play a vital role in accelerating innovation in these domains. Initiatives like TensorFlow and PyTorch provide accessible tools for researchers and developers to experiment with machine learning techniques.

Table 9.3 provides an overview of essential tools and frameworks commonly used in network automation. In network automation, projects like Open Daylight and Ansible offer open-source solutions for network

Table 9.3 Key tools and frameworks for network automation.

Tool/ framework	Purpose in network automation
TensorFlow	Used to build and train deep learning models for tasks such as network anomaly detection and predictive maintenance.
PyTorch	Employed to develop deep learning models, particularly in research and custom applications within network optimization.
Scikit-Learn	Utilized for various machine learning tasks, including classification, regression, and clustering for network data analysis and optimization.
Keras	Often used with TensorFlow to build neural networks and simplify deep learning model development within network automation.
Apache Spark	Enables distributed data processing and analytics for handling large-scale network data and performing batch and stream processing.
Ansible	Provides automation, configuration management, and orchestration for network device provisioning, configuration, and maintenance.
Puppet	Offers configuration management and automation capabilities for maintaining consistent network configurations and infrastructure.
Chef	Used for infrastructure automation and management, allowing network configurations to be defined as code and maintained efficiently.

configuration and management, fostering collaboration and standardization within the industry. Open-source contributions enable a wider community to benefit from shared knowledge and drive rapid progress [29]. It outlines the specific purposes for which each tool is employed, from deep learning and data analysis to automation and configuration management, highlighting their significant roles in optimizing and simplifying network operations. In summary, current research trends in machine learning and network automation are focused on improving model performance, privacy-preserving techniques, and autonomous decision-making. Industry collaborations with academia facilitate practical applications of research findings, while open-source projects provide accessible tools and solutions that promote innovation and standardization in these rapidly evolving fields. These trends collectively contribute to the development of more efficient, intelligent, and autonomous network systems.

9.6 Conclusion

The fields of machine learning–based communication and network automation have witnessed significant advancements, encountered notable challenges, and offer promising prospects for the future. Advancements in these fields include the integration of machine learning for predictive analytics and self-optimization in networks, paving the way for more efficient and responsive systems. The emergence of 5G and beyond, coupled with edge computing, has created new opportunities for real-time data processing and application deployment. Collaborations between industry and academia, along with the importance of open-source projects, have accelerated innovation and knowledge sharing. However, challenges persist, such as ensuring the security and privacy of increasingly interconnected networks and managing the complexity of autonomous systems. Achieving true autonomy in network management while maintaining human oversight remains a delicate balance. Moreover, addressing ethical considerations in machine learning and network automation, including bias and transparency, is crucial. Ongoing research and development efforts are paramount in addressing these challenges and unlocking the full potential of machine learning–based communication and network automation. Continuous advancements in algorithms, data collection, and computing power will drive innovation in these fields. Moreover, interdisciplinary collaboration and knowledge sharing will play a critical role in addressing the complex, evolving nature of network automation.

In conclusion, the future of network automation is promising, with the potential to revolutionize industries, enhance user experiences, and optimize resource allocation. As technology continues to evolve, it is essential to approach these advancements with responsibility, ethics, and a commitment to ensuring network security and privacy. With ongoing research and development efforts, machine learning-based communication and network automation are poised to shape the digital landscape, enabling more efficient, intelligent, and responsive networks in the years to come.

References

1. Ahmad, I., *et al.*, Machine Learning Meets Communication Networks: Current Trends and Future Challenges. *IEEE Access*, 8, 223418–223460, 2020, doi: 10.1109/ACCESS.2020.3041765.
2. Quarteroni, S., Natural Language Processing for Industry. *Informatik-Spektrum*, 41, 2, 105–112, Apr. 2018, doi: 10.1007/s00287-018-1094-1.
3. Reddy M, S.P. and Ambareesh, S., Network Automation. *Int. J. Innov. Res. Adv. Eng.*, 9, 8, 203–206, Aug. 2022, doi: 10.26562/ijirae.2022.v0908.10.
4. Bringhenti, D., Marchetto, G., Sisto, R., Valenza, F., Yusupov, J., Towards a fully automated and optimized network security functions orchestration, in: *2019 4th International Conference on Computing, Communications and Security (ICCCS)*, pp. 1–7, Oct. 2019, doi: 10.1109/CCCS.2019.8888130.
5. Rahman, S., Machine Learning and Data-Driven Solutions for Cost-efficient Network Automation, in: *Asia Communications and Photonics Conference/International Conference on Information Photonics and Optical Communications 2020 (ACP/IPOC)*, p. T3C.1, 2020, doi: 10.1364/ACPC.2020.T3C.1.
6. Latif, Z., Umer, Q., Lee, C., Sharif, K., Li, F., Biswas, S., A Machine Learning-Based Anomaly Prediction Service for Software-Defined Networks. *Sensors*, 22, 21, 8434, Nov. 2022, doi: 10.3390/s22218434.
7. López-Vizcaíno, M., Dafonte, C., Nóvoa, F., Garabato, D., Álvarez, M., Network Data Unsupervised Clustering to Anomaly Detection, in: *XoveTIC Congress 2018*, p. 1173, Sep. 2018, doi: 10.3390/proceedings2181173.
8. Nguyen, G., Dlugolinsky, S., Tran, V., Lopez Garcia, A., Deep Learning for Proactive Network Monitoring and Security Protection. *IEEE Access*, 8, 19696–19716, 2020, doi: 10.1109/ACCESS.2020.2968718.
9. Dev, R., Kundu, K., Sharma, A., Gupta, S.N., *Application of Machine Learning in Finger Vein Pattern Recognition*, pp. 113–128, 2023, doi: 10.1007/978-981-99-0109-8_7.
10. Ridwan, M.A., Radzi, N.A.M., Abdullah, F., Jalil, Y.E., Applications of Machine Learning in Networking: A Survey of Current Issues and

Future Challenges. *IEEE Access*, 9, 52523–52556, 2021, doi: 10.1109/ACCESS.2021.3069210.

11. Sapkale, P.V. and Kolekar, U.D., Modified Naïve Bayes Classifier for Mode Switching and Mobility Management Using Cellular Networks. *Wirel. Pers. Commun.*, 116, 3, 2345–2366, Feb. 2021, doi: 10.1007/s11277-020-07794-1.
12. Zhou, D., Yan, Z., Liu, G., Atiquzzaman, M., An Adaptive Network Data Collection System in SDN. *IEEE Trans. Cogn. Commun. Netw.*, 6, 2, 562–574, Jun. 2020, doi: 10.1109/TCCN.2019.2956141.
13. Fan, C., Chen, M., Wang, X., Wang, J., Huang, B., A Review on Data Preprocessing Techniques Toward Efficient and Reliable Knowledge Discovery From Building Operational Data. *Front. Energy Res.*, 9, 1–17, Mar. 2021, doi: 10.3389/fenrg.2021.652801.
14. Pannakkong, W., Thiwa-Anont, K., Singthong, K., Buddhakulsomsiri, J., Hyperparameter Tuning of Machine Learning Algorithms Using Response Surface Methodology: A Case Study of ANN, SVM, and DBN. *Math. Probl. Eng.*, 2022, 1–17, Jan. 2022, doi: 10.1155/2022/8513719.
15. Solozabal, R., Ceberio, J., Sanchoyerto, A., Zabala, L., Blanco, B., Liberal, F., Virtual Network Function Placement Optimization With Deep Reinforcement Learning. *IEEE J. Sel. Areas Commun.*, 38, 2, 292–303, Feb. 2020, doi: 10.1109/JSAC.2019.2959183.
16. Paleyes, A., Urma, R.-G., Lawrence, N.D., Challenges in Deploying Machine Learning: A Survey of Case Studies. *ACM Comput. Surv.*, 55, 6, 1–29, Jul. 2023, doi: 10.1145/3533378.
17. Liu, X., Yu, J., Wang, J., Gao, Y., Resource Allocation With Edge Computing in IoT Networks via Machine Learning. *IEEE Internet Things J.*, 7, 4, 3415–3426, Apr. 2020, doi: 10.1109/JIOT.2020.2970110.
18. Wang, S., *et al.*, Adaptive Federated Learning in Resource Constrained Edge Computing Systems. *IEEE J. Sel. Areas Commun.*, 37, 6, 1205–1221, Jun. 2019, doi: 10.1109/JSAC.2019.2904348.
19. Corici, M., Reichel, B., Bochow, B., Magedanz, T., An SDN-based solution for increasing flexibility and reliability of dedicated network environments, in: *2016 IEEE 21st International Conference on Emerging Technologies and Factory Automation (ETFA)*, pp. 1–6, Sep. 2016, doi: 10.1109/ETFA.2016.7733560.
20. Kafle, V.P., Hirayama, T., Miyazawa, T., Jibiki, M., Harai, H., Network Control and Management Automation: Architecture Standardization Perspective. *IEEE Commun. Stand. Mag.*, 5, 3, 106–114, Sep. 2021, doi: 10.1109/MCOMSTD.121.2100043.
21. Le Rouzic, E., *et al.*, Automation Journey in Core and Metro Networks: an Operator View, in: *2021 European Conference on Optical Communication (ECOC)*, pp. 1–4, Sep. 2021, doi: 10.1109/ECOC52684.2021.9606000.
22. Zhou, N., Zhang, Z., Nair, V.N., Singhal, H., Chen, J., Bias, Fairness and Accountability with Artificial Intelligence and Machine Learning Algorithms. *Int. Stat. Rev.*, 90, 3, 468–480, Dec. 2022, doi: 10.1111/insr.12492.

23. Awasthi, M., Verifiable and Practical Compliance for Data Privacy Laws, in: *2022 IEEE 29th International Conference on High Performance Computing, Data and Analytics Workshop (HiPCW)*, pp. 59–60, Dec. 2022, doi: 10.1109/HiPCW57629.2022.00013.
24. Kerr, A., Barry, M., Kelleher, J.D., Expectations of artificial intelligence and the performativity of ethics: Implications for communication governance. *Big Data Soc.*, 7, 1, 205395172091593, Jan. 2020, doi: 10.1177/2053951720915939.
25. Rahimi, H., Picaud, Y., Singh, K.D., Madhusudan, G., Costanzo, S., Boissier, O., Design and Simulation of a Hybrid Architecture for Edge Computing in 5G and Beyond. *IEEE Trans. Comput.*, 70, 8, 1213–1224, Aug. 2021, doi: 10.1109/TC.2021.3066579.
26. Elsayed, M. and Erol-Kantarci, M., AI-Enabled Future Wireless Networks: Challenges, Opportunities, and Open Issues. *IEEE Veh. Technol. Mag.*, 14, 3, 70–77, Sep. 2019, doi: 10.1109/MVT.2019.2919236.
27. Treleaven, P., Smietanka, M., Pithadia, H., Federated Learning: The Pioneering Distributed Machine Learning and Privacy-Preserving Data Technology. *Comput. (Long. Beach. Calif).*, 55, 4, 20–29, Apr. 2022, doi: 10.1109/MC.2021.3052390.
28. Sannö, A., Öberg, A.E., Flores-Garcia, E., Jackson, M., Increasing the Impact of Industry–Academia Collaboration through Co-Production. *Technol. Innov. Manag. Rev.*, 9, 4, 37–47, Apr. 2019, doi: 10.22215/timreview/1232.
29. Khan, A., Li, S., Chen, D., Li, Y., Open-source projects for autonomous robotics and systems: A survey. *Filomat*, 34, 15, 4953–4966, 2020, doi: 10.2298/FIL2015953K.

10

Empowering 6G Communication Systems: Harnessing Machine Learning for Advancements in Flexible and 3D-Printed Antennas

Duygu Nazan Gençoğlan[1]* and Shilpa Mehta[2]

[1]Adana Alparslan Türkeş Science and Technology University, Faculty of Engineering, Department of Electrical and Electronics Engineering, Adana, Türkiye
[2]Department of Electrical and Electronic Engineering, Auckland University of Technology, Auckland, New Zealand

Abstract
The emergence of 6G communication systems has ushered in a new era of wireless communication characterized by extremely high speeds and low latency requirements. There is, therefore, a need for innovative antenna solutions that meet these special requirements. In this sense, flexible and 3D-printed antennas have attracted wide attention due to their adaptability and cost-effectiveness. This study examines the critical role that machine learning (ML) techniques play in advancing the design, optimization, and performance improvement of these antennas for 6G communication systems. The first aspect covered in this study concerns the design and optimization of flexible and 3D-printed antennas using ML-based approaches. Second, ML techniques are used to monitor real-time performance and adapt flexible antennas in dynamic 6G communication environments. The ability to reconfigure antennas on the fly based on changing channel conditions, interference, and user mobility is critical to maintaining high-performance and reliable connections. ML algorithms enable adaptive beamforming, polarization adjustment, and frequency adjustment, ensuring optimal communication quality. This, in turn, leads to higher reliability and efficiency for the antenna. In conclusion, this study highlights the mutually beneficial relationship between ML

**Corresponding author*: dngencoglan@atu.edu.tr

Pallavi Sapkale, Shilpa Mehta and S. Balamurugan (eds.) Quantum Computing and Machine Learning for 6G, (217–242) © 2026 Scrivener Publishing LLC

techniques and flexible 3D-printed antennas in the context of 6G communication systems. The integration of ML-driven design, real-time adaptation, optimization, and fault tolerance promises to usher in a new era of highly efficient, adaptable, and resilient antenna solutions that will be instrumental in meeting the demands.

***Keywords*:** 3D-printed antennas, 6G communication systems, flexible antennas, machine learning techniques, real-time adaptation, intelligence, optimization

10.1 Introduction

Modern technological advancements such as 3D printing, artificial intelligence (AI), the Internet of Things (IoT), and extended reality (XR) have increased traffic, necessitating the improvement of current communication systems. Technology can make society smarter, but dependable and fast connectivity is necessary. In order to meet the demands of the contemporary market and society at large, fifth-generation (5G) technology came into play at this point. 5G is currently being widely deployed in many different nations throughout the world, and it can provide significant advantages over current systems. Compared to fourth generation (4G), 5G communications offer better quality of service. Advanced features also include the integration of licensed and unlicensed frequencies, improved management and utilization of the spectrum, and new frequency bands like millimeter wave and optical spectrum. On the other hand, cutting-edge intelligent systems might be too sophisticated for 5G wireless networks of the future. Thus, to meet the demands of future intelligent systems, it requires beyond 5G communication with new advanced features. Sixth-generation (6G) communication emerged as a result, successfully combining cutting-edge technologies while also addressing the shortcomings of 5G systems [1].

Due to the convergence of 5G to 6G, it is worth noting that use cases will increase, leading to an increase in connected devices that can connect almost anything. This requires more bandwidth and spectrum to meet the ongoing requirement for higher data capacity. A new spectrum will be accessible where there are numerous frequency bands that can be adopted for efficient wireless communications [2]. Antennas are one of the most important building blocks of wireless communication systems, responsible for transmitting and receiving electromagnetic signals. A multitude of antenna types are currently available, and this field is the subject of extensive research. In recent years, there has been a significant increase in the use of flexible antennas due to the need for global positioning systems (GPS), wearable technology, military applications, health monitoring systems, wireless sensor networks, IoT, and communication gadgets. Moreover, the choice of flexible antenna is influenced by a multitude of factors, such as the substrate, processing method, types of materials utilized, antenna performance, and surrounding environment. A microstrip patch antenna, monopole antenna, magneto dipole antenna, fractal patch antenna, substrate-integrated waveguide antenna (SIW), and planar inverted-F antenna are a few examples of flexible antennas. The high conductivity of conductive materials like copper, silver, and gold makes them popular choices for use as radiating elements, which guarantees high gain, bandwidth, and efficiency [3, 4].

Flexible antennas meet the high standards needed for wearable and implantable health monitoring systems, making them appropriate for use in biomedical applications. Higher education institutions, businesses, and federal agencies that deal with harsh environments can also benefit from these antennas. The majority of the works are focused on the materials, fabrications, and applications of these antennas. The most widely used materials are those that are conductive, and there are many different ways to fabricate them, such as screen printing, 3D printing, and inkjet printing. Although inkjet printing is a good substitute for traditional fabrication methods, it has problems with adequate resolution when dealing with uneven surfaces. Screen printing is another fabrication technique that is not only cost-effective but also simple and quick with flexible substrates. Nonetheless, it suffers from different challenges, such as fixed layer control, a dependency on substrate surface quality, and a lack of control over the thickness of the conductive layer. A chemical etching technique involves the fabrication of metallic patterns with photoresist and etchants, then milling the chosen area by corrosive means. While this process can be used to fabricate complex flexible antennas, there are numerous problems associated with it, including dangerous chemicals, a lengthy process, costly cleanroom equipment, photomasks, and chemicals that require human resources to handle. Due to its benefits, such as in-house development, the ability to vary the density of printed objects, the capability of fabricating complex 3D objects quickly with various materials, and the flexibility of material printing, additive 3D printing is considered one of the best fabrication approaches for flexible antennas [4]. By utilizing 3D printer fabrication techniques, flexible antenna materials can be categorized according to their materials, such as polymers, ceramics, metals, composites, and multi-material integration. A polymer material can be easily printed and is suitable for dielectric antenna fabrication. Furthermore, they can meet the requirements of current wireless communication systems, but their mechanical robustness is lacking. There is no doubt that metallic 3D antennas provide strong mechanical robustness and low electrostatic discharge;

however, they are relatively heavy, and it is difficult to print conductive materials for EM applications. A lighter, more cost-effective alternative would be to print metallized antennas using filaments or resins followed by conductive coatings. In addition, dielectric ceramics play a significant role in 5G wireless communication systems. Furthermore, ceramics are well known for their wide range of dielectric permittivity and their stable mechanical properties. In order to solve the problem of a fixed dielectric constant range and meet the size requirements of 5G communication systems, the composite material approach mixes polymer with nanoparticles in different ratios along with ceramic mixing in various ratios. Integrated multi-material antennas, as their name implies, are multi-material antennas in which various antenna parts are made from various materials, such as metals, polymers, ceramics, and composts, to meet high-performance requirements. This flexibility control results in an antenna that is lightweight and inexpensive [5].

Numerous studies demonstrating the application of 3D printing in flexible antennas have been put forth in the literature [6]. 3D-printed fingernail antennas were suggested in one of the works [7] for IoT applications to send massive volumes of sensor data in the millimeter and microwave spectrum of advanced 5G communications. The proposed nail antenna design has a small surface area and is lightweight, inexpensive, simple to install, and comfortable to wear. Antenna arrays and diversity systems, however, can be made practical for even better signal reception with the use of multiple human fingers. The proposed work is only suitable for 5G IoT applications. Furthermore, in another work [8], the authors demonstrated how to create a patch antenna out of conductive (CI) and dielectric (DI) ink using lights-out digital additive manufacturing (LDM), an advanced 3D printing technique. Although the results were promising, there are a number of drawbacks, including the extremely fragile nature of the printed objects and the limited ability to shape or bend them. Furthermore, extreme caution must be used when handling the printed objects. In order to address the shortcomings of the earlier methods, a reconfigurable antenna array was created by combining additive manufacturing techniques with 3D printing and inkjet printing. It resolves conventional designs' issues with size, flexibility, and IC assembly while also improving performance. The proposed work establishes the foundation for the development of flexible hybrid electronics and phased-array on-package modules, especially for massive MIMO, digital twin, wearable and conformal smart skin, and flexible modules for the next generation of 5G mmWave broadband communication [9]. The aforementioned antennas are unsuitable for use in 6G applications. As a result, in [10], two 3D-printed antennas appropriate for mmWave 6G and 5G applications were presented. For these applications, the proposed antennas not only proved to be economical but also attained satisfactory performance. Nevertheless, ML approaches show promise in solving complex problems, given the current state of technological innovation. Because ML techniques can offer an effective, adaptable, and dependable framework for identifying optimal design parameters, the primary goal of this chapter is to ascertain the role of ML techniques in addressing the issues associated with additive manufactured 3D-printed antennas and leading to automated antenna geometries suitable for a variety of applications. Drawing from this concept, a study has been suggested in [11], wherein the authors evaluated the effectiveness of a T-shaped monopole antenna and a 3D-printed slotted waveguide antenna created through HFSS. They also optimized the performance of both designs through machine learning techniques, yielding encouraging outcomes. The primary goal of this research is to tackle the challenges in antenna design and streamline the process for a variety of applications through the development of machine learning models. These models aim to pinpoint the connections between different design elements and performance metrics. This advancement will be beneficial for IoT applications that demand diverse antennas with specific objectives and limitations. A theoretical antenna optimization using machine learning was subsequently proposed by the authors [12], and the outcome was high accuracy, low calculation error, and short calculation time. It is, therefore, simple to apply ML techniques to antennas. However, to fully comprehend printed antenna applications in 6G, more research is necessary.

With the aid of ML techniques, this chapter thus discusses the most recent advancements in printed antenna technology for 6G. Section 10.2 discusses flexible and 3D-printed antennas, followed by the challenges faced by 6G antenna designs in Section 10.3. Section 10.4 focuses on ML for antenna design, followed by data-driven antenna optimization in Section 10.5, aiming to discuss the role of ML in determining the best antenna designs for various 6G applications by analyzing antenna parameters, simulation outcomes, and various performance metrics data. Section 10.6 covers various topology optimization approaches for 3D-printed antennas, enabling the development of various complex antennas with enhanced performance via design refinements, and Section 10.7 shows how material selection and optimization is done for flexible and 3D-printed antennas using ML. Section 10.8 shows how ML-based simulations and modeling approaches can improve the efficiency and accuracy of performed simulations, and Section 10.9 talks about the approaches that show the integration of ML with antenna designs and hardware-software co-design for real-time applications. Section 10.10 shows some case studies depicting the practical implementation of ML in 3D-printed and flexible antennas for 6G communication and concludes the chapter with future developments.

10.2 Flexible and 3D-Printed Antennas

Flexible antennas offer flexibility for any used purpose since these structures are capable of easily being integrated into various surfaces [3, 4, 13, 14]. Such antennas provide a great deal of advantages for various emerging technologies, including wearable technologies [15], IoT devices [16], and bionic devices [17]. The materials used in the production of flexible antennas generally consist of polymers, flexible metals, and nanomaterials [3, 4, 13–18]. Flexibility makes the antennas user-friendly and offers a wide range of uses in a variety of applications [19–21]. On the other hand, the 3D printing technique has been a promising method since the 1980s because of its contribution to the structure, including fast fabrication response, cost-effectiveness, and easy implementation [5]. Another contribution of 3D printing technology is to design complex structures in various application areas [22–25]. These pros of the promising technology also make any antenna structure design effective [25]. A myriad of antenna types, including dielectric lens antennas [26], reflect array antennas [27], and microstrip patch antennas [28, 29], have been devised through this contemporary method. Additionally, 3D printing has been applicable for developing advanced antenna designs, namely, all-metal terahertz multi-beam lens antennas [30] and dual-band stacked antennas [31]. Moreover, the application of 3D printing in antenna technology broadens traditional communication systems to contain millimeter-wave sensing applications [32] and passive UHF RFID tags [33].

The ability to fabricate flexible and stretchable antennas using 3D printing contributes to new opportunities for applications requiring conformal or unconventional antenna designs [34]. It can be deduced that the integration of 3D printing technology with antenna design and fabrication encourages the solutions for developing innovative, cost-effective, and high-performance antennas for various wireless communication and sensing systems. On the other hand, the integration of flexible and 3D-printed antennas is pivotal for the development and implementation of 6G communication systems [35]. 6G communication systems are planning to emerge in the 2030s [36–38]. With the advancements and requirements for higher data rates, lower latency, and improved connectivity, the unique characteristics of flexible and 3D-printed antennas might provide several benefits that comply with the requirements of 6G networks. Additionally, the use of 3D printing in antenna fabrication allows for the integration of novel materials and structures, such as meta-materials and dielectric lenses, which can enhance the functionality and efficiency of antennas operating in the terahertz frequency range characteristic of 6G systems [39–41]. Furthermore, the development of reconfigurable and beamforming antennas using 3D printing technology can support dynamic beam steering and adaptive communication strategies crucial for 6G networks [42–45]. The application of 3D printing in antenna manufacturing aligns with the trend toward space-air-ground integrated communication networks, where compact and lightweight antennas are essential for deployment in diverse environments, including aerial drones and satellite communication systems [46]. By taking everything into account, the pros provided by flexible and 3D-printed antennas for 6G technology stimulate research and development efforts in this field. In the future, new materials and manufacturing techniques may be developed to further improve the performance of these antennas. Additionally, studies on the reliability and longevity of flexible and 3D-printed antennas will contribute to the widespread adoption of this technology. Future research and development in this area will further improve the performance of flexible and 3D-printed antennas and contribute to maximizing the potential of 6G technology. At this point, flexible and 3D-printed antennas are depicted in Table 10.1 with respect to fabrication techniques, material compatibility, and shape complexity.

Table 10.1 Comparison of flexible and 3D-printed antennas along with fabrication technique, material compatibility, and shape complexity.

Aspect	Flexible antennas	3D-printed antennas
Fabrication technique	Inkjet printing [47, 48], screen printing [49, 50]	Metal casting [51], direct 3D printing [52–54]
Material compatibility	Flexible substrates [4, 55, 56], conductive inks [3, 57, 58]	Various materials (e.g., metals and polymers) [59–61]
Shape complexity	Limited by bending and folding capabilities [4]	Complex shapes achievable [5]

10.3 Challenges in 6G Antenna Design

Developing 6G antennas is challenging due to the numerous objectives and technological demands. The challenges involved in designing 6G antennas are briefly described below and depicted in Figure 10.1.

- **High Frequency Operation:** 6G is expected to operate in the terahertz spectrum (0.1–10 THz). As a result, it will be difficult to deploy antennas at these high frequencies economically. At these frequencies, free-space path loss is increased, and atmospheric absorption is greater [62]. Moreover, the material selection for novel antennas operating at 6G frequencies should be carefully considered, keeping in mind the loss and thermal stability [63].
- **Miniaturization:** As operating frequencies increase, small antenna elements are desirable to maintain high performance and efficiency [64].
- **Beamforming and Massive MIMO:** To direct terahertz signals, which have low diffraction and high path loss, it is essential to develop accurate and effective beamforming techniques [65].
- **Massive MIMO:** The massive MIMO system requires multiple antennas for noise, fading, and interference reduction. More antennas, however, increase complexity and, consequently, hardware costs. Therefore, it is necessary to have miniaturized components, which will help reduce both the overall complexity and the size of the hardware, as well as increase its affordability [66].
- **Integration:** It is challenging to meet the demand of communication systems when integrating 6G antennas due to

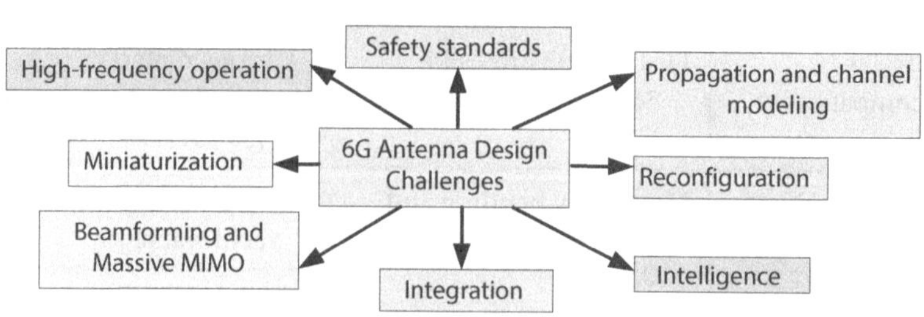

Figure 10.1 6G antenna design challenges.

different materials, size, complexity, signal loss, and thermal issue requirements [67].

- **Intelligence:** AI and ML are important technological advancements for antenna parameter optimizations for overall performance enhancements and efficient use of spectrum; however, they are also linked with computation and design issues [68].
- **Reconfiguration:** It is worth noting that reconfigurable intelligent surface (RIS) can help enhance the propagation environment and further improve the spectral efficiency of communication while controlling cost-effective passive reflective elements. However, as per the present communication systems, not much progress can be seen in RIS as they are developed as per earlier communication theories and several challenges [69].
- **Propagation and channel modeling:** Considering penetration, path losses, and atmospheric absorption, precise channel modeling is desirable at terahertz frequencies [70].
- **Safety standards:** There is a demand for new standards and advanced research to ensure human safety in 6G networks [71].

10.4 Machine Learning for Antenna Design

ML plays a pivotal role in antenna design engineering since this robust method provides innovative aspects for complicated structures, including 3D-printed antennas and emerging communication systems [72–76]. First of all, ML algorithms are generally preferred to optimize antenna performance parameters such as the shape, size, and material properties of the substrate materials, as well as the placement and orientation of the antenna structure. Secondly, the ML method can also curtail the evaluation time of the antenna performance parameter by learning existing designs. Furthermore, performance parameter predictions, inverse design, and array antenna design are exploited by using ML methods [77–83]. Figure 10.2. details the various aspects of the ML methods for antenna engineering applications.

ML plays an important role in advanced communication systems, especially in antenna design, since it offers effective and flexible solutions for emerging technologies, including 6G [83]. The advancement of 6G communication systems is expected to revolutionize wireless communication

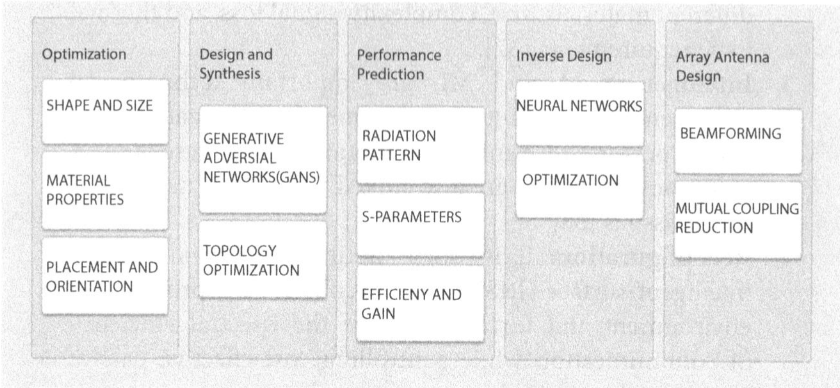

Figure 10.2 Application of the ML method along with various aspects.

because of extremely higher data rates and lower latency as compared to the 5G [36–38, 62–71]. At this point, ML may play an important role in the development of complex antenna designs with higher frequency bands. On the other hand, 3D-printed and flexible antennas may provide a novel solution for 6G communication systems due to their inherent characteristics. But, due to the system restrictions, new questions and research gaps might need to be solved. By leveraging ML, researchers and scientists can find solutions for these kinds of challenging tasks and realize a newer aspect for efficient and sustainable communication systems for the future.

10.5 Data-Driven Antenna Optimization

The purpose of this section is to discuss how ML is used in determining the best antenna designs for various 6G applications based on antenna parameters, simulation outcomes and performance metrics. Listed below are some steps in choosing the best antennas for 6G.

Data collection and preparation: The purpose of this step is to collect simulated data obtainable through simulation software such as CST and HFSS or any other software to analyze the performance of developed antennas in accordance with their specifications and requirements. Also, experimental data obtained from hardware prototypes serve as a valuable supplement to simulated data. Moreover, preprocessing data is vital after obtaining it to make it available for model training.

Key parameters selection: Antenna parameters are selected, which can affect overall performance.
Algorithm/model selection and training: Algorithm or model is selected based on the specifications and requirements such as problem complexity and type of preprocessed data from previous stage. Furthermore, training the model and optimization of performance parameters is done.
Design optimization: Design optimization is another important step where, fine-tuning of hyperparameters is done to enhance the overall performance and optimization algorithms such as genetic algorithms can be employed to attain optimal antenna configurations.
Performance prediction and validation: This step involves a quick performance prediction based on available data without a physical test. The accuracy of predictions can also be checked by comparing them with experimental results using cross-validation approaches. Alternative options include generating additional training data or using another suitable machine learning model if validation fails [84].

Antenna design has been the subject of several studies involving ML. By using machine learning methods, antenna design can be accelerated, with high accuracy levels maintained, time saved, and error minimization, along with a reduction of errors, the possibility of predicting antenna behavior, improved computing efficiency, and fewer simulation cycles required [85]. Based on the study [86], the authors demonstrated that ML can be an effective and suitable solution for designing and predicting antenna performance. Advanced wireless applications can benefit from this approach. Similarly, in [87], the authors proposed an integrated optimization method using ML and particle swarm optimization (PSO) algorithms for dielectric resonator antennas. It was found that the optimized results were superior to those of the conventional antenna optimization method. Moreover, other works discussed in [88–91] showed how ML is used for antenna design and performance optimization purposes to attain better results. In the upcoming sections, more works that are relevant to flexible and 3D-printed antennas will be discussed, depicting how material selection and optimization are done for such antennas to attain better performance than traditional approaches.

10.6 Topology Optimization with ML

Topology optimization with ML has gained significant attention in recent years due to its ability to enhance the design process by efficiently distributing materials within a defined design space to achieve optimal performance [92, 93]. By integrating ML techniques into established topology optimization methods, researchers have been able to address complex challenges in solid mechanics and structural design, leading to the creation of unique geometries that may not be achievable through traditional optimization approaches [94, 95]. The use of ML in topology optimization allows for the exploration of high-performing solutions while managing computational resources effectively [94]. This approach has been particularly beneficial in applications such as acoustic meta-material design and the optimal design of topological waveguides, where multiple iterations and analyses are required to obtain the final optimized design [94, 95]. Additionally, these optimization algorithms have been developed to optimize various structures, including rotating electric machines and photonic devices, showcasing the versatility and effectiveness of this approach [96, 97]. Furthermore, the combination of ML and topology optimization has been applied in diverse fields, such as airfoil design, battery optimization, and solar panel deployment, demonstrating the broad applicability and impact of this methodology [98]. By leveraging ML algorithms, researchers have been able to automate the design process, improve performance, and optimize complex systems efficiently. In conclusion, the integration of machine learning in topology optimization offers a powerful tool for enhancing design processes, achieving optimal performance, and exploring innovative solutions across various engineering disciplines. Topology optimization with ML in the context of 6G networks offers a promising approach to enhance network performance and efficiency. By utilizing ML techniques in topology optimization, researchers can address design challenges and achieve optimal network configurations tailored to the specific requirements of 6G technology [99, 100]. The incorporation of ML in topology optimization for 6G networks enables the development of intelligent networks capable of analyzing and optimizing end-to-end behavior, managing large volumes of real-time data, and achieving data rates of up to terabits per second [100]. This strategy facilitates the effective allocation of resources within the network, leading to enhanced spectral efficiency, network reliability, and energy efficiency [92, 101]. ML-based topology optimization algorithms can be employed in various aspects of 6G networks, including radio access network (RAN) design, signal processing, and resource allocation, to optimize network performance and enhance user experience [93, 102]. Furthermore, the utilization of ML in topology optimization can support the implementation of intelligent reflecting surfaces, energy-efficient communication strategies, and federated learning mechanisms in 6G networks [103–105]. Moreover, the amalgamation of ML and topology optimization in 6G networks can tackle security challenges, facilitate machine-type communications, and enable real-time optimization for diverse applications such as autonomous driving cars and IoT devices [106–108]. By harnessing ML in topology optimization, 6G networks can achieve heightened levels of efficiency, reliability, and intelligence to meet the evolving demands of future wireless communication systems. In conclusion, the integration of machine learning in topology optimization for 6G networks holds significant potential for transforming network design, enhancing performance, and enabling a variety of innovative applications in the era of next-generation wireless communication.

10.7 Material Selection and Optimization

Wearables, GPS, and other health monitoring and communication devices have become a significant part of society due to market demand [109]. This resulted in flexible antennas becoming widely accepted and used. Numerous factors, such as substrate, processing method, material use, antenna performance, and other ambient conditions, can be taken into consideration when choosing these antennas [3]. These antennas can be classified into 3D-printed flexible antennas, active wearable textile antennas, passive wearable textile antennas, substrate-integrated waveguide antennas, and membrane-based antennas, respectively [110]. This section, however, focuses on the optimization and targeted material selection process for 3D flexible antennas using ML. Based on this, researchers in [111, 112] proposed and optimized compact and folded antennas using ML. These antennas utilized regression-based algorithms and flexible substrates, resulting in high-performance antennas as compared to unoptimized or optimized ones using other optimization algorithms. This section additionally addresses 3D-printed antennas. The development of intricate structures at a reduced cost and with less material wastage is made possible by 3D printing technology, which is why it is so popular today. Healthcare, buildings, and other industries like transportation and automobiles can all benefit from this technology [113]. This section's main goal is to demonstrate how ML can be applied to the selection and optimization of antenna materials, resulting in time-saving and high-performance solutions. Based on this, in [112], the authors suggested that 3D-printed dielectrics around monopole antennas can be optimized and modeled using the ML approach. The main purpose is to model the gain performance of the antenna by modifying radiation characteristics by surrounding it with a dielectric material. The dielectric constant values can be mapped to the proposed design's reinforcement pattern using this method. When compared to heuristic optimization techniques, the results of the proposed study, which employed artificial neural network (ANN) and Gaussian regression approaches, looked promising. Likewise, the authors in [76] used ANN to optimize the 3D-printed W-band slot waveguide antenna, and the obtained results were promising. Furthermore, the authors in [114] proposed a wideband ML-based 3D-printed waveguide-based MIMO array antenna that maintains stable gain and reasonable radiation efficiency at the operating frequency. In addition, according to the authors in [115], differential evolution algorithms can be another suitable algorithm for optimizing the material selection and other parameters of the antennas. Thus, ML can be used for both flexible and 3D-printed antennas for material selection and parameter optimization.

10.8 Simulation and Modeling with ML

Simulation and modeling with ML in the context of 6G networks offer a transformative approach to optimize network performance, enhance efficiency, and address complex challenges. By leveraging ML techniques in simulation and modeling, researchers can develop intelligent networks capable of adapting to dynamic environments, predicting network behavior, and optimizing resource allocation [102, 103]. The integration of ML in simulation and modeling for 6G networks enables the creation of predictive models that can accurately forecast network performance, analyze data in real time, and optimize network configurations [5, 116]. This approach facilitates the development of advanced communication systems that can adapt to changing conditions, improve spectral efficiency, and enhance overall network reliability [48, 117]. ML-based simulation and modeling algorithms can be applied in various aspects of 6G networks, including signal processing, resource management, and network optimization, to optimize network performance and ensure seamless connectivity [100, 118]. Furthermore, the utilization of ML in simulation and modeling can support the implementation of federated learning mechanisms, intelligent reflecting surfaces, and energy-efficient communication strategies in 6G networks [101, 108]. Moreover, the amalgamation of ML and simulation in 6G networks can address security challenges, enable real-time optimization, and support a wide range of applications, such as IoT devices and autonomous vehicles [99]. By harnessing ML in simulation and modeling, 6G networks can achieve higher levels of efficiency, reliability, and intelligence to meet the evolving demands of future wireless communication systems. In conclusion, the integration of machine learning in simulation and modeling for 6G networks holds significant promise for revolutionizing network design, optimizing performance, and enabling a variety of innovative applications in the era of next-generation wireless communication.

10.9 Hardware-Software Co-Design for ML-Aided Antennas

The integration of hardware and software, wherein ML algorithms are implemented in tandem with hardware designs, is covered in this section. These domains can be combined to create extremely effective, flexible, and dependable antennas that can meet the needs of 6G networks [119]. One of the most relevant works is discussed in [120], where the authors developed a 6G antenna and used ML algorithms to predict and optimize the proposed antenna's return loss performance. This was found to be effective and appropriate for use in upcoming high-speed communication applications. A different study also demonstrated that ML can be used to decrease mutual coupling in a 2x2 microstrip antenna array by replacing a defective ground structure through a replacement-assisted design. The study's drawback, though, was that the envelope correlation coefficient did not improve noticeably [121]. A review of the literature revealed that ML can be used to develop and optimize different kinds of antennas; some of these works were covered in [82, 122–124]. There have been limited advancements in the field of 3D-printed and flexible antennas for 6G applications incorporating machine learning, with only a few works found in the literature. In [114], a flexible meta-material–based ultra-wideband antenna is proposed, which attained high performance compared to similar previous works; however, the study has not incorporated ML. Likewise, one of the best examples of a 3D-printed antenna is discussed in [125]. The authors proposed a W-band antenna in which ML played an important role in design optimization, and the design was fabricated using a 3D printing approach. The simulated results were validated with promising measurement results. Subsequently, a different study utilized machine learning algorithms to enhance the gain performance of monopole antennas, yielding encouraging outcomes [76]. Thus, more research is needed in the development of flexible and 3D-printed antennas with effective integration of ML, making them suitable for 6G communication systems [112].

10.10 Experimental Validation and Prototyping

To enhance the accuracy, efficiency, and effectiveness of experimental validation and prototyping in the context of 6G networks, researchers can utilize ML techniques in simulation and modeling processes. By integrating ML into these processes, researchers can optimize network configurations, materials, components, machine learning models, user scheduling, and resource allocation in 6G network prototypes. Here are some relevant references supporting the application of ML in experimental validation and prototyping for 6G networks:

- In [92], Yago *et al.* explore the application of machine learning techniques in solid mechanics, which are beneficial for optimizing materials and components in 6G network prototypes.
- Luo *et al.* focus on optimization approaches for federated learning in heterogeneous networks, which are relevant for optimizing machine learning models during experimental validation in 6G networks [126].
- Dahrouj *et al.* discuss machine learning–based user scheduling, which are applicable for optimizing user scheduling and resource allocation during experimental validation in integrated 6G networks [127].

By incorporating insights from these references, researchers can explore the application of machine learning in experimental validation and prototyping for 6G networks, leading to more efficient and effective network design and optimization.

10.11 Conclusion and Future Directions

Designing and optimizing flexible and 3D-printed antennas with ML is a significant step forward for 6G technology. ML has the capability to meet the demands of 6G networks, such as high frequencies, ultralow latency, and extensive connectivity. ML also aids in optimizing material properties, designs, and adaptive features, resulting in high-performance, highly flexible, and reliable antennas.

10.12 Future Directions

1. Introducing novel eco-friendly and sustainable materials using ML and testing their feasibility with flexible and 3D-printed antennas.
2. Using hybrid and advanced ML algorithms for better optimization.
3. Integrating ML with edge computing and quantum computing can become a more effective solution for flexible and 3D-printed antennas.

References

1. Chowdhury, M.Z., Shahjalal, M., *et al.*, 6G Wireless Communication Systems: Applications, Requirements, Technologies, Challenges, and Research Directions. *IEEE Open J. Commun. Soc.*, 1, 957–975, 2020.
2. Andersson, I., Manholm, L., Brazalez, A.A., *et al.*, Antenna System Requirements and Challenges Towards 6G - An Industrial View. *2023 International Workshop on Antenna Technology (iWAT)*, pp. 1–4, 2023.
3. AL-Haddad, M.A.S.M., *et al.*, Flexible Antenna: A Review of Design, Materials, Fabrication, and Applications. *J. Phys. Conf. Ser.*, 1878, 1, 012068, 2021.
4. Kirtania, S.G., Elger, A.W., *et al.*, Flexible Antennas: A Review. *Micromachines*, 11, 9, 847, 1–43, 2020.
5. Wang, A., Zhang, X., *et al.*, 3D Printed Antennas for 5G Communication: Current Progress and Future Challenges. *Chin. J. Mech. Eng.: Addit. Manuf. Front.*, 2, 1, 10006, 1–18, 2023.
6. Saleh, S., Saeidi, T., *et al.*, A comprehensive review of recent methods for compactness and performance enhancement in 5G and 6G wearable antennas. *Alexandria Eng. J.*, 95, 132–163, 2024.
7. Njogu, P., Sanz-Izquierdo, B., *et al.*, 3D Printed Fingernail Antennas for 5G Applications. *IEEE Access*, 8, 228711–228719, 2020.
8. Popela, M., Olivova, J., *et al.*, A Novel Approach to the Production of printed Patch Antennas. *Appl. Sci.*, 14, 1–15, 2024.
9. Hu, K., Zhou, Y., *et al.*, Additively manufactured flexible on-package phased array antennas for 5G/mmWave wearable and conformal digital twin and massive MIMO applications. *Sci. Rep.*, 13, 1–11, 2023.
10. Li, S., Izquierdo, B.S., *et al.*, 3D Printing Antennas for 5G and Millimeter Wave 6G Applications. *2022 IEEE 33rd Annual International Symposium on Personal, Indoor and Mobile Radio Communication (PIMRC)*, pp. 1–5.
11. Sharma, Y., Machine Learning and Additive Manufacturing Based Antenna Design Techniques, The University of Arizona, 2020, PhD Thesis.

12. Yong, T., Machine learning-based theoretical implementation of antenna design. *Highlights Sci. Eng. Technol.*, 27, 681–690, 2022.
13. Huang, H., Flexible wireless antenna sensor: A review. *IEEE Sens. J.*, 13, 10, 3865–3872, 2013.
14. El Gharbi, M., Fernández-García, R., Ahyoud, S., Gil, I., A review of flexible wearable antenna sensors: design, fabrication methods, and applications. *Materials*, 13, 17, 3781, 2020.
15. Hamouda, Z., Wojkiewicz, J.L., Pud, A.A., Kone, L., Bergheul, S., Lasri, T., Flexible UWB organic antenna for wearable technologies application. *IET Microwaves Antennas Propag.*, 12, 2, 160–166, 2018.
16. Al-Sehemi, A., Al-Ghamdi, A., Dishovsky, N., Atanasova, G., Atanasov, N., A flexible broadband antenna for IoT applications. *Int. J. Microwave Wireless Technolog.*, 12, 6, 531–540, 2020.
17. Lin, D., Wang, E., Wang, J., Zhang, W., Zhang, H., A Novel Dual Material Bionic Flexible Logo Antenna with EBG Structure. *Prog. Electromagn. Res. M*, 109, 13–23, 2022.
18. Kishk, A., Advancement in Microstrip Antennas with Recent Applications. *InTech*, 2013.
19. Venkatachalam, D., Jagadeesan, V., Ismail, K.B.M., Arun Kumar, M., Mahalingam, S., Kim, J., Compact Flexible Planar Antennas for Biomedical Applications: Insight into Materials and Systems Design. *Bioengineering*, 10, 10, 1137, 2023.
20. Ali, U., Ullah, S., Kamal, B., Matekovits, L., Altaf, A., Design, Analysis and Applications of Wearable Antennas: A Review. *IEEE Access*, 11, 14458–14486, 2023.
21. Ali, S.M., Sovuthy, C., Imran, M.A., Socheatra, S., Abbasi, Q.H., Abidin, Z.Z., Recent advances of wearable antennas in materials, fabrication methods, designs, and their applications: State-of-the-art. *Micromachines*, 11, 10, 888, 2020.
22. Feng, J., Fu, J., Lin, Z., Shang, C., Li, B., A review of the design methods of complex topology structures for 3D printing. *Vis. Comput. Ind. Biomed. Art*, 1, 1–16, 2018.
23. Datta, S. and Barua, R., 3D Printing in Modern Healthcare: An Overview of Materials, Methods, Applications, and Challenges, in: *Emerging Technologies for Health Literacy and Medical Practice*, M.B. Garcia and R.P. Pereira de Almeida (Eds.), pp. 132–152, IGI Global, Hershey, PA, 2024.
24. Raja, S., Al-Tmimi, H.M., Ghadir, G.K., Mustafa, M.A., Alani, Z.K., Rusho, M.A., Rajeswari, N., An analysis of polymer material selection and design optimization to improve Structural Integrity in 3D printed aerospace components. *Appl. Chem. Eng.*, 7, 2, 1–11, 2024.
25. Liu, Y., Shu, D.W., Lu, H., Lau, D., Fu, Y.Q., 3D printable spatial fractal structures undergoing auxetic elasticity. *Extreme Mech. Lett.*, 66, 102112, 2024.

26. Das, S., Clavin, H., Debbarma, K., Sharma, S.K., Lambert, P.M., Hobart, C.O., Design and Development of a High-Gain Broadband Balanced Antipodal Vivaldi Antenna using a 3D-Printed Shaped Dielectric Lens. *IEEE Access*, 12, 56836–56846, 2024.
27. Wang, Y., Han, M., Dou, W., Li, T., 3-D Printed All-Metal Conformal Circularly Polarized Reflectarray Antenna at X-Band. *IEEE Trans. Antennas Propag.*, 72, 6, 4989–4998, June 2024.
28. Fougeroux, T., Douyère, A., Murad, N.M., Sibille, J., Oree, S., Dubard, J.L., Performance enhancement of low-cost microstrip patch antennas through 3D-printed conductive geometric forms. *AEU Int. J. Electron. Commun.*, 177, 155211, 2024.
29. Khouser, G.H., Choukiker, Y.K., Bhowmick, A., Gain Enhancement in Microstrip Patch Antenna With High Negative Refractive Index 3D-Metamaterial Inspired Superstrate for Wireless Applications. *IEEE Access*, 12, 7372–7381, 2024.
30. Wu, G.B., Chen, J., Yang, C., Chan, K.F., Chen, M.K., Tsai, D.P., Chan, C.H., 3-D-Printed Terahertz Metalenses for Next-Generation Communication and Imaging Applications. *Proc. IEEE*, 112, 8, 1033–1050, August 2024.
31. Jang, D., Lee, J.Y., Choo, H., Design of a Stacked Dual-Patch Antenna with 3D Printed Thick Quasi-Air Substrates and a Cavity Wall for Wideband Applications. *Appl. Sci.*, 14, 4, 1571, 1–9, 2024.
32. Melouki, N., Ahmed, F., PourMohammadi, P., Naseri, H., Bizan, M.S., Iqbal, A., Denidni, T.A., 3D-Printed Conformal Meta-Lens with Multiple Beam-Shaping Functionalities for Mm-Wave Sensing Applications. *Sensors*, 24, 9, 2826, 1–18, 2024.
33. Pekgor, M., Arablouei, R., Nikzad, M., Masood, S., Displacement Estimation *via* 3D-Printed RFID Sensors for Structural Health Monitoring: Leveraging Machine Learning and Photoluminescence to Overcome Data Gaps. *Sensors*, 24, 4, 1233, 2024.
34. Sharma, P.K., Bansal, A., Chung, J.Y., Conformal holographic Metasurface-Based Beamforming Antenna using a 3D-Printed Flexible Substrate. *Commun. Netw. Broadcast Technol.*, 7, 1, 1–6, 2025.
35. Poyanco Acevedo, J.M., Innovative 3D-Printed Designs for Millimeter-Wave Lenses and Meta-Lens Antennas, 2024.
36. Sa'don, S.N.H., Kamarudin, M.R., Dahri, M.H., Ashyap, A.Y., II, Seman, F.C., Abbasi, M., II, Abidin, Z.Z., The review and analysis of antenna for sixth generation (6G) applications. *2020 IEEE Int. RF Microwave Conf. (RFM)*, 1–5, 2020.
37. Latva-Aho, M. and Leppänen, K. (Eds.), *Key drivers and research challenges for 6G ubiquitous wireless intelligence*, University of Oulu, Oulu, 2019.
38. Hajiyat, Z.R., Ismail, A., Sali, A., Hamidon, M.N., Antenna in 6G wireless communication system: Specifications, challenges, and research directions. *Optik*, 231, 166415, 2021.

39. Zhou, Z., *et al.*, Flexible Liquid Crystal Polymer Technologies from Microwave to Terahertz Frequencies. *Molecules*, 27, 4, 1–24, 2022.
40. Wu, G.B., Zeng, Y.-S., Chan, K.F., Qu, S.-W., Chan, C.H., High-Gain Circularly Polarized Lens Antenna for Terahertz Applications. *IEEE Antennas Wirel. Propag. Lett.*, 18, 5, 921–925, May 2019.
41. Xu, R., *et al.*, A Review of Broadband Low-Cost and High-Gain Low-Terahertz Antennas for Wireless Communications Applications. *IEEE Access*, 8, 57615–57629, 2020.
42. Patel, P. and Subramanian, K.S., Development of microfluidically reconfigurable antenna using additive manufacturing. *AEU Int. J. Electron. Commun.*, 178, 155290, 2024.
43. Sivasubramani, D.N., Additively Manufactured Stress-strain Dependant Frequency Reconfigurable Antenna for Pressure Sensor Applications. *Mater. Sci.*, 30, 2, 143–148, 2024.
44. Zhang, L., Zou, Q., Chu, H., Ning, Y., Li, D., Xiao, P., *et al.*, A., Multifunctional Magneto-Electric Dipole Antenna with Pattern and Polarized Reconfigurability. *IEEE Antennas Wirel. Propag. Lett.*, 23, 8, 2396–2400, August 2024.
45. Park, E., Lee, M., Jeong, H., Phon, R., Kim, K., Park, S., Lim, S., 3-D/4-D-Printed Reconfigurable Metasurfaces for Controlling Electromagnetic Waves. *Proc. IEEE*, 112, 8, 1000–1032, Aug. 2024.
46. Adeleke, A.K., Montero, D.J.P., Lottu, O.A., Ninduwezuor-Ehiobu, N., Ani, E.C., 3D printing in aerospace and defense: A review of technological breakthroughs and applications. *World J. Adv. Res. Rev.*, 21, 02, 1149–1160, 2024.
47. Yu, H., Zhang, X., Zheng, H., Li, D., Pu, Z., An inkjet-printed bendable antenna for wearable electronics. *Int. J. Bioprinting*, 9, 4, 722, 11, 2023.
48. Hossain, A.R., Sagar, M.S., II, Tran, N.H., Sekhar, P.K., Karacolak, T., Inkjet Printed Flexible High Isolation Patch Antenna for 5.8 GHz Full-Duplex Applications. *Prog. Electromagn. Res. C*, 127, 127–143, 2022.
49. Ibanez-Labiano, I., Arslan, D., Yenigun, E.O., Asadi, A., Cebeci, H., Alomainy, A., Screen printing carbon nanotubes textiles antennas for smart wearables. *Sensors*, 21, 14, 4934, 1–28, 2021.
50. Du, C., Li, X., Zhong, S., Compact Liquid Crystal Polymer Based TriBand Flexible Antenna for WLAN/WiMAX/5G Applications. *IEEE Access*, 1–10, 2024.
51. Gautam, K., Gogoi, D., Kongnyui, T.D., Devi, S., Kumar, C., Kumar, M., A comprehensive review on surface modifications of polymer-based 3d-printed structures: metal coating prospects and challenges. *Polym. Adv. Technol.*, 35, 4, 2024.
52. Alkaraki, S. and Gao, Y., mm-Wave Low-Cost 3D Printed MIMO Antennas With Beam Switching Capabilities for 5G Communication Systems. *IEEE Access*, 8, 32531–32541, 2020.
53. Bjorgaard, J., Hoyack, M., Huber, E., Mirzaee, M., Chang, Y.H., Noghanian, S., Design and fabrication of antennas using 3D printing. *Prog. Electromagn. Res. C*, 84, 119–134, 2018.

54. Mirzaee, M., Noghanian, S., Wiest, L., Chang, I., Developing flexible 3D printed antenna using conductive ABS materials. *2015 IEEE International Symposium on Antennas and Propagation & USNC/URSI National Radio Science Meeting*, IEEE Xplore, pp. 1308–1309, 2015.
55. John, D.M., Vincent, S., Pathan, S., Kumar, P., Ali, T., Flexible Antennas for a Sub-6 GHz 5G Band: A Comprehensive Review. *Sensors*, 22, 19, 7615, 1–46, 2022.
56. Khaleel, H.R., Al-Rizzo, H.M., Abbosh, A., II, Design, fabrication, and testing of flexible antennas in. *Adv. Microstrip Antennas Recent Appl.*, 363–383, 2013.
57. Ramli, M.R., Ibrahim, S., Ahmad, Z., Abidin, I.S.Z., Ain, M.F., Stretchable conductive ink based on polysiloxane–silver composite and its application as a frequency reconfigurable patch antenna for wearable electronics. *ACS Appl. Mater. Interfaces*, 11, 31, 28033–28042, 2019.
58. Rida, A., Yang, L., Vyas, R., Tentzeris, M.M., Conductive inkjet-printed antennas on flexible low-cost paper-based substrates for RFID and WSN applications. *IEEE Antennas Propag. Mag.*, 51, 3, 13–23, 2009.
59. Carvalho, S.S., Reis, J.R., Mateus, A., Caldeirinha, R.F., Exploring Design Approaches for 3D Printed Antennas. *IEEE Access*, 12, 10718–10735, 2024.
60. Myllymäki, S., Hannila, E., Kokkonen, M., Jantunen, H., Fabritius, T., Design thinking-driven development of a modular X-Band antenna using multimaterial 3D printing. *Int. J. Interact. Des. Manuf. (IJIDeM)*, 18, 2, 901–910, 2024.
61. Richhariya, G., Shukla, R.K., Sawale, M., Vishwakarma, N., Singh, N., *Recent trends in 3D printing antennas in: Array and Wearable Antennas*, P. Gour, N. Singh, R.K. Nema, R.S. Mishra, A.K. Srivastava (Eds.), pp. 218–233, CRC Press, Boca Raton, 2024.
62. Rappaport, T.S., Xing, Y., *et al.*, 6G Wireless Communication and Applications Above 100 GHz: Opportunities and Challenges for 6G and Beyond. *IEEE Access*, 7, 78729–78757, 2019.
63. Nagatsuma, T., Ducournau, G., *et al.*, Advances in terahertz communications accelerated by photonics. *Nat. Photonics*, 10, 371–379, 2016.
64. Akyildiz, I.F., Jornet, J.M., *et al.*, Terahertz band: Next frontier for wireless communications. *Phys. Commun.*, 12, 16–32, 2014.
65. Han, Y., Tang, W., *et al.*, Large Intelligent Surface-Assisted Wireless Communication Exploiting Statistical CSI. *IEEE Trans. Veh. Technol.*, 68, 8, 8238–8242, Aug. 2019.
66. Chataut, R. and Akl, R., Massive MIMO Systems for 5G and beyond Networks- Overview, Recent Trends, Challenges, and Future Research Direction. *Sensors*, 20, 10, 1–35, 2020.
67. Hajiyat, Z.R.M., Ismail, A., *et al.*, Antenna is 6G wireless communication system: Specifications, challenges and research directions. *Optik*, 231, 1–14, 2021.

68. Rajatheva, N., Atzeni, I., *et al.*, White Paper on Broadband Connectivity in 6G, pp. 1–46, 2020, arXiv.
69. Chen, Z., Chen, G., *et al.*, Reconfigurable-Intelligent-Surface-Assisted B5G/6G Wireless Communications: Challenges, Solution, and Future Opportunities. *IEEE Commun. Mag.*, 61, 1, 16–22, January 2023.
70. Patel, A., Shukla, A., Bhalani, J., A Comprehensive Survey on 6G Networks: Key Technologies and Challenges. *2021 International Conference on Simulation, Automation & Smart Manufacturing (SASM)*, pp. 1–6, 2021.
71. Zhang, Z., Xiao, Y., Ma, Z., *et al.*, 6G Wireless Networks: Vision, Requirements, Architecture, and Key Technologies. *IEEE Veh. Technol. Mag.*, 14, 3, 28–41, 2019.
72. Pandey, A.K. and Singh, Antenna Optimization using Machine Learning Algorithms and their Applications: A Review, Antenna Optimization using Machine Learning Algorithms and their Applications: A Review. *J. Eng. Sci. Technol. Rev.*, 17, 2, 128–144, 2024.
73. Sreelakshmy, R., *et al.*, Antenna design exploration and optimization using machine learning, in: *Array and Wearable Antennas, Design, Optimization, and Applications*, CRC Press, Boca Raton, 2024.
74. Prabha, K.R. and Jagadeeswari, M., High Directivity Microstrip Patch Antenna design using Binary Ebola Search Optimization for Radio Frequency Identification Application. *Appl. Soft Comput.*, 162, 111682, 2024.
75. Babale, S.A., *et al.*, Machine Learning-based Optimized 3G/LTE/5G Planar Wideband Antenna with Tri-bands Filtering Notches. *IEEE Access*, 12, 80669–80686, 2024.
76. Tak, J., *et al.*, A 3-D-Printed W-Band Slotted Waveguide Array Antenna Optimized Using Machine Learning. *IEEE Antennas Wirel. Propag. Lett.*, 17, 11, 2008–2012, Nov. 2018.
77. Dai, X.W., Mi, D.L., Wu, H.T., Zhang, Y.H., Design of Compact Patch Antenna Based on Support Vector Regression. *Radioengineering*, 31, 3, 339–345, 2022.
78. El Misilmani, H.M., Naous, T., Al Khatib, S.K., A review on the design and optimization of antennas using machine learning algorithms and techniques. *Int. J. RF Microwave Comput. Aided Eng.*, 30, 10, e22356, 2020.
79. Sharma, Y., Zhang, H.H., Xin, H., Machine learning techniques for optimizing design of double T-shaped monopole antenna. *IEEE Trans. Antennas Propag.*, 68, 7, 5658–5663, 2020.
80. Sarker, N., Applications of Machine Learning and Deep Learning in Antenna Design, Optimization and Selection: A Review. *IEEE Access*, 11, 103890–103915, 2023.
81. Wu, Q., *et al.*, Machine Learning-Assisted Optimization for Antenna Geometry Design. *IEEE Trans. Antennas Propag.*, 72, 3, 2083–2095, 2024.
82. Wu, Q., *et al.*, Multilayer Machine Learning-Assisted Optimization-Based Robust Design and Its Applications to Antennas and Array. *IEEE Trans. Antennas Propag.*, 69, 9, 6052–6057, 2021.

83. Ibarra-Hernández, R.F., Castillo-Soria, F.R., Gutiérrez, C.A., García-Barrientos, A., Vásquez-Toledo, L.A., Del-Puerto-Flores, J.A., Machine Learning Strategies for Reconfigurable Intelligent Surface-Assisted Communication Systems—A Review. *Future Internet*, 16, 5, 173, 1–29, 2024.
84. Gampala, G. and Reddy, C.J., Fast and Intelligent Antenna Design Optimization using Machine Learning. *2020 International Applied Computational Electromagnetics Society Symposium (ACES)*, pp. 1–2, 2020.
85. Misilmani, H.M.E. and Naous, T., Machine Learning in Antenna Design: An Overview on Machine Learning Concept and Algorithms. *2019 International Conference on High Performance Computing & Simulation (HPCS)*, pp. 600–607, 2019.
86. Reddy, B.V., Krishna, D.V.S., Sharma, A., *et al.*, Accelerated Antenna Design Assisted by Enhanced Machine Learning Techniques. *2021 International Conference on Intelligent Technologies (CONIT)*, pp. 1–4, 2021.
87. Hu, C., Zhao, J.P., *et al.*, Optimization of Dielectric Resonator Antenna based on Machine Learning and PSO Methods. *2020 International Conference on Microwave and Millimeter Wave Technology (ICMMT)*, pp. 1–3, 2020.
88. Jain, R., Ranjan, P., Singhal, P.K., *et al.*, Estimation of S11 Values of Patch Antenna Using Various Machine Learning Models. *2022 IEEE Conference on Interdisciplinary Approaches in Technology and Management for Social Innovation (IATMSI)*, pp. 1–4, 2022.
89. Indharapu, S.S., Caruso, A.N., Durbhakula, K.C., Study of Machine Learning Algorithms for Output Response Prediction of an UWB Fractal Antenna. *2021 IEEE Indian Conference on Antennas and Propagation (InCAP)*, pp. 510–512, 2021.
90. Zhang, L., Chen, L., Yuan, Z., *et al.*, Optimization of a Metasurface Antenna Composed of Dual T-shaped Antenna Elements Based on Machine Learning. *2021 International Symposium on Antennas and Propagation (ISAP)*, pp. 1–2, 2021.
91. Lalhriatpuii, R., Unlocking the Power of Machine Learning: Antenna Design Optimization in the Digital Age. *2023 International Conference on Advanced Computing & Communication Technologies (ICACCTech)*, pp. 419–425, 2023.
92. Yago, D., *et al.*, Machine learning in solid mechanics: application to acoustic metamaterial design. *Int. J. Numer. Methods Eng.*, 125, 14, 2024.
93. Du, Z., Chen, H., Liu, C., Zhang, W., Luo, J., Guo, X., Optimal design of topological waveguides by machine learning. *Front. Mater.*, 9, 1–12, 2022.
94. Gangl, P. and Krenn, N., Topology optimization of a rotating electric machine by the topological derivative. *Proc. Appl. Math. Mech.*, 23, 1, 2023.
95. Сафин, A. and Behera, R., Additive manufacturing and topology optimization of magnetic materials for electrical machines. *Power Eng. Res. Equip. Technol.*, 23, 3, 14–33, 2021.
96. Ge, M., *et al.*, Proactive defense for internet-of-things: integrating moving target defense with cyberdeception, pp. 1–19, 2020, arXiv:2005.04220.

97. Baudart, G., Hirzel, M., Kate, K., Ram, P., Shinnar, A., Lale: consistent automated machine learning, pp. 1–10, 2020, arXiv:2007.01977.
98. Li, Y., Lei, G., Bramerdorfer, G., Sheng, P., Sun, X., Zhu, J., Machine learning for design optimization of electromagnetic devices: recent developments and future directions. *Appl. Sci.*, 11, 41627, 1–24, 2021.
99. Alhaj, N.A., *et al.*, Integration of Hybrid Networks, AI, Ultra Massive-MIMO, THz Frequency, and FBMC Modulation Toward 6G Requirements: A Review. *IEEE Access*, 12, 483–513, 2024.
100. Elaziz, M.A., *et al.*, Evolution toward intelligent communications: Impact of deep learning applications on the future of 6G technology. *WIREs Data Min. Knowl. Discov.*, 14, 1, e1521, 2024.
101. Ayaz, H., *et al.*, Physical layer security analysis using radio frequency-fingerprinting in cellular-V2X for 6G communication. *IET Signal Process.*, 17, 5, e12225, 2023.
102. Klautau, A., Oliveira, A., Trindade, I.P., Alves, W., Generating Mimo Channels for 6G Virtual Worlds Using Ray-Tracing Simulations. *2021 IEEE Statistical Signal Processing Workshop (SSP)*, pp. 595–599, 2021.
103. Shi, Y., *et al.*, Machine Learning for Large-Scale Optimization in 6G Wireless Networks. *IEEE Commun. Surv. Tutor.*, 25, 4, 2088–2132, 2023.
104. Mucchi, L., *et al.*, Signal Processing Techniques for 6G. *J. Signal Process. Syst.*, 95, 4, 435–457, 2023.
105. Yazar, A. and Arslan, H., A Waveform Parameter Assignment Framework for 6G With the Role of Machine Learning. *IEEE Open J. Veh. Technol.*, 1, 156–172, 2020.
106. Hossain, M.A., Hossain, A.R., Ansari, N., AI in 6G: Energy-Efficient Distributed Machine Learning for Multilayer Heterogeneous Networks. *IEEE Network*, 36, 6, 84–91, 2022.
107. Khalid, W., Kaleem, Z., Ullah, R., Chien, T., Noh, S., Yu, H., Simultaneous Transmitting and Reflecting-Reconfigurable Intelligent Surface in 6G: Design Guidelines and Future Perspectives. *IEEE Network*, 37, 5, 173–181, 2023.
108. Batarseh, F., *et al.*, In-design DFM pattern optimization with ML models for dynamic fixing guidance selection and implementation. *SPIE Advanced Lithography + Patterning*, 2024.
109. Khan, M.M., Hossain, S., *et al.*, A review on machine learning and deep learning for various antenna design applications. *Heliyon*, 8, 4, 1–22, 2022.
110. Monne, M.A., *et al.*, Material Selection and Fabrication Processes for flexible Conformal Antennas. *Int. J. Antennas Propag.*, 2018, 1–14, 2018.
111. Bicer, M.B., Analysis and synthesis of L- and T-shaped flexible compact microstrip antennas using regression-based machine learning approaches. *Frequenz*, 77, 5–6, 281-292, 2023.

112. Sharma, Y., Chen, X., *et al.*, Machine Learning Methods-Based Modeling and Optimization of 3-D-Printed Dielectrics Around Monopole Antenna. *IEEE Trans. Antennas Propag.*, 70, 7, 4997–5006, July 2022.
113. Helena, D., Ramos, A., *et al.*, Antenna Design Using Modern Additive Manufacturing Technology: A Review. *IEEE Access*, 8, 177064–177083, 2020.
114. Nakmouche, M.F., *et al.*, Machine Learning Aided Design of Sub-Array MIMO Antennas for CubeSats Based on 3D Printed Metallic Ridge Gap Waveguides. *2022 IEEE Future Networks World Forum (FNWF)*, pp. 418-421, 2022.
115. Zheng, S.Y., *et al.*, Simultaneous Optimization of Material Selection and Structure for Antenna Design using Differential Evolution Algorithm. *2019 IEEE International Conference on Computational Electromagnetics (ICCEM)*, pp. 1–3, 2019.
116. Tariq, M., Naeem, F., Poor, H., Toward Experience-Driven Traffic Management and Orchestration in Digital-Twin-Enabled 6G Networks, pp. 1–7, 2022, arXiv:2201.04259.
117. Muscinelli, E., Shinde, S., Tarchi, D., Overview of Distributed Machine Learning Techniques for 6G Networks. *Algorithms*, 15, 6, 210, 1–28, 2022.
118. Zhou, X., Liang, W., She, J., Yan, Z., Wang, K., Two-Layer Federated Learning With Heterogeneous Model Aggregation for 6G Supported Internet of Vehicles. *IEEE Trans. Veh. Technol.*, 70, 6, 5308–5317, 2021.
119. Muttair, K.S., Shareef, O.A., Taher, H.B., Machine Learning Based on Antennas Modeling for 5G and 6G Communication Systems: A Systematic Review. *Int. J. Commun. Syst.*, 38, 9, e70105, 2025.
120. Iannacci, J., Towards Future 6G from the Hardware Components Perspective – A Focus on the Hardware-Software Divide, its Limiting Factors and the Envisioned Benefits in Going Beyond it. *2021 IEEE 4th 5G World Forum (5GWF)*, pp. 1–6, 2021.
121. Jain, R., Thakare, V.V., *et al.*, Design and Comparative Analysis of THz Antenna through Machine Learning for 6G Connectivity. *IEEE Lat. Am. Trans.*, 22, 2, 82–91, Feb. 2024.
122. Qian, B., Huang, X., *et al.*, Surrogate-Assisted Defected Ground Structure Design for Reducing Mutual Coupling in 2 × 2 Microstrip Antenna Array. *IEEE Antennas Wirel. Propag. Lett.*, 21, 2, 351–355, Feb. 2022.
123. Alsharari, M., Armghan, A., *et al.*, Monopole Antenna Modeling and Optimization for 5G Communication System using Machine Learning. *2023 International Wireless Communications and Mobile Computing (IWCMC)*, pp. 390–393, 2023.
124. Wu, Q., Wang, H., *et al.*, Broadband Millimeter-Wave SIW Cavity-Backed Slot Antenna for 5G Applications Using Machine-Learning-Assisted Optimization Method. *2019 International Workshop on Antenna Technology (iWAT)*, pp. 9–12, 2019.

125. Saeidi, T., Mahmood, S.N., *et al.*, Sub-6G Metamaterial-Based Flexible Wearable UWB Antenna for IoT and WBAN. 2020 IEEE Intl Conf on Dependable, Autonomic and Secure Computing. *Intl. Conf. on Pervasive Intelligence and Computing, Intl. Conf. on Cloud and Big Data ComputingIntl. Conf. on Cyber Science and Technology Congress (DASC/PiCom/CBDCom/CyberSciTech)*, pp. 7–1, 2020.
126. Luo, B., Ouyang, X., Sun, P., Han, P., Ding, N., Huang, J., Optimization Design for Federated Learning in Heterogeneous 6G Networks, pp. 1–7, 2023, arXiv:2303.08322.
127. Dahrouj, H., Li, S., Alouini, M., Machine Learning-Based User Scheduling in Integrated Satellite-HAPS-Ground Networks. *IEEE Network*, 37, 2, 102–109, March/April 2023.

11

Potential Communication in B5G Networks Through Hybrid Millimeter-Wave Beamforming and Machine Learning: Basics, Challenges, and Future Path

Snehasis Dey

College of Engineering, Bhubaneswar, BPUT University, Odisha, India

Abstract

B5G and 6G are still in their infancy, but the technological advancement and curiosity about the potential inclusion of ML in today's wireless communication have shown many dimensions to current researchers and academicians. Smartest as proposed and advanced as suggested, ML has proven that it will rule for at least another decade in the field of wireless communication. Basic challenges in the current communication network, like proper bandwidth utilization, security enhancement, interference limitations to a lower level, and data rate increments to some high expectation level, have been solved and maintained by the proper inclusion of millimeter-wave and ML algorithms. As stated, the pros of mmWave are quite impressive, as is the ML algorithm's performance in the field of wireless communication. Algorithms, like supervised, unsupervised, and reinforced learning, are the building blocks of today's huge data optimizations in wireless communication. Together, they have revolutionized the current scenario of smart networking. This chapter dives into the basics of mmWave beamforming and the subsequent contribution of ML techniques toward the deployment of mmWave in B5G communications. It also studies the challenges for implementation and the future path in this regard.

***Keywords*:** mmWave beamforming, ML algorithms, B5G communication, optimization, efficient network

---

Email: Snehasis9dey@gmail.com; ORCID: https://orcid.org/0000-0002-0490-8628

Pallavi Sapkale, Shilpa Mehta and S. Balamurugan (eds.) Quantum Computing and Machine Learning for 6G, (243–260) © 2026 Scrivener Publishing LLC

11.1 Introduction

Next-generation communication has attracted different research on high-speed communication, a higher data rate, and low latency. Due to its potential advantages in many ways, the millimeter wave is gaining immense attraction in current times. It promised to provide high transmission quality and exceptional bandwidth utilization by inculcating different antenna beamforming techniques. In reality, the deployment scenario is very important and crucial because of hardware constraints and the complexity of the design. Today, network design and user demands have reached a maximum level, which in turn makes it very difficult to propose and realize an ideal network for the billions of devices connected through the same network, which is heterogeneous in nature through different technologies and techniques. The basic solutions to these uncalled problems are the technological advancements in B5G wireless communication, like massive multiple input, multiple output antenna arrays (MIMO), beamforming (BF), and non-orthogonal multiple access (NOMA). For proper utilization of available bandwidth and properly optimizing the system's energy efficiency, the millimeter-wave (30–300 GHz) band is chosen as the best option for B5G communication. But, due to the high operating frequencies, mmWave exhibits bad propagation characteristics. For effective mmWave beam forming in B5G communication, it is essential to have analog beamformers or hybrid analog/digital beamformers. In analog beamformers, a single RF chain is utilized by all antenna elements, but in hybrid analog and digital beamformers, without having as many RF chains, the system will surely emerge to retain a high number of antennas. Hybrid beamformers are designed to provide good performance and secure transmission for multiuser and multistream. The art of the act is to design a secure and improved SINR-based mmWave transmission scheme for B5G communication. Figure 11.1 shows the typical structure of hybrid analog/digital BF for mmWave, clearly mentioning the RF chains.

In the Tx section, we have a series of RF chains labeled RF chain 1, RF chain 2,..., RF chain N, and similarly, in the Rx section, we also have RF chain 1, RF chain 2,..., RF chain N. Contrary to the technological advancement, there has been a big discovery in the past decade, perhaps the growth of ML and its relevant utilization in the recent wireless communication system. It provides numerous advantages, like proper optimization, channel allocation, routing, and efficient and intelligent resource allocation. Various ML schemes have been taken into consideration for the design of ideal mmWave communication in B5G networks. ML has also proven to be impactful in handling different complex problems like efficient spectrum management, recovery of channel state information (CSI), and security management in communication systems.

Hybrid precoding shows great promise for mmWave communication networks by significantly reducing the required number of RF chains, along with the associated energy consumption and cost compared to digital precoding. The implementation of this hybrid configuration involves using a small digital precoder along with a limited number of RF chains to initially eliminate interference. Subsequently, a large analog beamformer with numerous phase shifters (without RF chains) is employed to boost the antenna array gain. This is shown in Figure 11.1.

This chapter provides an overview of hybrid BF and different ML schemes and their subsequent effectiveness in communication. Both hybrid BF for mmWave communication and ML algorithms have no doubt revolutionized B5G communication in recent times.

11.2 Literature Survey

Ahmad et al. [24], in their article, surveyed some of the of the most recent papers on hybrid BF and described a vivid study about hybrid beamforming techniques in 5G. He also mentioned some key advantages of implementing this BF in 5G. This paper provided a comprehensive review of hybrid BF, which is an integral part of the mmWave massive MIMO system. The research path toward integrating ML and different algorithms into hybrid BF for mmWave communication was not proposed in this study.

Rihan et al. [3] described hybrid BF and its classification based on different scenarios and criteria. It also mentioned the procedure to evaluate the best performance of hybrid BF with the lowest cost and complexity. Some key research directions have been discussed, like deep learning–based hybrid BF, interference management, antenna selection management, and BF for green communication. Although hybrid beamforming is extensively discussed, key issues like ML-based hybrid BF, proper interference management, and optimization of antenna selections were not proposed accordingly.

Busari et al. [1] studied mmWave communication and open issues in 5G and B5G communication. Their research highlighted the different system models and presented the current scenarios involving the standardization of mmWave in relation to socioeconomic and environmental concerns about this type of architecture.

Elhalawany et al. [14] proposed a comprehensive study related to ML-based algorithms in the field of mmWave BF. In his study, different ML schemes and their practical implementations have been proposed. A lot of research challenges and future scope have been studied related to mmWave BF in B5G communication.
Rappaport et al. [25] explained the basic overview of mmWave propagation in 5th-generation communication. It also provided different propagation models associated with mmWave communication. The study basically provided the mmWave importance in 5G communications.
Hashima et al. [26] designed different ML schemes and mentioned their basic importance in 5G and B5G communication. It also identified different challenges and issues related to the establishment of practical ML-based solutions in D2D communication (B5G).
Antón-Haro and X. Mestre et al. [27] studied how deep learning and ML approaches can be used in selecting the beam in hybrid BF. Different multi-class classification problems have been identified and solved by the application of efficient ML algorithms.
Alkhateeb et al. [22] proposed a basic study regarding ML schemes for reliable mmWave communication. In their study, they specified blockage prediction and its relevant solution in communication systems.

This chapter has studied some relevant literature related to ML-based mmWave and concluded that each and every study proposed different ML schemes for optimizing and solving some difficult tasks in mmWave communication. This ML-based setup for B5G communication is crucial for higher precision, security, and effective data transmission. This chapter contributes to the current research in B5G communication by proposing different ML setups and hybrid BF scenarios that persist in the need for today's higher demand in communication systems. The basic problem statement from the literature study is to design and create a hybrid BF architecture inculcating different ML schemes for efficient B5G communication. Also, it dives into the ML application in real-life use cases in mmWave communication.

Hybrid Beamforming and Beamforming Training in mmWave:
Beamforming is a technique in which the signals produced by an antenna array are directed in a specific angular direction as per requirements. BF transmits redundant symbols over each transmitting antenna with a weighting factor, and at Rx, the separate set of weighting factors combines the received signal to improve the SNR value. The increment in SNR value is called the BF gain.

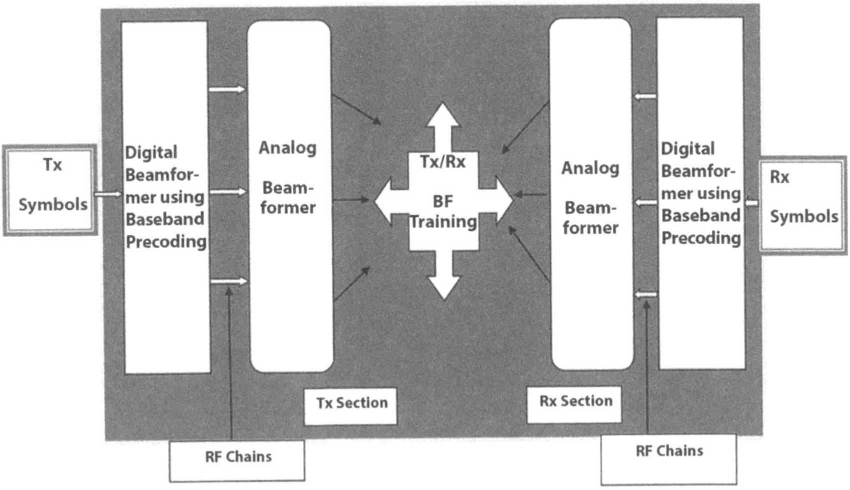

Figure 11.1 Typical architecture of hybrid analog/digital BF for mmWave in B5G communication.

Due to the large bandwidth and available spectrum, mmWave is considered to be the key technology in B5G communication. Similarly, hybrid beamforming provides an excellent beamforming scenario, which is generally a combination of both analog and digital beamforming. But, mmWave needs a specific scenario where a single RF chain can be shared by all antenna elements, which will definitely control the power consumption and complexity involved in designing the beamforming in mmWave. Thus, hybrid BF is suitable for mmWave because it provides enough advantages over other beamforms like power consumption, complexity, easy transmission, and a sufficient signal-to-noise ratio (SNR).

Hybrid BF employs a small digital/analog precoder with small RF chains to cancel interference, which ultimately increases the antenna gain. The hybrid BF uses digital precoding and analog BF for cost and performance balancing. Figure 11.1 shows the typical architecture of hybrid BF.

Similarly, the ML and its subsequent applications in different fields of communication are shown in Figure 11.2. It describes the advantages of hybrid BF for mmWave communication as well as the benefits of ML inclusion in recent wireless communication.

HBF (hybrid beamformer) may be of two types: fully connected and partially connected HBF.

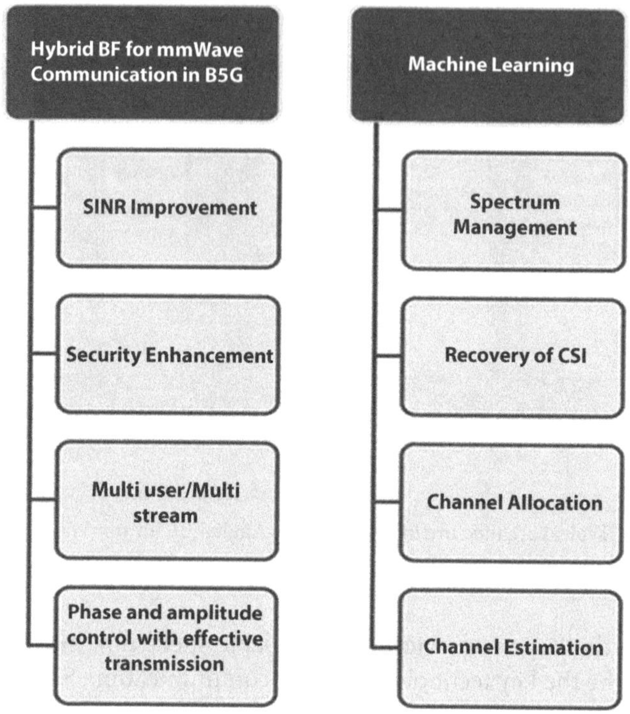

Figure 11.2 Key advantages of Hybrid BF in mmWave and ML in recent B5G communication.

- Fully connected HBF (Here, all the RF chains are connected to all the antennas).
- Partially connected HBF (Here, every RF chain is connected to only a subset of antennas, and every antenna is attached to a phase shifter).

Similarly, beamforming training (BT) in mmWave is a technique of optimization and finding out the best beam pair that maximizes the required throughput in bits per second.

Let us consider that in mmWave communication with hybrid BF, the best beam pair is given by $bp_{tx}{}^{*}$ and $bp_{rx}{}^{*}$.

So, we can write

$$(bp_{tx}{}^{*}, bp_{rx}{}^{*}) = W\,[T_D/\,(KT_{BT} + T_D)]$$

where "W" represents the available bandwidth and [TD/(KTBT + T_D)] represents the BT overhead. *K* is the total number of (*b*tx, *b*rx) beam pairs

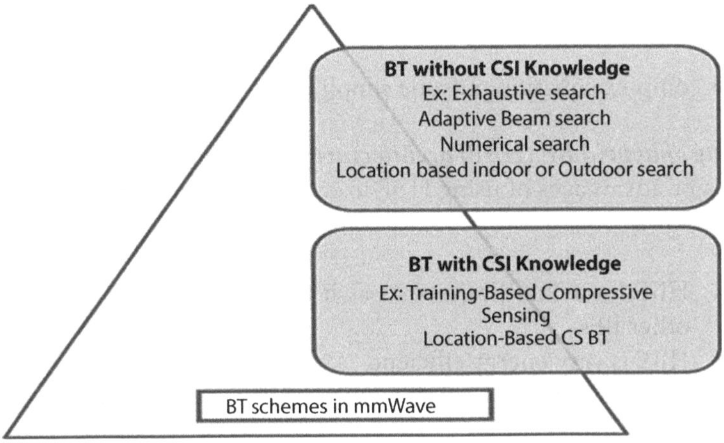

Figure 11.3 BT schemes in mmWave.

involved in the BT process, T_D is the time required for data transmission, and T_{BT} is the time for BT for one pair.

Figure 11.3 provides different beamforming training schemes for mmWave communication. These are basically without channel state information (CSI) knowledge types or with CSI types. Without CSI, there may be direct training, numerical search, or location-based types, but with CSI, there may be training-based compressive sensing or location-based compressive sensing types.

A complex hybrid beamformer can be designed by considering some basic formulations and matrixes into account. The below equation represents the same:

$$\text{Minimize } F_{RF}, F_{BB}$$

$$\text{That is, minimize } ||F_{opt} - F_{RF}, F_{BB}||^2_F$$

$$\text{Subject to } ||F_{RF}, F_{BB}||^2 \leq K\,Ns\,F$$

$$\text{And } F_{RF} \in A$$

where the combined fully digital beamformer is denoted as

$$F_{opt} = [\,F_{opt1,1,\ldots}, F_{optk,f}, \ldots, F_{opt\,K,F}\,] \in C^{Nt \times KNsF}$$

$$\text{and } F_{BB} = [F_{BB1,1},\ldots, F_{BBk,f},\ldots, F_{BBK,F}].$$

This complex equation must be simplified to design a hybrid BF.

Benefits of hybrid BF (HBF) architectures in mmWave communication: The major advantages of using HBF in mmWave communication for B5G are as follows:

- HBF limits hardware costs as it uses fewer RF chains than other BFs.
- HBF is very energy efficient.
- HBF minimizes power consumption without affecting performance.
- HBF exploits the practical and efficient use of the massive MIMO mmWave systems with great capacity enhancements.
- HBF provides easy transmission and sufficient enhancement in SINR values.

In Figure 11.4, a typical HBF is shown, which is an arrangement of an analog beamformer with a large number of antennas and a digital beamformer with a small number of RF chains. HBF is broadly implemented in mMIMO systems where baseband signals are generated in DBF and the analog beamformer is responsible for the RF chain that ultimately enhances the amplifier performance. HBF will definitely provide enhanced value with less cost effectiveness.

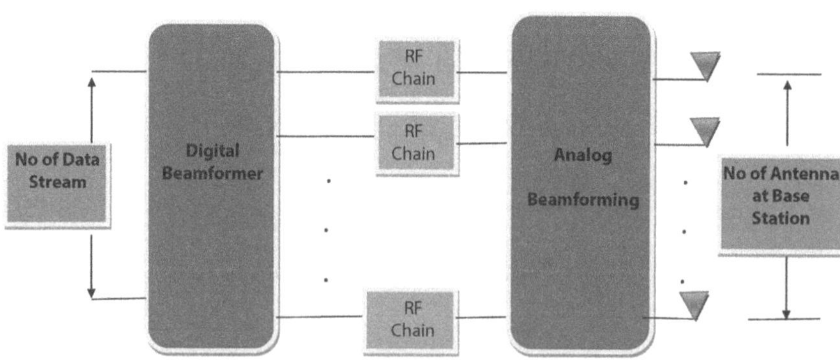

Figure 11.4 Typical HBF architecture, where ABF connects a large number of antennas and the DBF connects a small number of RF chains.

Benefits of HBF over traditional BF in the B5G network context:
Hybrid BF has several advantages over traditional in the B5G network context, which are as follows:

- Enhanced flexibility and performances
- Improved spectral efficiency
- Efficient energy efficiency
- Cost effectiveness
- Flexible to different environments
- Enhanced user experiences with low latency and consistent connectivity

11.3 HBF Open Challenges

With lots of advantages, there are also some challenges or practical implications in HBF realization in B5G communication.

I. *Channel estimation and beamforming realization:* Channel estimation and beamforming realization are much more important in B5G communication, which inculcates mmWAVE. But, in HBF, the task at hand is much more difficult than in other counterparts like analog or digital due to the fact that the number of RF chains is very small. It leads to the complexity and requirements of proper optimization that are actually hard to solve. Therefore, ML implementations are evident and important. When designing channel estimation techniques for HBF-based systems, it is necessary to minimize the cost of channel estimation in the system, which limits spectral efficiency. Compressive sensing methods can be used to exploit the sparsity of mmWave channels in the corner domain to reduce the number of estimated channel parameters and the complexity of the process. This will significantly reduce the size of the channel array and the complexity of the precoder and combiner design. Additionally, in situations with high MD mobility, rapid channel variations lead to estimation delays, which can impact performance.

II. *Ideal number of RF chains:* Having a large number of antenna elements, it is very essential to fix optimal numbers of RF chains in designing the HBF in mmWave-based B5G communication. Thus, the challenge lies in the ideal number of RF chains for optimal performance and limitations in power consumption.

III. *Challenge in precoder design and beam training:* Hybrid precoder and combiner design is a challenge that aims to maximize spectral efficiency. Therefore, proper algorithms may be designed for adequate signal processing and performance enhancement.

The above three important open challenges are generally brought into play when we employ HBF in mmWave communication. The common idea is to mitigate these challenges for the betterment of performance enhancement through effective communication. In the next section, we will discuss the ML applications in the mmWave BF.

ML Conceptualization and its Application in mmWave BF:
Machine learning is the most promising technique that has been employed in mmWave communication in recent times, which provides better utilization of spectrum, effective networking, proper optimization, and a stable network. Adding to the above features, channel estimation, security management, and handoff management are also some key strengths of ML techniques. ML in communication can be of three types: supervised, unsupervised, and reinforced.

Supervised Learning:
ML models are trained to learn a mapping function, y = f(x), using a historical dataset that provides patterns of input-output relationships (x, y), while the goal of the model is to predict future outputs (y_0) for a given test input (x_0). The two main predictive models that can be used are regression models and classification models. Regression models use statistical techniques to model the relationships between explanatory variables and real-valued outcomes to predict outputs using approximations of linear or sigmoid functions. Classification, on the other hand, is the most widely used ML technique, which classifies data samples into one of many patterns. The general classical classification models for mmWave BF are K-nearest neighbor (KNN), support vector machines (SVMs), and decision trees.

Unsupervised Learning:
This technique looks for patterns and hidden structures in the input data in the absence of data labels. Unsupervised learning tasks can be divided into

classification, estimation, and dimension reduction. First, the main purpose of clustering is to divide samples into groups or clusters. This means that initially, we do not know which class each instance of the dataset belongs to. Clustering has many applications in data analysis, image, audio, and video processing, and, more recently, in wireless communications. K-means is frequently used as a clustering method. Second, the purpose of density estimation is to estimate the density of the data distribution in image space, which may indicate some important features at high points. The Gaussian mixture model (GMM) is a popular method of this type.

Reinforcement Learning:

RL uses different learning methods based on trial and error. The RL agent is rewarded or penalized for his action to increase the price in the long run. A responsive environment is provided to the customer to help choose the appropriate action at each step by following a specific policy that maps the customer's behavior from one state to another. Because of the uncertainty of the environment, the system dynamics can be modeled using a Markov decision process to optimize the objectives. Q-learning is the best RL method. The ML basic application in mmWave hybrid BFs is proposed here below:

- Efficient hybrid BF design through the KNN algorithm, which achieves target BER at higher data rates.
- Beam alignment and tracking by RL learning schemes for a faster learning environment.
- Beam selection with low latency with DL methods for 99% throughput achievement.

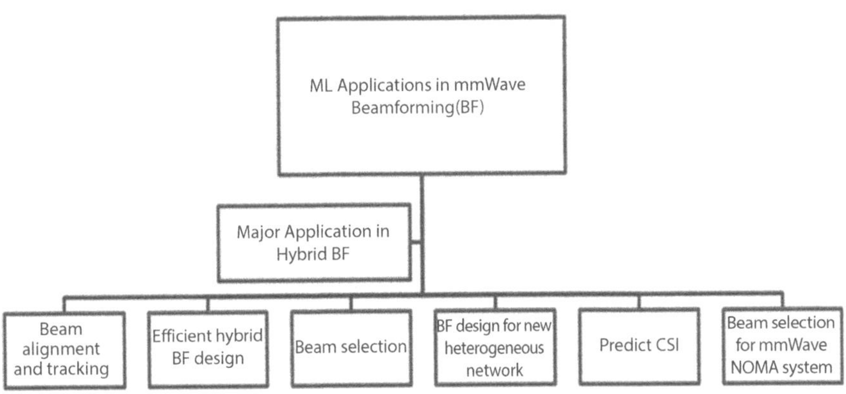

Figure 11.5 Structural overview of ML applications in mmWave hybrid BF.

- Beam selection for the mmWave NOMA system.
- Develop efficient beam selection designs using deep neural network (DNN) methods with more than 95% accuracy.
- BF design for a new heterogeneous network for unknown entities or users.
- Predict CSI.

The figure above (Figure 11.5) provides an overview of ML inclusion and its respective applications in mmWave hybrid beamforming. In B5G communication employing mmWave communication, beam tracking is a challenging and vital task, mostly in high-mobile environments or scenarios. Therefore, smart networking with AI and ML inclusion is quite a necessity for this purpose, which in turn predicts the secured surrounding environment for enhanced performance. Different promising ML schemes are being employed, like recurrent neural network (RNN)–based beam tracking, for these purposes. ML is a useful tool for beam selection, tracking, searching, and alignment.

Investigating the optimal beamformers in large MIMO systems is a large non-convex optimization problem that is solved by expensive optimization methods. This problem becomes even more complicated in mmWave-based HetNet scenarios, where BSs are equipped with multiple transmit antennas and different inter-BS distances. Attempts have been made to solve such problems using ML techniques. Despite the innovative ML algorithms and their latest progress, there are many open challenges in this field, which are discussed below.

ML algorithms to handle high mobility in B5G communication:
ML acts as a perfect tool for B5G communication in providing high mobility in devices by adopting different strategies and techniques like dynamic resource allocation, mobility prediction, edge computing, anomaly detection, network slicing, and, of course, adaptive beamforming.

- ***Dynamic resource allocation:*** It provides the opportunity to network to establish resources based on real time data. This has the ability to maintain quality of services (QoS) and network efficiently by the application of reinforced learning.
- ***Network Slicing:*** Different MLs can establish, create, and manage virtual network slices for specific user groups as per demand. It gives low latency connections also.

- ***Edge Computing:*** ML adaptation at the edge of the network reduces latency and fastens the connectivity as well as data processing in the networks.
- ***Adaptive Beamforming:*** In moving devices, ML has the potential to adjust and control the directions of the signal beams for consistent connectivity.

Potential Applications of HBF with ML in Real-World Scenarios: Hybrid beamforming, when integrated with machine learning (ML) techniques, presents numerous advantageous applications in practical contexts such as smart cities and autonomous vehicles:

Smart Cities

- ***Augmented Connectivity:*** The implementation of hybrid beamforming has the potential to significantly enhance the connectivity of Internet-of-Things (IoT) devices within smart cities by adaptively modifying signal beams to maintain stable connections, even in areas characterized by high population density.
- ***Optimized Resource Allocation:*** Machine learning algorithms can effectively streamline the distribution of network resources, ensuring optimal utilization of bandwidth while simultaneously mitigating congestion.
- ***Enhanced Public Safety:*** The fusion of hybrid beamforming with machine learning enables smart city infrastructures to facilitate real-time surveillance and prompt interventions in emergency situations, thereby improving public safety outcomes.

Autonomous Vehicles

- ***Enhanced Navigation:*** The implementation of hybrid beamforming can significantly improve the precision of vehicle-to-everything (V2X) communication, thereby providing consistent and reliable data for navigation and obstacle identification.
- ***Accident Prevention:*** Machine learning–augmented hybrid beamforming can optimize radar and communication systems, thereby assisting autonomous vehicles in more effectively detecting and circumventing obstacles.

- ***Uninterrupted Connectivity:*** The establishment of continuous and dependable communication between autonomous vehicles and infrastructural elements, even in dynamic mobility conditions, is essential for ensuring both safety and operational efficiency.

Open Challenges in ML-assisted mmWave hybrid BF and subsequent future directions:

- The availability of a large number of labeled datasets for training purposes in ML-assisted mmWave HBF is really a big challenge in B5G communication. Future research may be done to find a solution for this.
- Proposing an optimal ML-assisted algorithm with fast interference time is also another big task in ML-assisted mmWave hybrid BF. So, future research can be propelled toward finding an optimal ML algorithm with fast interference times.
- Always finding adaptive ML schemes for a perfect environment is quite challenging, so research can be done in this regard.
- ML assistance with precision in frequent mobility is also very hard to achieve.
- The performance of the network is also dependent on the best ML schemes.
- The complexity of optimization and networking is present in many cases.

As shown in the below (Figure 11.6), there are huge research opportunities in the prospect of ML assisted mmWave hybrid BF. It may be in

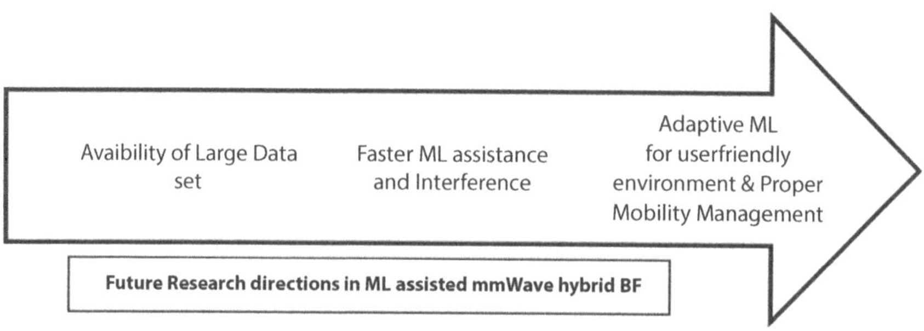

Figure 11.6 Future research direction of ML-assisted mmWave hybrid BF.

fields like faster ML assistance and interfacing, adaptive ML for sustainable environments, and dataset training and optimization.

Challenges to Overcome the Limited Labelled Datasets for Training ML Models in B5G Communication:

The endeavor to surmount the limitations posed by constrained labeled datasets for the training of machine learning models in B5G communications encompasses a multitude of innovative methodologies:

Data Augmentation: Methodologies such as the introduction of noise, the transformation of signals, and the generation of synthetic data serve to enhance the current datasets. This facilitates the formation of a more heterogeneous array of training samples.

Transfer Learning: Utilizing pre-trained models that have been developed for analogous tasks or domains can markedly diminish the necessity for extensive labeled datasets. These pre-trained models may be fine-tuned utilizing a limited quantity of B5G-specific data.

Federated Learning: This paradigm enables a consortium of devices to collaboratively develop a model without the exchange of their datasets. Each device engages in local model training and subsequently shares only the model updates, thereby safeguarding data privacy and mitigating the necessity for centralized labeled datasets.

Active Learning: In this framework, the model proactively identifies the most informative samples from the unlabeled dataset for labeling. This strategy diminishes the effort required for labeling while ensuring that the model is trained on the most pertinent data.

Machine learning (ML) assumes a pivotal role in optimizing the efficacy of hybrid beamforming (BF) in beyond 5G (B5G) networks through several fundamental mechanisms:

Optimal Beam Selection: ML algorithms possess the capability to scrutinize extensive datasets to ascertain the most effective beam patterns pertinent to various scenarios. This process guarantees the maximization of signal strength and quality, even amidst fluctuating environmental conditions.

Adaptive Beamforming: ML models are equipped to dynamically modify beamforming parameters in real time, contingent upon the evolving network conditions and user mobility. Such adaptability is instrumental in preserving consistent connectivity and sustaining elevated data transmission rates.

Interference Management: Through the anticipation and alleviation of interference, ML can significantly enhance the performance of hybrid beamforming. This capability is particularly critical in densely populated urban settings where multiple signals may interfere with one another.
Energy Efficiency: ML has the potential to optimize the energy consumption associated with beamforming operations, thereby ensuring that the network functions efficiently without compromising its performance. This aspect is vital for the sustainability of network operations.
Resource Allocation: ML algorithms are proficient in the strategic allocation of network resources, including bandwidth and power, to various beams in accordance with real-time demand and prevailing network conditions. This practice ensures the optimal utilization of the available resources.
Predictive Maintenance: ML can foresee potential malfunctions or degradations in beamforming apparatus, facilitating proactive maintenance interventions and minimizing operational downtime.

11.4 Conclusion

This chapter studies vividly the concepts of beamforming, hybrid BF, hybrid BF architecture, and the role of ML in designing hybrid BF. Hybrid beamforming is very crucial in mmWave B5G communication. We also analyze how different ML schemes can enhance the performance of the B5G network as it is secure, stable, and optimized as compared to the conventional way of communication. ML learning assistance in mmWave hybrid BF will provide adequate utilization of spectrum and resources by limiting the power factor. As there are different challenges to face, this chapter also provides ample research directions in the field of ML-assisted hybrid BF.

Bibliography

1. Busari, S.A., Huq, K., Mumtaz, S., Dai, L., Rodriguez, J., Millimeter-Wave Massive MIMO Communication for Future Wireless Systems: A Survey. *IEEE Commun. Surv. Tutorials*, 20, 836–869, 2017, 10.1109/COMST.2017.2787460.
2. Dey, S., Phenomenon of Excess of Artificial Intelligence: Quantifying the Native AI, Its Leverages in 5G/6G and Beyond. *Radar RF Front End Syst. Des. Wireless Systems. IGI Global*, 2 Scientific Publishing, 45–274, 2024. https://doi.org/10.4018/979-8-3693-0916-2.ch010.

3. Rihan, M., Abed Soliman, T., Xu, C., Huang, L., Dessouky, M., II, Taxonomy and Performance Evaluation of Hybrid Beamforming for 5G and Beyond Systems. in. *IEEE Access*, 8, 74605–74626, 2020, doi: 10.1109/ACCESS.2020.2984548.
4. Chen, T., Matinmikko, M., Chen, X., Zhou, X., Ahokangas, P., Software-defined mobile networks: concept, survey, and research directions. *IEEE Commun. Mag.*, 53, 11, 126–133, November 2015.
5. Satyanarayana, K., El-Hajjar, M., Mourad, A.A.M., Hanzo, L., Multiuser hybrid beamforming relying on learning-aided link-adaptation for mmWave systems. *IEEE Access*, 7, 23197–23209, 2019.
6. Vahid, S., Tafazolli, R., Filo, M., Small Cells for 5G Mobile Networks, in: *Fundamentals of 5G Mobile Networks*, J. Rodriguez (Ed.), pp. 63–104, John Wiley & Sons, Ltd., West Sussex, UK, 2015.
7. Health, R.W., Lozano, A., Marzetta, T.L., Popovski, P., Five disruptive technology directions for 5G. *IEEE Commun. Mag.*, 52, 2, 74–80, February 2014.
8. Swindlehurst, L., Ayanoglu, E., Heydasri, P., Capolino, F., Millimeter-wave massive MIMO: The Next Wireless Revolution? *IEEE Commun. Mag.*, 52, 9, 56–62, September 2014.
9. Li, Q.C., Niu, H., Papathanassiou, A.T., Wu, G., 5G Network Capacity: Key Elements and Technologies. in. *IEEE Veh. Technol. Mag.*, 9, 1, 71–78, March 2014.
10. Bojkovic, Z.S., Bakmaz, M.R., Bakmaz, B.M., Research challenges for 5G cellular architecture. *12th International Conference on Telecommunication in Modern Satellite, Cable, and Broadcasting Services (TELSIKS)*, pp. 215–222, 2015.
11. Dey, S., Khampariya, P., Jain, M., Analysis of various AI-based algorithms and learning perspectives for 5G wireless. *IJME*, 7.5, 1234–124, 2022.
12. Dey, S. and Sahoo, B.B., Link Budget of LEO Satellite (Sky Bridge) For Communication Operated At Ku Band Frequency Range (12–14) GHz. *Int. J. Innov. Eng. Technol. (IJIET)*, 4.1, 173–179, 2014.
13. Dey, S., Mohapatra, D., Archana, S.D.R.P., An approach to calculate the performance and link budget of a leo satellite (iridium) for communication operated at a frequency range of 1650–1550 mhz. *Int. J. Latest Trends Eng. Technol.*, 4.4, 96–103, 2014.
14. ElHalawany, B.M., Hashima, S., Hatano, K., Wu, K., Mohamed, E.M., Leveraging Machine Learning for Millimeter Wave Beamforming in Beyond 5G Networks. In: *IEEE Syst. J.*, 16, 2, 1739–1750, 2022, doi: 10.1109/JSYST.2021.3089536.
15. Hur, S., Kim, T., Love, D.J., Krogmeier, J.V., Thomas, T.A., Ghosh, A., Multilevel millimeterwave beamforming for wireless backhaul. In: *Proc. IEEE GLOBECOM Workshops*, 61, 253–257, 2011.
16. Li, B., Zhou, Z., Zhang, H., Nallanathan, A., Efficient beamforming training for 60-GHz millimeter-wave communications: A novel numerical optimization framework. *IEEE Trans. Veh. Technol.*, 63, 2, 703–717, Feb. 2014.

17. Mubarak, A.S., Esmaiel, H., Mohamed, E.M., LTE/Wi-Fi/mmWave RAN-level interworking using 2 C/U plane splitting for future 5G networks. *IEEE Access*, 6, 53473–53488, 2018.
18. Nor, A.M. and Mohamed, E.M., Millimeter wave beamforming training based on Li-Fi localization in indoor environments, in: *Proc. IEEE Global Commun. Conf.*, pp. 1–6, 2017.
19. Chiu, S., Ronquillo, N., Javidi, T., Active learning and CSI acquisition for mmWave initial alignment. *IEEE J. Sel. Areas Commun.*, 37, 11, 2474–2489, Nov. 2019.
20. Cheng, M., Wang, J., Wang, J., Lin, M., Wu, Y., Zhu, H., A fast beam searching scheme in mmWave communications for high-speed trains, in: *Proc. IEEE Int. Conf. Commun.*, pp. 1–6, May 2019.
21. Raj, V., Nayak, N., Kalyani, S., Deep reinforcement learning based blind mmWave MIMO beam alignment, 2021, [Online], Available: https://arxiv.org/abs/2001.09251.
22. Alkhateeb, A., ElAyach, O., Leus, G., Heath, R.W., Channel estimation and hybrid precoding for millimeter wave cellular systems. *IEEE J. Sel. Top. Signal Process.*, 8, 5, 831–846, Oct. 2014.
23. Dey, S., *et al.*, The potential solutions to next generation wireless communication: AI and Massive MIMO technology design and development. *J. Emerging Technol. Innovative Res.*, 9, 4, 80–87, April 2022.
24. Ahmed, I., Khammari, H., Shahid, A., Musa, A., Kim, K.S., De Poorter, E., Moerman, I., A survey on hybrid beamforming techniques in 5G: Architecture and system model perspectives. *IEEE Commun. Surv. Tutor.,* 20, 4, 3060–3097, 2018. Article 8371237. https://doi.org/10.1109/COMST.2018.2843719.
25. Rappaport, T., Overview of Millimeter Wave Communications for Fifth-Generation (5G) Wireless Networks-with a focus on Propagation Models. *IEEE Trans. Antennas Propag.,* https://doi.org/10.1109/TAP.2017.2734243.
26. Hashima, S., ElHalawany, B.M., Hatano, K., Wu, K., Mohamed, E.M., Leveraging Machine-Learning for D2D Communications in 5G/Beyond 5G Networks. *Electronics,* 10, 2, 169, 2021. https://doi.org/10.3390/electronics10020169.
27. Anton, C. and Mestre, X., Learning and Data-Driven Beam Selection for mmWave Communications: An Angle of Arrival-Based Approach. *IEEE Access,* 1–1, 2019. 10.1109/ACCESS.2019.2895594.

12

Device-to-Device Communication in 6G Using Machine Learning

J. Shanthalakshmi Revathy[1]*, J. Mangaiyarkkarasi[2] and J. Matcha Rani[1]

[1]Department of Computer Science and Engineering, Velammal College of Engineering and Technology, Viraganoor, Madurai, India
[2]PG and Research Department of Physics, Nadar Mahajana Sangam S. Vellaichamy Nadar College, Nagamalai, Madurai, India

Abstract

Device-to-device (D2D) communication is poised to play a pivotal role in the evolution of 6G networks, offering enhanced connectivity, lower latency, and increased spectral efficiency. This chapter explores the integration of machine learning (ML) techniques with D2D communication in 6G, focusing on how ML can optimize network performance, resource allocation, and security in decentralized environments. The chapter begins by outlining the fundamental concepts of D2D communication, highlighting its importance in 6G networks. It then delves into various ML algorithms that can be applied to D2D communication, such as reinforcement learning for dynamic spectrum management, supervised learning for link quality prediction, and unsupervised learning for anomaly detection. The chapter also discusses the role of deep learning in enhancing the adaptability and intelligence of D2D systems, enabling real-time decision-making and autonomous operation.

Moreover, the chapter addresses the challenges and limitations associated with implementing ML in D2D communication, such as the need for large-scale data, the complexity of real-time processing, and the potential for security vulnerabilities. It offers solutions to these challenges, including federated learning approaches for decentralized data processing and advanced cryptographic techniques for secure communication. The chapter concludes by envisioning the future of D2D communication in 6G networks, emphasizing the transformative potential of ML in creating intelligent, self-organizing networks that can meet the demands of emerging applications such as augmented reality, autonomous vehicles, and the Internet of Things (IoT).

**Corresponding author*: revathyjeganathan@gmail.com

Pallavi Sapkale, Shilpa Mehta and S. Balamurugan (eds.) Quantum Computing and Machine Learning for 6G, (261–282) © 2026 Scrivener Publishing LLC

***Keywords*:** Device-to-device communication, 6G networks, machine learning, resource allocation, network optimization

12.1 Introduction

The sixth generation of wireless technology is 6G, which is defined as a cellular network and the successor of 5G. While 5G substantially improves speed, capacity, and latency, 6G will transcend these boundaries by integrating technologies like artificial intelligence (AI) and machine learning (ML). It provided significant advancements in speed, capacity, and latency [15]. It uses cognitive technology like AI to enable high speed. 6G will operate on higher frequencies in the radio spectrum, potentially enabling unprecedented data transfer rates and ultralow latency. The primary goal of 6G is to achieve one-microsecond latency, which is 1,000 times faster than the one-millisecond latency in 5G. 6G, which will make major improvements in imaging, presence technology, and location awareness. It will dynamically determine the optimal location for computing tasks like deciding data storage, processing, and sharing. The integration of AI will make 6G networks more efficient, perform better, and be more adaptive.

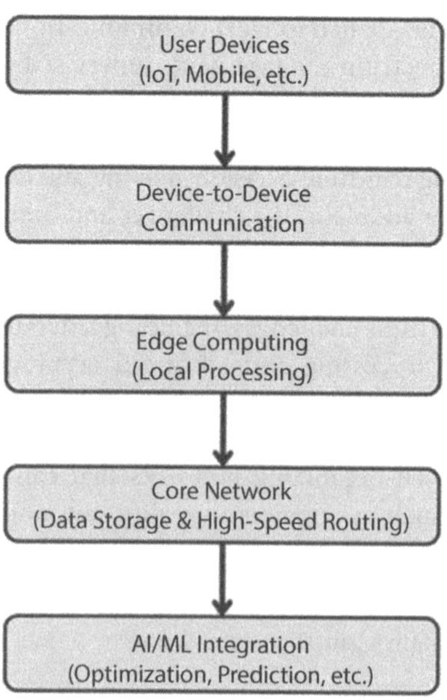

Figure 12.1 The architecture of 6G networks.

In 5G, the human users and the Internet of Things are the use cases, whereas in 6G, it will focus more on device-to-device connectivity (machine to machine). The 5G-led ultrareliable low-latency communication service will be developed in 6G. 6G will be implemented in heterogeneous cloud settings, including a combination of private, public, and hybrid clouds. 6G allows AI/ML to determine the optimal method of communication between two endpoints [21]. Figure 12.1 illustrates the architecture of 6G networks.

Device-to-device communication is communication between two-user equipment without relying on intermediate network infrastructure. It lowers latency, improves the network spectrum, reduces the system overhead, and enhances the reliability of communication. It reduces the data transfer time and makes a faster response, and this is particularly important for IoT devices that will function for a period without recharging [3].

D2D communication includes data privacy and security, as data are exchanged directly between the devices without passing through the central network elements. It efficiently utilizes the network resources. In 6G, D2D communication plays a vital role in enabling ultrareliable and high-capacity networks.

12.2 Fundamentals of Device-to-Device Communication

Device-to-device (D2D) communication is a communication model where user devices communicate directly with each other without the central base station or access point. This direct communication is made by establishing a direct link between the devices, allowing for the exchange of data, voice, and video without relying on the traditional cellular network infrastructure. D2D communication can be categorized into various types, including peer-to-peer (P2P) communication, where devices communicate directly, and relay communication, where one device acts as a relay for communication between other devices [7].

The key concept in D2D communications is device discovery, where devices identify each other and establish communication through link and resource allocation, whereas communication resources such as spectrum and power are allocated to the devices. Another critical concept is interference management, which involves minimizing the interference between D2D communication and traditional cellular communication to ensure efficient and reliable communication. D2D communication can operate in

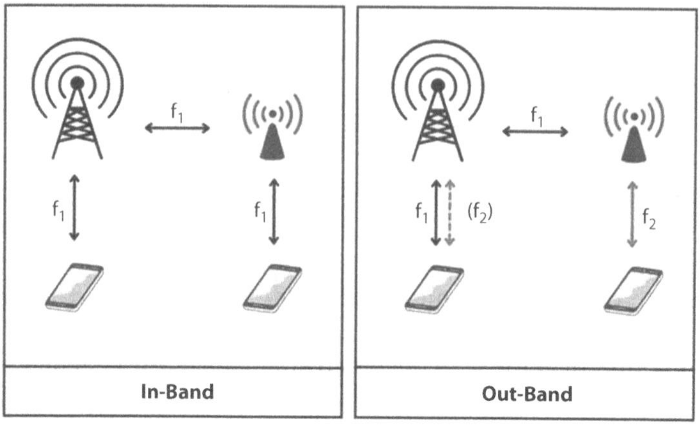

Figure 12.2 In-band and out-band communications.

both licensed and unlicensed spectrum bands, which provides flexibility in how communication is managed and maintained. In licensed bands, D2D communication can be integrated with the cellular networks, allowing for better control and management. In unlicensed bands, D2D communication operates independently and provides an alternative means of communication when the network is unavailable or congested [13].

Nowadays, information transmission has evolved from physical cables to radio frequency (RF) technology. The radio signals enable communication without physical connections; the radio signals travel from the user mobile to the base station (BS), and then the base station to another user mobile is standard in cellular networks. Because of the limitations in radio frequency, device-to-device communication (D2D) has been introduced. D2D communication allows direct communication without the need to route messages through a base station.

D2D communication is classified into two main categories based on spectrum utilization: In-Band D2D communication (IBD) and Out-Band D2D communication (OBD). Figure 12.2 explains In-Band and Out-Band communications.

In-Band Communication (IBD)

In IBD, it shares the same wireless resource in cellular communication, known as underlay mode. It is intended to use the spectrum efficiently, enhance cellular coverage, and reduce latency and energy consumption. It also allocates separate wireless resources for cellular communication,

Table 12.1 Comparison between In-Band and Out-Band D2D communications.

Feature	In-band D2D (IBD)	Out-band D2D (OBD)
Spectrum	Licensed	Unlicensed
Interference	Potential interference with cellular links	Minimal interference with cellular links
Modes	Underlay, overlay	Controlled, autonomous
Deployment	Requires spectrum management	Uses interfaces like Bluetooth or Wi-Fi Direct

preventing interference from cellular links while still experiencing interferences in device-to-device links, known as overlay mode [8].

Out-Band Communication (OBD)

It uses unlicensed spectrum like Wi-Fi and Bluetooth, and it avoids interference with cellular communications. The base station manages the communication and improves reliability and efficiency over communication, which is called the controlled mode. Out-band communication can operate independently of cellular networks, reducing network overhead and using an interface like Bluetooth or Wi-Fi, which is autonomous mode [10]. Table 12.1 explains the comparison between In-Band and Out-Band D2D communications.

12.3 Evolution from Previous Generations

Device-to-device communication has evolved rapidly, with the need for faster access and more efficiency. Here, we learn how the evolution of device-to-device communication has been in detail [2].

12.3.1 Early Foundations: Peer-to-Peer and Ad Hoc Networks

Early on, device-to-device communication used peer-to-peer (P2P) and ad hoc networks. In this P2P network, the devices are connected directly to each other without a base server. This network is used to share files or resources, functioning as a file-sharing network. Mobile ad hoc networks (MANETs) are especially used to fix impractical issues, and these networks are self-organized by acting as both routers and terminals [4].

12.3.2 Device-to-Device Communications in Cellular Networks

With the increase in technology, traditional cellular networks based on the base station are used to manage all communications, but they become more complex and useful when the number of communications increases. The 3rd Generation Partnership Project is the standardized cellular network that allows devices to communicate directly. It introduced LTE Direct, which makes direct communication through links, and it includes many advantages listed below. Figure 12.3 shows D2D in cellular networks.

Network Offloading: It allows the device to communicate directly by reducing the bandwidth of the user's communication.
Lower Latency: In this, the data do not need to travel through the core network.
Improved Spectrum Efficiency: It is more useful in wireless communication by the use of available spectrum.

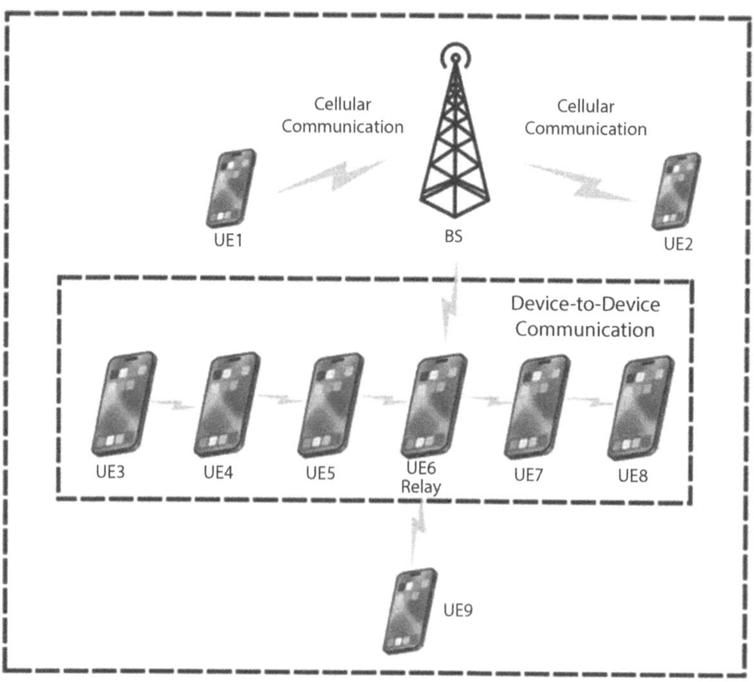

Figure 12.3 D2D in cellular networks.

12.3.3 The 5G Era

Device-to-device communication is enhanced in 5G; it is designed to make ultrareliable low-latency communication (URLLC), which is used in the applications like autonomous driving and remote surgery [18].

The Enhancement in 5G

Improves Device Discovery: It uses a mechanism to discover each other in dense areas.

Synchronization: Device-to-device communication is made more effective by reducing the interference and helps to improve the quality of communication through links.

Enhanced Security and Privacy: In D2D, the devices communicate directly with each other, strengthening the security measures to protect the data from unauthorized access.

12.3.4 Enhancement in 6G

In the future, the 6G networks are expected to reach new heights in D2D communications. They will manage data and ensure that the communication is efficient [17].

Artificial Intelligence (AI) and Machine Learning (ML) will be Integrated into D2D Communication in 6G by Enabling Resource Allocation

The AI algorithms are used to reduce spectrum resources, improve efficiency, and gradually reduce congestion.

Predictive Maintenance

In this, the devices can also use AI to predict the need for communication maintenance, controlling the network.

Security

In D2D communication using AI, it is easy to detect and respond to security threats in real time, which it shows that D2D communication is secure in complex networks.

12.4 Role of Machine Learning in 6G D2D Communication

Machine learning (ML) models are high-functioning computational structures that were designed to figure out patterns within data that the traditional mathematical models are incapable of doing. They are exquisitely good at jobs like regression, classification, and situations with an intelligent system working in an environment. The training and testing set allows the ML model to learn and gain insight into human interaction long enough to make its own decisions based on data not yet analyzed by the model. Besides that, they do not make many mistakes so it can be said that they work accurately as well [9].

12.4.1 Supervised Learning

Supervised learning is a type of algorithm that allows one to label the dataset as both the input and the desired output. That approach depends largely on enough data to accomplish the goal. Generally speaking, training is the use of supervised learning where classification and regression tasks predominate. There are several rooftop buildings in the supervised learning landscape, such as logistic regression, artificial neural networks (ANNs), k-nearest neighbors (kNN), naive Bayes, random forests, and decision trees.

Artificial Neural Networks (ANNs): ANNs, which imitate the system of brains, can predict through the model that their hidden layers create so that young people understand the music in terms of matter. They are the ones who create music using self-sufficient methods as well as complicated deep learning with deep neural networks (DNNs). Autoencoders, another kind of ANN, are the main unsupervised learning ANN, but other forms are utilized in reinforcement learning [19].

k-Nearest Neighbors (kNN): A machine learning strategy that predicts the category of an instance based on the categories of the training points close to it is an algorithm called k-nearest neighbors (k-NN). Multiclass classification tasks can be performed with it, and its advantages are that it is not mostly affected by anomalies in terms of predictions, although time does not allow its effectiveness with big data and datasets.

Naive Bayes: The reason why classification is so simple here is that naive Bayes uses the theorem of Bayes, which describes the probability of a certain result given some input parameters. Naive Bayes, due to its simplicity, is extremely efficient with large, high-dimensional datasets, where it allows to bypass of the difficult process of density estimation [14].

Random Forests: A random forest is an ensemble of decision trees, which is constructed using a random subset of features. The final decision is taken based on the majority vote of all the trees. This technique guards against the dangers of overfitting observed in the case of a single decision tree, as it involves the averaging of multiple tree results.

Convolutional Neural Networks (CNNs): CNNs are especially useful for image recognition purposes. To be more specific, they are made up of layers such as the convolutional, pooling, and fully connected layers, which, in groups, analyze images to find patterns. On the one hand, CNNs are both supervised and unsupervised if we determine the concrete application.

Recurrent Neural Networks (RNNs): RNNs are inherently sequential, so in most cases, they are used for jobs such as language translation, speech recognition, and time series prediction. LSTM (long short-term memory) networks are a special case of RNN in which the vanishing gradient problem is solved, and therefore, the network can remember information over long sequences.

12.4.2 Unsupervised Learning

In unsupervised learning, no help is given in the form of labels to the model as it processes the data; it has to identify the patterns in the data by itself by searching the data for patterns or structures. These algorithms are often used for clustering and aggregation, but they can also handle regression tasks.

K-means: It is one of the most commonly used clustering algorithms that groups similar data points together into clusters based on their proximity to the nearest centroid. The values of the cells are tallied and the centroid is adjusted. It is done iteratively until the cells remain in the cluster for which they are dedicated. The value of K, which determines the number of clusters the model has to identify, has a critical impact on the performance of the algorithm.

Self-Organizing Maps (SOMs): SOMs are the neural network given the task of clustering and dimensionality reduction. The neural network model is composed of an input layer and a map layer, where every node is trying to recognize the input data. The output node that wins becomes the missing link in the topological chain that shapes up the clusters. During the process, dimensions are collapsed by projecting the high-dimensional data onto a lower-dimensional grid that forms clusters. SOMs are the ideal tools for orientation in the n-dimensional space [6].

Autoencoders: These are neural networks that are designed to extract the internal information of data, and then the dimensions are reduced. Usually, the modeling target is obtaining the most compact and efficient representations of data. Autoencoders work in the following way: They encode the input into a lower-dimensional space encoding and then decode back to the original space; hence, the minimization of the error in the reconstruction is the goal of the input.

12.4.3 Reinforcement Learning

Reinforcement learning (RL) is related to behavioral psychology, where an organism learns to do something by trial and error, as it gets positive or negative feedback, i.e., rewards or penalties. It is pertinent to note that reinforcement learning (RL) does not, like supervised learning, rely upon labeled datasets. It is rather a kind of learning that is based on interactions with the environment.

Policy Gradient (PG): The agent was trained to select actions that would secure the best outcomes for the expected rewards of threading and simulation. These methods are similar to policy gradient methods but from the point of view of control variates, which makes them more compatible with continuous action spaces [12].

SARSA: Complementing the above algorithms, SARSA is an on-policy learning algorithm besides TD learning and Q-learning, which means that the policy followed is the one used to update the Q-value function.

Q-learning: A popular RL algorithm, Q-learning, is an off-policy method that learns the value of taking certain actions in a given state, even if it is not currently the best policy. The Q-values are saved in a table, and the agent chooses the next action according to the maximal value of the Q-values.

Actor-Critic: This RL method intertwines policy and value functions. The actor identifies the best action to do, while the critic judges the action by giving a value to the function, hence correcting the policy among the way.

Deep Reinforcement Learning: With the introduction of artificial intelligence technologies, which include neural networks in reinforcement learning, it can be applied to tasks where the state space is very large and which can be modeled in recognition tasks, such as breaking a code.

In D2D communication, machine learning (ML) algorithms significantly impact performance optimization, resource management, and security enhancement. Reinforcement learning (RL) excels in dynamic resource allocation and interference management. By learning through interaction, RL allows devices to make real-time decisions, such as adjusting transmission power or selecting optimal frequency bands. This capability is crucial in decentralized environments, where network conditions change rapidly. RL's adaptability ensures efficient spectrum usage, minimizing collisions and boosting overall throughput.

Supervised learning, on the other hand, contributes through data-driven prediction and classification. It can predict link quality, user mobility, and traffic patterns by leveraging historical data, which aids in optimizing routing and handover decisions. For instance, in high-mobility environments, supervised learning models can forecast when a device will need to switch base stations, ensuring seamless connectivity.

Furthermore, both RL and supervised learning enhance security in D2D networks. RL can adapt to evolving threats and develop optimal defense strategies over time. Supervised learning models, which are trained on previous network behaviors, can detect anomalies and potential attacks. Together, these approaches enable D2D networks to become more adaptive, resource-efficient, and secure, making them integral to 6G networks and beyond.

12.4.4 Integration of Machine Learning in 6G Networks

The combination of machine learning (ML) and 6G is the next step in wireless communication, where modern algorithms and the sixth generation of mobile technology coexist, aiming to build a smarter, more efficient, and adaptive network and device that change not only the view but also the interaction of humans with wireless communication [20].

The subsequent wireless technology, 6G, will be the faster, more reliable, and more intelligent solution to the problem of connectivity. If put in very simple words, it is a better version of 5G, but it is expected to increase the speed of data transmission, reduce the latency to milliseconds, and improve the overall network efficiency. And it is not just about the internet being faster; we are talking about a network that should be able to support more devices, handle more data, and introduce a new category of capabilities such as AR and worldwide connectivity. This communications revolution will not only conquer the limits of the existing technology but also let us perform tasks beyond our imagination.

In D2D communication, integrating machine learning (ML) enhances network performance, with various use cases demonstrating its impact. Reinforcement learning (RL), for instance, is widely applied in dynamic spectrum allocation. In a congested urban environment, RL enables devices to autonomously select optimal frequency bands by learning from real-time feedback, reducing interference, and boosting network throughput. A practical example is using RL in smart city IoT systems, where thousands of devices need to communicate without centralized control. RL dynamically manages these devices' resources, ensuring efficient communication.

Supervised learning is useful for predicting user mobility and improving handover decisions in vehicular networks. For example, in a V2V (vehicle-to-vehicle) communication scenario, supervised learning models can predict when vehicles will move out of range of each other based on historical mobility data, ensuring seamless handover to new communication links without interruption. In another use case, supervised learning helps in traffic offloading, where high-bandwidth content is transferred between nearby devices, optimizing data traffic and reducing the burden on central networks.

These ML techniques also enhance security. For instance, RL can detect and respond to jamming attacks in D2D networks by dynamically adapting defense strategies, while supervised models can identify suspicious behavior patterns based on historical data.

Amplifying 6G Capabilities through Machine Learning

The main feature of machine learning in 6G networking is that the system learns, without being explicitly programmed, and marshals data, becoming context-aware as well as making intelligent decisions. When all these are added, 6G will be transformed from a network of data pipes to an organic-invisible-intelligent fabric. Above all, ML can use a more fine-grained optimization of resource allocation to attain ubiquitous low-delay communication in addition to ultrareliable communication in challenging environments. ML can also be the source of predictive technology that allows the network to forecast problems and take steps to prevent them before performance is affected. Moreover, ML can secure the network through real-time threat detection and response, personalized services by grasping and anticipating individuals, etc., so you will not only get a quicker but also an organic-invisible-intelligent fabric [11].

Advantages of Machine Learning in 6G

The ML technology can be used in 6G networks to dynamically manage the network resources in terms of bandwidth and latency and thus to achieve more effective performance.

Improved Connectivity: In a 6G network, ML can be used for up to end-to-end connectivity, which ensures that more global connectivity is being connected and multifunctional networks are being done.

New Methods: ML employs advanced algorithms such as supervised, unsupervised, deep learning, reinforcement learning, and federated learning to tackle resource allocation, task offloading, and handover management issues.

Energy Efficiency: Techniques of ML can highly increase the energy efficiency of 6G networks and, in return, diminish the latency and optimize the overall network operation.

Absolute Decentralization: AI and ML are among the tools integrated into 6G to come up with the optimal network design, manage dynamically the allocation of resources, and deal with the traffic flow in the interference-rich environment [5].

Large-Scale Optimization: ML is the most apt for the solution of problems connected to 6G and large-scale optimization through its ability to ensure the desired performance, high efficiency, expandability, and supposition.

Utmost Usage Scenarios: ML would be the natural enabler in applications 6G such as smart imaging, proximate technologies, and location awareness operated with the support of massive data warehouses and rich services.

12.5 Applications of Machine Learning in D2D Communication Resource Allocation and Spectrum Management

Resource Allocation and Spectrum Management:

Dynamic Spectrum Allocation: It can be noted that the oral use of 'spectrum congestion' was made by the non-technical members in the course of discussion as the ML algorithms are capable of analyzing the real-time network conditions and predicting the future congestion pattern of spectrum usage. This makes it possible to support the dynamic sharing of the physical spectrum resources, hence the available bandwidth, and mitigate interference in the flow of D2D data. Table 12.2 outlines various applications of machine learning (ML) in modern cellular networks:

Power Control: In the context of D2D, power control can be one of the areas in which ML can be applied to enhance the system and adapt to the environment to minimize power levels capable of interfering while guaranteeing the communication flow [16].

Interference Management

Interference Prediction: It is noted that interference is a potential problem in D2D communication; however, with the help of the ML models, it is possible to make an analysis based on historical information, and thus, the system will be able to foresee potential interference scenarios and prevent them in advance.

Table 12.2 Applications of machine learning for modern cellular networks.

Physical and mac layer	Network layer	SON	Network economy	New use cases and applications	Description
Channel estimation Channel coding Spectrum sensing and access	Energy consumption Resource management Fault detection	Organization Optimization Healing	Maintenance cost Management cost Service cost	Intelligent transmission Human-centric communication User behavior analysis Customized services for individual users	Small cell clustering Wi-Fi association D2D user clustering HetNet clustering

Adaptive Interference Cancellation: Some of the applications that can be achieved with the aid of ML include the ability of devices to adapt the communication parameters and cancel or at least minimize interference from other devices or other forms of interference.

Security and Privacy

Anomaly Detection: ML can be used to discover one or multiple suspicious P2P communication patterns that indicate such security risks as eavesdropping and unauthorized connection.

Privacy-Preserving Techniques: Some of the ML algorithms such as federated learning can be adopted in a manner that makes data processing be done locally on the devices without having to share any sensitive information with other people other than the intended recipient, while at the same time facilitating D2D communication.

Energy Efficiency

Energy-Aware Routing: ML can decide the best route to be taken depending on energy consumption patterns and, hence, increase the battery lifetime of devices that are participating in D2D communication.

Sleep Mode Optimization: That means that through the ML approach, they can be able to forecast the time when the devices are idle, and hence, they can switch them off to low power modes and only switch them back on to actively engage in communication.

Mobility Management

Handover Optimization: Control algorithms can estimate likely opportunities of leaving the range, hence when to perform the handover to achieve continuity during D2D communication.

Location Prediction: Mobility patterns can be used to predict the location of devices in the future; this will allow proper coordination and utilize resources in D2D communication.

12.6 Challenges and Solutions

First of all, the scalability and complexity of a project always remain big questions in the agile approach. Another potential concern that needs to be considered in the setting of ML in 6G D2D communication is the problem of a large number of variables required in the execution of the complex models of ML. With the increase in the number of devices in the network, the total amount of data generated in the network also increases, and therefore, there

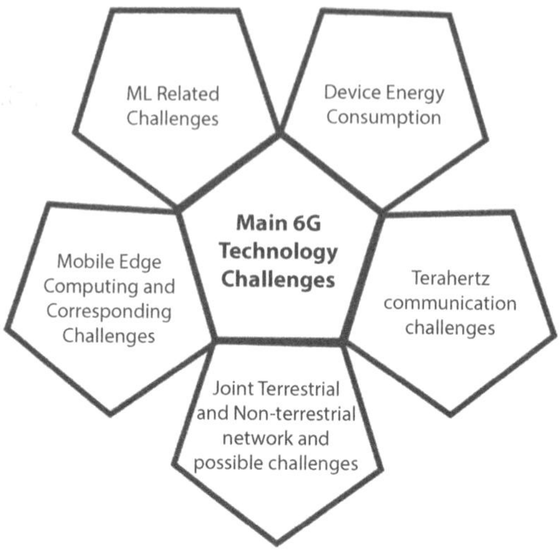

Figure 12.4 Main challenges in 6G technology.

is a considerable challenge in processing the data in real time, if not impossible. About the ML models that can be deployed into D2D communication, it is also vital to note that they may also be complex and may need large computational resources and power. This is a challenge because such a system can be hard to deploy in environments with limited resources such as IOT devices or edge-computing nodes. To tackle these issues, there are ongoing studies on methods of simplifying ML models and increasing the size of the models that can be handled. For instance, model compression, pruning, and quantization are some of the methods that can be employed to transform the ML modes to suit the limited environment. Furthermore, it is possible to use such approaches as federated learning and distributed learning to distribute the computation load related to ML models across multiple devices [14]. Figure 12.4 explains the main challenges in 6G technology.

Latency and Real-Time Handling

Overall, another challenge that needs to be addressed in 6G D2D communication is the solution's latency since numerous applications demand low response time. The incorporation of the ML into the D2D communication may lead to new sources of delay, which include the time taken by the models to analyze data before making decisions. To overcome this challenge, there are ongoing investigations on how to miniaturize its latency in a bid to enhance its real-time feature. For instance, edge computing and fog computing are the approaches that can be applied to employ the ML model closer to the data source; thus, the time needed for data transfer to a centralized processing unit is minimized, and the real-time applications will be enhanced [1].

Energy Efficiency and Battery Life

Energy efficiency and battery life are two factors that are capable of having a major impact on our work. Power consumption optimization is an important factor in Life Energy D2D communication especially for IoT devices that require long durations of use at a single charge. If we include ML in D2D communication, it will add an overhead as the models used in machine learning mean increased energy consumption of devices, as most of the models need computation power. This avenue is particularly problematic, and to this end, researchers are looking at ways to make the ML models consume less power and less time from the battery. For instance, energy-efficient inference and lightweight machine learning are some of the approaches that can be employed to enhance the efficiency of the ML models in the consumption of energy. Furthermore, self-powering concerns energy harvesting and energy-sensitive resource control that can be employed in managing the energy consumption of these devices.

12.7 Case Studies

Several real-world implementations and case studies have emerged as researchers, industries, and governments explore the potential of D2D communication in 6G networks using ML techniques.

12.7.1 Smart Cities and Urban IoT Networks

Location: South Korea
Overview: South Korea is one of the leading nations in exploring 6G technologies and smart cities. In Seoul, smart city initiatives leverage D2D communication for real-time traffic monitoring, pollution control, and energy management. Machine learning models predict congestion patterns and optimize resource allocation between devices for smoother communication.
Implementation: A real-world trial used ML algorithms for dynamic spectrum management, allowing devices to communicate directly based on their proximity and network conditions. The system used reinforcement

learning to allocate communication channels in real time, leading to a 30% reduction in communication delays.
Outcome: Enhanced traffic management systems, with reduced latency and improved real-time responses to incidents, provide smoother urban operations.

12.7.2 Autonomous Vehicles and Vehicular Communication

Location: Silicon Valley, USA
Overview: The push for autonomous vehicles has driven the need for reliable and low-latency communication. D2D communication plays a critical role by enabling vehicles to communicate directly with each other to share information about traffic, road conditions, and potential hazards. Machine learning facilitates better decision-making in dynamic environments.
Implementation: A project by Tesla integrated D2D communication with machine learning algorithms to predict and optimize vehicle paths. The ML models continuously learned from vehicle interactions, weather patterns, and traffic conditions to make real-time decisions about when to switch from centralized communication to D2D for more efficient data exchange.
Outcome: The implementation showed improved traffic flow, reduced collisions, and better energy management through optimized routes and communication paths.

12.7.3 Healthcare and Wearable Devices

Location: Japan
Overview: In the healthcare sector, wearable devices connected *via* D2D communication are being explored for patient monitoring, especially in elderly care. Devices can directly communicate with each other to monitor heart rates, glucose levels, and other vital signs, with machine learning providing predictive analytics for early diagnosis and intervention.
Implementation: Japan's health sector trailed D2D communication in elderly care homes. Wearable devices, equipped with ML algorithms, dynamically adjusted their communication protocols based on the health conditions of the wearer. Anomalies detected by one device were instantly communicated to other devices and central monitoring systems using D2D protocols.
Outcome: The trial reported a 40% improvement in early detection of health issues, such as falls and heart attacks, due to real-time device communication and predictive health analytics.

12.7.4 Augmented Reality (AR) and Immersive Media

Location: China
Overview: In the field of entertainment and AR, China has been pioneering 6G-based AR experiences that use D2D communication for real-time rendering and interaction. Machine learning algorithms enable devices to predict user movements and actions to optimize the flow of data between devices.
Implementation: A large-scale AR gaming event in Beijing demonstrated the capabilities of D2D communication, where users' devices communicated directly to maintain the synchronization of game environments. ML models predict user interactions to allocate bandwidth dynamically and reduce latency.
Outcome: The event saw a marked improvement in user experience, with smoother interactions and less lag, setting the foundation for future large-scale AR applications.

12.8 Challenges and Future Scope

The future of integrating machine learning (ML) in D2D communication offers immense potential but also presents several gaps and challenges. As 6G networks develop, ML will become essential for managing the increasing complexity of D2D systems, enabling self-organizing, efficient, and secure communication. However, scalability remains a challenge. Current ML models often struggle to handle the vast number of devices in dense environments, necessitating future research into more efficient algorithms that can manage these large-scale deployments.

Another area for growth is in energy efficiency. While ML enhances resource allocation, many current models require significant computational power, which may drain battery life in D2D devices. Future work needs to focus on lightweight, low-energy algorithms that balance performance with device limitations.

Security is another crucial aspect. While supervised learning and reinforcement learning improve anomaly detection, evolving threats such as sophisticated cyberattacks in 6G environments require more robust models. Future research must explore integrating advanced techniques, such as federated learning, which enhances security by training models locally without sharing sensitive data.

Lastly, there is a need for real-world implementations and large-scale testing to move ML-driven D2D from theory to practice. Bridging these gaps will be key to realizing the full potential of ML in future D2D systems.

12.9 Conclusion

Machine learning–enhanced D2D communication supports the personalization and customization of services, particularly in environments where diverse devices and applications are involved. For example, in healthcare, wearable devices equipped with ML algorithms can adapt their communication patterns based on the real-time health status of users, ensuring timely and accurate transmission of critical data. Similarly, in autonomous vehicular networks, ML enables real-time decision-making for routing, collision avoidance, and traffic management by allowing vehicles to communicate directly and intelligently with each other. In immersive media and augmented reality (AR), D2D communication enhanced by ML facilitates real-time interaction and synchronization of experiences between users. ML models can predict user actions and adjust bandwidth allocation, allowing for smoother and more responsive AR experiences. This is especially important in large-scale events or densely populated environments where centralized communication systems may struggle to handle the load efficiently. By leveraging D2D communication, devices can share data directly and optimize their performance based on local conditions, resulting in better user experiences. The success of ML-enhanced D2D communication in 6G also depends on the development of standardized protocols and frameworks that can support the seamless integration of AI-driven decision-making processes. Collaboration between industries, governments, and research institutions will be essential to establish these standards and drive innovation in this field. Furthermore, real-world testing and experimentation will be crucial in validating the performance of ML-based D2D communication systems and ensuring their readiness for deployment in commercial networks. However, achieving the full potential of ML-enhanced D2D communication will require overcoming technical challenges related to security, scalability, and interference management. With continued research and collaboration, the future of wireless communication in the 6G era promises to be more dynamic, efficient, and intelligent than ever before.

References

1. Alhammadi, A., *et al.*, Artificial Intelligence in 6G Wireless Networks: Opportunities, Applications, and Challenges, in: *International Journal of Intelligent Systems*, El Kafhali, S. (Ed.), 2024, pp. 1–27, 2024, https://www.hindawi.com/journals/ijis/2024/8845070/.
2. Amer, A., Ahmad, A.-M., S.H., Resource Allocation for Downlink Full-Duplex Cooperative NOMA-Based Cellular System with Imperfect SI Cancellation and Underlaying D2D Communications. *Sensors*, 21, 8, 2768, 2021, https://www.mdpi.com/1424-8220/21/8/2768.
3. Basar, E., *et al.*, Wireless Communications Through Reconfigurable Intelligent Surfaces. *IEEE Access*, 7, 116753–73, 2019, https://ieeexplore.ieee.org/document/8796365/.
4. Cai, Y., *et al.*, Power Allocation for NOMA in D2D Relay Communications. *China Commun.*, 18, 1, 61–69, 2021, https://ieeexplore.ieee.org/document/9339830/.
5. Fang, C., *et al.*, Deep-Reinforcement-Learning-Based Resource Allocation for Content Distribution in Fog Radio Access Networks. *IEEE Internet Things J.*, 9, 18, 16874–83, 2022, https://ieeexplore.ieee.org/document/9691477/.
6. Gismalla, M.S.M., *et al.*, Survey on Device to Device (D2D) Communication for 5GB/6G Networks: Concept, Applications, Challenges, and Future Directions. *IEEE Access*, 10, 30792–821, 2022, https://ieeexplore.ieee.org/document/9737127/.
7. Al-Bowarab, H., Mustafa, N.A.Z., Abidin, Z.Z., Maseer, Z.K., Review on Device-to-Device Communication in Cellular Based Network Systems. *Int. J. Eng. Technol.*, 7, 3.20, 435–40, 2018, https://www.sciencepubco.com/index.php/ijet/article/view/20587.
8. Hmila, M., Fernández-Veiga, M., Rodríguez-Pérez, M., Herrería-Alonso, S., Non-Orthogonal Multiple Access for Unicast and Multicast D2D: Channel Assignment, Power Allocation and Energy Efficiency. *Sensors*, 21, 10, 3436, 2021, https://www.mdpi.com/1424-8220/21/10/3436.
9. Ioannou, I., Christophorou, C., Vassiliou, V., Pitsillides, A., A Novel Distributed AI Framework with ML for D2D Communication in 5G/6G Networks. *Comput. Netw.*, 211, 108987, 2022, https://linkinghub.elsevier.com/retrieve/pii/S138912862200158X.
10. Lam, T.T. and Di Renzo, M., On the Energy Efficiency of Heterogeneous Cellular Networks With Renewable Energy Sources—A Stochastic Geometry Framework. *IEEE Trans. Wireless Commun.*, 19, 10, 6752–70, 2020, https://ieeexplore.ieee.org/document/9134826/.
11. Lee, W. and Schober, R., Deep Learning-Based Resource Allocation for Device-to-Device Communication. *IEEE Trans. Wireless Commun.*, 21, 7, 5235–50, 2022, https://ieeexplore.ieee.org/document/9673099/.

12. Letaief, K.B., Shi, Y., Lu, J., Lu, J., Edge Artificial Intelligence for 6G: Vision, Enabling Technologies, and Applications. *IEEE J. Sel. Areas Commun.*, 40, 1, 5–36, 2022, https://ieeexplore.ieee.org/document/9606720/.
13. Nguyen, T.N., *et al.*, On the Performance of Underlay Device-to-Device Communications. *Sensors*, 22, 4, 1456, 2022, https://www.mdpi.com/1424-8220/22/4/1456.
14. Noman, H.M.F., *et al.*, Machine Learning Empowered Emerging Wireless Networks in 6G: Recent Advancements, Challenges and Future Trends. *IEEE Access*, 11, 83017–51, 2023, https://ieeexplore.ieee.org/document/10209158/.
15. Puspitasari, A.A., An, T.T., Alsharif, M.H., Lee, B.M., Emerging Technologies for 6G Communication Networks: Machine Learning Approaches. *Sensors*, 23, 18, 7709, 2023, https://www.mdpi.com/1424-8220/23/18/7709.
16. Sun, Y., *et al.*, Harmonizing Artificial Intelligence with Radio Access Networks: Advances, Case Study, and Open Issues. *IEEE Network*, 35, 4, 144–51, 2021, https://ieeexplore.ieee.org/document/9520336/.
17. Tu, L.-T., Bradai, A., Pousset, Y., A., II, Energy Efficiency Analysis of LoRa Networks. *IEEE Wireless Commun. Lett.*, 10, 9, 1881–85, 2021, https://ieeexplore.ieee.org/document/9444332/.
18. Wang, J., Song, X., Ma, Y., A Novel Resource Allocation Scheme in NOMA-Based Cellular Network with D2D Communications. *Future Internet*, 12, 1, 8, 2020, https://www.mdpi.com/1999-5903/12/1/8.
19. Wang, L., *et al.*, Phase Separation and Sample Size Independence of Fracture Strength for (Mg0.585Cu0.305Y0.11)95Be5 Bulk Metallic Glass. *J. Non-Cryst. Solids*, 370, 1–5, 2013, https://linkinghub.elsevier.com/retrieve/pii/S0022309313001798.
20. Wu, W., Liu, R., Yang, Q., Quek, T.Q.S., Learning-Based Robust Resource Allocation for D2D Underlaying Cellular Network. *IEEE Trans. Wireless Commun.*, 21, 8, 6731–45, 2022, https://ieeexplore.ieee.org/document/9720998/.
21. Yang, F., *et al.*, Multi-IRS-Assisted MmWave MIMO Communication Using Twin-Timescale Channel State Information. *IEEE Trans. Commun.*, 70, 9, 6370–84, 2022, https://ieeexplore.ieee.org/document/9819898/.

Part IV

QUANTUM COMPUTING AND MACHINE LEARNING

13

Integrating Quantum Computing and Machine Learning in 6G Networks

Ogobuchi D. Okey[1,2*], Theodore T. Chiagunye[2], Henrietta U. Udeani[2], Ikechukwu Nicholas[2], Renata L. Rosa[3] and Demóstenes R. Zegarra[3]

[1]*Center for Engineering, Modelling and Applied Science (CECS), Federal University of ABC, Santo Andre, Sao Paulo, Brazil*
[2]*Department of Computer Engineering, Michael Okpara University of Agriculture, Umudike, Abia State, Nigeria*
[3]*Department of Computer Science, Federal University of Lavras, Minas Gerais, Brazil*

Abstract
The sixth-generation (6G) wireless networks are anticipated to have a transformative impact on communication methods, facilitating high-speed data transfer rates, extensive connectivity, and applications with minimal latency. The escalating intricacy and magnitude of 6G networks present noteworthy obstacles for conventional computing paradigms. In order to tackle these obstacles, the integration of quantum computing (QC) and machine learning (ML) methodologies within the framework of 6G networks is needed to improve its robustness and handle issues relating to resource allocation, bandwidth, and spectrum management. This chapter provides a thorough examination of the latest advancements in the field of fusing QC and ML to cater to the requirements of 6G technology. We highlight and discuss how quantum computing's unique features, like superposition and entanglement, could improve the effectiveness of machine learning algorithms in the context of 6G networks. Additionally, this study explores the utilization of quantum machine learning (QML) techniques within the confines of 6G, aimed at improving the dynamics required to meet the sophisticated architecture of 6G. On top of the foregoing, we explore in detail the security implications and frameworks for implementing QML in 6G networks. Quantum cryptography methods, exemplified by quantum key distribution, offer heightened protection against unauthorized access and data breaches, thereby safeguarding the confidentiality and

**Corresponding author*: okey.ogobuchi@mouau.edu.ng

Pallavi Sapkale, Shilpa Mehta and S. Balamurugan (eds.) Quantum Computing and Machine Learning for 6G, (285–310) © 2026 Scrivener Publishing LLC

integrity of data conveyed through 6G networks. Ultimately, the benefits of QML and a roadmap outlining potential avenues for future research in this nascent field are presented. The study highlights the importance of the creation of quantum computing architectures that are both scalable and fault-tolerant, as well as the development of QML algorithms, which are optimized for 6G networks. The findings of this research are robust and enable students to gain in-depth knowledge of the concept of QML and assist in further research.

Keywords: Quantum computing, 6G network, quantum machine learning, 6G security, artificial intelligence, QML algorithms

13.1 Introduction

The increasing demand for faster, more secure, and reliable Internet services, driven by the widespread increase in Internet usage and the proliferation of complex computing devices, continues to stimulate innovative research and development efforts. The undeniable success of fifth-generation (5G) networks, praised by both individuals and businesses for improving Internet experiences and accelerating information exchange, has sparked an unyielding pursuit of even faster and more adaptable communication solutions. As a result, the relentless quest for sixth-generation (6G) networks remains a major focus of exploration [1].

Extensive research has demonstrated that beyond 5G (B5G) technology possesses the potential to usher in novel network deployment models, ushering in higher data rates, extensive network capacity, seamless connectivity, and ultrareliable low-latency communication empowered with high-level intelligence to meet the emerging network demands [2]. The 6G paradigm represents an evolutionary communication platform that harnesses the power of network software and satellite communication to deliver rapid response times and cost-efficient ultradense networks [3]. Moreover, the defining characteristics of 6G, including ultralow latency, expansive network coverage, ultrahigh-speed capabilities, the infusion of network intelligence, and unmatched reliability, lay the groundwork for innovative technologies spanning virtual reality, interconnected robotics, autonomous systems that enable intelligent, self-managed operations, disseminated blockchain that offers secure, decentralized ledger for transactions and data storage, and augmented reality that empowers our perception of the world in real time [4, 5].

Efforts to provide the vast connectivity required by 6G coupled with the efficient processing of copious data at both user and network endpoints necessitate a substantial degree of automation and intelligence [5–7].

Integrating artificial intelligence (AI), quantum computing (QC), machine learning (ML), and quantum machine learning (QML) into the 6G architectural framework promises to unlock the full potential of this forthcoming technology set to debut by 2030 [8]. ML currently shows great potential to enhance network management across various layers, aiding the recovery of information using investigative and predictive intelligence to determine system behaviors, data mining, and adequately configure communications rules, resource allocation, and service provisioning at scale. However, ML-based processes, especially deep learning algorithms, require a heavy learning phase, hence the need for higher computational resources [9]. Unfortunately, these are not adequately provided by the current computing power offered through classical computing [10].

Furthermore, the complexities of 6G necessitate swifter computing functionalities, a feat that classical computers alone cannot achieve. QC has rapidly emerged as a field that allows for efficient quantum computations, enabling us to address complex challenges and previously unsolvable tasks more effectively than traditional computers [11]. QC technology excels at addressing formidable computational problems, including non-convex optimization, intensive computation, and algorithmic search functions. Prevailing research highlights the vast potential and capabilities of QC in improving practical usage and accelerating computational processes with exceptional efficiency. QC utilizes quantum phenomena to solve complex mathematical problems that classical computers find challenging, often utilizing advanced processing hardware units [12].

As a result, some scientific contributions have highlighted the possibilities of integrating QML into the design of 6G architecture. These contributions leverage ML algorithms based on quantum computing as a building block for the intelligent network [13–15]. In reference [16], a detailed analysis regarding the specifications pertaining to the 6G network was presented, highlighting such areas' air interface and inherent ancillary know-how. The critical examination of key performance indicators (KPIs) pertinent to both 5G and 6G was evaluated, shedding light on latent challenges and possibilities for investigations. Reference [17] undertook a rigorous exploration of the synergy between quantum information technology (QIT) and QKD to support the evolving 6G systems. Their investigation extends to elucidating the ways in which QIT stands to elevate and contribute to the development of 6G-enabled systems, particularly in information sharing and problem-solving. Reference [18] emphasized the significance of QKD in ensuring secure communication in upcoming wireless networks, while [19] explained how QML contributes to enhancing the efficiency and accuracy of optimization algorithms, suggesting that

QML holds the promise of significantly improving the performance and adaptability of 6G networks. The authors of reference [7] investigated the opportunities and challenges of AI's adoption into 6G wireless networks. Notwithstanding the inclusion of QC in 6G systems, the exploration of resultant network architectures and the assessment of design ramifications arising from the implementation of extensive network intelligence schemes remain uncharted territories in current research [5].

This chapter considers in detail the theory and implications of integrating QC and ML in 6G. It highlights the major concerns with resource allocation and security, discusses the various QML algorithms, and elucidates the frameworks that empower the application of QML algorithms. We explore some challenges that impact the practical deployment of 6G and conclude with prominent research directions.

13.2 Background Study

13.2.1 Technology Evolutionary Trends Toward 6G Network

Mobile communication has undergone significant development and expansion since the early 1980s. Extensive research has identified distinct eras characterized by improvements in data rates, connectivity, and functionality. These advancements have given rise to different generations of mobile communication, from 1G to 6G [20].

The initial 1G network [21] had low data transfer rates and subpar audio quality, primarily used for voice communication in areas such as the Nordic mobile telephone (NMT) and total access communication system (TACS). In the 1990s, the introduction of 2G improved upon 1G, incorporating features like short message services and basic email functionality. This success led to the development of technologies like the global system for mobile communication (GSM) and personal digital service (PDS) [22].

In the 2000s and 2010s, 3G and 4G were introduced, respectively [23, 24]. Each new generation built upon the previous one, offering higher data transfer rates and introducing new technologies like code division multiple access 2000 (CDMA) in 3G and long-term evolution (LTE) in 4G. The fifth-generation (5G) network, introduced with the aim of improved data rates and security, brought even more impressive capabilities, including expanded network coverage, higher speeds, and ultralow latency [25]. This laid the foundation for the emergence of the Internet of Things (IoT), the Fourth Industrial Revolution, and smart cities in the 2020s.

While artificial intelligence (AI) was introduced for optimization and automation during these decades, it was not integrated into the core network architecture. This integration is a key feature of the sixth-generation (6G) architecture, which has the potential to provide unparalleled transmission speed, ultralow latency, and advanced coverage. 6G is expected to incorporate newer technologies, such as terahertz communication, millimeter-wave communication, reconfigurable intelligent surfaces, and ultra-massive MIMO. Researchers have identified that the emerging 6G network can bring immense benefits to sectors such as healthcare, entertainment and media, finance and banking, transportation, and education.

13.2.2 Unique Features of 6G Networks

With the expectation that 6G will advance the current 5G technology, there are key features that empower 6G over previous networks, thereby increasing its possibilities. They include increased spectral efficiency of up to 10 times above those of 5G, extended coverage to include deep-sea, underground areas and space, and enhanced user experience (UX) by amplifying the capabilities and usage of extended reality such as virtual reality (VR) and augmented reality (AR). The 6G also includes a fast data exchange rate of up to 10 Tbps, ultralow latency within the range of 0.1 ms, a wide range

Figure 13.1 Core features of 6G network.

Table 13.1 Summary of the comparison of the mobile communication trends.

Evaluation metric	1G	2G	3G	4G	5G	6G
Maximum data transfer rate	Up to 2.4 kbps	Up to 64 kbps	Up to 2 Mbps	Up to 1 Gbps	Up to 10 Gbps	Up to 10 Tbps
Minimum latency	Not specified	200–400 ms	100–150 ms	10–20 ms	1 ms	0.1 ms
Device density per km^2	Not specified	Not specified	± 1000	±100,000	±1 million	±10 million
Energy efficiency	Relatively low	More than 1G	Moderate	1x previous	100x more than 4G	100x more than 5G with optimization
Spectral efficiency	Not specified	Not specified	Moderate	Higher than 3G	Up to 5x more than 4G	10x more than 5G
Spectrum availability	Limited	Expanded	1x more than 2G	Higher frequency bands	mmWave and sub-6 GHz	mmWave, THz, and others
Maximum mobility	Vehicular mobility	Handheld devices	More enhancement	200 km/h	300 km/h	600 km/h
AI integration	Nil	Nil	Nile	Nil	Available	Advanced
Available technology	Analog cellular	Digital voice and SMS	Mobile broadband	LTE, WiMAX	mmWave, Massive MIMO	THz, Orbital angular momentum

of broadband connection for over 1 million devices per square kilometer, full integration with AI, and a high level of energy efficiency. Figure 13.1 summarizes the core features and advantages of 6G networks. Based on some evaluation metrics, we summarize the key differences between the six mobile communication generations in Table 13.1.

13.2.3 The Principle of Quantum Computing

Quantum computing is an advanced technology that has recently achieved a great audience for addressing complex problems that defy conventional approaches [26] using quantum mechanics. It hinges on three fundamental properties: superposition, entanglement, and interference. In the realm of quantum computing, superposition allows a quantum-based system to exist simultaneously in multiple states, thereby allowing quantum computers to process information in parallel, an approach that is fundamentally different from classical procedures. It enables quantum computers to explore multiple solutions to a problem at once, potentially leading to exponential speedup tasks. Entanglement, intrinsic to quantum mechanics, binds entities together indefinitely, thus enabling quantum computers to perform operations on qubits distributed over long distances without any loss of coherence. It forms the basis for quantum teleportation and is vital for various quantum algorithms. Meanwhile, interference may alter quantum states by magnifying impulses in the desired path and attenuating signals in the opposite way [8].

In contrast to classical computing, which employs binary bits representing information as either 0 or 1, quantum computing employs qubits capable of existing in multiple states simultaneously. This facilitates parallel processing and accelerates problem-solving beyond the capabilities of classical computers. At the same time, classical computers use bits, and QC uses "qubit" for its operations. In a conventional computer process, data are encoded using bits that can either be a 0 or 1. Unlike classical bits, it is easy to encode qubit in one of the states, $|0\rangle$ or $|1\rangle$, or in a direct combination of the two states, as illustrated in Figure 13.2. Qubits serve as data storage units and are conventionally denoted by $|\psi\rangle = \alpha|0\rangle + \beta|1\rangle$, where $|0\rangle$ and $|1\rangle$ represents the binary computational positions, and α and β represent the intricate elevation associated with the state, subject to $|\alpha|^2 + |\beta|^2 = 1$ as constraints.

QC leverages the power of quantum parallelism to unlock considerably higher processing speeds compared to traditional computing approaches. Considering some scenarios, it achieves quantum supremacy, especially in optimization problems. To further bolster quantum computing's

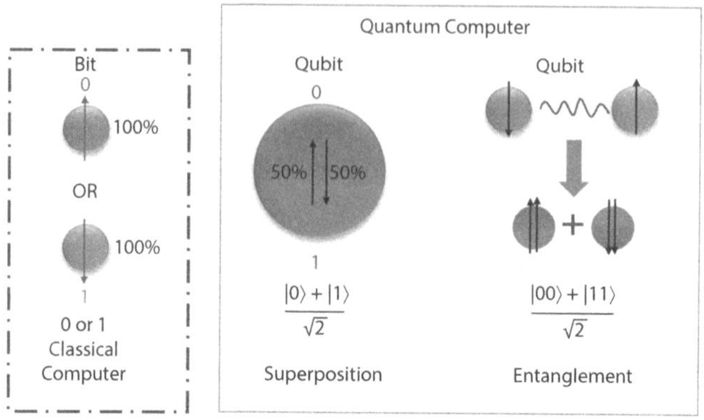

Figure 13.2 Demonstration of bits (classical) and qubit (quantum) computing. In a classical state, the probability of obtaining a "1" or "0" during computation is 100%. However, in a superposed state, a qubit can be in a state of 0⟩ or 1⟩ of both 0⟩ and 1⟩. This means that the chances of getting an outcome are 50% each. In the entanglement scenario, the properties of two qubits are linked to each other such that observing one of them will reveal the other qubits, even when they are at physically large separations.

capabilities, machine learning algorithms can be distributed across interconnected quantum computers, augmenting the number of operational qubits and sometimes leveraging on QPUs [3].

13.2.4 Machine Learning

ML is a subset of AI that focuses on the creation of algorithmic systems that use information from the input to produce predicted outcomes. These algorithms facilitate various tasks, including categorization, regression analysis, and enabling intelligent agents to interact effectively within wireless environments [17]. Generally, ML can be grouped into three categories, namely, supervised, unsupervised, and reinforcement learning [27]. Supervised learning models are instrumental in predicting and classifying predefined attributes. They undergo training using a dataset comprising input-output pairs, allowing them to refine their predictive capabilities over time. Unsupervised learning, on the other hand, directly examines unlabeled input data to uncover hidden structures within the data. This exploration can yield valuable insights from the dataset. Finally, models that use reinforcement learning generate decisions by choosing a pattern of behaviors that optimize compounded rewards based on input from the environment at every phase.

In line with the vast possibilities offered by ML algorithms in problem-solving and intelligent decision-making, they are applied in various domains to handle a variety of tasks. Authors in [27, 28] have applied ML to develop intrusion detection system (IDS) models to improve computer networks and Internet-of-Things (IoT) security. In the computer network scenario and at different levels of the open systems interconnection (OSI) paradigm, ML can offer different assistance in improving its functionality. For instance, convolutional neural networks (CNNs) are used in the physical layer for optimizing orthogonal frequency-division multiplexing receivers, channel decoding, and detecting and classifying signals [9]. ML also plays an important role in channel estimation, improving the appropriate selection of transmission frequencies and accurate management of the reflection angles of intelligent reflective surfaces (IRS). This, in turn, mitigates the adverse effects of attenuation in high-frequency communications [5]. Furthermore, inside the data-link layer, ML-based algorithms improve data transfer efficiency and dynamically distribute network bandwidth and other resources, as well as reduce network overhead and delay, even in diverse settings.

ML methods assist in different purposes, including predicting cacheable data contents at specific network locations, making decisions regarding target cells during handovers, cum effectively managing the load on the network by classifying the traffic in the network layer [4]. Additionally, user mobility predictions support software-defined networking (SDN) as well as network function virtualization (NFV) paradigms, allowing optimal network configuration and the allocation of computing and communication assets. Within the application layer, ML analyzes packet characteristics like size and inter-arrival times to categorize data streams by application type, hence enabling the implementation of highly optimized resource distribution strategies [9, 29].

Despite the foregoing unquestionable benefits, the learning process is still challenged by long computation times and high computational power requirements. In the 6G ecosystem, the timing and resource constraints should be balanced, especially communication latency. Aggregating QC and ML, referred to as QML, holds high possibilities. Based on the foregoing, the convergence of QC, ML, and 6G networks holds the capacity to improve telecommunications by enhancing data acquisition, processing, and analysis, as well as providing more secure communications.

13.3 Quantum Machine Learning Algorithms and Implementation Frameworks

Processing the colossal volumes of data that are envisaged in 6G use cases presents a formidable challenge, demanding computational power and time capabilities that exceed current system capabilities. Conventional machine learning techniques, while effective, suffer from protracted processing times as data scales. The extensive, sometimes iterative, learning phases mandated by traditional ML algorithms [13] necessitate substantial computational resources. In response, the superior speed of QC, when addressing specific challenges compared to classical computing, has spurred an increasing number of researchers to explore the utilization of QC for more efficient problem-solving, ushering in a burgeoning area of research known as quantum machine learning (QML).

QML employs the principles of quantum superposition, intertwined with quantum entanglement, cum some fundamental aspects of quantum physics to execute computational tasks. QML finds application in optimizing 6G network communication, where it combines ML and QC as pivotal enabling assets. This convergence attempts to apply quantum mechanics to improve learning and inference processes by adapting traditional algorithms into quantum-computing frameworks [8].

QML focuses on developing algorithms that can harness the capabilities of quantum computers to supercharge ML tasks and promises to offer solutions to problems that are currently considered complex using classical systems, such as efficiently analyzing massive datasets and identifying complex patterns. This breakthrough can transform spectrum optimization and network management. Within this context, in [11], the authors delve into the landscape of 6G, exploring its vision and essential prerequisites, particularly focusing on its core enabling technologies of ML and QC. The authors conducted a comprehensive examination and exploration of machine learning, deep learning, and quality control in relation to 6G systems and highlighted prospective advantages, limitations, and potential use cases.

The implementation of QML in 6G aimed at solving pertinent challenges follows the paradigm used in classical ML tasks, which involve data collection, data preparation, model training, testing, and deployment, as in Figure 13.3.

A comprehensive exploration of QML algorithms reveals a rich landscape within the literature [8]. In this overview, we aim to provide a concise summary of the most prevalent QML algorithms while elucidating their

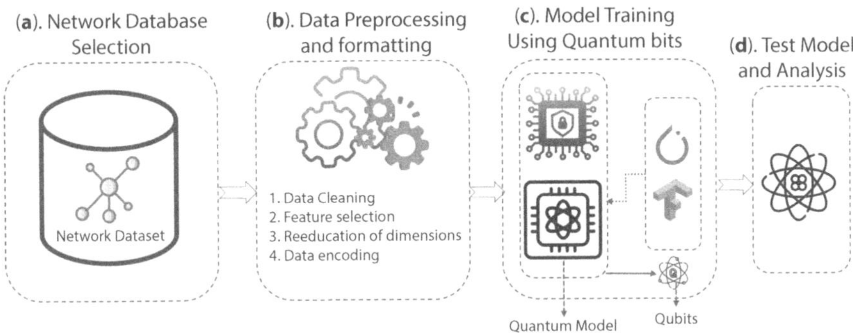

Figure 13.3 Method for implementing QML in 6G scenario.

suitability for specific task categories, namely, supervised, unsupervised, and reinforcement learning paradigms, as shown in Table 13.2.

Quantum support vector machine (QSVM) [30] extends classical SVMs to the quantum realm. They use quantum feature maps and quantum kernels to encode and classify data in quantum states. QSVM has the potential for quantum speedup and is suited for quantum data and high-dimensional problems. In 6G networks, QSVM can be used for tasks like network optimization, anomaly detection, and real-time resource allocation, enhancing network efficiency and security.

Quantum neural networks (QNN) aggregate classical artificial neural networks (ANN) and quantum information to design algorithms that are more robust. However, the training process is similar to that of the classical approach. In both cases, the effectiveness of the neural network (NN) is determined with the cost function, defining the relationship between the actual and expected output. For instance, given that weights (ω) at each step with biases (b) is defined by the mathematical expression $C(\omega,b)$, then, in a classical scenario, (ω) and (b) are adequately adjusted according to Equation 13.1.

$$C(\omega,b)=\frac{1}{N}\sum_{i}\frac{||y(i)-a^{out}(i)||}{2} \tag{13.1}$$

with $y(i)$ being the anticipated output and $a^{out}(i)$ being the real output, where $C(\omega,b)=0$, indicates a fully optimized function. Conversely, in QNN, we estimate the cost function considering how reliable the outcome information state ρ^{out} is in relation to the ideal outcome ϕ^{out}. This results in the modification of the unitary transformers at each iteration and achieving optimization at $C = 1$, as expressed in Equation 13.2 [4, 31, 32].

$$C = \frac{1}{N}\sum_{i}^{N}\langle \phi^{out} | \rho^{out} | \phi^{out} \rangle \tag{13.2}$$

Quantum CNN (QCNN) [33] is inspired by classical CNNs that employs quantum circuits and qubits to process and extract features from quantum data suitable for image processing and quantum pattern recognition. QCNN find relevance in 6G networks for quantum data classification, security, and optimizing quantum communication protocols.

Other QML algorithms include but are not limited to a continuous-variable instantaneous quantum polynomial (CV-IQP) [33–35], variational quantum Boltzmann machines (VarQBM) [36], variational quantum linear solver (VarQLS) [37, 38], circuit-centric quantum classifiers (CCQC) [39], and quantum k-means algorithm (QKA) [40, 41]. CV-IQP shines in solving polynomial optimization problems, while the VarQLS is more efficient with linear systems of equations. VarQBM leverages variational quantum circuits to represent and learn complex probability distributions, making it suitable for generative modeling.

These QML algorithms utilize different quantum search algorithms (QSA), such as Shor's period-finding and Grover's search algorithm, to optimize complex processes and improve QC efficiency. Shor's approach improves speed in determining a function's terminal using quantum knowledge to efficiently factorize integers with reduced cost function [42]. The use of quantum parallelism in Shor's algorithm gives it an edge in the QML process. On the other hand, Grover's search is suitable for searches in unstructured data that portray a high probability of yielding a target result, thereby handling the frequent black box challenge in ML [43, 44] with easier implementation compared with the Shor's search algorithm.

In addition to the various algorithms, there are several frameworks that integrate multiple of them to facilitate experimental studies. Frameworks such as Qiskit [45], Amazon Braket [46], Strawberry Fields [47], Pennylane [48], Forest [49], Microsoft Qdk, Tensorflow Quantum [50], and Qibo [51] offer platforms for experimenting with various QML algorithms. Each framework provides support for different kinds of quantum-enabled algorithms for either classification or regression tasks in supervised, unsupervised, or reinforcement learning scenarios, as summarized in Tables 13.2 and 13.3.

Table 13.2 Commonly used quantum machine learning algorithms.

Algorithm	Description	Type of ML	Use case in 6G network
Quantum kernel machine (QKM)	A supervised learning algorithm that uses a quantum circuit to learn a kernel function.	Supervised	Regression, classification, and clustering
Quantum neural network (QNN)	An NN that employs quantum circuits as its nodes and edges.	Supervised, unsupervised, or reinforcement	Image classification, natural language processing, and network segmentation
Quantum principal component analysis (QPCA)	An unsupervised learning approach that implements a quantum circuit to identify principal components datasets.	Unsupervised	Dimensionality reduction, clustering, and anomaly detection
Variational quantum classifier (VQC)	Uses a quantum circuit–based supervised approach for solving classification tasks.	Supervised	Classification of network traffic, modulation schemes, and channel conditions
Quantum-enabled support vector machine (QSVM)	SVM algorithms that enhance its performance using qubits.	Supervised	Classification of network traffic, modulation schemes, and channel conditions

(*Continued*)

Table 13.2 Commonly used quantum machine learning algorithms. (*Continued*)

Algorithm	Description	Type of ML	Use case in 6G network
Quantum Boltzmann machine (QBM)	Learn a probabilistic graphical model.	Unsupervised	Dimensionality reduction, clustering, and anomaly detection
Quantum annealing (QA)	A heuristic optimization algorithm that helps to ascertain the quantum system's ground state.	Reinforcement learning	Resource allocation, scheduling, and routing
Quantum error correction (QEC)	A technique for correcting errors that occur during quantum computation.	Unsupervised	Improving the reliability of QML

Table 13.3 Description of available frameworks for QML experiments.

Framework	Description	Strengths	Weaknesses
TensorFlow quantum (TFQ)	A framework developed by Google that allows you to build and train hybrid quantum-classical machine learning models. It integrates with TensorFlow, a popular ML framework, and provides high-performance quantum circuit simulators.	Easy to use, well-documented, large community	Not yet as mature as some other frameworks

(*Continued*)

Table 13.3 Description of available frameworks for QML experiments. (*Continued*)

Framework	Description	Strengths	Weaknesses
Qiskit	It includes a quantum circuit simulator, a compiler for translating quantum programs to different hardware backends, and a library of quantum algorithms.	Wide range of features and capabilities, well-supported by IBM	Can be complex to use, not as well-documented as some other frameworks
ProjectQ	It provides a high-level API for creating and manipulating quantum circuits, as well as a compiler for translating circuits to different hardware backends.	Easy to use, open-source, well-documented	Not as many features as some other frameworks
Forest	A framework developed by Rigetti Computing that provides a high-level API for creating and manipulating quantum circuits. It is designed to be efficient and scalable, and it includes a number of quantum machine learning algorithms.	Efficient, scalable, well-documented	Not as many features as some other frameworks

(*Continued*)

Table 13.3 Description of available frameworks for QML experiments. (*Continued*)

Framework	Description	Strengths	Weaknesses
Xanadu Strawberry Fields	A framework for quantum computing in Python. It supports a variety of quantum machine learning algorithms, including variational quantum circuits, quantum annealing, and quantum error correction.	Easy to use, well-documented, actively developed	Not as many features as some other frameworks

13.4 Resource Allocation in QML-Enabled 6G Network

The complexity of the 6G network cum the integration of QML require an established mechanism to properly manage the available resources to achieve the desired performance. The 6G network needs to allocate QC resources, including qubits and quantum gates, efficiently, which includes determining how many qubits are needed for specific tasks and ensuring that quantum processors are allocated to perform quantum algorithms effectively. Some of the resources that need to be allocated efficiently include bandwidth, processing power, energy, network slicing, security resources, traffic polarization, qubit, and resource optimization algorithms. Resource allocation is a multifaceted process that requires different approaches, including specific network requirements, network architecture, cum use cases. Whichever technique is adopted in achieving the efficient utilization of the resources can be static, dynamic, or AI-engineered [4, 11, 12, 17].

In a static resource allocation scenario, predefined network configuration and demands are the basis for resource allocation, and these factors have been determined to remain the same over time. This technique is essential where the applications function with predictable resource demands. Resources can also be allocated dynamically, which can either be an on-demand allocation where real-time assessment is used to determine the required resources or queue-based allocation in which the queuing models and polarization are factors that determine which resources are allocated. This particularly ensures that high-priority tasks receive resources before others. Leveraging the AI intelligence integrated into the 6G network, deep learning algorithms and reinforcement learning agents can aid resource management.

Other approaches, including the use of optimization algorithms, modeling and simulation, application of quantum Markov chain theory (QMCT—acronym provided by the authors), and quantum theoretic game theory [4], have been evaluated as a possible aid to the resource allocation issues in QML-assisted 6G network. Authors in [4] have postulated that quantum methods can provide a high-level reduction in time consumption when deciding the optimal resource demand for a particular task in 6G. Also, beam-based problem solutions and spectrum optimizations can also be proffered using this technology.

13.5 Security Challenges and Prospects in QML 6G

The integration of QML into 6G networks not only brings forth numerous opportunities but also ushers in a new spectrum of security concerns. As quantum technologies advance, adversaries may exploit quantum capabilities to compromise network security. The authors of [12] identified the role of AI in mitigating the security challenges in 6G. Below, we outline some of the key security concerns associated with QML integration and propose mitigation strategies. A summary of the key challenges in presented in Figure 13.4.

i. Quantum Attacks on Classical Cryptography

Quantum computers can potentially decipher the most adopted encryption mechanisms like Rivest-Shamir-Adleman (RSA) and Elliptic-curve cryptography (ECC) using algorithms like Shor's algorithm, rendering classical cryptographic methods obsolete. Applying cryptographic search algorithms that are based on post-quantum techniques holds the potential to provide high-level security against quantum threats. Such cryptographic methods based on lattice, hash functions, and code-centric cryptography can help protect against these security issues. In addition, quantum key distribution (QKD) that leverages quantum properties to enable the exchange of encryption keys that are immune to quantum attacks can ensure the confidentiality and integrity of data [52].

ii. Data Privacy and Quantum Eavesdropping

Quantum eavesdropping attacks could potentially compromise the privacy of data transmitted over quantum channels, posing a threat to sensitive information. To mitigate this, it is imperative to leverage encryption methods that are quantum-resistant, ensuring data privacy in the post-quantum era, and implement quantum-secure authentication that uses authentication protocols that can detect and thwart quantum eavesdropping attempts, ensuring secure data transmission.

iii. Quantum Adversarial Machine Learning

Quantum computing can potentially help to enhance adversarial machine learning attacks, leading to more sophisticated and effective attacks against machine learning models. Possible solutions can be to develop quantum-enhanced machine learning models for robust anomaly detection and intrusion detection systems that can adapt to quantum-enhanced threats. When ML models are deployed, it is necessary to include techniques for model verification and integrity checking to ensure the trustworthiness of machine learning models in quantum adversarial environments.

iv. Resource-Intensive Quantum Attacks

Future adversaries with access to quantum computing power may launch resource-intensive attacks on networks, such as brute-force attacks on encryption keys. An increase in the key length of cryptographic algorithms can provide more complexity in the algorithms such that they become more computationally infeasible for attackers, even with quantum resources. On top of the above, a continuous monitoring of the development of quantum computing technology and adapting new security measures accordingly are crucial.

v. Quantum Side-Channel Attacks

New side-channel attack vectors can exploit vulnerabilities in quantum hardware or algorithms due to the complexity of the architecture of the network. Quantum hardware systems to be used for the implementation of 6G networks needs to be enhanced with more security protocols to protect against side-channel attacks, including measures such as tamper-proofing and intrusion detection. In addition, quantum algorithms should be designed with built-in defenses against side-channel attacks.

Additionally, outside the security-specific challenges identified, there are some other drawbacks to the deployment of the 6G network, including investment, technology innovation and standardization, spectrum scarcity, regulation and policy, power consumption, and energy efficiency. Deploying 6G infrastructure at its full capacity is identified to be cost-demanding as it requires advanced technologies [53]. New regulatory

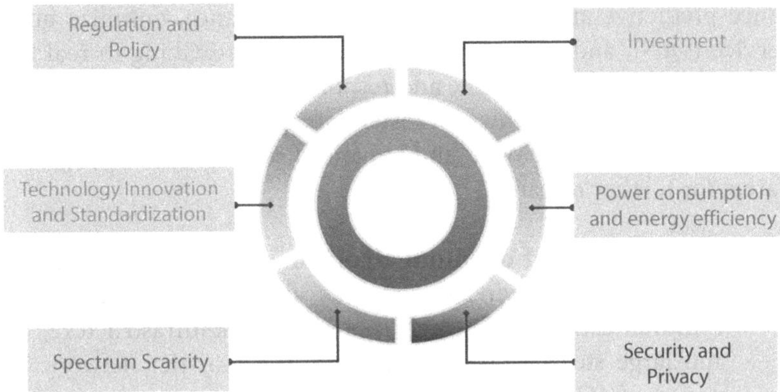

Figure 13.4 Challenges for the deployment of 6G [55].

policies may be developed to respond to the demand for more spectra and technologies [54], which can impact on the time for implementation.

13.6 Limitations, Benefits, and Future Directions

Currently, experimental studies have shown the possibilities of the integration of QML into 6G deployment [7, 19, 55, 56]. However, there are practical implementation challenges that can be investigated, such as hardware limitation, algorithmic complexity, and data access and training to achieve the goal of 6G. Hardware limitation results in high error rates and limited qubit coherence times in QC, making it challenging to scale quantum processors to meet the computational requirements of 6G networks while ensuring reliability and performance. Hence, developing advanced error correction techniques, qubit stabilization methods, and scalable quantum architectures can aid in solving the challenge. Additionally, QML algorithms often exhibit high computational complexity, making their implementation and optimization for real-time applications in 6G networks quite challenging. Machine learning models rely on large volumes of high-quality training data to achieve optimal performance. However, accessing and pre-processing data in quantum-enhanced 6G networks presents logistical challenges due to the distributed nature of network resources and privacy concerns associated with sensitive data.

The integration of QML into the 6G network provides for high-level network orientation and intelligence, making them continually learn from data and adapt to changing conditions. Enabling 6G with QML can enhance predictive analytics on network performance, optimize quality of service (QoS), and enable autonomous decision-making in real time, thereby creating a more dynamic and responsive network. In addition, the synergy provides opportunities for faster data processing, reduced latency, efficient resource management, and enhanced security. We highlight four key areas for further research.

1. **Hybridization of quantum algorithms:** The heterogeneity characteristics in wireless networks, along with advances in communication intelligence, robust network infrastructure, and large storage properties, define the four-tier network design of 6G, which integrates millimeter-wave and quantum communication, offering more dynamic functionalities that may surpass a single algorithm that has a high possibility of occurrence. Therefore, the hybridized quantum algorithm can be a solution in such scenarios.
2. **Redesigning cryptographic algorithms:** Many of the QML algorithms leverage Grover's and Shor's methods in optimizing performance. However, the fast-growing technologies have identified some vulnerabilities in these algorithms, which presents threats to future networks. It is, hence, worthwhile to investigate the redesign of the public keys and hash functions using quantum knowledge to achieve a quantum-resistant cryptosystem.
3. **Quantum-enabled blockchain communications:** An integration of the blockchain technology to develop quantum-enabled blockchain communications in 6G can be a step toward enhancing data security on the communication channels and mitigate certain attacks.
4. **QML-assisted optimization technique:** The bourgeoning demand for IoT in different sectors, including military, health, education, banking, insurance, and more, and the massive connectivity and communications it provides require high accuracy in data analytics to achieve an optimal IoT ecosystem. Since most IoT systems function in real time, utilizing the 6G network on them demands the design of a novel QML-assisted optimization technique to maximize data accuracy and cater to the resource constraint challenges of IoT.

13.7 Conclusion

Integrating QC and ML within 6G architecture is a promising adventure in the scientific community with the potential to enhance wireless communication design and operation. This chapter has vigorously examined the emerging technologies of QC, ML, and 6G networks and the merging of quantum ML algorithms. Most importantly, several potential QML algorithms have been identified. In addition, we highlight the frameworks for implementing QML, measures for dealing with resource allocation, security challenges, and future directions. The current study encapsulates a comprehensive understanding of applying QML in 6G, making it suitable as a guide to quantum researchers and enthusiasts to investigate future developments in 6G. Additionally, the study is limited in its practical evaluation of the discussed methods, which will be investigated in future work.

References

1. Bang, A., Kamal, K.K., Joshi, P., Bhatia, K., 6G: The Next Giant Leap for AI and ML. *Procedia Comput. Sci.*, 218, 310–317, 2023.
2. Akbar, M.A., Khan, A.A., Hyrynsalmi, S., Khan, J.A., 6G secure quantum communication: a success probability prediction model. *Autom. Softw. Eng.*, 31, 1, 31, 2024.
3. Giordani, M., Polese, M., Mezzavilla, M., Rangan, S., Zorzi, M., Toward 6G networks: Use cases and technologies. *IEEE Commun. Mag.*, 58, 3, 55–61, 2020.
4. Duong, T.Q., Ansere, J.A., Narottama, B., Sharma, V., Dobre, O.A., Shin, H., Quantum-Inspired Machine Learning for 6G: Fundamentals, Security, Resource Allocations, Challenges, and Future Research Directions. *IEEE Open J. Veh. Technol.*, 375–387, 3 September, 2022.
5. Vista, F., Musa, V., Piro, G., Grieco, L.A., Boggia, G., Network Intelligence with Quantum Computing in 6G and B6G: Design Principles and Future Directions. *2021 IEEE Globecom Work. (GC Wkshps)*, pp. 1–6, 2021.
6. Haldorai, A., Ramu, A., Murugan, S., *Artificial Intelligence and Machine Learning for Future Urban Development BT - Computing and Communication Systems in Urban Development: A Detailed Perspective*, A. Haldorai, A. Ramu, S. Murugan, (Eds.), pp. 91–113, Springer International Publishing, Cham, 2019.
7. Alhammadi, A., Shayea, I., El-Saleh, A.A., Azmi, M.H., Ismail, Z.H., Kouhalvandi, L., Saad, S.A., Artificial Intelligence in 6G Wireless Networks: Opportunities, Applications, and Challenges. *Int. J. Intell. Syst.*, 2024, 8845070, 2024.

8. Suriya, M., Machine learning and quantum computing for 5G/6G communication networks - A survey. *Int. J. Intell. Netw.*, 197–203, 3 July, 2022.
9. Zhang, C., Patras, P., Haddadi, H., Deep learning in mobile and wireless networking: A survey. *IEEE Commun. Surv. Tutorials*, 21, 3, 2224–2287, 2019.
10. Akyildiz, I.F., Kak, A., Nie, S., 6G and beyond: The future of wireless communications systems. *IEEE Access*, 8, 133995–134030, 2020.
11. Nawaz, S.J., Sharma, S.K., Wyne, S., Patwary, M.N., Asaduzzaman, M., Quantum Machine Learning for 6G Communication Networks: State-of-the-Art and Vision for the Future. *IEEE Access*, 7, Ml, 46317–46350, 2019.
12. Siriwardhana, Y., Porambage, P., Liyanage, M., Ylianttila, M., AI and 6G security: Opportunities and challenges. *2021 Jt. Eur. Conf. Netw. Commun. 6G Summit, EuCNC/6G Summit, 2021*, 616–621, 2021.
13. Khan, T.M. and Robles-Kelly, A., Machine learning: Quantum vs classical. *IEEE Access*, 8, 219275–219294, 2020.
14. Sergioli, G., Quantum and quantum-like machine learning: a note on differences and similarities. *Soft Comput.*, 24, 14, 10247–10255, 2020.
15. Monserrat, J.F., Martin-Sacristan, D., Bouchmal, F., Carrasco, O., de Valgas, J.F., Cardona, N., Key technologies for the advent of the 6G. *2020 IEEE Wirel. Commun. Netw. Conf. Work*, 1–6, 2020.
16. Akhtar, M.W., Hassan, S.A., Ghaffar, R., Jung, H., Garg, S., Hossain, M.S., The shift to 6G communications: Vision and requirements. *Human-centric Comput. Inf. Sci.*, 10, 1–27, 2020.
17. Wang, C. and Rahman, A., Quantum-Enabled 6G Wireless Networks: Opportunities and Challenges. *IEEE Wirel. Commun.*, 29, 1, 58–69, 2022.
18. Adil, M., Song, H., Khan, M.K., Farouk, A., Jin, Z., 5G/6G-enabled metaverse technologies: Taxonomy, applications, and open security challenges with future research directions. *J. Netw. Comput. Appl.*, 223, 103828, 2024.
19. Urgelles, H., Maheshwari, S., Nande, S.S., Bassoli, R., Fitzek, F.H.P., Monserrat, J.F., In-Network Quantum Computing for Future 6G Networks. *Adv. Quantum Technol.*, 8, 2, 2300334, 2024.
20. Bhandari, N., Devra, S., Singh, K., Evolution of cellular network: from 1G to 5G. *Int. J. Eng. Tech.*, 3, 5, 98–105, 2017.
21. Quy, V.K., Chehri, A., Quy, N.M., Han, N.D., Ban, N.T., Innovative Trends in the 6G Era: A Comprehensive Survey of Architecture, Applications, Technologies, and Challenges. *IEEE Access*, 11, 39824–39844, 2023.
22. Serôdio, C., Cunha, J., Candela, G., Rodriguez, S., Sousa, X.R., Branco, F., The 6G Ecosystem as Support for IoE and Private Networks: Vision, Requirements, and Challenges. *Futur. Internet*, 15, 11, 2023.
23. Garg, V.K., Halpern, S., Smolik, K.F., Third generation (3G) mobile communications systems. *1999 IEEE Int. Conf. Pers. Wirel. Commun. (Cat. No.99TH8366)*, 39–43, 1999.
24. Dahlman, E., Parkvall, S., Sköld, J., 4G L.-A.P. and T.R. @ to 5G (Third E.), Introduction, in: *4g, LTE Evolution and the Road to 5G*, E. Dahlman, S. Parkvall, J.B.T. Sköld, (Eds.), pp. 1–5, Academic Press, Elsevier Science and Technology Books, Incorporated, 2016.

25. Deepender, M., Shrivastava, U., Verma, J.K., A Study on 5G Technology and Its Applications in Telecommunications. *2021 Int. Conf. Comput. Perform. Eval.*, 365–371, 2021.
26. Fastovets, D.V., Bogdanov, Y.I., Bantysh, B.I., Lukichev, V.F., Machine learning methods in quantum computing theory. *Int. Conf. Micro-and Nano-Electronics 2018*, 11022, 752–761, 2019.
27. Okey, O.D., Maidin, S.S., Adasme, P., Lopes Rosa, R., Saadi, M., Carrillo Melgarejo, D., Zegarra Rodríguez, D., BoostedEnML: Efficient Technique for Detecting Cyberattacks in IoT Systems Using Boosted Ensemble Machine Learning. *Sensors*, 22, 19, 7409, 2022.
28. Okey, O.D., Melgarejo, D.C., Saadi, M., Rosa, R.L., Kleinschmidt, J.H., Rodríguez, D.Z., Transfer Learning Approach to IDS on Cloud IoT Devices Using Optimized CNN. *IEEE Access*, 11, 1023–1038, 2023.
29. Bhat, J.R. and Alqahtani, S.A., 6G ecosystem: Current status and future perspective. *IEEE Access*, 9, 43134–43167, 2021.
30. Singh, G., Kaur, M., Singh, M., Kumar, Y., Implementation of quantum support vector machine algorithm using a benchmarking dataset. *Indian J. Pure Appl. Phys.*, 60, 5, 2022.
31. Beer, K., Bondarenko, D., Farrelly, T., Osborne, T.J., Salzmann, R., Scheiermann, D., Wolf, R., Training deep quantum neural networks. *Nat. Commun.*, 11, 1, 808, 2020.
32. Nguyen, N.H., Behrman, E.C., Moustafa, M.A., Steck, J.E., Benchmarking neural networks for quantum computations. *IEEE Trans. Neural Netw. Learn. Syst.*, 31, 7, 2522–2531, 2019.
33. Cong, I., Choi, S., Lukin, M.D., Quantum convolutional neural networks. *Nat. Phys.*, 15, 12, 1273–1278, 2019.
34. Šćekić, M., Šćepanović, S., Mitrović, S., Implementation of Quantum Machine Learning Algorithms: A Literature Review. *2022 11th Mediterr. Conf. Embed. Comput.*, 1–4, 2022.
35. Douce, T., Markham, D., Kashefi, E., Diamanti, E., Coudreau, T., Milman, P., Van Loock, P., Ferrini, G., Continuous-variable instantaneous quantum computing is hard to sample. *Phys. Rev. Lett.*, 118, 7, 70503, 2017.
36. Lehtonen, L., Analysis and implementation of quantum Boltzmann machines, 2021.
37. Bravo-Prieto, C., LaRose, R., Cerezo, M., Subasi, Y., Cincio, L., Coles, P.J., Variational quantum linear solver, 2019, *arXiv Prepr. arXiv1909.05820.*
38. Cerezo, M., Arrasmith, A., Babbush, R., Benjamin, S.C., Endo, S., Fujii, K., McClean, J.R., Mitarai, K., Yuan, X., Cincio, L., Variational quantum algorithms. *Nat. Rev. Phys.*, 3, 9, 625–644, 2021.
39. Schuld, M., Bocharov, A., Svore, K.M., Wiebe, N., Circuit-centric quantum classifiers. *Phys. Rev. A*, 101, 3, 32308, 2020.
40. Zhong, J., Lin, C., Sheng, Z., Zhang, S., Quantum K-Means algorithm based on Hamming distance. *J. Comput. Appl.*, 43, 8, 2493, 2023.

41. Kerenidis, I., Landman, J., Luongo, A., Prakash, A., q-means: A quantum algorithm for unsupervised machine learning. *Adv. Neural Inf. Process. Syst.*, 32, 2019.
42. Bhatia, V. and Ramkumar, K.R., An efficient quantum computing technique for cracking RSA using Shor's algorithm. *2020 IEEE 5th Int. Conf. Comput. Commun. Autom.*, 89–94, 2020.
43. Rahman, M. and Paul, G., Grover on KATAN: Quantum resource estimation. *IEEE Trans. Quantum Eng.*, 3, 1–9, 2022.
44. Duong, T.Q., Nguyen, L.D., Narottama, B., Ansere, J.A., Van Huynh, D., and Shin, H., Quantum-Inspired Real-Time Optimization for 6G Networks: Opportunities, Challenges, and the Road Ahead. *IEEE Open J. Commun. Soc.*, 3, 1347–1359, June 2022, doi: 10.1109/OJCOMS.2022.3195219.
45. Qiskit, C., Qiskit: An Open-source Framework for Quantum Computing, 2023.
46. Amazon, Quantum Cloud Service - Quantum Computing Tool - Amazon Braket - AWS, 2023.
47. Killoran, N., Izaac, J., Quesada, N., Bergholm, V., Amy, M., Weedbrook, C., Strawberry fields: A software platform for photonic quantum computing. *Quantum*, 3, 129, 2019.
48. Bergholm, V., Izaac, J., Schuld, M., Gogolin, C., Ahmed, S., Ajith, V., Alam, M.S., Alonso-Linaje, G., AkashNarayanan, B., Asadi, A., Pennylane: Automatic differentiation of hybrid quantum-classical computations, 2018, *arXiv Prepr. arXiv1811*.04968.
49. Rigetti Computing, Welcome to Quantum Cloud Services - QCS Documentation. *Rigetti Comput.*, 2023, https://docs.rigetti.com/qcs. Accessed: 2023-09-11.
50. Broughton, M., Verdon, G., McCourt, T., Martinez, A.J., Yoo, J.H., Isakov, S.V., Massey, P., Halavati, R., Niu, M.Y., Zlokapa, A., Peters, E., Lockwood, O., Skolik, A., Jerbi, S., Dunjko, V., Leib, M., Streif, M., Von Dollen, D., Chen, H., Cao, S., Wiersema, R., Huang, H.-Y., McClean, J.R., Babbush, R., Boixo, S., Bacon, D., Ho, A.K., Neven, H., Mohseni, M., TensorFlow Quantum: A Software Framework for Quantum Machine Learning, pp. 1–56, 2020.
51. Efthymiou, S., Ramos-Calderer, S., Bravo-Prieto, C., Pérez-Salinas, A., García-Martín, D., Garcia-Saez, A., Latorre, J.I., Carrazza, S., Qibo: a framework for quantum simulation with hardware acceleration. *Quantum Sci. Technol.*, 7, 1, 15018, 2021.
52. Okey, O.D., Maidin, S.S., Lopes Rosa, R., Toor, W.T., Carrillo Melgarejo, D., Wuttisittikulkij, L., Saadi, M., Zegarra Rodríguez, D., Quantum Key Distribution Protocol Selector Based on Machine Learning for Next-Generation Networks. *Sustainability*, 14, 23, 15901, 2022.
53. Tataria, H., Shafi, M., Dohler, M., Sun, S., Six Critical Challenges for 6G Wireless Systems: A Summary and Some Solutions. *IEEE Veh. Technol. Mag.*, 17, 1, 16–26, 2022.

54. Ariyanti, S. and Suryanegara, M., Visible Light Communication (VLC) for 6G Technology: The Potency and Research Challenges. *2020 Fourth World Conf. Smart Trends Syst. Secur. Sustain.*, 490–493, 2020.
55. Chataut, R., Nankya, M., Akl, R., 6G Networks and the AI Revolution—Exploring Technologies, Applications, and Emerging Challenges. *Sensors*, 24, 1888, 2024.
56. Akbar, M.A., Khan, A.A., Hyrynsalmi, S., Role of Quantum Computing in Shaping the Future of 6G Technology. *Inf. Softw. Technol.*, 170, 107454, 2024.

14

A Quantum Computing Perspective in 6G Networks: The Challenge of Adaptive Network Intelligence

Pallavi Sapkale

Department of Computer Science and Engineering, Ramrao Adik Institute of Technology, Nerul, Navi Mumbai, India

Abstract

6G networks will provide previously unheard-of connection and data rates, bringing in a new age of ubiquitous connectivity and game-changing technology. This chapter highlights the existing challenges in networks and how quantum computing provides an advanced approach to addressing the demands by leveraging quantum phenomena such as superposition and entanglement to process large amounts of data and solve optimization problems more efficiently. In 6G systems and beyond, network intelligence would need processing power and computation time, which are difficult in existing installations. Though, the quantum computing with the QML became a feasible way to address this problem, incorporating these machines into the structure of networks. To fill this gap, this chapter demonstrates the design concepts of distributed design principles, in which quantum computing systems are placed in the cloud. Incorporating quantum computing, a novel model that uses the laws of quantum physics to execute estimated values beyond the capacity of classical computers, is essential to this progress. In the framework of 6G networks, we examine the possible synergy between quantum computing and network intelligence in this chapter.

Keywords: Quantum computing, machine learning, artificial intelligence, 6G networks

Email: pme932@gmail.com

Pallavi Sapkale, Shilpa Mehta and S. Balamurugan (eds.) Quantum Computing and Machine Learning for 6G, (311–326) © 2026 Scrivener Publishing LLC

14.1 Introduction

Over time, mobile radio networks experienced numerous modifications. As of now, the 3GPP Release marks the conclusion of the standardization process for the fifth generation (5G) of mobile systems. Scientific groups started to look at the next generation of wireless communication systems, which includes beyond 6G (B6G) and sixth generation (6G) [1].

6G networks will provide previously unheard-of connection and data rates, bringing in a new age of ubiquitous connectivity and game-changing technology. The incorporation of quantum computing, a novel model that uses the laws of quantum physics to estimate beyond the capacity of classical computers, is essential to this progress. In the framework of 6G networks, we focus on the possible synergy between quantum computing and network intelligence. Based on quantum physics, quantum computing is a novel computer that works with uncertain and unpredictable physical environments. "Network intelligence" describes a network's capacity to self-optimize its performance, adjust to changing circumstances, and provide users with customized services. Conventional methods for network intelligence depend on antiquated algorithms and heuristics, which might not be able to handle the intricacy and enormity of 6G networks [2]. To handle enormous volumes of data and solve optimization problems more quickly, quantum computing provides a fresh solution to these difficulties. Network intelligence will have a major impact on how 6G and B6G develop [4].

14.1.1 Quantum Computing in 6G

However, machine learning techniques have a laborious and occasionally recursive learning phase, requiring enormous computational power. Because of this, the large volumes of data anticipated to be handled in 6G use cases will require processing power and computation time capabilities that are difficult to provide in current systems. In such instances, the advantages resulting from the cooperative integration of the previously used critical techniques may potentially be eliminated by the lack of abundant processing capacity throughout the network. Another potential solution to this problem is quantum computing (QC) in 6G [5]. In particular, QC uses the basic concepts of quantum physics to create novel kinds of algorithms that quickly address complicated issues compared to traditional methods. QC has the potential to accelerate machine learning algorithms and render them appropriate for real-time, computationally intensive applications.

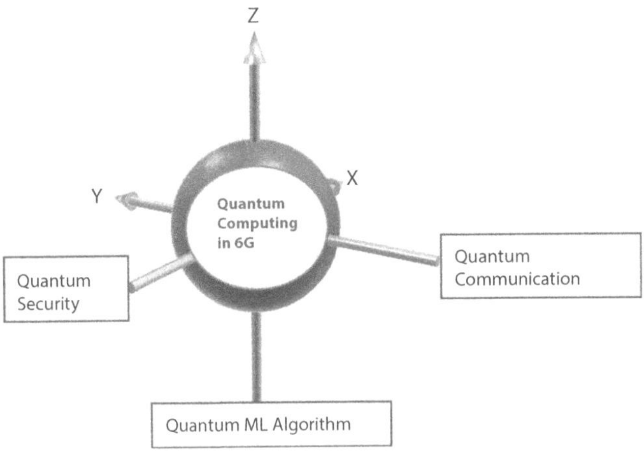

Figure 14.1 Quantum computing in 6G.

The method that emerged is called quantum machine learning (QML). Quantum computers are currently in their infancy, with limited scalability and error rates that hinder their practical deployment. Moreover, quantum algorithms and protocols for network intelligence uses are still in the initial phase of development. The potential benefits of quantum-enhanced network intelligence in 6G are enormous, considering these difficulties. The development of quantum computing has the potential to completely transform how we plan, implement, and oversee next-generation wireless networks. In the framework of 6G networks, this concept illustrates the potential and difficulties of using quantum computing for network intelligence, opening the door to a new age of innovation and connectedness. Figure 14.1 shows the basic structure of quantum computing in 6G.

In 6G, deploying and implementing a network intelligence system presents big challenges. Considering this direction, our work represents design principles for a quantum computing–aided network intelligence and also highlights the related emerging research challenges [6]. Table 14.1 shows the quantum-based 6G systems.

14.2 What is Network Intelligence in Quantum Computing?

In the context of quantum computing, network intelligence is the application of quantum computing techniques and algorithms to improve the security [7], flexibility, and efficiency of network administration and operations.

Table 14.1 Quantum-related 6G systems.

Features	Communication	Computing	Entanglement	Advance quantum
Quantum-RAN	✓	✓		
Quantum SIN	✓		✓	✓
Quantum-EDGE	✓			
Quantum-DC	✓			
Quantum-Blockchain	✓	✓	✓	
Quantum-WAI	✓	✓	Optional	
Quantum Service	✓	✓	Optional	
Quantum Applications	✓	✓	✓	

The special powers of quantum computing have the potential to change network management, security, and optimization completely. In the conventional method, deep packet inspection is used for network intelligence optimization and is less secure. In quantum computing network intelligence, packet inspection, which comprises examining the data packets traveling over the computer network and applying their data to comprehend network performance, is typically how network intelligence functions. To provide fast insights into user-application interactions, internet protocol interactions, and other network elements, this procedure examines packet pathways and traffic levels. When the data are combined, it can show connections and provide "intelligence" about the network. To analyze these data packets, it is necessary to determine if the data are in the anticipated format, if any malicious code or unexpected data are included in any of the packets, and if there are any anomalous traffic variations or spikes.

Optimization: This feature may be used to optimize resource allocation, routing protocols, and network settings in network management, which will increase effectiveness and performance.
Machine Learning: Quantum machine learning models can handle and analyze massive amounts of network data more quickly by utilizing quantum concepts like superposition and entanglement. This improves prediction accuracy and facilitates more intelligent decision-making [8].

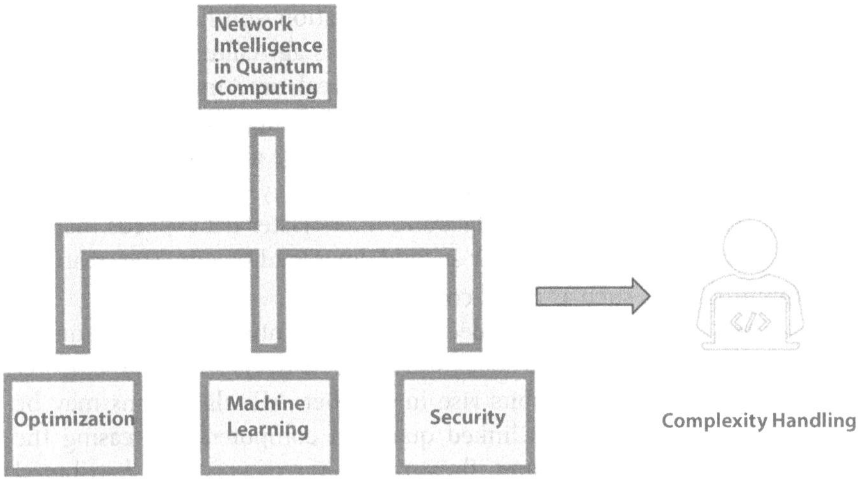

Figure 14.2 Network intelligence in quantum computing.

Security: The safety of networks is affected by quantum computing as well. Using the laws of quantum physics, quantum cryptography systems, such as quantum key distribution (QKD), provide unmatched levels of security by enabling secure communication channels impervious to manipulation or eavesdropping.

Handling Complexity: Compared with standard computing, quantum computing is more adept at managing the inherent complexity of contemporary networks. Complex combinatorial optimization issues, such as those involving network topology design, traffic engineering, and protocol optimization, can be effectively solved by quantum algorithms.

Real-time Adaptability: Large volumes of network data may be processed in real time thanks to quantum computing, which enables networking to rapidly adapt to shifting needs and conditions. For networks to function at their best and respond to changes in unexpected and dynamic contexts, real-time flexibility is essential. Above Figure 14.2 describes the intelligence of network.

6G Objective and Quantum Computing in the Network

Although 5G is still under expansion, the studies are currently focusing on 6G wireless communication. The introduction of 5G technology has ushered in a new age of digitalization across a variety of businesses. It is currently concentrating on providing automation and linking to a wide range of applications beyond industry, such as agriculture, construction, and energy, using intelligent networks and real-time Internet-of-Things (IoT) technologies. 5G aims to provide extensive support for a wide range of devices, improving video streaming, gaming, and augmented reality experiences while maintaining minimal latency. It reduces the delay between sending and receiving data and offers faster data speeds than its predecessors, reaching gigabit-per-second download speeds. The creativity in combining ideas such as cloud computing.

Quantum computing is encoded with the quantum bits called qubits (0, 1) [9]; n qubits encode 2n states simultaneously. As a result, the power of QC grows linearly as qubits rise in number. ML algorithms may be dispersed among numerous linked quantum computers, increasing the number of qubits working and, thus, the power of QC. The distributed computing resources are controlled by a control system. Quantum information, unlike conventional data, cannot be replicated due to the no-cloning theorem. This limits the use of typical error-correcting procedures. On the other hand, quantum communication and entanglement allow for the transmission of quantum states *via* quantum communications. Two particles share a quantum state when there is quantum entanglement, and the measurement of one particle affects the measurement of the entangled one.

A representation for qubit space [15], considering the polar coordinates θ and φ, is

$$|\psi\rangle = \cos\left(\frac{\theta}{2}\right)|0\rangle + e^{i\phi}\sin\left(\frac{\theta}{2}\right)|1\rangle,$$

Here, $0 \leq \varphi \leq \pi$ and $0 \leq \theta \leq \pi$.

Networks running on 6G will require highly precise time and phase synchronization, with near-perfect coverage across the globe, sub-centimeter tracking accuracy, and millisecond geographic location improvements to handle a variety of use cases and advanced applications. Whereas 5G uses millimeter-wave (mmW) technology to deliver information at speeds in the Gbps range, 6G will need broadcast data rates in the Tbps range to support services such as high-quality 3D video, virtual reality (VR), and hybrids of VR and augmented reality. With a user plane latency of a mobility speed of roughly 100, it can handle several moving platforms. Terahertz (THz) and optical frequency bands may be suitable for achieving these speeds.

14.2.1 Methods to Achieve the Network Intelligence in Quantum Computing

The combination of 6G with QC promises a revolutionary change in communication technology: improved security, better network performance, and the development of new applications that take advantage of quantum computing's special powers [10]. This convergence is expected to affect the future of telecommunications and technology. The foundational pillars at the core of 6G's vision are sustainability and reliability, which include privacy, endurance, dependability, flexibility, and digital accessibility. In this section, we look at the connection of QC with these pillars, evaluating their alignment, possible synergies, and barriers in their convergence.

Achieving network intelligence with quantum computing in the context of 6G networks involves several key steps and considerations:

1. **6G URLLC:** is a traditional machine-learning technique that creates challenges in the realm of 6G URLLC due to the constraints of traditional machine-learning techniques. Quantum machine intelligence, which leverages superposition and entanglement, offers a solution to these challenges through the improvement of learning speeds and the efficient optimization of tasks [11]. In 6G URLLC, ML is used to identify patterns, classify the collected data, adapt communication features based on environmental conditions, and predict the users' mobility by using THZ and cell-free technology, which gives a connectivity density of 10^7 d/km^2 and an energy efficiency of 10 to 100x.
2. **Creation of Quantum Algorithms:** Create and modify quantum algorithms that are specific to the use cases that have been found. This entails investigating and creating quantum algorithms that take advantage of special features of quantum computing, such as superposition and entanglement, to resolve cryptography, machine learning, and optimization issues pertinent to network intelligence.
3. **Hardware Development:** Invest in the creation and implementation of quantum computing hardware appropriate for applications related to network intelligence. Investing in internal quantum computing research and development projects or working with producers of quantum hardware might be necessary for this.

4. **Security and Privacy Considerations:** Ensure that network intelligence solutions built on quantum computing platforms incorporate robust security and privacy measures. This may involve leveraging quantum cryptographic techniques, such as quantum key distribution (QKD), to secure network communications and sensitive data.
5. **Testing and Validation:** Conduct extensive testing and validation of quantum-enabled network intelligence solutions in simulated and real-world network environments. This ensures that the solutions perform as expected and meet the requirements of 6G networks in terms of performance, reliability, and scalability.

By considering these steps, we can work toward achieving network intelligence with quantum computing in 6G networks, unlocking new levels of efficiency, adaptability, and security in future wireless communication systems. Following Figure 14.3 shows the connectivity with 6G.

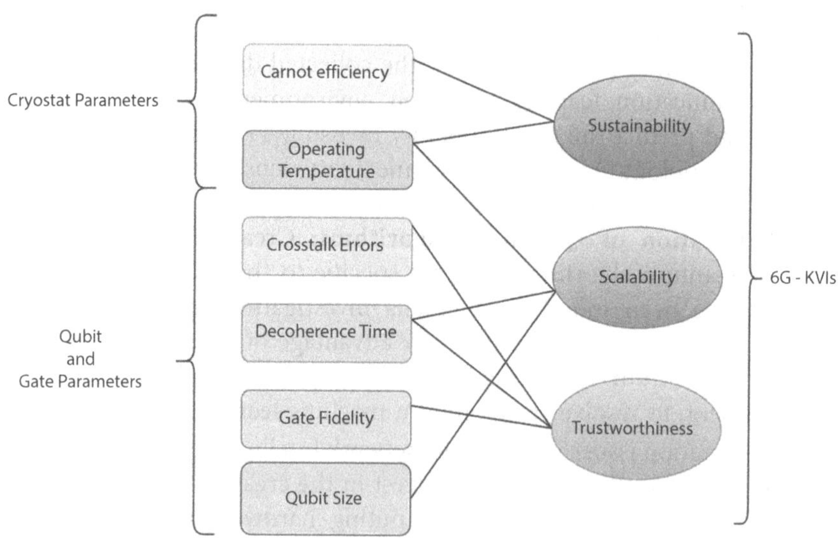

Figure 14.3 A representation of the connection of 6G with quantum computing (Source: [13]).

14.3 How to Accomplish Network Intelligence

Machine learning (ML) and quantum machine learning are key instruments for achieving network intelligence. ML techniques involve supervised, unsupervised, and reinforcement learning. Achieving network intelligence with quantum computing in the context of 6G networks involves several key steps and considerations, such as understanding use cases and quantum algorithm development.

Quantum Machine Learning (QML) for Faster Decision Making: It works with accuracy and speed. Machine learning models can produce more accurate results in real-time because of quantum computers' ability to analyze enormous datasets at a rate that is significantly quicker than that of conventional computers. It also helps to manage network traffic. QML can analyze real-time network traffic patterns and predict congestion points. This allows 6G networks to reallocate resources or reroute data to less congested paths instantly [12].

Optimizing Edge Computing with ML and Quantum Intelligence:
Distributed AI at the Edge: Machine learning models learned on quantum computers may be deployed at network edges, allowing devices to make real-time choices without communicating with the central network. This minimizes latency and improves response times for applications such as autonomous driving and AR/VR. Energy Efficiency: Machine learning algorithms operating on quantum-enhanced hardware may improve energy usage by selecting the most effective method to process data at the edge, hence boosting the overall sustainability of the 6G network.

14.4 Quantum Computing Opportunities with 6G

Quantum-Assisted Wireless Artificial Intelligence: Quantum-assisted wireless artificial intelligence (QAWAI) connects cutting-edge systems to revolutionize different fields, from communication to computing. For the QAWAI, the major term is quantum computing power, which is based on quantum algorithms that enable complex calculations that are impractical for traditional AI systems, enhancing data analysis and decision-making capabilities. The second important term is using quantum encryption for secure communication with sensitive AI-driven data from cyber threats. 6G network will be more intelligent, which will get the massive available data from devices and connected nodes. The main applications are the AI algorithms.

14.5 Challenges and Research Scope in Quantum Computing with 6G

If there is anticipated to be a greater demand for computational activities, then additional quantum computers should be deployed. The load balancing between quantum and conventional computers may be optimized by the use of fine-grained control of the computing resources and an understanding of the complexity of the challenge. In addition, to safeguard the data integrity and confidentiality of shared information and provide quick access control, it is essential to introduce new security methods that make use of quantum principles. Last but not least, it is critical to use both simulation and physical implementations to measure the performance gain (and the margins of improvement of existing solutions) supplied by distributed and centralized QML in comparison to conventional ML techniques.

14.5.1 Main Challenges in Quantum Computing with 6G

Although quantum computing is a fascinating and quickly developing topic, there are many obstacles and research possibilities to overcome. Figure 14.4 shows the basics of quantum error correction (QEC). The following are some major issues and possible study areas:

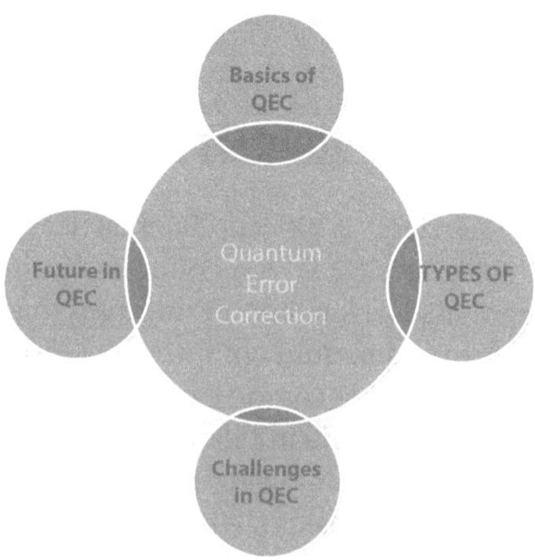

Figure 14.4 Basics of quantum error correction.

Error Rates and Quantum Decoherence:
Important ideas in quantum computing that affect the dependability and efficiency of quantum systems include error rates and quantum decoherence. Here is a closer look at each, along with some tips for lessening its impact. The primary element limiting quantum computers' computing capacity is decoherence [14]. It happens when qubits—the fundamental building blocks of quantum computing—interact with their surroundings in their quantum states. Coherence is lost as a result of this connection, which results in calculation mistakes. To tackle this difficulty, researchers have created a spectrum of quantum error correction algorithms that can identify and repair defects in a quantum system.

Challenge: Quantum bits (qubits) are highly susceptible to errors due to decoherence and noise. Due to its many drawbacks, quantum error correction (QEC) is not an ideal option. The requirement for several ancilla qubits, which raises the system's complexity and expense, is one of the primary obstacles. A further difficulty is the ancilla qubits' error-proneness, which can cause faults to spread throughout the system. Furthermore, QEC codes demand a high degree of precision in the gates and measurements, which is tough to attain in practice.

Research/Future Scope:
In network intelligence systems, a huge number of smart devices connected to the network will boom by more than 11 billion to 110 billion in 6G networks. This new model system significantly affects the security processes. These are the major issues in building secure 6G networks, which determine the algorithms for the protection of data transmission. Resource allocation is also the main research scope in quantum 6G networking. To improve the quality of service (QoS) for users, resource allocation needs to be considered. During mobility, the radio waves fluctuate, and frequency problems are generated. Hence, it provides a quantum algorithm that is precise and reliable to address the 6G communication. Also, architecture and standardization are important in quantum 6G [3, 17]. The following are the main future scopes.

Quantum Software and Programming Languages:

- **Challenge:** There is a lack of robust programming languages and software frameworks tailored for quantum computing.

- **Research Scope:** Creating new programming paradigms, tools, and high-level languages for quantum software development.

Hardware Limitations:

- **Challenge:** Existing quantum hardware often has limited qubit connectivity and reliability.
- **Research Scope:** Innovating new materials and fabrication techniques to improve qubit performance and connectivity.

Interfacing with Classical Systems:

- **Challenge:** Efficiently integrating quantum computers with classical systems for practical applications.
- **Research Scope:** Developing hybrid algorithms and systems that combine classical and quantum computing resources.

Resource Optimization:

- **Challenge:** Quantum algorithms often require a significant amount of resources, which may not be feasible with current technology.
- **Research Scope:** Research ways to optimize resource usage in quantum computations.

14.5.2 Research Scope in Quantum Computing

1. Quantum Cryptography:

- Exploring protocols like quantum key distribution (QKD) and their practical implementations in secure communication [16].

2. Quantum Machine Learning:

- Developing algorithms that utilize quantum properties for data analysis and pattern recognition, improving efficiency over classical methods.

3. Quantum Networks:

- Investigating the development of quantum communication networks and their architectures for secure information exchange.

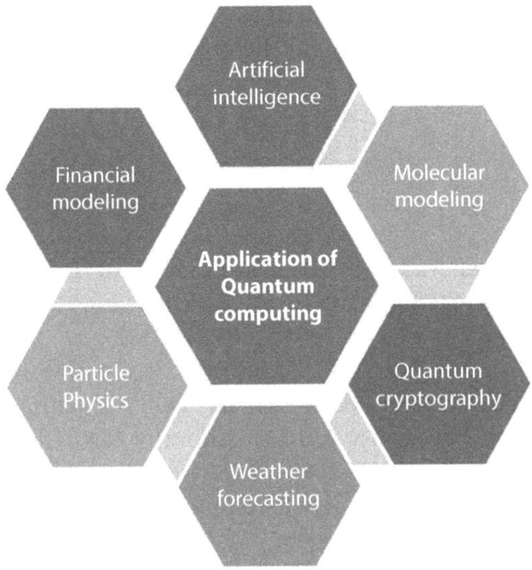

Figure 14.5 Research scope and application for quantum computing.

4. **Quantum Information Theory:**
   - Studying the theoretical foundations of quantum information and its implications for computing, cryptography, and communication.

5. **Education and Workforce Development:**
   - Addressing the skills gap by creating educational programs and resources to train the next generation of quantum scientists and engineers.

Figure 14.5 depicts the research scope in quantum computing.

14.6 Conclusion

In conclusion, this chapter has brought to light the pivotal role of quantum computing in shaping the future of networking. The research study serves as a guideline for both industry and academia. Overall, this chapter reframes quantum computing in 6G technology and builds a foundation for researchers. The basic ideas and principles relating to quantum computing for 6G and network intelligence applications highlighted in this chapter, outlining QML concepts and relative algorithms for network intelligence in 6G communication, are described in this work. In future work, we will expand this research by developing the challenges in quantum computing in future networking.

References

1. Zaman, F., Farooq, A., Ullah, M. A., Jung, H., Shin, H., Win, M.Z., Quantum Machine Intelligence for 6G URLLC. *IEEE Wireless Commun.*, 30, 2, 22–30, 2023, https://doi.org/10.1109/MWC.003.2200382.
2. Ogobuchi, D.O., Maidin, S.S.B., Lopes Rosa, R., Toor, W.T., Melgarejo, D.C., Wuttisittikulkij, L., Saadi, M., Rodriguez, D.Z., Quantum Key Distribution Protocol Selector Based on Machine Learning for Next-Generation Networks. *Sustainability*, 14, 23, 15901–15901, 2022, doi: 10.3390/su142315901.
3. Corcoles, A., Kandala, A., Javadi-Abhari, A., McClure, D., Cross, A.W., Temme, K., Nation, P.D, Steffen, M., Gambetta, J.M., Challenges and Opportunities of Near-Term Quantum Computing Systems, 2020, doi: 10.1109/JPROC.2019.2954005.
4. Sukhpal, S.G., Adarsh, K., Harvinder, S., Manmeet, S., Manmeet, S., Kamalpreet, K., Muhammad, U., Rajkumar, B., Quantum computing: A taxonomy, systematic review and future directions. Software - Practice and Experience, 2021, doi: 10.1002/SPE.3039.
5. Matthias, M. and Cornelis, V., On the impact of quantum computing technology on future developments in high-performance scientific computing. *Ethics Inf. Technol.*, 19, 4, 253–269, 2017, doi: 10.1007/S10676-017-9438-0.
6. Jozef, G., Quantum Computing Challenges, doi: 10.1007/978-3-642-56478-9_27.
7. Golec, M., Hatay, E.S., Golec, M., Uyar, M., Golec, M., Gill, S.S., Quantum Cloud Computing: Trends and Challenges. *J. Economy Technol.*, 2, 190–199, 2024, https://doi.org/10.1016/j.ject.2024.05.001.
8. Jin, Y., Current Status and Future Development of Quantum Computing. *Theor. Nat. Sci.*, 36, 1, 165–174, 2024. https://doi.org/10.54254/2753-8818/36/20240606.
9. Gongsheng, Y., Yuxing, C., Jiaheng, L., Sai, W., Zhiwei, Y., Ling, Q., Gang, C., Quantum Computing for Databases: Overview and Challenges, 2024, doi: 10.48550/arxiv.2405.12511.
10. Muhammed, G., Emir, S., Hatay, M., Golec, M., Uyar, M., Golec, S., Singh, G., Quantum Cloud Computing: Trends and Challenges, 2024, doi: 10.48550/arxiv.2404.19612.
11. Kar, A.K., He, W., Payton, F.C., Grover, V., Al-Busaidi, A.S., Dwivedi, Y.K., How Could Quantum Computing Shape Information Systems Research – An Editorial Perspective and Future Research Directions. *Int. J. Inf. Manage.*, 80, 102776, 2024. https://doi.org/10.1016/j.ijinfomgt.2024.102776.

12. Atadoga, A., Chimezie, O., Osasona, F., Onwusinkwue, S., Onwusinkwue, S., Daraojimba, A., II, Dawodu, S.O., Quantum computing in big data analytics: a comprehensive review: assessing the advancements, challenges, and potential implications of quantum approaches in handling massive data sets. *Comput. Sci. IT Res. J.*, 2024, doi: 10.51594/csitrj.v5i2.794.
13. Urgelles, H., *et al.*, In-Network Quantum Computing for Future 6G Networks, March 2024, https://doi.org/10.1002/qute.202300334.
14. Shuford, J., Quantum Computing and Artificial Intelligence: Synergies and Challenges, 2024, doi: 10.60087/jaigs.v1i1.35.
15. Pagano, A.., Angelelli, M., Calvano, M., Curci, A., Piccinno, A., Quantum Computing for Learning Analytics: An Overview of Challenges and Integration Strategies, 2023, doi: 10.1145/3617570.3617867.
16. Paudel, H.P., Syamlal, M., *et al.*, Quantum Computing and Simulations for Energy Applications: Review and Perspective, 2022, https://doi.org/10.1021/acsengineeringau.1c00033.
17. Duong, T.Q., Ansere, J.A., Narottama, B., Sharma, V., Dobre, O. A., Shin, H., Quantum-Inspired Machine Learning for 6G: Fundamentals, Security, Resource Allocations, Challenges, and Future Research Directions. IEEE Open *J. Veh. Technol.*, 3, 375–387, 2022, https://doi.org/10.1109/OJVT.2022.3202876.

15

Role of QML in 6G Integrated Vehicular Networks

R. Palanivel[1*], Muthulakshmi P.[1], Snehasis Dey[2], Shilpa Mehta[3] and Pallavi Sapkale[4]

[1]*Department of Computer Science, Faculty of Science and Humanities, SRM Institute of Science and Technology, Kattankulathur, Chennai, Tamil Nadu, India*
[2]*Department of Electronics & Telecommunication Engineering, College of Engineering, Bhubaneswar, BPUT University, Odisha, India*
[3]*Department of Electrical and Electronic Engineering, Auckland University of Technology, Auckland, New Zealand*
[4]*Department of Computer Science and Engineering, Ramrao Adik Institute of Technology, Nerul, Navi Mumbai, India*

Abstract
The continuous evolution of communication technologies has ushered in the era of 6G networks, promising unparalleled connectivity, speed, and reliability. Central to this transformative landscape is the adoption of quantum machine learning (QML) as a cutting-edge tool for network resource allocation. This research encapsulates a groundbreaking study combining quantum computing, machine learning, and 6G network management. The study explores QML's potential to optimize resource allocation in 6G networks by harnessing the unmatched processing capabilities of quantum computing. QML algorithms, empowered by quantum parallelism and superposition, provide innovative solutions for dynamic spectrum management, routing, and quality-of-service (QoS) optimization. The research delves into the design and implementation of quantum circuits tailored to resource allocation challenges, highlighting their effectiveness in alleviating network congestion and elevating QoS.

Furthermore, it explores the quantum-inspired reinforcement learning paradigm, enabling autonomous decision-making by network components. Quantum neural networks are deployed to decipher complex patterns in network traffic,

**Corresponding author*: pr8874@srmist.edu.in

Pallavi Sapkale, Shilpa Mehta and S. Balamurugan (eds.) Quantum Computing and Machine Learning for 6G, (327–348) © 2026 Scrivener Publishing LLC

facilitating real-time, context-aware resource allocation. These advancements hold the promise of reducing latency, optimizing throughput, and enhancing the overall efficiency of 6G networks.

Keywords: Quantum machine learning, 6G network, traffic prediction, network security in vehicular communication, resource management, quality of service

15.1 Introduction

The insistent walk of technology has brought us to the dawn of the 6G network era, where promises of extraordinary connectivity, speed, and reliability are poised to redefine the way we communicate and interact with our surroundings [1]. At the heart of this transformative journey lies quantum machine learning (QML) [2, 3], a convergence of quantum computing and machine learning, ready to shape the future of 6G network management (Figure 15.1).

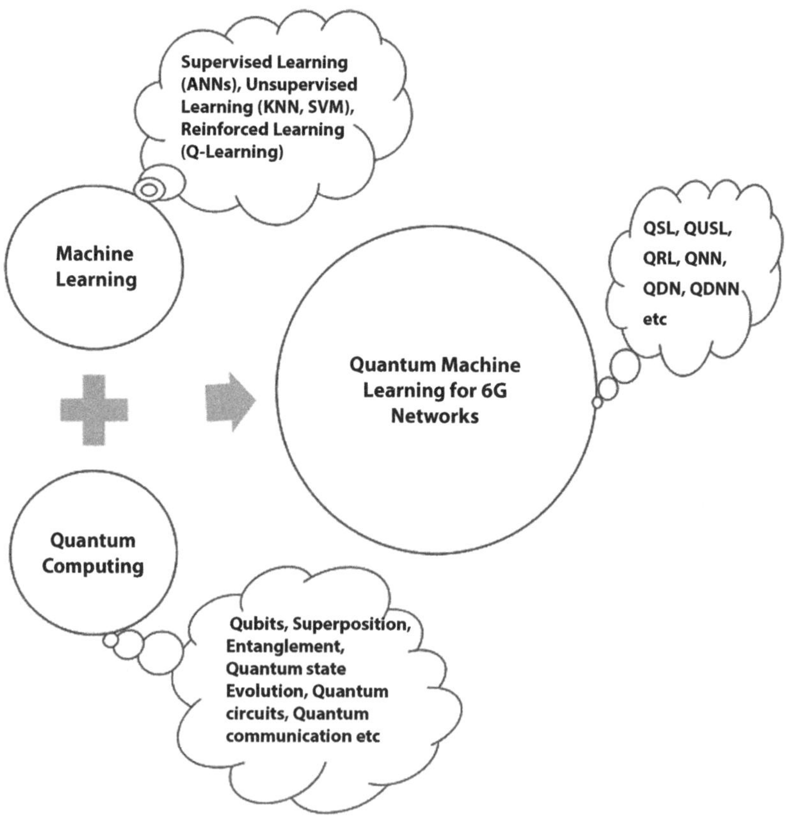

Figure 15.1 QML for 6G networks.

Quantum computing and machine learning are both the pillars of next-generation communication. When it emerges into a hybrid framework, then it is known as quantum machine learning (QML). That phenomenon has evolved with the advantages of quantum computations, such as the speed of computing, merits of statistical patterns, and uncertainty theory along with optimization, which can be resolved by the potentiality of ML algorithms. The adequate synergy of these frameworks can be deployed to vehicular communication in 6G, which will need priority in the coming days. Also, ML has the potential to analyze big data and provide possible stability to global connectivity. The different ML algorithms, like supervised and unsupervised, have paced unprecedented growth in security, stability, robustness, and data-driven learning solutions to the networks, whereas the QC will foster the processing and computation capability to the next level. Figure 15.1 shows the details of QML for 6G networks.

This research is a general exploration of QML's transformative potential in the world of 6G networks, where the fusion of quantum computing's immense processing power and machine learning's adaptability offers novel solutions to complex challenges. These challenges encompass dynamic spectrum management, intelligent routing, and quality-of-service (QoS) optimization, all critical in ensuring the seamless operation of the 6G ecosystem.

In the following sections, four distinct divisions are embarked on, each illuminating a unique facet of QML's application in 6G networks (Figure 15.7).

Section 1: The first section introduces the application of quantum machine learning (QML) in the domain of autonomous vehicles, focusing on traffic prediction. By combining advanced simulations with machine learning integration, this section provides valuable insights into vehicle behavior and safety (Figure 15.1).

Section 2: The second section explores the integration of autonomous vehicle control with quantum key distribution (QKD), aimed at enhancing security in vehicle-to-vehicle communication [4]. It discusses the complexities of QKD and its role in strengthening the safety mechanisms of autonomous vehicle control systems (Figures 15.2 and 15.3).

Section 3: The third section shifts attention to quantum-inspired optimization techniques for resource management in network slicing. This approach highlights how QML can dynamically optimize resource allocation in emerging 6G networks, ensuring efficiency and scalability (Figure 15.4).

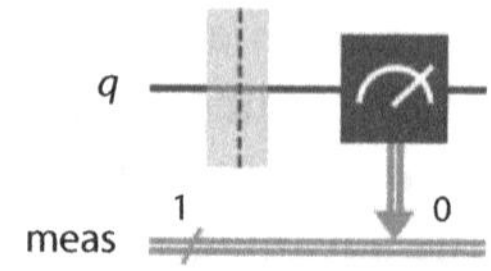

Figure 15.2 Single-qubit circuit setup.

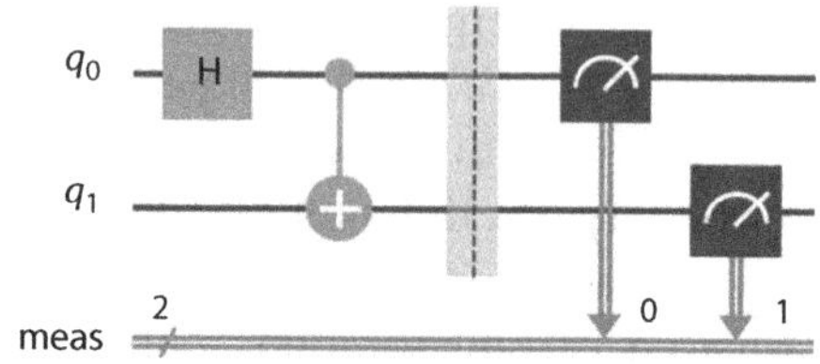

Figure 15.3 Two qubits circuit setup.

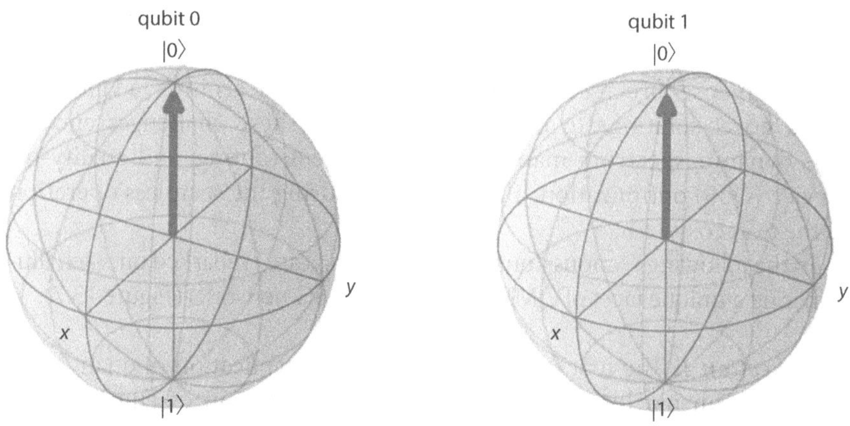

Figure 15.4 Quantum state vector.

***Section 4*:** The fourth section addresses quality-of-service (QoS) optimization using QML [5]. It explains how QML-driven approaches can enhance service reliability and performance in next-generation communication systems (Figure 15.5).

Exploring these sections is a testament to the transformative power of QML, showcasing its potential to enhance efficiency, security, and resource allocation in the 6G landscape. In a world that demands lightning-fast connectivity and unfailing reliability, QML emerges as powerfully capable of redefining what is possible in modern communication systems. As we explore these sections, we are invited to envision a future where technology transcends its limitations, ushering in a new era of seamless communication and unparalleled connectivity.

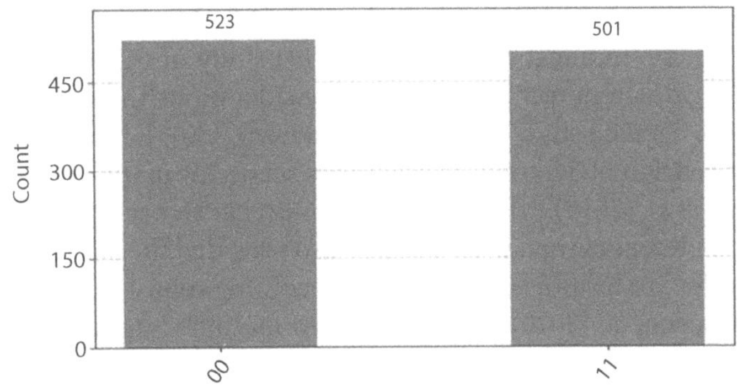

Figure 15.5 Qubit state of measurement.

15.2 Literature Survey

For fast globalization of connectivity and uninterrupted communication, 6G needs the extensive inclusion of quantum computing (QC) and quantum machine learning (QML). These three enabling technologies (ML, QC, and QML) are the building blocks of 6G and beyond networks [6–9]. They solve various optimization problems that develop in different layers of the communication system and thus make QML the best solution for forthcoming wireless communication systems. In this literature survey part, we study numerous articles regarding QC, ML, and QML and their collective applications in the communication system.

Suriya M (2022), in his survey article, mentioned the significance of QC and QML in the intelligent 5G/6G communication system. Different QC and QML principles, along with algorithms, have been analyzed for the upcoming intelligent networks. Quantum models like QKNN, QSVM, and QNN are also broadly defined for upcoming global networking in this study [26].

Duong *et al.* (2022) proposed a framework model called quantum-inspired real-time optimization for 6G networks, which basically implemented QML techniques for its best optimization by implementing the true concept of QC and QML. That also provided the roadmap for real-time optimization problem-solving capabilities of the networks [27].

V. Kulkarni *et al.* (2021) described the advantages of quantum computing methods for machine learning, like supervised machine learning, which studied the vivid methodology involved in the process [28].

Gyongyosi, Laszlo, and Imre (2019) provided the basic idea of quantum computation and discussed the open challenges associated with it. In this study, the authors emphasized the positive outcomes of QC and its relative applications in real use cases [29].

M. Chiani *et al.* (2018) and F. Tariq *et al.* (2019) studied open issues in beyond 5G communication and speculative study of 6G, respectively, by considering different technologies into consideration. This resulted in and propelled a detailed study of QC, ML, and QML [30]. F. Tariq *et al.* (2020) extend the vision of 5G to more ambitious scenarios in this work [31].

W. Saad *et al.* (2019) demonstrated a comprehensive study of 6G systems based on different new analytic tools. It also provided the different research areas that had to be looked into for the upcoming robust networking [32].

S. J. Nawaz *et al.* (2019) studied quantum machine learning for 6G communication networks. In that paper, they provided a comprehensive review of ML, QC, and QML for 5G and beyond networks, which in turn made a road map to enable the QML emerging technology for 6G systems. They proposed a framework for the same and discussed various open research directions [33].

Through the detailed study in the literature survey section, it has been found that QC, ML, and QML are emerging technologies in the wireless communication system. Each and every study mentioned its merits and future research directions, but a vivid and solid foundation for the same has been missing. In this article, some very précised context related to the detailed study has been mentioned here. These are as follows:

- Earlier work separately analyzed ML, QC, QML, and intelligent communication networks, but there is a huge gap in the detailed study that will give a proper framework for the 6G system that deploys all these. This article aims to minimize this gap.
- The state-of-the-art designing of the QML and its role in 6G integrated vehicular networks is done here.
- The proposed design will include different enabling algorithms, technologies, and optimization frameworks for 6G networks that, in turn, meet the expectations of global infrastructure.
- State-of-the-art optimization model for intelligent decision-making and its possible solutions for the 6G vehicular networks are also done.

15.3 Methodology

15.3.1 Quantum Machine Learning for Traffic Prediction in 6G Networks

In the rapidly evolving landscape of 6G networks, quantum machine learning (QML) catalyzes groundbreaking innovations [2, 8]. This first section explores the convergence of quantum technologies and autonomous vehicles, offering a glimpse into the future of traffic prediction. By leveraging quantum principles, advanced algorithms, and a safety-centric approach, this simulation covers the way for a safer, more efficient, and transformative era in 6G network applications.

15.3.1.1 Environment Setup

In this section, we lay the foundation for a comprehensive exploration of quantum machine learning (QML) within the realm of 6G networks. The initial step involves setting up an environment that simulates the movement of an autonomous vehicle over a specified time frame, providing a realistic context for further investigations. The simulation spans 10 seconds, with a time step of 0.1 seconds, allowing for the precise tracking of the vehicle's behavior. The autonomous vehicle has initial parameters, including position, velocity, maximum acceleration, maximum deceleration, and target velocity [9].

Representation of Quantum

- Position of the autonomous vehicle: p(t), a function of time (t).
- Velocity of the vehicle: $v(t) = \frac{dp(t)}{dt}$
- Initial conditions: p(0) for the initial position and v(0) for the initial velocity.

A basic environment setup for single qubits and measures is used to construct the quantum-based network to communicate with each other.

15.3.1.2 Quantum Traffic Prediction Model

This phase introduces the quantum machine learning model, a pinnacle of innovation within the 6G network landscape [10]. Leveraging the versatile capabilities of the PennyLane python library, this model takes the stage to address a fundamental challenge in modern transportation traffic prediction. By employing a quantum circuit equipped with two qubits, characterized by quantum embedding and strongly entangling layers, the model enters the realm of quantum-inspired solutions.

15.3.1.3 Quantum Circuit Representation

Quantum gates, qubits, and quantum states are described using quantum mechanics principles [11]. The specific representation depends on the quantum algorithms used in the model. Figure 15.2 and Figure 15.3 describes the single-qubit and two qubits circuit setup respectively.

This two-qubit quantum circuit, as shown in Figure 15.3, leverages quantum superposition and entanglement to enable secure and efficient communication between vehicle nodes in the 6G network traffic prediction model.

Figure 15.4 illustrates the state vector of two qubits with initial \00> position. Once the communication starts, it will change its status to transfer the signal [12].

Figure 15.5 illustrates the qubit state of measurement of the outcome. This shows the probability of communication to reach the nodes.

15.3.1.4 Safety Analysis

With the quantum model's predictions, the research progresses to the critical safety analysis phase. This step is imperative as it assesses not only the accuracy of the quantum model's predictions but also the safety and efficiency of the autonomous vehicle's behavior [9]. Visualizing the position of the 6G vehicle over time offers deep insights into its movement patterns and safety precautions.

Position-time graph: Figure 15.6 illustrates the position of the vehicle over time.
Safety metrics: Figure 15.7 shows safety, such as acceleration, deceleration, and time to reach the target velocity.

15.3.1.5 Interpretation

Position-Time Graph
Figure 15.6 displays the position of the 6G vehicle over time. The x-axis represents time in seconds, and the y-axis represents the vehicle's position in meters. The place is calculated using a simple quadratic curve, commonly used to describe smooth acceleration and deceleration patterns. As time progresses, the vehicle's position increases, following a quadratic curve. This indicates that the vehicle is accelerating and then decelerating in a controlled manner. Figure 15.6 visually shows the position changes over time, providing insights into the vehicle's movement patterns.

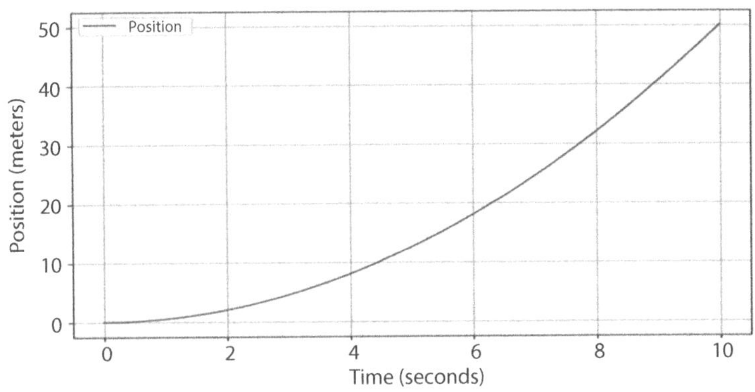

Figure 15.6 Position-time graph.

Safety Metric (Acceleration) Graph

Figure 15.7 displays the acceleration of the 6G vehicle over time. The x-axis represents time in seconds, and the y-axis represents the vehicle's acceleration in meters per second squared (m/s^2). Figure 15.7 features a horizontal red dashed line at zero acceleration, serving as a reference point for zero acceleration. Positive values above the reference line indicate acceleration, while negative values below the line represent deceleration. Figure 15.7 allows you to assess the vehicle's acceleration patterns. A smooth curve suggests controlled and safe acceleration and deceleration. The reference line at zero acceleration indicates moments when the vehicle is not accelerating or decelerating.

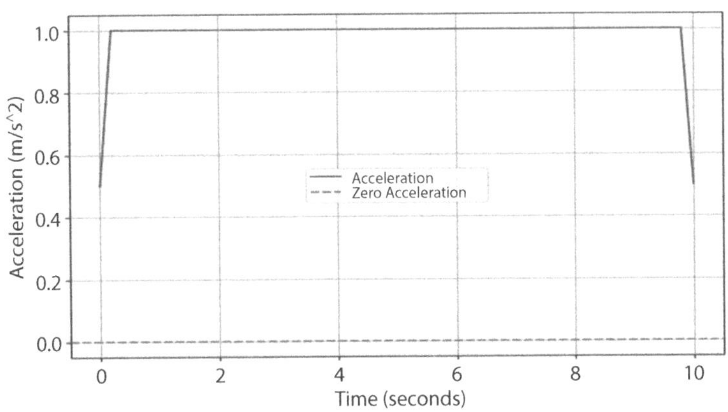

Figure 15.7 Safety metrics.

Figure 15.7 provides a visual representation of the vehicle's position and safety metrics, helping to analyze its behavior over time. They are based on mathematical models, and the specific functions used for position and acceleration calculations can be customized to match real-world scenarios and safety criteria. Its core strength lies in its ability to tackle the complexities of traffic prediction, merging quantum principles, advanced algorithms, and quantum states.

15.3.2 QML for Network Security in Vehicular Communication

In the dynamic landscape of 6G networks and autonomous vehicle systems, the fusion of quantum machine learning (QML) and quantum key distribution (QKD) is set to revolutionize network security and communication [2, 13]. This simulation embarks on a journey that encompasses the setup of an autonomous vehicle environment and explores the transformative potential of quantum technologies. From quantum traffic prediction models to quantum communication security, this scenario exemplifies the innovative strides made toward enhancing safety, efficiency, and security in 6G networks and vehicular communication.

15.3.2.1 Environment Setup

In this intricate simulation, we lay the foundation for integrating quantum communication security within autonomous vehicle systems [14]. The journey begins with establishing a virtual environment that encapsulates an autonomous vehicle's movement. The autonomous vehicle commences its expedition from an initial position of 0 meters and an initial velocity of 10 m/s. Key parameters come into play, including the maximum acceleration (2 m/s^2), maximum deceleration (-3 m/s^2), and a target velocity of 20 m/s. These parameters set the stage for a secure and efficient vehicular communication system. Figure 15.8 shows an arrangement for two-qubit primary environment circuit.

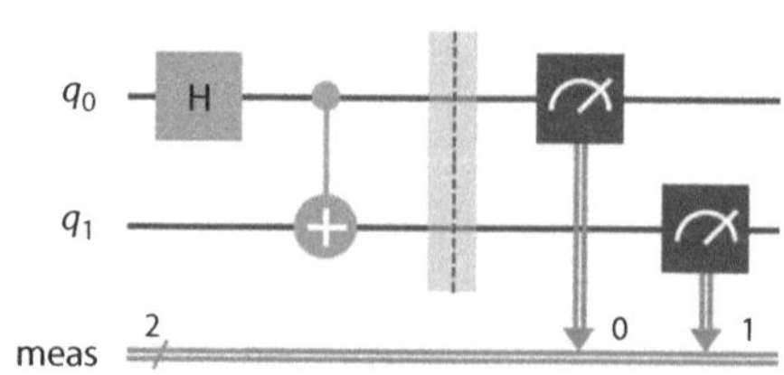

Figure 15.8 Two-qubit primary environment circuit.

15.3.2.2 Quantum Key Distribution (QKD)

A progressive feature of this simulation is the introduction of quantum key distribution (QKD) as a robust mechanism for ensuring secure communication between the autonomous vehicle and other entities [15]. The QKD takes center stage, representing the QKD protocol. Within the quantum realm, a circuit with two qubits materializes, symbolizing the communication between Node1 and Node2—the principal actors in this security narrative. Figure 15.9 and Figure 15.10 shows the Node 1 and Node 2 setups.

15.3.2.3 Node1's Side (Initialization)

The narrative explores the quantum side of security. On Node1's end, the stage is set for quantum charm. The first qubit (qubit 0) is meticulously prepared with an initial state. The Hadamard gate (H gate) is invoked, creating a superposition state that forms the bedrock of secure communication. The superposition state represents the fundamental choice of encoding for sensitive information [16, 17].

15.3.2.4 Quantum Communication Channel (Simulated)

This simulation section mirrors the quantum communication channel, a critical component in the secure transmission of information. While the term "simulated" is used here, in practical applications, this step represents

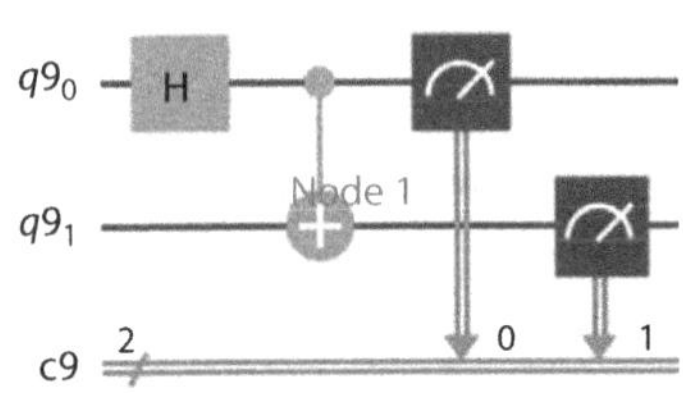

Figure 15.9 Node 1 setup.

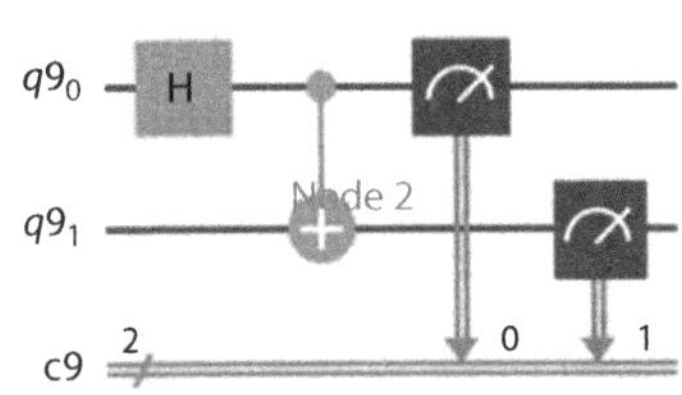

Figure 15.10 Node 2 setup.

the actual transmission of qubits between Node1 and Node2 over a secure quantum channel, ensuring the integrity and confidentiality of data [18].

15.3.2.5 Node2's Measurement

Node2, the recipient of the secure information, takes center stage as it measures its designated qubit (qubit 1). Its measurement carries the responsibility of extracting concealed information and ensuring its security [17].

15.3.2.6 Security and Key Sharing

A key milestone in the simulation represents the secure sharing of measurement results between Node1 and Node2. These shared results, devoid of interference or eavesdropping, assume the role of a shared key. This key is the cornerstone of secure and confidential communication during the expedition [19].

The rest of the description remains the same, with the terminology adjusted to feature Node1 and Node2 instead of Alice and Bob. This simulation, featuring Node1 and Node2, is an illustrative example of the seamless integration of quantum communication security into autonomous vehicle systems. It illustrates the potential to safeguard vehicular communication against threats and intrusions with real-world applications involving advanced QKD protocols and comprehensive security measures to ensure robust security in autonomous vehicle networks.

15.3.2.7 Interpretation

This simulation represents a new stride toward enhancing the security and integrity of communication in autonomous vehicle systems within the scope of 6G networks. Integrating quantum key distribution (QKD) and quantum principles demonstrates the potential to establish a secure communication channel that safeguards sensitive data during transmission. The simulation, featuring Node1 and Node2, exemplifies the successful exchange of a shared key, free from external interference, highlighting the promising application of quantum-inspired security mechanisms in vehicular communication. This innovative approach not only secures data but also ensures the efficiency and trustworthiness of communication in an era where autonomous vehicles play a pivotal role. It provides a foundational glimpse into the transformative potential of quantum technologies in the evolving landscape of 6G networks and autonomous systems. Figure 15.11 demonstrates the quantum key distribution for security communication.

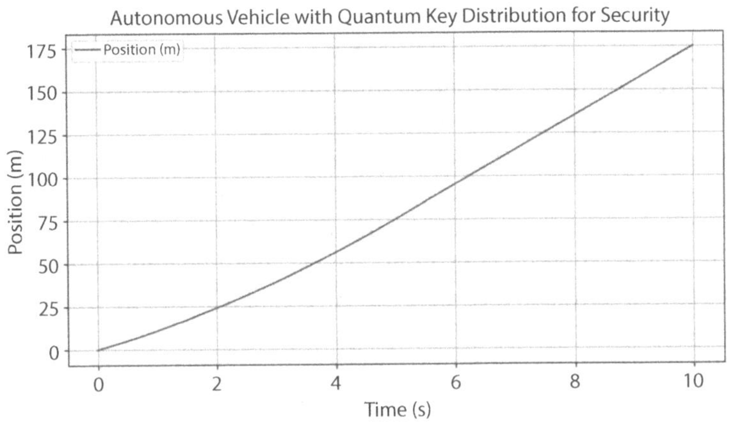

Figure 15.11 Quantum key distribution for security communication.

15.3.3 6G Network Slicing and Resource Management by QML

Network slicing is a cutting-edge technology that has revolutionized the management and optimization of network resources, effectively catering to the diverse and ever-evolving requirements of modern communication systems [16]. In this document, we delve into network slicing and introduce the concept of quantum-inspired optimization techniques, which have shown immense promise in efficiently allocating and managing these valuable network resources. Our simulation showcases the practical application of quantum-inspired resource management within network slicing.

15.3.3.1 Environment Setup

Figure 15.12 shows the single-qubit quantum circuit with Hadamard and R family gate. In this quantum circuit setup, a single qubit is initialized, and a Hadamard gate is applied to place it in a superposition state. Subsequently, X- and Y-axis rotations are executed on the qubit, with the rotation angles determined by the values in the "params" array [20]. This configuration forms the foundation for quantum operations and manipulations within the circuit.

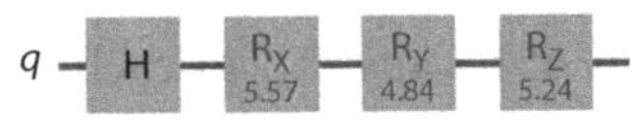

Figure 15.12 Single-qubit quantum circuit with Hadamard and R family gate.

15.3.3.1.1 Implementation Parameters

In our exploration, we have established essential parameters that govern the simulation's dynamics. The total simulation time encompasses a 10-second window, allowing for a comprehensive investigation. We intricately dissect the resource allocation process using a time step of 0.1 seconds, enabling a detailed examination of resource adjustments over time.

Our focus centers on managing five distinct network slices, each with unique requirements and constraints. To provide a reference point, we initiate the simulation with an initial bandwidth allocation of 5 Gbps for each network slice.

Furthermore, our quantum-inspired resource management adds a layer of dynamism to the allocation process. To achieve this, we introduce three randomly chosen parameters for quantum rotations, ensuring that the resource allocation adapts dynamically to changing conditions. This combination of parameters and time frame facilitates a comprehensive exploration of resource management in the context of network slicing.

The simulation progresses systematically through stages: initialization, quantum-inspired optimization, iterative resource adjustments, optimized outcomes, and visual representation of bandwidth allocation.

15.3.3.2 Implementation Process

Classical Resource Management

In the classical resource management phase, the initial bandwidth allocations for network slices are determined based on traditional principles. These allocations serve as a benchmark for comparison with the quantum-inspired approach, providing a foundation to assess the improvements achieved through quantum techniques [10].

Quantum-Inspired Resource Management

The true innovation emerges with quantum-inspired optimization techniques. This phase dynamically adjusts bandwidth allocations for the network slices, introducing adaptability and efficiency. Random changes to bandwidth allocations during the simulation showcase the dynamic nature of this approach, allowing for real-time adjustments [21].

Resource Allocation Over Time

Over time, the allocation of bandwidth to each network slice is meticulously documented. This temporal tracking enables the observation of quantum-inspired resource management's dynamic nature and ability to adapt and optimize resource allocation as network conditions evolve.

Quantum Circuit Visualization
A visual representation of the quantum circuit used in the resource management model is provided. This circuit incorporates single-qubit operations, including the Hadamard gate and rotations along the x-, y-, and z-axes. Parameters for these operations are determined by random values, illustrating the versatility of quantum-inspired techniques [22].

Resource Allocation Plot
To conclude the simulation, a graphical representation of resource allocation for each network slice over time is presented. This plot visually emphasizes the dynamic adaptability and optimization brought about by quantum-inspired resource management, showcasing the benefits of this innovative approach in network slicing.

15.3.3.3 *Interpretation*

Figure 15.13 paints a vivid picture of the dynamic resource management capabilities achieved through quantum-inspired optimization techniques. The innovation's ability to adapt resource allocation in real time highlights its potential advantages over conventional static resource allocation methods [9]. It is important to note that real-world quantum-inspired algorithms are typically more intricate and tailored to the specific requirements of communication networks. Still, this demonstration serves as a starting point for exploring the broader application of quantum computing in network optimization and slicing. The fusion of quantum-inspired techniques

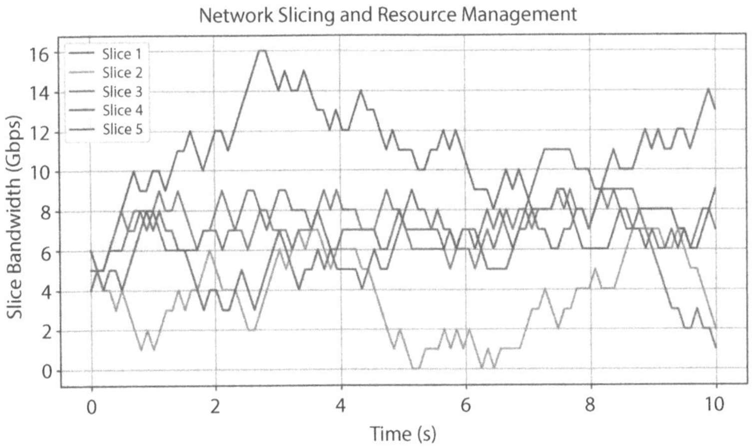

Figure 15.13 Network slicing and resource management.

with network slicing has the potential to transform the efficiency and adaptability of communication systems in the digital age.

15.3.4 Quality-of-Service (QoS) Optimization by QML

Efficiently allocating bandwidth in communication networks is paramount to ensure optimal resource utilization. In this document, we embark on an exploration of quantum-inspired optimization to manage bandwidth allocation in a network-slicing scenario dynamically [23]. The primary objective is to maximize the total allocated bandwidth while adhering to the constraints inherent in this context.

15.3.4.1 Environment Setup and Parameters

In our experimental framework, we have defined crucial parameters to underpin our simulation. These parameters include the management of bandwidth allocation for five distinct network slices, leveraging a total available bandwidth of 100 Gbps as the resource for optimal distribution. To maximize bandwidth allocation, we introduce a simplified cost function as the guiding principle. The innovative aspect of our simulation lies in the introduction of quantum-inspired optimization, a dynamic approach that harnesses quantum principles to allocate resources in real-time adaptively. This infusion of quantum-inspired techniques introduces a new dimension of dynamism and efficiency to the resource allocation process, promising enhanced performance and adaptability.

15.3.4.2 Implementation Process

Initialization: We begin with the initiation of the simulation, where each network slice is assigned an initial allocation of bandwidth. For this example, we maintain an equitable distribution, with each slice receiving an equal portion of the available bandwidth.
Quantum-Inspired Bandwidth Allocation: Here is where the heart of the quantum-inspired optimization beats. We deploy a quantum-inspired optimization algorithm, employing PennyLane as the instrument of choice for this endeavor. The primary goal is maximizing the allocated bandwidth while adhering to the predefined constraints.
Optimization Iterations: The simulation unfurls across 100 iterations, during which the optimization algorithm dynamically adjusts the bandwidth allocations. This iterative process captures the essence of quantum-inspired adaptability.

Optimized Bandwidth Allocation: Following the optimization process, we extract the fruit of our labor—the optimized bandwidth allocations for each network slice.
Visualization: The results take on a visual form as we craft a bar plot. This visualization effectively conveys the optimized bandwidth allocations for each network slice.

15.3.4.3 Interpretation

In Figure 15.14, we have harnessed the power of quantum-inspired optimization to maximize the total allocated bandwidth across the network slices. The outcome reflects a balanced allocation strategy where each network slice receives approximately 90.45 Gbps. This equilibrium in allocation not only leads to efficient resource utilization but also ensures that all slices enjoy fair and equitable access to the available bandwidth.

The cost function introduced in this example signifies maximizing bandwidth allocation. In practical scenarios, such as real-world network environments, the cost function would extend its considerations to encompass more complex factors like latency, quality of service (QoS), and other specific network requirements.

Quantum-inspired optimization introduces an exciting potential to adapt dynamically to changing network conditions and allocate resources with precision and efficiency. It offers a glimpse into how quantum principles can be harnessed to address real-world resource management challenges.

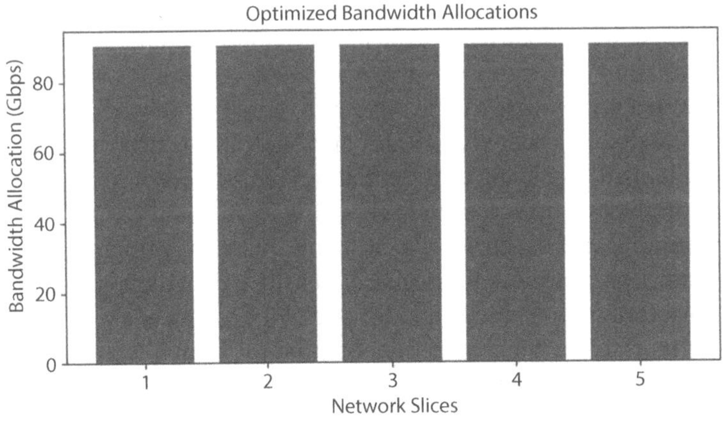

Figure 15.14 Optimized bandwidth allocation.

This chapter acts as an introduction to the concept of quantum-inspired bandwidth allocation and the potential it holds for application in network slicing. It is important to note that in real-world scenarios, quantum-inspired algorithms would be meticulously tailored to the unique requirements and constraints of specific network environments, thereby enhancing the overall quality of service (QoS) and resource management.

15.4 Results and Discussion

- *Quantum Machine Learning for Traffic Prediction in 6G Networks*:

The simulation demonstrates the practical application of quantum machine learning (QML) for traffic prediction in 6G networks. It successfully predicts the behavior of an autonomous vehicle over a 10-second timeframe. The vehicle's movement, including acceleration and deceleration, is tracked precisely. The quantum model, powered by PennyLane, offers real-time traffic predictions.

Using QML in traffic prediction showcases the transformative potential of quantum technologies in enhancing autonomous vehicle behavior. Analyzing the vehicle's journey, we find that it efficiently accelerates to reach its target velocity and judiciously decelerates, demonstrating safety and optimal behavior. In real-world traffic scenarios, where complexities like traffic conditions and obstacles are involved, the quantum model's adaptability and predictive capabilities can revolutionize traffic management.

The fusion of quantum principles and machine learning techniques in traffic prediction holds promise in enhancing transportation safety and efficiency within the dynamic landscape of 6G networks.

- *QML for Network Security in Vehicular Communication*:

This simulation illustrates the integration of quantum key distribution (QKD) into autonomous vehicle systems to enhance network security. The shared vital exchange between Node1 and Node2 is secured through quantum mechanisms, ensuring confidential and tamper-proof communication.

The simulation showcases the promising application of QKD in vehicular communication security. By utilizing quantum principles to secure communication channels, it safeguards sensitive data during transmission between autonomous vehicles. Node1 and Node2's successful key exchange without interference highlights the potential for robust security measures in independent vehicle networks.

Quantum-inspired security mechanisms can provide a trustworthy framework for communication, which is vital for ensuring the integrity and confidentiality of data in vehicular networks.

• *6G Network Slicing and Resource Management by QML:*
The simulation explores quantum-inspired optimization techniques for resource allocation in the context of network slicing. It dynamically manages the bandwidth allocation for five network slices and achieves an equitable distribution of resources.

Quantum-inspired optimization techniques have been showcased to allocate resources across network slices efficiently. The equitable bandwidth distribution ensures fair access for each network slice while maximizing the allocated bandwidth. In real-world scenarios, quantum-inspired algorithms can adapt to changing network conditions and offer precise resource management.

This simulation introduces the concept of quantum-inspired resource allocation, laying the foundation for future applications in network slicing, where dynamically managing resources is crucial for maintaining quality of service and network efficiency.

• *Quality-of-Service (QoS) Optimization by QML:*
The simulation demonstrates quantum-inspired optimization techniques for maximizing allocated bandwidth in a network slicing scenario. It achieves a balanced allocation of approximately 90.45 Gbps for each network slice.

Quantum-inspired optimization techniques provide a solution to dynamically allocate bandwidth resources while ensuring equitable access for network slices. The results indicate efficient resource utilization, maintaining a balance in resource allocation among slices. In practical applications, the cost function can encompass more complex factors to enhance the quality of service (QoS).

This simulation introduces the concept of quantum-inspired bandwidth allocation and its potential to address real-world resource management challenges. It highlights the adaptability of quantum-inspired algorithms in optimizing resource allocation for improved network efficiency.

The simulations demonstrate the substantial potential of quantum machine learning (QML) and quantum-inspired techniques in enhancing 6G network capabilities. These advancements can revolutionize traffic prediction, network security, resource management, and quality of service in the evolving landscape of 6G networks, ultimately delivering unparalleled connectivity, efficiency, and reliability [24, 25].

15.5 Conclusion

It integrates quantum machine learning (QML) and quantum-inspired techniques within the scope of 6G networks, ushering in a new era of transformative capabilities. Through the simulations presented, it becomes evident that QML is vital in addressing critical aspects of 6G network management.

The application of QML in traffic prediction not only enhances our understanding of autonomous vehicle behavior but also promises to revolutionize traffic management within dynamic 6G network scenarios, offering a safer and more efficient transportation landscape.

In the context of network security, the integration of quantum key distribution (QKD) ensures secure and confidential communication between autonomous vehicles, safeguarding sensitive data against potential threats and intrusions. This quantum-inspired approach represents a vital advancement in ensuring the integrity of vehicular communication systems.

Moreover, quantum-inspired techniques in resource management and bandwidth allocation exhibit a dynamic and adaptive approach to network slicing, efficiently catering to the diverse requirements of modern communication systems. By maximizing allocated bandwidth while adhering to constraints, this approach paves the way for optimal resource utilization and equitable access among network slices.

The QML and quantum-inspired methods in 6G networks promise unparalleled connectivity, efficiency, and reliability. These innovations exemplify the power of quantum technologies in reshaping the future of communication systems, providing the seamless and transformative connectivity that our increasingly interconnected world demands. The chapter also dives into the different emerging technologies and QML-based optimization techniques in the 6G networks and provides key research directions toward the upcoming communication systems. Extensive studies may be done in the field of specific algorithm-based QML for optimization in 6G integrated vehicular networks. As QML plays a key role in 6G networks, its proper application in 6G also may be studied in the future.

References

1. Ge, X., Li, Z., Li, S., 5G software defined vehicular networks. *IEEE Commun. Mag.*, 55, 7, 87–93, 2017, doi: 10.1109/MCOM.2017.1601144.
2. Biamonte, J., Wittek, P., Pancotti, N., Rebentrost, P., *et al.*, Quantum machine learning. *Nature*, 549, 7671, 195–202, 2017, doi: 10.1038/nature23474.

3. Dong, D., Chen, C., Li, H., Tarn, T.J., Quantum reinforcement learning. *IEEE Trans. Syst. Man Cybern. Part B Cybern.*, 38, 5, 1207–1220, 2008, doi: 10.1109/TSMCB.2008.925743.
4. Broadbent, A. and Schaffner, C., Quantum cryptography beyond quantum key distribution. *Des. Codes Cryptogr.*, 78, 1, 351–382, 2016, doi: 10.1007/s10623-015-0157-4.
5. Li, Y., Tian, M., Liu, G., Peng, C., *et al.*, Quantum optimization and quantum learning: A survey. *IEEE Access*, 8, 23568–23593, 2020, doi: 10.1109/ACCESS.2020.2970105.
6. Dey, S., Phenomenon of Excess of Artificial Intelligence: Quantifying the Native AI, Its Leverages in 5G/6G and Beyond, in: *Radar and RF Front End System Designs for Wireless Systems*, pp. 245–274, IGI Global, Hershey, PA, USA, 2024.
7. Dey, S., Panda, A.K., Pati, C., Unlocking the potential of machine learning and deep learning algorithms in recent communication: AI the best revolutionary tool in current era. *CPPPT*, 23, 2, 2794–2805, 2023.
8. Chen, S.Y.-C., Quantum deep Q learning with distributed prioritized experience replay, 2023, [Online], Available: http://arxiv.org/abs/2304.09648.
9. Shah, S.A.A., Ahmed, E., Imran, M., *et al.*, 5G for Vehicular Communications. *IEEE Commun. Mag.*, 56, 1, 111–117, 2018, doi: 10.1109/MCOM.2018.1700467.
10. Suciu, G., Hussain, I., Esanu, I.A., Beceanu, C., *et al.*, Role of 5G in Vehicular Network for Smart Vehicles in Smart Cities, in: *2021 IEEE 27th International Symposium for Design and Technology in Electronic Packaging (SIITME)*, pp. 382–387, 2021, doi: 10.1109/SIITME53254.2021.9663700.
11. Feynman, R.P., Feynman, R., *et al.*, *Gate1*, 1959, 2011, doi: 10.1007/978-1-84628-887-6.
12. Barenco, A., *et al.*, Elementary gates for quantum computation. *Phys. Rev. A*, 52, 3457–3467, 1995, doi: 10.1103/PhysRevA.52.3457.
13. Scarani, V., Bechmann-Pasquinucci, H., Cerf, N.J., Dušek, M., *et al.*, The security of practical quantum key distribution. *Rev. Mod. Phys.*, 81, 3, 1301–1350, 2009, doi: 10.1103/RevModPhys.81.1301.
14. Carsten, P., Andel, T.R., Yampolskiy, M., McDonald, J.T., In-vehicle networks: Attacks, vulnerabilities, and proposed solutions. *ACM Int. Conf. Proc. Ser.*, 1–8, 2015, doi: 10.1145/2746266.2746267.
15. Yoon, C.S., Hong, C.H., Kang, M.S., *et al.*, Quantum asymmetric key crypto scheme using Grover iteration. *Sci. Rep.*, 13, 1, 1–6, 2023, doi: 10.1038/s41598-023-30860-0.
16. Ansere, J.A., *et al.*, Quantum agents in the Gym: a variational quantum algorithm for deep Q-learning. *Quantum*, 4, 2, 1–12, 2023, doi: 10.22331/Q-2022-05-24-720.
17. Johansson, K.H., Törngren, M., Nielsen, L., Vehicle Applications of Controller Area Network. *Handb. Networked Embed. Control Syst.*, 741–765, 2005, doi: 10.1007/0-8176-4404-0_32.

18. Rieffel, E. and Polak, W., An introduction to quantum computing for non-physicists, vol. 32, 2000, doi: 10.1145/367701.367709.
19. Cleve, R., An Introduction to Quantum Complexity Theory. *Quantum Comput. Quantum Inf. Theory*, 103–127, 2001, doi: 10.1142/9789810248185_0004.
20. Zhou, X., Feng, Y., Li, S., Quantum Circuit Transformation: A Monte Carlo Tree Search Framework. *ACM Trans. Des. Autom. Electron. Syst.*, 27, 6, 2022, doi: 10.1145/3514239.
21. Wang, B., Zhang, B.F., Zou, F.C., Xia, Y., A kind of improved quantum key distribution scheme. *Opt. (Stuttg).*, 235, 166628, 2021, doi: 10.1016/j.ijleo.2021.166628.
22. Wei, Q., Ma, H., Chen, C., Dong, D., Deep Reinforcement Learning With Quantum-Inspired Experience Replay. *IEEE Trans. Cybern.*, 1–12, 2021, doi: 10.1109/TCYB.2021.3053414.
23. Krishan, R. *et al.*, *Innovative Smart Materials Used in Wireless Communication Technology*, IGI Global, Hershey, PA, 2023.
24. Krishan, R., *et al.*, Innovative Smart Materials Used in Wireless Communication Technology, Global, I.G.I., 2023.
25. Jaganathan, R., *et al.*, Intelligent Decision Making Through Bio-Inspired Optimization, Global, I.G.I., 2024.
26. Suriya, M., Machine Learning and Quantum Computing for 5G/6G Communication Networks: A Survey. *Int. J. Intell. Netw.*, 3, 1–8, 2022, https://doi.org/10.1016/j.ijin.2022.06.001.
27. Duong, Trung Q. *et al.*, Quantum-Inspired Real-Time Optimization for 6G Networks: Opportunities, Challenges, and the Road Ahead. *IEEE Open J. Commun. Soc.*, 3, 1347–1361, 2022, https://doi.org/10.1109/OJCOMS.2022.3199932.
28. Kulkarni, V., Kulkarni, M., Pant, A., Quantum Computing Methods for Supervised Learning. *SN Comput. Sci.*, 2, 5, article 377, 2021, https://doi.org/10.1007/s42979-021-00798-6.
29. Gyongyosi, L. and Imre, S., A Survey on Quantum Computing Technology. *Comput. Sci. Rev.*, 31, 51–71, 2019, https://doi.org/10.1016/j.cosrev.2018.11.003.
30. Chiani, M., *et al., Open Issues and Beyond 5G*, 5G Italy White eBook, pp. 1–22, 2018, https://www.5gitaly.eu/2018/wp-content/uploads/2019/01/5G-Italy-White-eBook-Beyond-5G.pdf.
31. Tariq, F., *et al.*, A Speculative Study on 6G. *IEEE Wirel. Commun.*, 27, 4, 118–125, 2020, https://doi.org/10.1109/MWC.001.1900488.
32. Saad, W., *et al.*, A Vision of 6G Wireless Systems: Applications, Trends, Technologies, and Open Research Problems. *IEEE Netw.*, 34, 3, 134–142, 2020, https://doi.org/10.1109/MNET.001.1900287.
33. Nawaz, S.J., *et al.*, Quantum Machine Learning for 6G Communication Networks: State-of-the-Art and Vision for the Future. *IEEE Access,* 7, 46317–46350, 2019, https://doi.org/10.1109/ACCESS.2019.2909490.

Part V
APPLICATIONS

16

Smart Irrigation Technique Using IoT Based on 5G

Jyoti B. Deone[1]* and Khan Rahat Afreen[2]

[1]*RAIT D.Y Patil Deemed to be University, Navi Mumbai, India*
[2]*CSE Dept. of DIEMS Dr. Babasaheb Ambedkar Marathwada University, Chh. Sambhaji Nagar, India*

Abstract
Agriculture is a demanding occupation that uses a lot of water, so we need systems that use water wisely. Farmers need to measure and irrigate their crops with the right amount of water. Farmers should go to the field and use their intuition and experience to estimate how much water they need to release. Intelligent agriculture has been made possible by the growing adoption of 5G and advanced information technologies like the Internet of Things and artificial intelligence. Smart agriculture will flourish in large part thanks to the 5G-based Internet of Things. The main goal is to provide an automatic irrigation system that saves farmers time, money, and energy. This system records various factors such as soil moisture and water level. Smart irrigation systems are evolving with new technologies, such as the Internet of Things (IoT), and are controlled automatically from remote locations. The system can also control the amount of water supplied to plants as needed. The device will send a notification to the farmer and automatically turn on the sprinkler system. The sprinkler will automatically turn off when the moisture level reaches the reference value. The system also checks incoming water for contamination and sends notifications to farmers so they can take further action.

***Keywords*:** Agriculture, irrigation, IoT, sprinkler, 5G

**Corresponding author*: done.jyoti@gmail.com

Pallavi Sapkale, Shilpa Mehta and S. Balamurugan (eds.) Quantum Computing and Machine Learning for 6G, (351–366) © 2026 Scrivener Publishing LLC

16.1 Introduction

India is an agricultural country. The agricultural sector is very important from the villagers' point of view. Farmland productivity does not depend on excess water sprinkled on the land but on better matching of crop demand and water supply to uniform environmental conditions suitable for agriculture. Irrigation is the scientific process of artificially watering cropland or soil. Traditionally, in arid regions with little or no rain, water had to be brought to the fields *via* canals, hand pumps, or tube wells [1]. Conventional irrigation methods have serious problems, such as increasing the burden on farmers, and often cause problems such as water shortages and soil leaching. Therefore, such areas should be properly irrigated. The new technology era has redefined communication [2]. Today, the world has truly become a global village as most people have access to mobile phones. You can get in touch with a specific person at any time on your mobile phone. However, mobile phone use is not limited to sending SMS and starting conversations [3, 4]. From this, we can generate new innovations and ideas that can further improve our performance. Technologies such as infrared, Bluetooth, and Wi-Fi developed in recent years have shown that improvements are indeed possible, and these improvements have made our lives and lifestyles easier.

A traditional irrigation system is someone who drives up to a grove at a specific time and runs a well pump, assuming proper irrigation work has been done. Thus, wells dry up, pumps suck air, and the amount of water entering the irrigation system is greatly reduced [5]. Sometimes, there was no water at all, and at the end of a period, only about half of the required amount was applied to the trees. Indeed, no one knew how much water was properly used. Of course, it was not very satisfying, and even the most conscientious helpers could not do anything [6, 7]. Also, when water levels are low in the well with air being sucked into the pump inlet, there is considerable agitation of the remaining water, considerable sand and dirt are sucked up into the system, and the sprinklers would plug badly. As we face different challenges in traditional agriculture, as illustrated in Fig. 16.1, it is important to address these issues effectively.

The automated control of irrigation is the main function of the system. The automated part is handled with Python programming [8]. The gadget consists of soil humidity sensors that measure and regulate temperature, humidity, and soil humidity in order to provide information about environmental conditions. The Raspberry Pi, powered by a 5V power source, completely monitors the whole gadget. The Python web framework is used

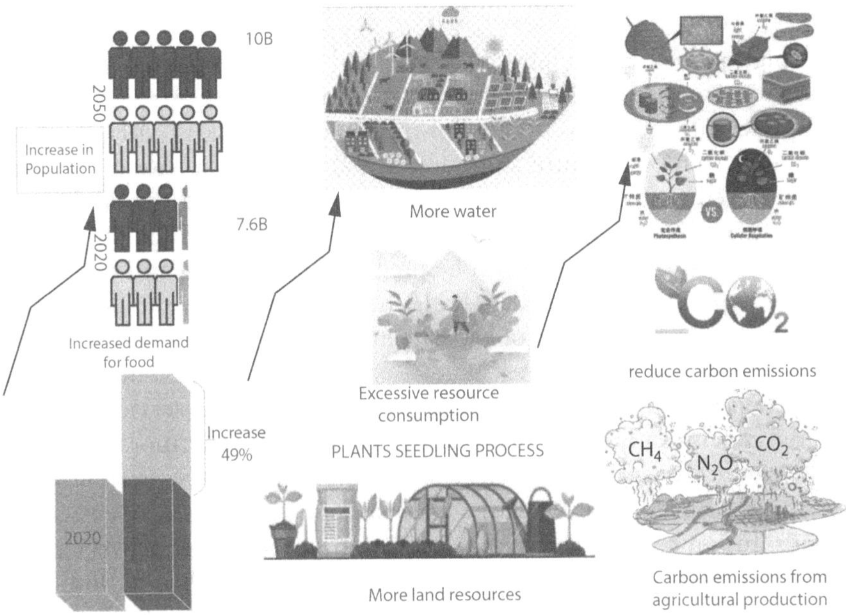

Fig. 16.1 Challenges to sustainable agricultural development in the future.

by a cloud service to understand the framework's IoT capabilities. There are several automation-enabled irrigation systems on the market right now. The irrigation systems designed by several academics to track plant development demand an amazing and expensive computer [9, 10].

Reducing the waste of water resources, electricity, and productive water consumption through the use of an intelligent soil moisture monitoring system is a successful strategy. The main selling point of the technology is its ability to simply track and manage irrigation at any time, anywhere on the Internet. Because of this, the ARM and IoT systems are quite versatile when it comes to providing pleasant drainage, soil control, and the best water preservation options.

16.2 Related Work

In order to create a smart management device that effectively uses the water at hand, an Internet-of-Things (IoT)–based smart irrigation system is employed in this study. Automatic time management, preventive and proactive irrigation, efficient water distribution and consumption, and management of water reserves are the goals of this management equipment [11].

A high-performance embedded MCU and a high-precision sensor configuration are used in the intelligent agriculture system presented in this study. Get information on the following topics: rainfall, EC, pH, diseases and pests, soil temperature and humidity, and air quality. Returned data can be saved to a distant server over a 5G network, and the data curve can be examined. The amount of water and nutrients that plants require at different times of the year can be predicted by building an experimental prototype and gathering data [12]. The cultivation plan should then be customized. An abundance of experimental evidence confirms the method's viability and efficacy. Pest prediction, intelligent irrigation, big data prediction, agricultural logistics, online experts, and other services are also offered concurrently by the management platform. Furthermore, it significantly increases agricultural yield and planting efficiency. Furthermore, for smart irrigation, this gadget uses field-deployed sensors, open-source clouds, fusion centers, and sinks. In relation to the packet delivery ratio, packets transmitted to the destination, network stability period, and energy consumption, the performance is compared with other existing approaches. The proposed management device is seen to offer greater network stability and can save up to 30% of energy consumption based on the observations of the trial findings.

The scope of the smart irrigation system (SIS) is to develop an automated irrigation system that includes sensing the moisture level of soil and watering the plants/crops accordingly. If rain is forecasted, then less water is supplied to the plants. Also, a GSM module is included so that the user can control the system *via* smartphone [3]. A water level indicator is to be included to know the amount of water used for irrigation. Furthermore, wireless sensors are also used [13].

The goals and objectives of our systems are the following:

a. To demonstrate the ability to use new methods for irrigation.
b. To reduce the workload of farmers.
c. To reduce the time spent on the whole irrigation process.
d. Implementation of automation in the irrigation system.

Fields need to be watered daily, often multiple times a day. Farmers must go to the fields to supply water and estimate the amount of water released, which is determined by different types of irrigation drips and sprinklers. Farmers have to work hard just to irrigate their crops. The system aims to enable farmers to focus on the agricultural aspect by automating the entire agricultural process. The parameters required to automate irrigation fall into three broad categories: soil, vegetation, and climatic factors [14, 15].

1. Moisture Content:
Soil Moisture

- The quantity of water in the soil is known as soil moisture. Gravimetric soil moisture content, volumetric soil moisture content, and soil moisture depth per soil depth are the methods used to characterize soil moisture content [16].

The main tool for calculating soil matric potential, or soil water suction, is a tensiometer (Fig. 16.2). This concept is frequently expressed in terms of negative pressure (soil water tension) or soil water suction. Only a small percentage spent on the whole range of accessible moisture is captured by a tensiometer, which only operates in the 0–1 range.

$$\text{Soil Moisture Content} = 100 - \left(\frac{\textit{Analog Moisture Reading}}{1023} \times 100 \right)$$

For the majority of crops, this lack of comprehensive coverage results in an imprecise assessment of the moisture-wilting threshold [1]. The farm's soil moisture sensor measures the soil's moisture content. Turning on the solenoid valve allows water to enter the farm for irrigation when the moisture content drops below a set point. The irrigation is stopped by the

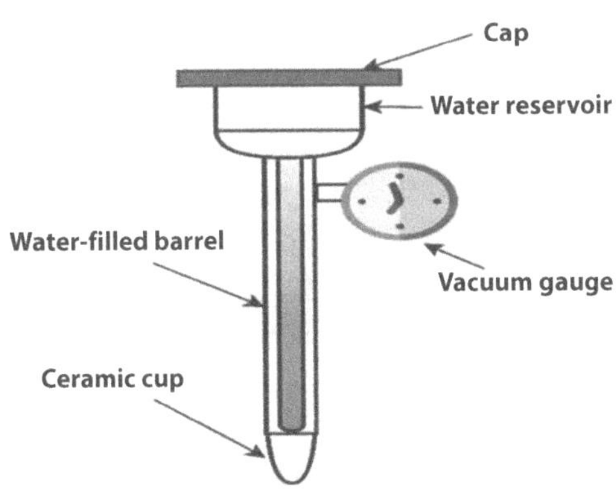

Fig. 16.2 Tensiometer.

solenoid valve turning OFF as soon as the soil's moisture content exceeds the desired level.

- The method works well in sandy soil, where moisture is often found at a depth of less than one meter; in fine-textured soil, however, it is ineffective. Although it is inexpensive and simple to install, it requires constant upkeep and has a destructive character.

2. Water Holding Capacity

- When evaluating the appropriate depth of irrigation water to apply, consider the soil's water holding ability. Plant signs operate as reservoirs in the root zone. Solid particles such as sand, silt, and clay are present in soil volume, as are spaces or pores. Air and water are used in this procedure. The volume of voids or pores containing air and water in the soil ranges from around 30% for sand to roughly 50% for clay. Although clay contains more holes than sand, its pores are smaller due to the finer particle size [17]. Because of its enormous particle size, clay sand has huge pore diameters. Both the pore volume and pore size are significant in water transport. Determines how much water is in the tank by measuring the water level or volume. To monitor the water levels, a water level sensor, shown in Fig. 16.3, is installed in the tank. The sensor is provided with the reference value as the minimal quantity needed. The user is informed of the water level if it falls below the reference level.

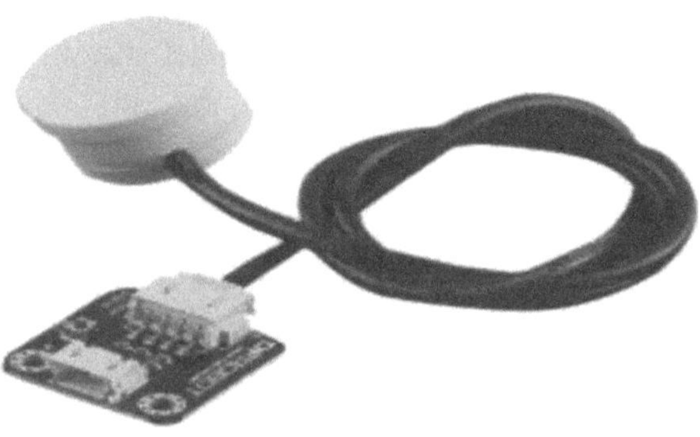

Fig. 16.3 Water level sensor.

- Saturated: A saturated soil has pores that are completely filled with water. In reality, saturated soil has air trapped in it, so it is never fully saturated. Air does not flow through the floor. Unsaturated soils have pores that are partially filled with water, allowing water to flow through the soil [18].
- Drainage: After watering, water is removed from the pores using gravity drainage and the moisture in the plant's soil. Saturated soil, therefore, becomes unsaturated. As drainage continues, the biggest pores are emptied first, followed by progressively smaller holes. Small holes are consequently filled with the residual soil moisture, and as drainage proceeds, water is held in ever smaller pores. Determines how much water is in the tank, with the primary determining variables being finely grained data inputs such as volume, pressure, and sensor readings. More accessible water can be absorbed by clay silt or loam than by sandy, coarsely structured soils.
- Soil Depth: Soil water storage capacity is also affected by soil depth. Virtually all vegetables and crops grown under irrigated conditions absorb water from the top two feet of the soil profile, but the roots of the same crops can reach much deeper.
- Frequency of watering: The proper frequency of watering is influenced by the water holding capacity of the soil and the water consumption rate of the plant and can be determined by monitoring soil moisture. A tensiometer is a simple and inexpensive device that can be used to monitor soil moisture.

16.3 5G Network on Smart Farming

The 3G, 4G, and NB-IoT wireless network technologies have been around for 10 years, and they are used to link smart devices through the Internet of Things (IoT) to share data for precise evaluation in the agricultural field. However, the effectiveness of the 4G network has diminished as a result of the improvement in information quality and quantity, as the data transfer has gotten worse than it was previously. The fifth-generation (5G) network represents the progression of communication networks by offering extremely fast data transformation speeds [15]. Due to a nearly 100-fold improvement in download and upload rates compared to the 4G network, the 5G network allows for quicker data transfer than existing networks [14].

For the first time in 2017, autonomous tractors and drones were employed in smart farming applications such as crop harvesting, fertilization, insecticides, and seed operations. Additionally, 5G provides benefits for the agriculture industry, as it enhances a variety of agricultural tasks, including drone control, interactive real-time monitoring, seeding operations, pesticide and fertilizer spraying, artificial intelligence robots, and data analytics [19].

16.3.1 The Following Decade Will See the Development of 5G and Smart Farming

High-bandwidth connection has been the primary emphasis of 5G's early phases. Centralized farms will be the most realistic use cases prior to the widespread adoption of 5G infrastructure. Thousands of transactional or triggered IoT sensors may be aggregated into one major corporate agricultural operation's private 5G network to support high-bandwidth use cases (such as drone-based crop monitoring). When a farming operation uses a lot of data from many sources, 5G will now be most useful. Thermostat and feeding machine data are collected at a hub on an industrial chicken farm. Each of these hundreds of sensors produces small amounts of data at a low cost or with too little complexity for a 5G broadband data connection [4]. The obtained bandwidth can be comparable to 5G mobile broadband capacity when combined in correctly sized clusters. The backhauling and aggregation of these data can be accomplished very well with 5G.

Smart agriculture will make extensive use of three 5G application scenarios: eMBB, mMTC, and uRLLC. The connectivity between key players in smart agriculture, user goods, and data will be greatly improved. The common application situations are shown in Fig. 16.4. To maximize plant growth and output, smart greenhouses employ cutting-edge technologies. In order to assess if the environment is favorable for plants, sensors keep an eye on variables, including temperature, humidity, soil moisture, and light. Climate control systems use these data to automatically regulate temperature, humidity, ventilation, lighting, and watering [12].

Although it has drawbacks, 5G technology offers precision agriculture a lot of potential advantages. Using IoT sensors, real-time monitoring of crop health, machinery, and soil conditions can be made possible by high-speed Internet. Farmers might operate drones and irrigation equipment from a distance. However, in order to cover huge stretches of countryside, 5G networks need a lot of cell towers.

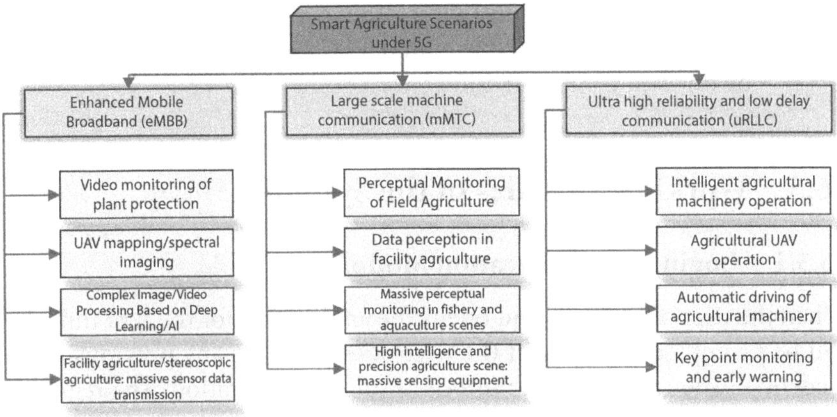

Fig. 16.4 5G application scenarios in smart agriculture.

16.4 Proposed Methodology

- ANDROID (Mobile Application Platform/OS): Android is a mobile operating system (OS) created by Google that is based on the Linux kernel and is primarily intended for touch screen mobile devices such as smartphones and tablets. That is correct. Swipe, tap, and pinch to interact with on-screen items and utilize the virtual keyboard for text entry. Google continues to develop Android TV for TVs, Android Auto for automobiles, and Android Wear for watches, each with its own user interface.
- SQLITE (SQLite) (Mobile Application Database): SQLite is a free and open-source SQL database that saves data on the device in text files. Android includes an SQLite database implementation. SQLite provides all aspects of relational databases. There is no need for JDBC, ODBC, or other database connectivity to access this database.
- The Arduino IDE (Integrated Development Environment): Arduino is an open-source initiative that developed microcontroller-based kits for the construction of digital gadgets and interactive objects capable of sensing and controlling physical items. The project is based on microcontroller board designs offered by a number of manufacturers and employs

a variety of microcontrollers. The Arduino programming language is simply a collection of C/C++ functions that may be invoked from your code.

16.5 Working Modules of the System

16.5.1 Login and Registration Module

When the user downloads and opens the application for the first time, he will be prompted to log in. If the user does not have any previous login credentials, he can register to use the Android application. The registration module asks for some basic information, such as the username and password. Once the user has successfully registered, he can now enter the application.

16.5.2 Change Number Module

The user can change the number anywhere and anytime in the Android application. The users simply have to log in with their previous credentials, such as username and password, then go to the "update account" section where the username and new number are to be entered. Thus, the number can be changed.

16.5.3 Check Status Module

Here, the user can check the current status of the soil field by clicking on "check status"; it will display the status of the soil and will also ask for permission to start the motor or not.

16.5.4 Start Water Pump Module

Users can start the water pump (i.e., motor) when required. Based on the current status of the soil and the water level in the tank, the motor can be turned on. There are various test cases that are being performed (such as when the soil moisture is wet and the tank is full; when the soil moisture is wet and there is no need to start the motor, unless a forced start is required; and when the soil moisture is dry and the tank is half full, among others.

16.5.5 Stop Water Pump Module

The user can stop the water pump (i.e., motor) based on the current status of the soil and the water level in the tank. The motor can be turned off. There are various test cases that are being performed (such as when the soil moisture is wet, the tank is full, and the motor is running, among others).

16.5.6 Force Start Water Pump Module

The user can force the water pump (i.e., motor) to start when there is sufficient water in the soil. If you still want to force start the motor, then click on "force start motor" in the app (if the soil moisture is wet, there is no need to start motor; otherwise, force start the motor).

16.5.7 Auto Stopped Module

When soil moisture is wet and the tank is full, the motor will automatically stop.

16.6 Experimental Result Analysis and Working

A Soil Moisture Smart Irrigation System uses sensors to monitor soil moisture and a microcontroller to control water flow, activating the pump only when needed. This optimizes plant health and conserves water, the complete process shown in Fig. 16.5. The soil moisture sensor, which was earlier included in the plant, is connected to the Arduino microcontroller as the primary working principle of this system. It is also connected, as seen in Fig. 16.6, to other electronic components mentioned above. Sensors measure soil moisture and transmit data and parameters to microcontrollers, which in turn drive pumps. When the soil moisture content falls below a predetermined point shown in Table 16.1, the microcontroller notifies the

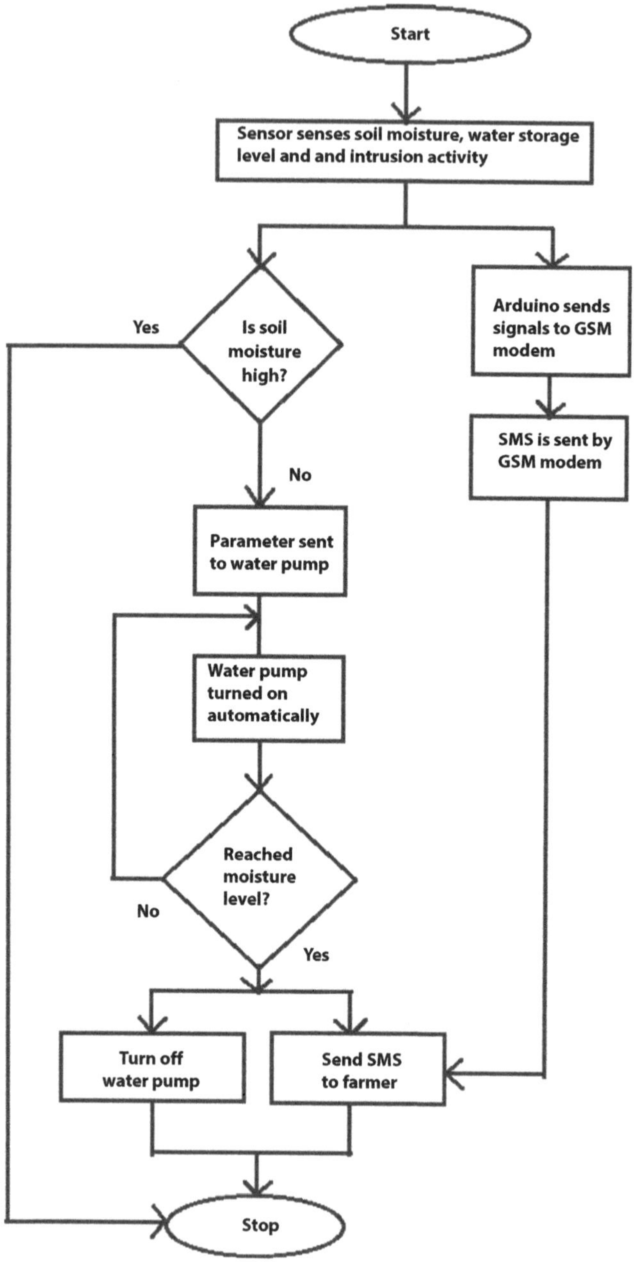

Fig. 16.5 Working diagram.

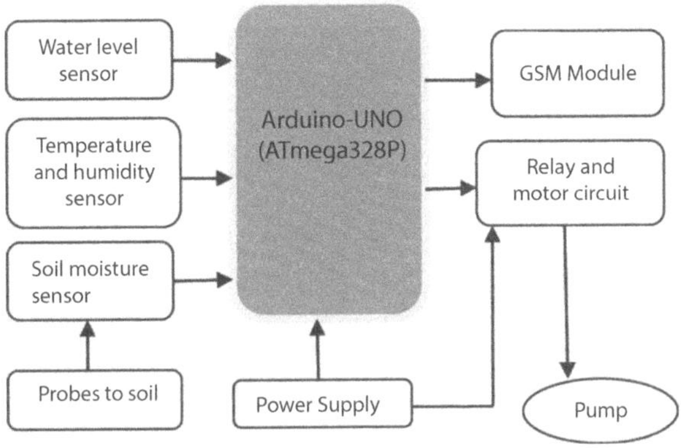

Fig. 16.6 The architecture of smart irrigation technique.

Table 16.1 Requirement of soil moisture.

Soil condition	Moisture content	Relay status	Water pump status	Test case status
Dry soil	<1100>500	On	On	True
Damp soil	<500 >300	Off	On	True
Wet soil	<300	Off	Off	True

relay module, which in turn activates a pump to provide a specific volume of water toward the plant. The pump ceases operation as soon as enough water is delivered. The power supply's job is to provide power to the entire system, and the suggested value should be between 7 and 12 volts, which is the microcontroller's input supply range.

The moisture content of soil and other comparable materials is measured using a soil moisture sensor (Fig. 16.7). The sensor includes two sizable exposed pads that serve as the sensor's probes and, when combined, operate as a variable resistor. This sensor determines the soil's moisture content. The analog voltage will be low while the soil's water content is low, and it will continue to rise when the conductivity between the electrodes in the soil changes.

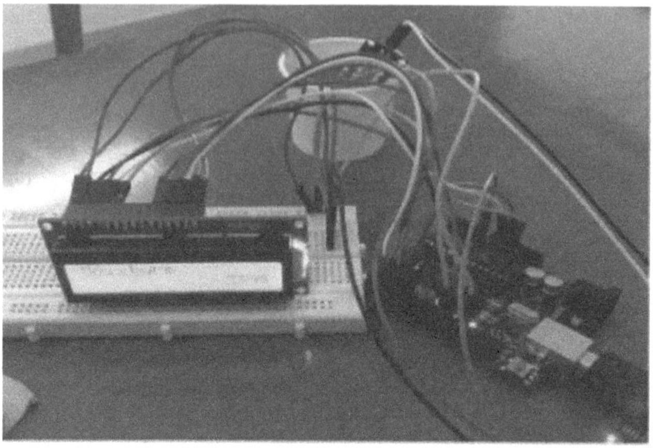

Fig. 16.7 Moisture level setting.

16.7 Conclusion

A smart irrigation system is designed to automate the process of irrigation. It helps to reduce the time and cost required for the irrigation process. It provides a simple and effective way for the entire irrigation process. It also helps to notify the farmer if an intrusion occurs. This study explains the entire workings of a smart irrigation system, along with the minimum requirements needed to implement it. As the monitoring device will always provide farmers a helping hand in receiving correct live feed of irrigation and soil moisture with more than 99% accurate findings, this study will aid farmers in enhancing the agriculture output and taking effective care of food production. Numerous agricultural applications have been created as a result of the integration of 5G with other technologies. These applications aim to lessen the negative effects of pesticides on the environment, safeguard natural resources, enhance animal welfare, and assist farmers in increasing yields and cutting expenses. This paper provides an overview of how 5G will affect connected devices, smart farming, and other relevant fields of technology.

References

1. Tephila, M.B., Sri, R.A., Abinaya, R., Lakshmi, J.A., Divya, V., Automated Smart Irrigation System using IoT with Sensor Parameter. *2022 International*

Conference on Electronics and Renewable Systems (ICEARS), pp. 543–549, 2022, doi: 10.1109/ICEARS53579.2022.9751993.

2. García, L., Parra, L., Jimenez, J.M., Lloret, J., Lorenz, P., IoT-based smart irrigation systems: An overview on the recent trends on sensors and IoT systems for irrigation in precision agriculture. *Sensors*, 20, 4, 1042, 2020.
3. Prathibha, S.R., Hongal, A., Jyothi, M.P., IOT Based Monitoring System in Smart Agriculture. *2017 International Conference on Recent Advances in Electronics and Communication Technology (ICRAECT)*, pp. 81–84, 2017, doi: 10.1109/ICRAECT.2017.52.
4. Mutyalamma, A.V., Yoshitha, G., Dakshyani, A., Padmavathi, B.V., Smart Agriculture to Measure Humidity Temperature Moisture Ph. of the Soil using IoT. *International Journal of Engineering and Advanced Technology (IJEAT)*, 2020.
5. Barik, L.B., IoT based Temperature and Humidity Controlling using Arduino and Raspberry Pi. *Int. J. Adv. Comput. Sci. Appl. (IJACSA)*, 10, 9, 2019, http://dx.doi.org/10.14569/IJACSA.2019.0100966.
6. MatLeh, N.A., Smart Irrigation System Using Internet of Things. *Inst. Electr. Electron. Eng. (IEEE)*, 2019.
7. Li, F., Intelligent agricultural monitoring system based on lot. *2022 IEEE 6th Information Technology and Mechatronics Engineering Conference (ITOEC)*, pp. 652–655, 2022, doi: 10.1109/ITOEC53115.2022.9734462.
8. Sangeetha, K. and Karishma, K., A study on smart irrigation system using IoT. *Publisher Int. Acad. J.*, 2019.
9. Ayaz, M., Ammad-Uddin, M., Sharif, Z., Mansour, A., Aggoune, E.-H.M., Internet-of-Things (IoT)-Based Smart Agriculture: Toward Making the Fields Talk, in: *IEEE Access*, vol. 7, pp. 129551–129583, 2019, doi: 10.1109/ACCESS.2019.2932609.
10. Marcu, I.M., Suciu, G., Balaceanu, C.M., Banaru, A., 2019 11th International Conference on Electronics, Computers and Artificial Intelligence (ECAI) IoT based System for Smart Agriculture, pp. 1–4, 2019.
11. Zhang, X. and Davidson, E.A., Improving nitrogen and water management in crop production on a national scale. *Proc. AGU Fall Meet. Abstr.*, Dec. 2018.
12. Tripathi, A.D., Mishra, R., Maurya, K.K., Singh, R.B., Wilson, D.W., Chapter 1 - Estimates for World Population and Global Food Availability for Global Health, in: *The Role of Functional Food Security in Global Health*. R.B. Singh, R.R. Watson, T. Takahashi (Eds.), pp. 3–24, Academic Press, 2019, ISBN 9780128131480, https://doi.org/10.1016/B978-0-12-813148-0.00001-3.
13. Kwon, S.-Y., Kim, Y.-H., Jung, D.-S., Cha, K.-R., and Lee, Y.-H., 5G Reference IoT Board for Smart Farm, *2022 International Conference on Computational Science and Computational Intelligence (CSCI)*, Las Vegas, NV, USA, 2022, pp. 1239–1240, doi: 10.1109/CSCI58124.2022.00223.

14. Anand, A., De Veciana, G., Shakkottai, S., Joint scheduling of URLLC and eMBB traffic in 5G wireless networks. *IEEE/ACM Trans. Netw.*, 28, 2, 477–490, 2020.
15. Sutton, A., 5G network architecture. *J. Inst. Telecommun. Prof.*, 12, 8–15, 2018. doi.org 10.1016 b 978-0-08-102267-2.00001-4.
16. Kalbande, K., Choudhary, S., Singru, A., Mukherjee, I., Bakshi, P., Multi-Way Controlled Feedback Oriented Smart System for Agricultural Application using Internet of Things. *2021 5th International Conference on Trends in Electronics and Informatics (ICOEI)*, pp. 96–101, 2021, doi: 10.1109/ICOEI51242.2021.9452946.
17. Kalaiselvi, V.K.G., Gopalakrishnan, J., Anand, S.S., Hariharan, S., Saravanan, S., Annamalai, H., Sustainable Algorithms using Artificial Intelligence and Various Stages for Precision Agricultural Cultivation. *2023 Second International Conference on Augmented Intelligence and Sustainable Systems (ICAISS)*, pp. 239–244, 2023, doi: 10.1109/ICAISS58487.2023.10250631.
18. Cáceres, G.B., Millán, P., Pereira, M., Lozano, D., Economic Model Predictive Control for Smart and Sustainable Farm Irrigation. *2021 European Control Conference (ECC)*, pp. 1255–1260, 2021, doi: 10.23919/ECC54610.2021.9655201.
19. Sott, M.K., Furstenau, L.B., Kipper, L.M., Giraldo, F.D., Lopez-Robles, J.R., Cobo, M.J., *et al.*, Precision techniques and agriculture 4.0 technologies to promote sustainability in the coffee sector: State of the art challenges and future trends. *IEEE Access*, 8, 149854–149867, 2020.

17

Modeling and Development of Low-Cost Visible Light Communication System

Mrinmoyee Mukherjee[1]*, Kevin Noronha[1] and Ravi Kumar Bandi[2]

[1]*Department of Electronics and Telecommunication Engineering, St. Francis Institute of Technology, Mumbai, Maharashtra, India*
[2]*Department of Electrical Engineering, Indian Institute of Technology-Bombay, Maharashtra, India*

Abstract

Visible light communication (VLC) is a supportive transient-scale last-mile wireless communication technology established on IEEE P802.15.7 that attempts to combine illumination with communication using existing infrastructure. VLC transmits data by employing intensity modulation in the frequency range of 430 THz to 790 THz. The extensive range of VLC applications encompasses VLC for indoor positioning systems, industrial applications, residential and workplace automation, VLC for advanced 5G and 6G communication systems, VLC for IoT-based smart cities, and vehicle-to-vehicle communication. This chapter endeavors to achieve **three objectives**: introduce VLC, its performance and evaluation parameters, introduce the procedures for modeling a VLC system using MATLAB2023®, and provide key technical insights for developing an economical VLC system employing commercial components. The ***first objective*** is designed to introduce the concept and working principle of VLC. It also elaborates on various VLC performance parameters for both the transmitter and the receiver such as semi-angle, luminous intensity, field of view (FOV), and area of the detector, to name a few. The ***second objective*** is targeted toward developing a hardware model to support VLC communication up to a maximum data speed of 1.2 Mbps for a line-of-sight distance of 1 meter using on-off keying non-return-to-zero (OOK-NRZ) modulation. The experimental VLC model is designed using low-cost ultra-bright 5-mm light-emitting diodes (LEDs), silicon photodiodes, and a TLO81CP FET operational amplifier (OPAMP). The ***third objective*** systematically navigates through the procedures to develop a software model to implement the VLC system

**Corresponding author*: mrinmoyeemukherjee@sfit.ac.in

Pallavi Sapkale, Shilpa Mehta and S. Balamurugan (eds.) Quantum Computing and Machine Learning for 6G, (367–422) © 2026 Scrivener Publishing LLC

by considering the effect of all the defined performance parameters. This will aid in understanding the effect of variation of performance parameters on evaluation parameters like received power, zero frequency gain, channel impulse response, and bit error rate. The last objective also aims to provide concluding remarks on how the developed VLC system can be improved upon to support 6G applications.

***Keywords*:** Bit error rate, channel model, DC channel gain, light-emitting diodes, photodiodes, quality factor, visible light communication

17.1 Learning Objectives

1. Literature review of recent comprehensive VLC papers
2. Literature review of most recent VLC application–based papers
3. Understanding VLC hardware system development and its components
4. Understanding VLC simulation system development
5. Few hands-on code

17.2 Introduction to VLC

VLC is a novel and appreciated personal area network (PAN) short-range wireless communication technology aimed to attenuate the electromagnetic scarcity problem [1]. VLC operates in the frequency range of 430 THz to 790 THz [1–3]. The proposed IEEE standard for VLC is IEEE 802.15.7, which defines the physical (PHY) and medium access control (MAC) layers. The objectives of standardization are the following: integrating VLC with existing technologies; providing data delivery services for audio and multimedia; resolving compatibility issues related to existing infrastructure, topology configuration, advanced modulation, and coding schemes; and resolving issues related to security, flicker and dimming control, health hazards, mobility, and association-disassociation and handover issues [4, 5]. The illustrious advantages of VLC as a complementary technology are as follows [1–4].

- Gigantic license-free bandwidth: VLC operates in the frequency range of 430 THz to 790 THz. This huge bandwidth supports the expansive surge in demand for data-hungry applications [1].
- VLC assures skin and eye protection directives set by divergent government bodies [1].

- VLC is acceptable and fitted for hazardous and precarious environments such as oil refineries, magnetic resonance imaging (MRI) zones in hospitals, and chemical laboratories, as RF signals do not impede VLC signals [1, 2].
- Certain properties of light-emitting diodes (LEDs), such as low cost, energy efficiency, and low energy diffuse, make it eco-friendly green technology [2].
- LEDs are cheap, radiate less heat, and are energy-efficient. This makes the technology "green communication technology."
- Radio waves have long wavelengths, and hence, they can easily penetrate walls. This makes it vulnerable to snooping. Light waves, on the other hand, cannot penetrate opaque objects and are more likely to get reflected. This characteristic of light can be exploited to build interference-free communication hot spots [4].

It will be interesting for the readers to comprehend some of the cardinal research papers in the area of VLC. The objective of Table 17.1 is to list the most recent and meticulous references that contribute a prodigious amount of information from straightforward topics like VLC standardization to the most contemporary ones involving the integration of VLC with 5G and 6G services and quantum communication. Most of the recent papers in VLC deal with the implementation of multiuser massive multiple-input–multiple-output (MIMO) [16, 17]. The direction of work in massive MIMO deals with the design of system and channel models, the use of advanced modulation techniques for downlink communication, and the analysis of data rates, including precoder design, channel estimation, and non-orthogonal multiple access (NOMA) MIMO techniques. Due to its enormous bandwidth of VLC, it is used in a variety of applications. Table 17.2 highlights some of the most recent papers on varied applications that can be developed using this technology.

The remainder of the chapter is arranged as follows: the aim of section 17.3 is to provide insights into the block diagram of the VLC system and define cardinal evaluation parameters related to the transmitter and receiver. Section 17.5 provides a detailed understanding of the simulation work for developing a VLC system: procedures, technical details, and mathematical relations. The section also provides a model with a few codes and discusses the results obtained. Section 17.4 deals with the experimental work done toward the implementation of VLC up to a maximum data speed of 1.2 Mbps for a line-of-sight distance of 1 meter using on-off

Table 17.1 Comprehensive literature survey papers for VLC.

Ref. no.→	**[2]**	**[3]**	**[6]**	**[7]**	**[8]**	**[9]**	**[10]**	**[11]**	**[12]**	**[13]**	**[14]**	**[15]**
Parameters/Year	2015	2015	2018	2019	2019	2019	2020	2020	2020	2021	2022	2022
VLC standard	✓	✓	✓	✓	*	✓	*	✓	✓	✓	✓	✓
VLC system model	✓	✓	✓	✓	✓	✓	✓	✓	✓	✓	✓	✓
VLC sources	✓	✓	✓	*	✓	*	✓	✓	✓	✓	*	✓
VLC detectors	✓	✓	*	*	✓	*	✓	✓	✓	✓	*	✓
VLC potentials	✓	✓	✓	✓	✓	*	✓	✓	*	✓	*	✓
VLC channel modeling	✓	*	*	✓	✓	*	✓	✓	*	*	*	*
Modulation techniques	✓	✓	✓	✓	✓	*	✓	✓	✓	✓	✓	✓
Access schemes	✓	*	*	✓	✓	*	✓	*	✓	*	*	*

(*Continued*)

Table 17.1 Comprehensive literature survey papers for VLC. (*Continued*)

Ref. no.→	[2]	[3]	[6]	[7]	[8]	[9]	[10]	[11]	[12]	[13]	[14]	[15]
VLC network architecture	✓	✓	*	✓	✓	✓	✓	✓	✓	*	*	*
Programmable testbeds	✓		*	✓	*	*	*	*	*	*	*	*
VLC applications	✓	✓	✓	✓	✓	✓	✓	✓	✓	✓	✓	✓
Research challenges	✓	✓	✓	✓	✓	✓	✓	✓	✓	✓	✓	✓
VLC data rate progression	*[1]	✓	✓	*	*	*	*	*	✓	✓	✓	✓
Recent advancements	*	✓	✓	*	✓	✓	✓	*	✓	*	✓	✓
Quantum communication	*	*	*	*	*	*	✓	*	*	✓	✓	✓
Integration with 5G and 6G	*	*	*	*	*	*	✓	*	*	*	*	*

Table 17.2 VLC applications.

Sr. No.	Application domains	Year	Ref. no.
	VLC for commercial application		
1	Communication technologies for industrial applications, discussing different applications like manufacturing, mines and pipelines, indoor positioning systems for vehicles, and research challenges	2020	[18]
2	Dimming control, encoding and decoding techniques, transmission capacity improvements for IoT-based VLC applications	2022	[19]
3	Prediction of trajectory positions and channel parameters using artificial intelligence (AI)–based algorithms for industrial applications	2023	[20]
4	Study of VLC channel characteristics for underground mines	2023	[21]
	VLC for residential and workplace		
5	Demonstrates 40-Mbps VLC using off-the-shelf components based on multi-band carrier-less amplitude and phase modulation for indoor environment	2020, 2021	[22, 23]
6	Develops VLC-enabled intelligent automation semantic vocabulary for an office setup	2022	[24]
7	Demonstrates VLC data transmission in clinical environment setup	2023	[25]
	VLC for 5G and 6G communication		
8	Overview of VLC, research work on VLC and VLC solutions for 5G	2019	[26]

(Continued)

Table 17.2 VLC applications. (*Continued*)

Sr. No.	Application domains		Ref. no.
9	IoT challenges, integration of VLC and VLP in IoT networks, supported modulation and multiplexing schemes, the potential of VLC for 6G communication, novel concepts and uses of VLC for 6G communication, challenges for 6G using VLC	2020	[27–29]
10	Underwater 5G communication using VLC, challenges, future prospects, and future research on 5G and 6G using VLC	2021	[30, 31]
	VLC for smart cities		
11	VLC generic system, low data rate and high data rate smart city VLC applications, outdoor VLC challenges	2020	[32, 33]
12	Developed long-range 1.5-km LED to solar panel communication	2022	[34]
13	Discusses the requirements of a 6G IoT network for smart cities, prospective challenges, and research conducted toward 6G IoT–based networks	2023	[35]
	VLC for Vehicle to Vehicle (V2V) communication		
14	Developed a V2V system using LEDs and photodiodes for a maximum data rate of 3.5 Mbps at a distance of 15 m.	2019	[36]
15	System design for V2V communication, result analysis w.r.t vehicle speed, throttle positioning system, brake pedal system, distance, light intensity, and light angle	2020	[37]
16	Presents a system for bidirectional data transfer, propagation model, transmission performance parameter analysis and discussion	2021	[38]

(*Continued*)

Table 17.2 VLC applications. (*Continued*)

Sr. No.	Application domains		Ref. no.
17	Developed a two-lane road-based V2V model to study the impact of different weather conditions on various parameters	2022	[39]
18	Proposes a multi-hop relay system to develop a direct transmission range of up to 19 m for V2V communication	2023	[40]
19	Implementation of a standalone VLC system model using an imaging receiver for a maximum range of 272.5 m	2024	[41]

keying non-return-to-zero (OOK-NRZ) modulation. The experimental VLC model is designed using low-cost ultrabright 5-mm light-emitting diodes (LEDs), silicon photodiodes, and a TLO81CP FET operational amplifier (OPAMP).

17.3 VLC System Description

The VLC working principle is based on the direct detection of intensity-modulated signals. To completely understand the working principle of VLC, it becomes imperative to understand the VLC system block diagram, as represented in Figure 17.1. The transmitter unit comprises the information source, the source and channel encoders, the driver unit, and LEDs. A source encoder is used to convert the continuous time-varying analog information in the form of text, audio, image, or video into bits. The three important steps employed by the source encoder are sampling, quantization, and data compression. The channel encoder converts the information bits into passband signals. The channel encoder implements four major steps: error correcting codes, symbol mapping, pulse shaping, and up-conversion to convert the baseband signal to a passband signal. Channel coding is also used to efficiently transmit the data over a noisy channel. The driver circuit is utilized to derive the required current to intensity modulate the passband signal. This electrical signal is now intensity-modulated by the LEDs. The modulation bandwidth of the LED defines its switching speed and restricts the supported data rate of the VLC system. Tai-Cheng *et al.* [13] list the achieved data rates

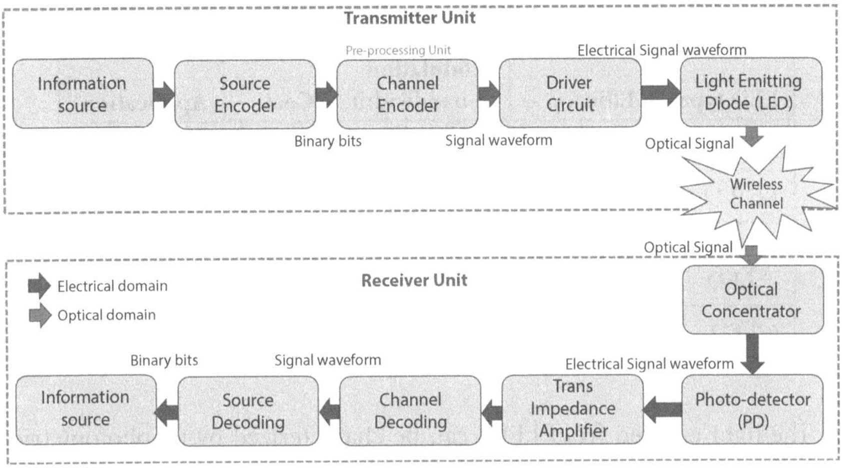

Figure 17.1 Block diagram of VLC communication system.

supported by different light sources like LEDs and laser diodes (LDs) for VLC systems. Direct detection of the received optical signal is done by the photodetector and converted to equivalent current. The current is transformed to voltage and magnified by the trans-impedance amplifier (TIA). This voltage signal then goes through channel and source decoding techniques to receive the information signal back.

It becomes imperative to understand that the two most important components for developing a VLC model are the optical transmitter [LED or laser diode (LD)] and the optical receiver (the photodetector). The remaining part of the section focuses on the principal parameters of LED and photodetectors.

17.3.1 Key Parameters - Light-Emitting Diode

A light-emitting diode is a solid-state semiconductor device that converts electrical energy to light energy using the process of radioactive reaction. The bandgap energy of the semiconductor material used for the construction of LED defines the emitted wavelength range or spectral width $(\Delta\lambda)$. Off-the-shelf LEDs have a $(\Delta\lambda)$ of approximately 60 nm to 170 nm. Phosphor-coated white LEDs (PC-LEDs) and multi-chip white (RGB) LEDs are the most frequently used LEDs for different applications in indoor VLC. The characteristics of different types of LEDs are listed in Table 17.3 [10]. The supported data rate for red LED is 50 Mbps, while for white LED, it is 1 to 2 Mbps.

Table 17.3 Characteristics of different LEDs [10].

LED types	Efficacy	Modulation bandwidth	Cost	Application
PC LED	130 lm/W	5–3 MHz	Low	Illumination
RGB LED	65 lm/W	10–20 MHz	High	Illumination
Organic LED	45 lm/W	≤1 MHz	Lowest	Display
μ-LED	....	≥300 MHz	High	Biosensors

The light emitted from LEDs can be characterized by its photometric or radiometric parameters [2, 10]. The photometric parameters quantify brightness and color and aid in understanding the illumination aspect of light. The radiometric parameters, on the other hand, quantify the radiant energy of light and help to understand the communication-related parameters—the transmitted output power of LED. Both radiometric and photometric parameters are cardinal for the design of a based system. The important radiometric and photometric parameters related to Lambertian source are listed as follows:

(a) Luminous Flux: It is interpreted as the comprehensive amount of power radiated per unit of time by the Lambertian source as "perceived" by mankind. It is measured in lumens or candela steradian.

(b) Luminous Intensity: It is interpreted as the brightness of light released from a source in a specific direction. It can also be factored as luminous flux per unit solid angle (1 steradian) and measured in candela. Figure 17.2 depicts the relative luminous intensity distribution of VLHW5100 from Vishay semiconductors. Relative luminous intensity is maximum at an angular displacement (θ) of θ=0° and decreases by a factor of cos(θ). The value is specified in the datasheets of LEDs. For VLHW5100, the minimum luminous intensity at a forward current $\left(I_{LED}\right)$ of 20 mA is 5600 mcd, and the maximum is 11,200 mcd.

(c) Half Beam Angle: It is also called an angle of half intensity (*hpa*) and is defined as the angle at which the light intensity reduces to half of its maximum luminous intensity. For VLHW5100 [42], the angle of half intensity is $\pm 10°$.

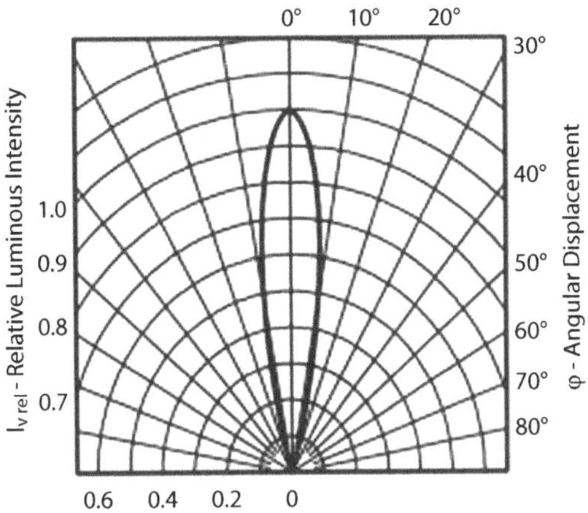

Figure 17.2 Luminous intensity distribution of VLHW5100 [42].

(d) Illuminance: Illuminance (I) is defined as the amount of light that shines onto the surface of a unit area. It is measured in lumens per square meter. For a Lambertial source, as shown in Figure 17.3, the horizontal illuminance at point (x, y, z) is given by equation (17.1) [43–45]. The transmitter and receiver are placed in the line-of-sight (LOS) propagation model, i.e., the power received from the reflections of walls, doors, and windows is not considered to evaluate the transmitted power.

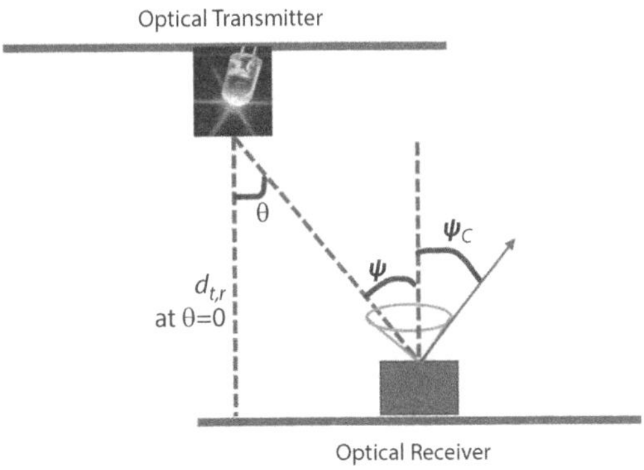

Figure 17.3 Geometry of LOS propagation model.

$$E_{hor} = \frac{I(\theta)\cos^m(\theta)}{d_{t,r}^2 \cos(\psi)} \tag{17.1}$$

In the above equation, I(θ) is the center luminous intensity of LED in candela, θ is the irradiation angle, Ψ is the incident angle with respect to the receiver, and $d_{t,r}$ is the vector distance from the source to the receiver.

17.3.2 Key Parameters - Photodiode

(a) Range of spectral bandwidth: The range of spectral bandwidth (Δλ) defines the entire range (λmin, λmax) of optical wavelength that the photodetector is capable of detecting. For silicon PIN photodetector BPW34, (λmin, λmax)=(430 nm, 1100 nm).

(b) 3-dB bandwidth and rise time: The 3-dB bandwidth and rise time are the two evaluation specifications that are used to represent the limit of a system's potential to change with the change of input signal. The rise time is listed in datasheets and can be used to evaluate the 3-dB bandwidth of the detector using equation (17.2). For BPW34 [46], the rise time is 100 ns.

$$f_{3dB} = \frac{0.35}{Rise\ time} \tag{17.2}$$

For BPW34,

$$f_{3dB} = \frac{0.35}{100 \times 10^{-9}} = 3.5\ MHz \tag{17.3}$$

It becomes imperative that the maximum transmitted signal frequency $f_{clk} \leq f_{3dB}$ of the photodetector.

(c) Responsivity (R): It is defined as the output current generated by the photodetector in response to the incident optical power. Responsivity is a wavelength-dependent parameter, as represented in Figure 17.4. In the visible range of 400 nm to 1100 nm, responsivity is in the range of 0.45 A/W to 0.65 A/W.

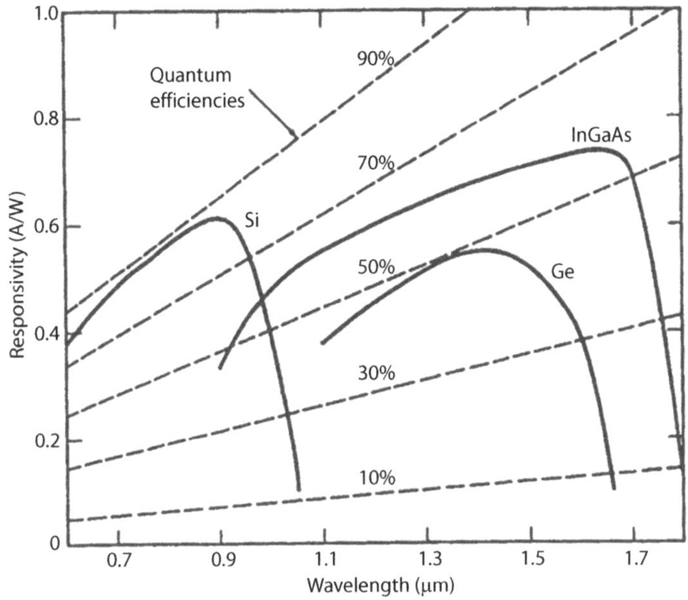

Figure 17.4 Responsivity curve [47].

(d) Radiant sensitive area (A_{PD}): It is the active detector area. Photons falling within the active region are converted to current by the photodetector. For BPW34 [46], the active sensitive area is 7.5 mm^2.

17.3.3 Key Parameters - VLC Channel

Channel modeling is the elemental step toward the structured design and implementation of a VLC system that helps us to characterize both physical and system-dependent parameters. VLC channel modeling is aimed at evaluating the multipath propagation results when light exerts an influence on the below-listed parameters:

- The phenomenon of reflection, refraction, scattering, and absorption
- Transmitter and receiver characteristics
- Number of objects in the given scenarios
- Possibility of movement of people and objects in a scenario
- Background light intensity
- Distance between transmitter and receiver
- Orientation and position of transmitter and receiver
- Size and application of room

(a) DC channel gain H(0): Since the parameters do not vary drastically over a period of time, VLC can be modeled as a system of linear time-invariant (LTI) nature. The equivalent baseband model of an LTI intensity modulated direct detection (IM/DD) optical wireless link can be represented numerically by Eq. (17.1) [43]

$$y(t) = RA_{PD}x(t) * h(t) + n(t) \tag{17.4}$$

where $y(t)$ is the output current generated by the photodetector in response to the received optical power, R represents the photodetector responsivity (A/W), A_{PD} is the area of the photodetector, $x(t)$ is the transmitted optical signal (or the input intensity), $n(t)$ is the additive noise that includes the thermal and shot noise, $h(t)$ is the channel impulse response, and * operator is the convolution. $h(t)$ is the total indoor channel impulse response (CIR) that can be modeled as Eq. (17.5), where the impulse responses of both the line of sight, $h_{LOS}(t)$, and non-line of sight (NLOS), $h_{NLOS}(t)$, are considered for evaluation.

$$h(t) = h_{LOS}(t) + h_{NLOS}(t) \tag{17.5}$$

In most cases, the value of the amplitude of channel direct current gain H(0) [43] is used to characterize the losses in the channel, which unites the average optical power received $\boldsymbol{P_r}$ and transmitter power P_t measured in watts or in dBm.

$$P_r = H(0)P_t \tag{17.6}$$

$$P_r = \left[H(0)_{LOS} + H(0)_{NLOS}\right]P_t \tag{17.7}$$

As per the geometry given in Figure 17.3 for LOS configuration, the DC channel gain is given by equation (17.8).

$$\begin{aligned} H(0)_{LOS} &= \frac{A_{PD}(m+1)}{2\pi d_{t,r}^2} cos^m(\theta) g_{filter} T(\psi)\cos(\psi); \quad 0 \le \psi \le \psi_c \\ H(0)_{LOS} &= 0; \quad \psi > \psi_c \end{aligned} \tag{17.8}$$

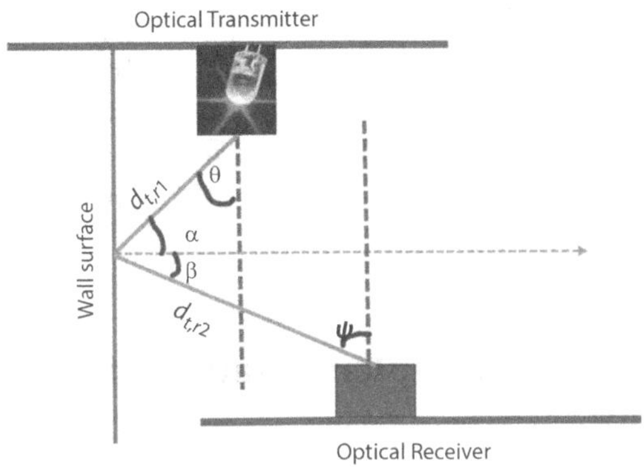

Figure 17.5 NLOS configuration [43].

The NLOS configuration that considers the power received from the k-reflections is represented in Figure 17.5. The DC channel gain is listed by equation (17.9)

$$H(0)_{NLOS} = \frac{m+1}{2\pi}\sum_{i=1}^{N} \frac{R\cos^{m}(\theta)\cos(\psi)}{d_{t,r1}^{2}d_{t,r2}^{2}} * rect\left(\frac{2\psi}{\pi}\right)h^{k-1}\left(t-\frac{d_{t,r}}{c};S_{i},R\right)X\Delta A \tag{17.9}$$

In the above equation, m is the mode number defined by equation (17.9), θ *is the irradiation angle, the incident angle with respect to the receiver is* Ψ, $d_{t,r1}$ is the vector distance between the transmitter and the first incidence on the wall, $d_{t,r2}$ is the distance from the wall to the receiver, *c* is the velocity of light in vacuum (3*10⁸ m/s), and ΔA is the differential area of the reflecting surface.

$$m = \frac{-ln(2)}{ln\left(cos(hpa)_{\frac{1}{2}}\right)} \tag{17.10}$$

Equation (17.7) can then be rewritten as

$$P_r = \sum^{NLEDs} P_t H_{LOS}(0) + \int_{Reflections} P_t H_{NLOS}(0) \tag{17.11}$$

After discussing the block diagram, the operating principle of VLC, and the key parameters related to the optical transmitter, receiver, and channel, the forthcoming section aims to build a low-cost VLC system that can successfully transmit and receive VLC data for a maximum distance of 1 meter at a data rate of 1.2 Mbps using on-off keying non-return-to-zero (OOK-NRZ) modulation.

17.4 Experimental Implementation of the VLC System

The focus of this section is to establish a ground for the implementation of a VLC system that operates at a data rate of 1.2 Mbps for a maximum distance of 1 meter, employing OOK-NRZ modulation and commercial components.

17.4.1 Block Diagram and Technical Specifications

This section evaluates the understanding of the technical details required to build a VLC system in a stepwise manner. The complete block diagram of the experimental setup is illustrated in Figure 17.6.

Step-1: Understand your application
The foremost step in the design and development of any hardware system is to understand the needs of the application. This step should be able to

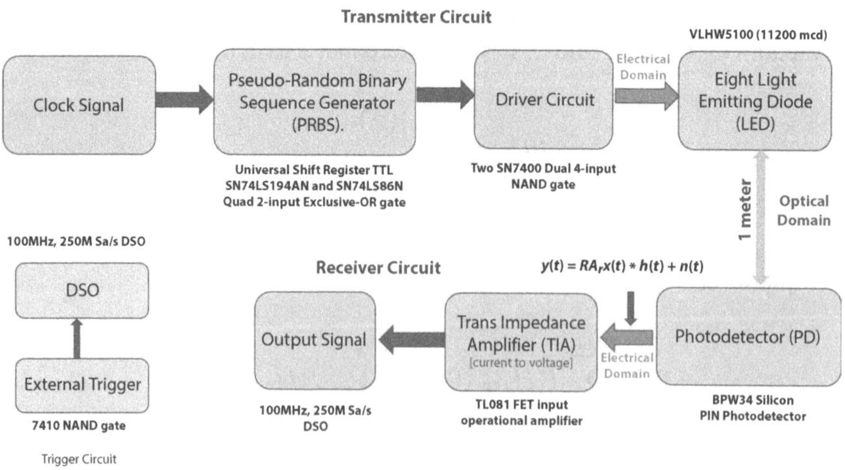

Figure 17.6 VLC experimental setup block diagram.

resolve the following set of queries, as listed in Table 17.4, with respect to the application. The table also reasons out the need to resolve the query.

The information signal or the clock signal (f_{clk}) is provided in the laboratory set by the 2-MHz Systronics function generator. The supported data rate (f_{clk}) of the developed VLC system is in the range of 500 kHz to 1.2 MHz. The setup employs LOS configuration and the maximum distance between the transmitter and receiver is set at 1 meter. The function generator provides data as a continuous sequence of zeros and ones.

Step-2: Selecting the right components

(a) The PRBS Unit: The PRBS unit aids in converting the sequential data into a random sequence of 0s and 1s and employs a universal shift register and Ex-Or gate. The selection of a universal shift register depends on how many random bits the application needs in each trigger pulse. The developed PRBS unit employs 4-bit $(N = 4)$ SN74LS194AN TTL high-speed 16-pin bidirectional universal shift register SN74LS194AN and 14-pin quad two input exclusive-or gate SN74LS86N. The length of a pseudorandom sequence that can be generated is of $(2^N - 1) = 15$ bits. The bit pattern repeats every 15th clock cycle. This experimental work uses three output pins $(Q_A, Q_B, \text{and } Q_C)$, hence generating a pseudorandom sequence of $(2^3 - 1) = 7$ bits that repeats after every 7th clock cycle, as shown in Figure 17.7.

Two examples of 8-bit (N=8) universal shift registers that can be used to generate a pseudorandom sequence of 255 bits per trigger pulse are

Table 17.4 Set of queries and reasons.

Sr. No.	Queries	Reason	Eq. no.
1.	The lowest and highest clock frequencies (f_{clk})	f_{clk} defines the lowest and highest data rates supported by your application.	......
2.	The maximum distance of communication	This helps to decide on the value of the luminous intensity of LEDs.	(17.1)
3.	Type of configuration: LOS or NLOS	Helps to finalize the set of equations for DC channel gain.	(17.8, 17.9)

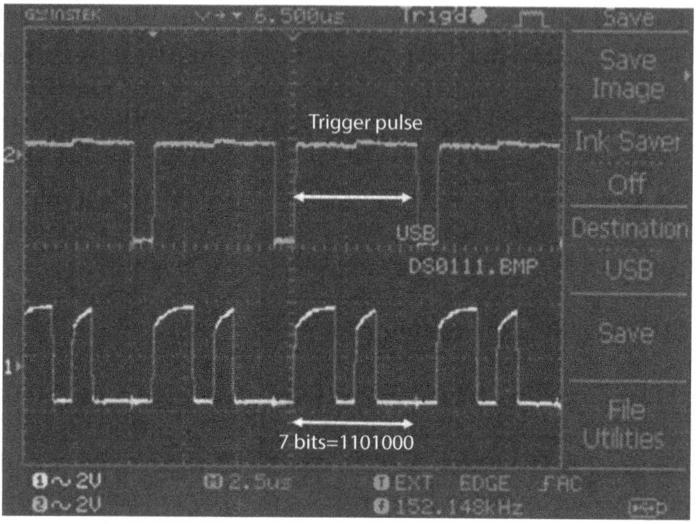

Figure 17.7 Trigger pulse and PRBS bits.

TTL-compatible CMOS SN74HCT595 and 74HC597PW. It is also worth noting that the typical clock frequency of the used universal shift register $(f_{usr}) > (f_{clk})$. The detailed technical specifications of all the components used in the design are tabulated in Table 17.5.

(b) Driver Circuit: The total output current to be drawn from the driver circuit depends on the total number of LEDs used in the circuit. The more LEDs are in the circuit, the more NAND gates are required to be connected in parallel. SN7400 quadruple two input positive NAND gate is used to build the LED current driver circuit. Each NAND gate of SN7400 is capable of sourcing 16 mA of current. The total sourced current by the driver circuit should be sufficient to drive the series or parallel connected LEDs into the linear region of operation.

(c) Light-Emitting Diodes: The LEDs are then employed to convert incoming electrical PRBS signal into optical signal (power) using intensity modulation. Primarily, the selection of LED is based on three important factors:

(i) Modulation Bandwidth: The modulation bandwidth of the selected LED, as listed in Table 17.3, has to be more than the maximum data of the application, as the modulation bandwidth directly determines the speed of communication [54]. The modulation bandwidth defines the switching speed of the

Table 17.5 Table of essential components.

Sr. No.	Component/IC details	Functionality of components	Technical specifications		Ref. no.
1.	SN74LS194AN universal shift register	PRBS unit consists of SN74LS194AN and SN74LS86N. Aids to generate random data with DC balance	Max. supply voltage	5.25 V	[48]
			Clock frequency	36 MHz	
			High-level output voltage (typical)	3.5 V	
			Low-level output voltage (typical)	0.25 V	
2.	SN74LS86N Exclusive-OR gate		Propagation delay time	14 ns	[49]

(*Continued*)

Table 17.5 Table of essential components. (*Continued*)

Sr. No.	Component/IC details	Functionality of components	Technical specifications		Ref. no.
3.	LED driver: SN7400 NAND gate.	Sourcing 16 mA (maximum) of current to modulate the LEDs at the rate of the incoming data signal.	Low-level output current	16 mA	[50]
4.	Photodetector: PIN silicon BPW34S	Conversion of the optical power signal to current signal	Spectral bandwidth range	430–1100 nm	[46]
			Peak sensitivity λ	900 nm	
			Rise time	100 ns	
			Radiant sensitive area	7.5 mm^2	
			Responsivity	0.5 A/W	

(*Continued*)

Table 17.5 Table of essential components. *(Continued)*

Sr. No.	Component/IC details	Functionality of components	Technical specifications		Ref. no.
5.	OPAMP TLO81	Current to a voltage conversion. Provides gain to the output signal.	Slew rate	13 V/μs	[51]
			Rise time	0.05 μs	
			Unity gain bandwidth	3 MHz	
6.	LED VLHW5100	Converts the electrical to optical signal	Luminous intensity	11,200 mcd	[52]
			Forward voltage	2.8 V	
7.	7410 dual 4-input NAND buffer	Triggering the circuit externally.	Low-level output current	8 mA	[53]
8.	2-MHz Systronics function generator	Clock signal	--------		---

(Continued)

Table 17.5 Table of essential components. *(Continued)*

Sr. No.	Component/IC details	Functionality of components	Technical specifications	Ref. no.
9.	GW INSTEK DSO 100 MHz, 250 M Sa/s digital storage oscilloscope	Voltage measurement, eye diagrams plotting, sample values of transmitted and received signals	--------	---
10.	Resistors	Used for current limiting and feedback	--------	---
11.	Capacitors (0.1 μF, 9.4 pF)	As feedback and for DC noise deletion	--------	---

LEDs and is restricted by the doping levels in the active region of the diode, the recombination lifetime of the carriers, and the parasitic capacitance of the LED. This experimental work uses PC LEDs whose modulation bandwidth is in the range of 3 to 5 MHz.

(ii) Luminous Intensity: It is also important to choose LEDs with high luminous intensity as this parameter defines the distance that the light signal travels. VLHW5100 has a maximum luminous intensity of 11,200 mcd.

(iii) Angle of Half Intensity (hpa): This parameter defines the spread of the light intensity as shown in Figure 17.2. It is preferred to have an LED with an angle of half intensity less than the field of view (FOV) of the detector used. This study uses VLHW5100 as an optical source with an hpa value of $\pm 10^{\circ}$ and FOV of the receiver as ±65. This will help to focus the light signal on the detector area effectively.

(d) Photodetector: The photodetector is used to convert the received optical power into the current signal. The 3-dB bandwidth of the photodetector has to be more than the targeted data rate of the application. As discussed earlier, the 3-dB bandwidth can be evaluated using Equations (17.2) and (17.3) from the rise time of the photodetector. The value of responsivity depends on whether a silicon or germanium photodetector is used in the application. This work uses Si-based PIN BPW34 with a modulation bandwidth of 3.5 MHz. The entire experimental setup built using the above-listed components is shown in Figure 17.8.

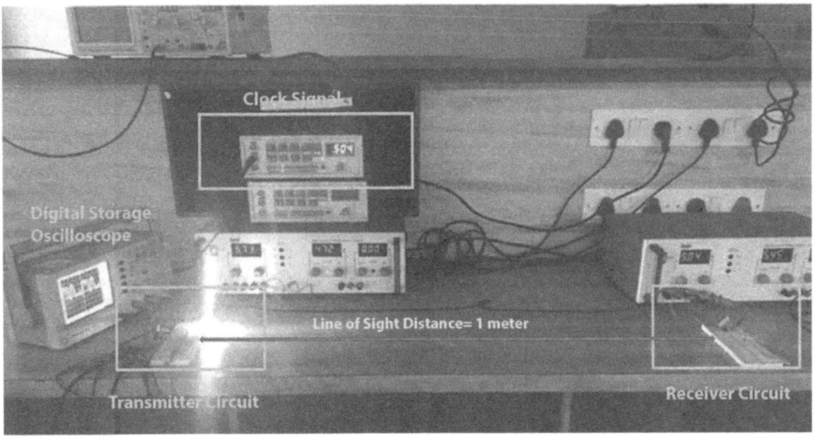

Figure 17.8 VLC experimental setup for a distance of 1 m at 1.2-MHz clock frequency.

(e) Trans-Impedance Amplifier: The trans-impedance amplifier (TIA) is an operational amplifier that is employed to convert the output current of the photodetector to a voltage signal. It also provides gain. TLO81CP is an FET operational amplifier with a rise time of 0.05 μs and a maximum slew rate of 13 V/μs. The 3-dB bandwidth of TIA is given by equation 17.12.

$$f_{3dB} = \frac{0.35}{0.05 \times 10^{-6}} = 7\ MHz \tag{17.12}$$

The detailed procedure to calculate the transmitted power is referenced in [55] by Mukherjee and Noronha. This also provides details about the values of resistors and capacitors that are needed in the receiver circuit.

17.4.2 Results and Discussions

This section highlights the input output graphs obtained at the transmitter and receiver at different clock frequencies (f_{clk}) for a distance of 1 m. The design of receiver circuit has an impact on the output signal received. The feedback resistor R_F in the TIA dictates the amount of feedback current I_F. As R_F increases, I_F decreases, thereby decreasing the 3-dB bandwidth of the TIA system. The feedback capacitor C_F is used to limit the bandwidth. Limiting the bandwidth of the TIA limits the addition of noises. Figure 17.9 illustrate the input-output signal obtained at different clock frequencies using $R_F = 100\ K\Omega$ and $C_F = 8.25\ pF$.

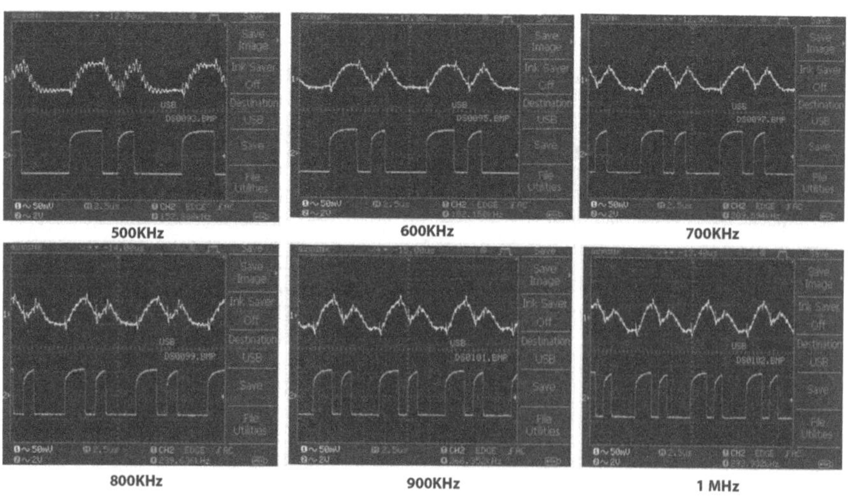

Figure 17.9 Input-output signal at different clock frequencies (f_{clk}) for $R_F = 100\ K\Omega$ and $C_F = 8.25\ pF$.

Figure 17.10 illustrates the input-output signal obtained at peak frequency of 1MHz at divergent values of R_F with $C_F = 4.7\ pF$.

Figure 17.11 illustrates the input-output signal obtained at peak frequency of 1MHz at divergent values of R_F with $C_F = 9.4\ pF$.

Case 1: Distance = 1 m, $(f_{clk}) = 500\ \text{kHz}^{-1}$ MHz, feedback resistor $R_F = 100\ K\Omega$, feedback capacitor $C_F = 8.25\ pF$. [Refer Figure 17.9].

Channel 1 (blue color) is the transmitted optical signal and channel 2 (yellow color) is the received signal.

Case 2: Distance = 1 m, $(f_{clk}) = 1\ \text{MHz}$, feedback resistor $R_F = 33\ K\Omega$ $-55\ K\Omega$, feedback capacitor $C_F = 4.7\ pF$. [Refer Figure 17.10].

Case 3: Distance = 1 m, $(f_{clk}) = 1\ \text{MHz}$, feedback resistor $R_F = 33\ K\Omega$ $-55\ K\Omega$, feedback capacitor $C_F = 9.4\ pF$ [Refer Figure 17.11].

All the above three cases highlight the significance of choosing the right value of (R_F, C_F) for a given value of transmitted power. It is up to the designers to optimize (R_F, C_F) values to reduce the effect of noise and improve the value of the bit error rate (BER). More detailed technical insights about the circuit diagram of transmitter and receiver and evaluation of quality-of-service parameters like eye diagram, quality factor, and bit error rate (BER) are listed by Mukherjee and Noronha in [56].

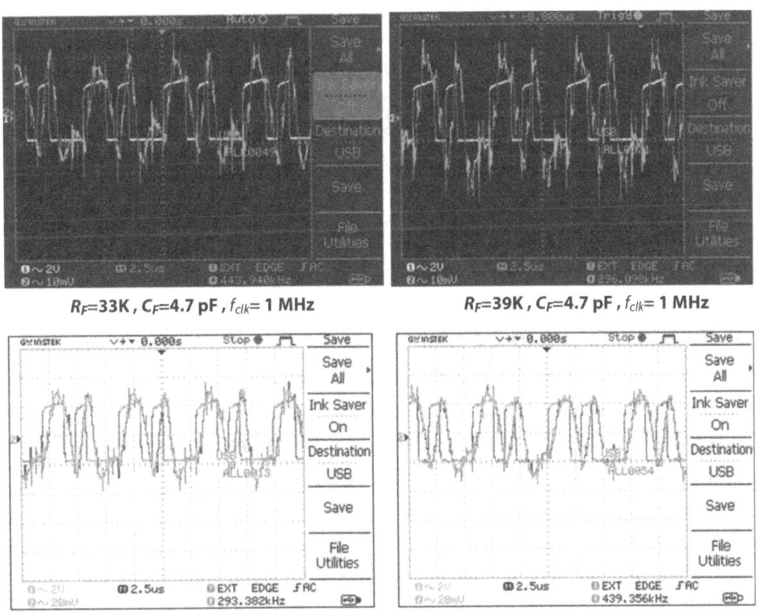

Figure 17.10 Input-output signal at $(f_{clk}) = 1\ \text{MHz}$ for $R_F = 33\ K\Omega - 55\ K\Omega$ and $C_F = 4.7\ pF$.

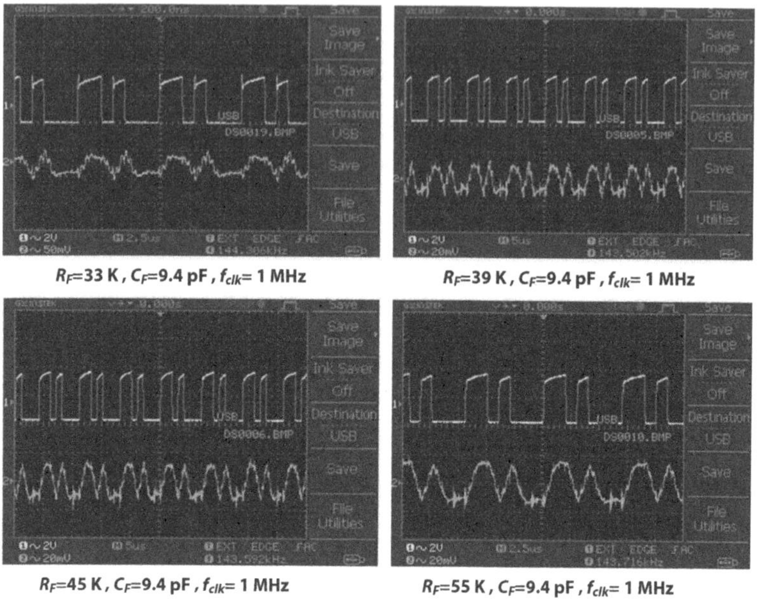

Figure 17.11 Input-output signal at $(f_{clk}) = 1\,\text{MHz}$ for $R_F = 33\,K\Omega - 55\,K\Omega$ and $C_F = 9.4\,pF$.

17.5 Simulation and Modeling of the VLC System

This section demonstrates the stepwise procedures for modeling an indoor VLC system. The programming tool used is MATLAB2023®. The latter part of the section provides a few MATLAB codes for the evaluation of illuminance, received power, channel impulse response, and rms delay spread.

Step-1: Simulation of room configuration
To simulate an indoor VLC system, the room dimensions must be first modeled. Consider a rectangular room of dimension $(l * b * h) = (5 * 5 * 3)$. These dimensions are to be mapped on $x - axis$, $y - axis$, and $z - axis$, respectively, as shown in Figure 17.12. Consider that all three axes originate from the center of the room.

As per Figure 17.12, the length of the room is mapped parallel to the x-axis, hence defined from -2.5 to +2.5 m; the breadth of the room is mapped parallel to the y-axis and defined from -2.5 to +2.5 m; and the height is -1.5 to +1.5 m. The part of MATLAB code is given in program 1. This code generates 75 points on the x- and y-axes and 45 points on the z-axis. The creation of more points will give better accuracy of distances measured between the transmitter and the receiver but at the cost

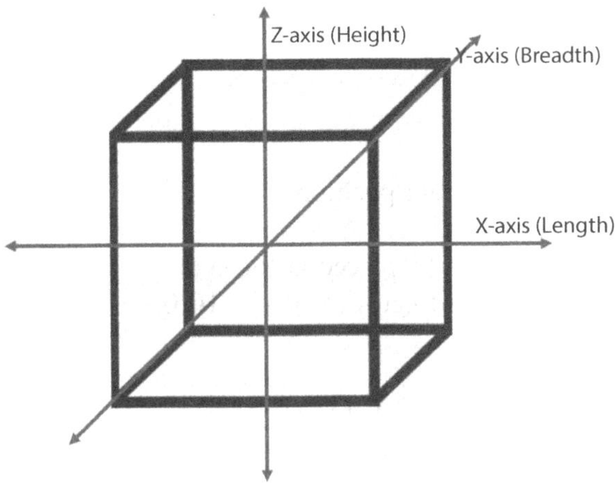

Figure 17.12 Visualization of an empty room w.r.t. x-, y-, and z-axes.

of computing speed and complexity. Code snippet 1 details the MATLAB code for room configuration.

Code snippet 1: Configuring room dimensions

```
%Defining room dimensions
lx=5; ly=5; lz=3;
Nx=lx*15;
Ny=ly*15;
Nz=round(lz*15);          %Generating multiple
                          points for x, y, and z
dA=lz*ly/(Ny*Nz);         %Will be used for diffuse
                          channel
x=linspace(-lx/2,lx       %75 points on x-axis from
/2,Nx);                   -2.5 to +2.5
y=linspce                 %75 points on y-axis from
(-ly/2,ly/2,Ny);          -2.5 to +2.5
z=linspace                %45 points on z-axis from
(-lz/2,lz/2,Nz);          -1.5 to +1.5
```

Step-2: Configuring the room mesh

The entire room mesh can be created using the command. Since the receiver is placed at the bottom of the room, mesh grid arguments are (x, y, and -lz/2). Code snippet 2 details the MATLAB code to create the mesh grid inside the room configuration.

Code snippet-2: Creating the mesh-grid

```
[XR,YR,ZR] = meshgrid(x,y,-lz/2);  %Receiver
mesh grid. The receiver is placed at the bottom
```

Step-3: Define the transmitter position
Case 1: Single transmitter
The single transmitter can be placed at the center of the room at the top. Hence, the positional coordinates $(x,y,z)=(0,0,+1.5)$

```
TP1=[0 0 lz/2];
```

Case 2: Four transmitters placed at four quadrants
Code snippet 3: Position of four transmitters

```
TP1=[lx/4 ly/4 lz/2]   %First LED in the first
                        quadrant
TP2=[-lx/4 ly/4 lz/2]  %Second LED in the second
                        quadrant
TP3=[-lx/4 -ly/4 lz/2] %Third LED in the third
                        quadrant
TP4=[lx/4 -ly/4 lz/2]  %Fourth LED in the fourth
                        quadrant.
```

Case 3: Any other LED layout position
The below code snippet shows the coding for the layout as shown in Figure 17.13.

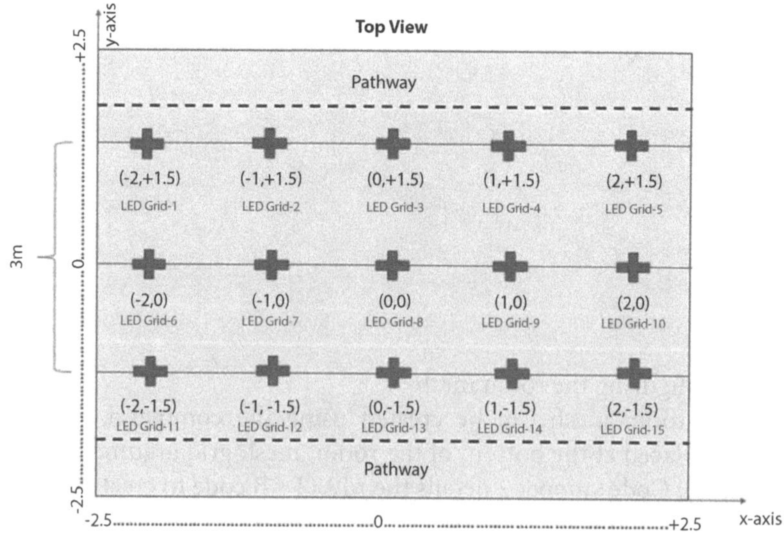

Figure 17.13 LED layout configuration using 15 LEDs.

Code snippet 4: Position of 15 transmitter

```
TP1=[-lx/2.5 ly/3.333     %This is TP1 position
lz/2];
TP2=[-lx/5 ly/3.333       %This is TP2 position
lz/2];
TP3=[0 ly/3.333 lz/2];    %This is TP3 position
TP4=[lx/5 ly/3.333        %This is TP4 position
lz/2];
TP5=[lx/2.5 ly/3.333      %This is TP5 position
lz/2];
TP6=[-lx/2.5 0 lz/2];     %This is TP6 position
TP7=[-lx/5 0 lz/2];       %This is TP7 position
TP8=[0 0 lz/2];           %This is TP8 position
TP9=[lx/5 0 lz/2];        %This is TP9 position
TP10=[lx/2.5 0 lz/2];     %This is TP10 position
TP11=[-lx/2.5 -ly/3.333   %This is TP11 position
lz/2];
TP12=[-lx/5 -ly/3.333     %This is TP12 position
lz/2];
TP13=[0 -ly/3.333 lz/2];  %This is TP13 position
TP14=[lx/5 -ly/3.333      %This is TP14 position
lz/2];
TP15=[lx/3.333 -ly/3.333  %This is TP15 position
lz/2];
```

Step-4: Define the transmitter and receiver parameters

```
p_total=100e-3;       %Transmitted optical power
                      for simulation=20dBm
C=3e8*1e-9;           %Distance traveled by light
                      in 1 ns=0.3
hpa=55;               %Semi angle at half power
m=-log(2)/log(cos-    %mode no; angle in degree
d(hpa));
I0=0.73;              %[defined in candela]
I0_total=I0*60*60;
delta_t=0.2;          %Delay parameter
Adet=5.5e-6;          %The detector physical area
                      of a PD in meters
rho=0.8;              %The reflection coefficient
                      of wall
FOV=80;               %FOV of the receiver
```

Step-5: Evaluate the vector distance between the transmitter position and the receiver

```
D1=sqrt((XR-XT(1,1)).^2+(YR-YT(1,1)).^2+h^2);
```

Step-6: Evaluate the irradiance angle

```
cosphi_A1=h./D1;  %adjacent side by hypotenuse
```

Step-7: Evaluate the illuminance

```
%requirement of illuminance
illuminance=I0_total.*cosphi_A1.^m./(D1.^2);
```

Code 1: Evaluation of illuminance for the LED layout, as shown in Figure 17.13

```
% LED Part No.:                VLHW5100
% Manufacturer:                Vishay Semiconductors
% Description Standard         5mm
LEDs:
% Luminous Intensity:          11200 mcd=12.2cd
% Viewing angle:               10
% Forward current:             20 mA
% Forward voltage:             2.7 V

%Transmitted optical power
p_total=100e-3;               %Power for simulation=20
                              dBm
g_fil=1;                      %The gain of optical
                              filter
rho=0.8;                      %The reflection coeffi-
                              cient of wall
R=0.55;                       %Responsivity of photo-
                              detector A/W
Adet=7.5e-6;                  %The detector physical
                              area of a PD in meters
index=1.5;                    %Refractive index of
                              lens
fov=60;                       %FOV of the receiver
g_con=(index^2)/(sind(-       %Gain of concentrator
FOV).^2);
```

```
%Listing of LED physical parameters from the data-
sheet
hpa=10;                        %Semi-angle at half pow-
                               er
LI=11.2;                       %Center luminous inten-
                               sity in candela of a
                               single LED
n=8;                           %Number of LEDs
LI_tot=n*LI;                   %Total center illumi-
                               nance
m=-log(2)/log(cosd(hpa));      %Mode number

%Define room dimensions in meters
lx=5; ly=5; lz=3;
Nx=lx*50; Ny=ly*50;            %Number of subpoints
x=-lx/2:lx/Nx:lx/2;            %Define x-axis
y=-ly/2:ly/Ny:ly/2;            %Define y-axis
[XR,YR]=meshgrid(x,y);         %Receiver plane grid

%Define distance between transmitter and receiver
dtr_1=1;

%Define the positions of the LEDs
XTrans1=-2;    YTrans1=1.5;     %LED-1
XTrans2=-1;    YTrans2=1.5;     %LED-2
XTrans3=0;     YTrans3=1.5;     %LED-3
XTrans4=1;     YTrans4=1.5;     %LED-4
XTrans5=2;     YTrans5=1.5;     %LED-5

XTrans6=-2;    YTrans6=0;       %LED-6
XTrans7=-1;    YTrans7=0;       %LED-7
XTrans8=0;     YTrans8=0;       %LED-8
XTrans9=1;     YTrans9=0;       %LED-9
XTrans10=2;    YTrans10=0;      %LED-10

XTrans11=-2;   YTrans11=-1.5;   %LED11
XTrans12=-1;   YTrans12=-1.5;   %LED12
XTrans13=0;    YTrans13=-1.5;   %LED13
XTrans14=1;    YTrans14=-1.5;   %LED14
XTrans15=2;    YTrans15=-1.5;   %LED15
```

```
%Evaluate the distance vector
D1=sqrt((XR-XTrans1(1,1)).^2+(YR-YTrans1(1,1)).^2+dtr_1^2);
D2=sqrt((XR-XTrans2(1,1)).^2+(YR-YTrans2(1,1)).^2+dtr_1^2);
D3=sqrt((XR-XTrans3(1,1)).^2+(YR-YTrans3(1,1)).^2+dtr_1^2);
D4=sqrt((XR-XTrans4(1,1)).^2+(YR-YTrans4(1,1)).^2+dtr_1^2);
D5=sqrt((XR-XTrans5(1,1)).^2+(YR-YTrans5(1,1)).^2+dtr_1^2);
D6=sqrt((XR-XTrans6(1,1)).^2+(YR-YTrans6(1,1)).^2+dtr_1^2);
D7=sqrt((XR-XTrans7(1,1)).^2+(YR-YTrans7(1,1)).^2+dtr_1^2);
D8=sqrt((XR-XTrans8(1,1)).^2+(YR-YTrans8(1,1)).^2+dtr_1^2);
D9=sqrt((XR-XTrans9(1,1)).^2+(YR-YTrans9(1,1)).^2+dtr_1^2);
D10=sqrt((XR-XTrans10(1,1)).^2+(YR-YTrans10(1,1)).^2+dtr_1^2);
D11=sqrt((XR-XTrans11(1,1)).^2+(YR-YTrans11(1,1)).^2+dtr_1^2);
D12=sqrt((XR-XTrans12(1,1)).^2+(YR-YTrans12(1,1)).^2+dtr_1^2);
D13=sqrt((XR-XTrans13(1,1)).^2+(YR-YTrans13(1,1)).^2+dtr_1^2);
D14=sqrt((XR-XTrans14(1,1)).^2+(YR-YTrans14(1,1)).^2+dtr_1^2);
D15=sqrt((XR-XTrans15(1,1)).^2+(YR-YTrans15(1,1)).^2+dtr_1^2);

%Evaluate the irrandiance angle
coseno_phi1=dtr_1./D1;
coseno_phi2=dtr_1./D2;
coseno_phi3=dtr_1./D3;
coseno_phi4=dtr_1./D4;
coseno_phi5=dtr_1./D5;
coseno_phi6=dtr_1./D6;
coseno_phi7=dtr_1./D7;
coseno_phi8=dtr_1./D8;
coseno_phi9=dtr_1./D9;
coseno_phi10=dtr_1./D10;
coseno_phi11=dtr_1./D11;
coseno_phi12=dtr_1./D12;
coseno_phi13=dtr_1./D13;
coseno_phi14=dtr_1./D14;
coseno_phi15=dtr_1./D15;

%Evaluate illuminance
E_lux1=(LI_tot*coseno_phi1.^m)./(D1.^2);
E_lux2=(LI_tot*coseno_phi2.^m)./(D2.^2);
E_lux3=(LI_tot*coseno_phi3.^m)./(D3.^2);
E_lux4=(LI_tot*coseno_phi4.^m)./(D4.^2);
E_lux5=(LI_tot*coseno_phi5.^m)./(D5.^2);
```

```
E_lux6=(LI_tot*coseno_phi6.^m)./(D6.^2);
E_lux7=(LI_tot*coseno_phi7.^m)./(D7.^2);
E_lux8=(LI_tot*coseno_phi8.^m)./(D8.^2);
E_lux9=(LI_tot*coseno_phi9.^m)./(D9.^2);
E_lux10=(LI_tot*coseno_phi10.^m)./(D10.^2);
E_lux11=(LI_tot*coseno_phi11.^m)./(D11.^2);
E_lux12=(LI_tot*coseno_phi12.^m)./(D12.^2);
E_lux13=(LI_tot*coseno_phi13.^m)./(D13.^2);
E_lux14=(LI_tot*coseno_phi14.^m)./(D14.^2);
E_lux15=(LI_tot*coseno_phi15.^m)./(D15.^2);

%Evaluate the total illuminance
E_lux=E_lux1+E_lux2+E_lux3+E_lux4+E_lux5+E_lux6+E_lux-
7+E_lux8+E_lux9+E_lux10+E_lux11+E_lux12+E_lux13+E_lux14+E_
lux15;

%Display the illuminance model
figure(1)
meshc(x,y,E_lux);
colorbar;
xlabel('x length in meters');
ylabel('y breadth in meters');
zlabel('Illuminance(lux)');
title('Illumination Pattern(n=5)');

figure(2)
contour(x,y, E_lux,'ShowText','on');
xlabel('Length in meters');
ylabel('Breadth in meters');
title('Contour plot (n=5)');
```

Observations

It is observed that illuminance depends on the number of LEDs (n) used, the luminous intensity of each LED, and the vector distance between the transmitter and the receiver. It is observed in Figure 17.14(a) that an illuminance of only 80 lux is achieved with eight LEDs, each of luminous intensity 11,200 mcd. The Lambertian spread of the signal depends on the semi-angle of the LED.

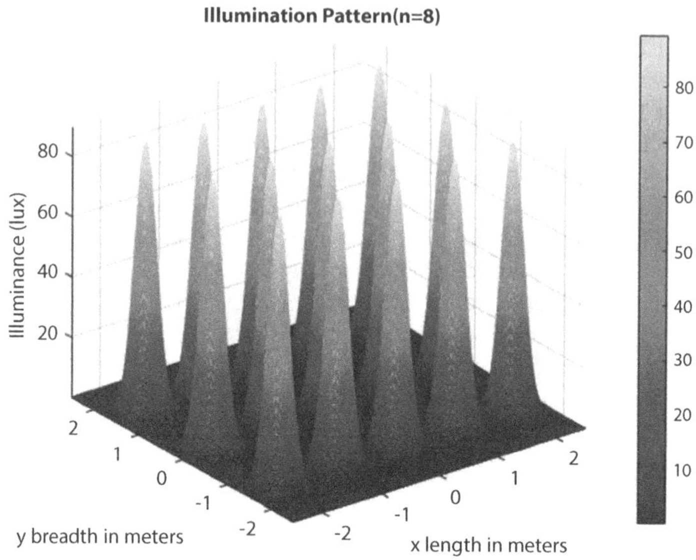

(a)

Figure 17.14(a) Illuminance plot for n=8.

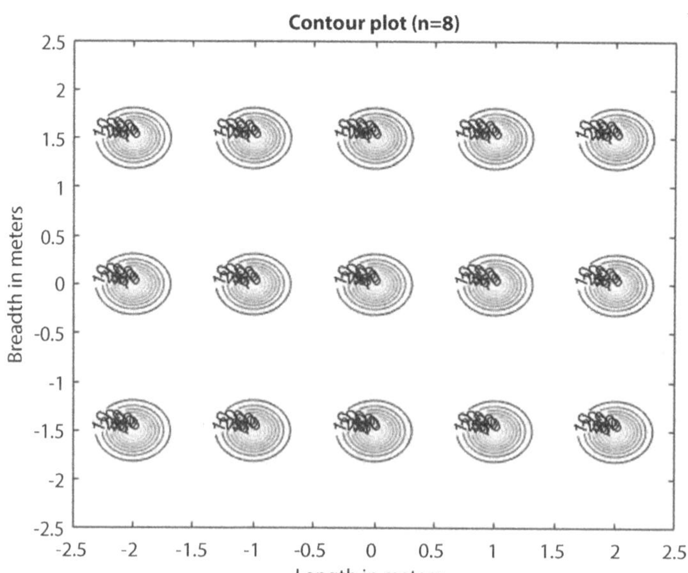

(b)

Figure 17.14(b) Contour plot for n=8.

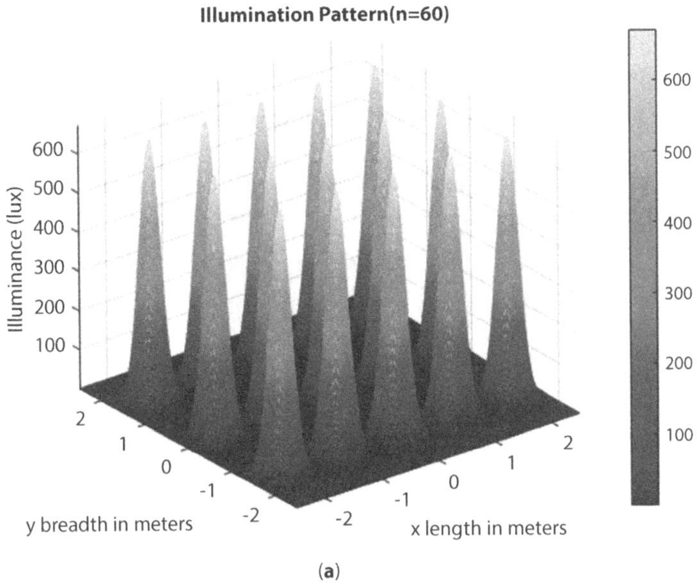

Figure 17.15(a) Illuminance plot for n=60.

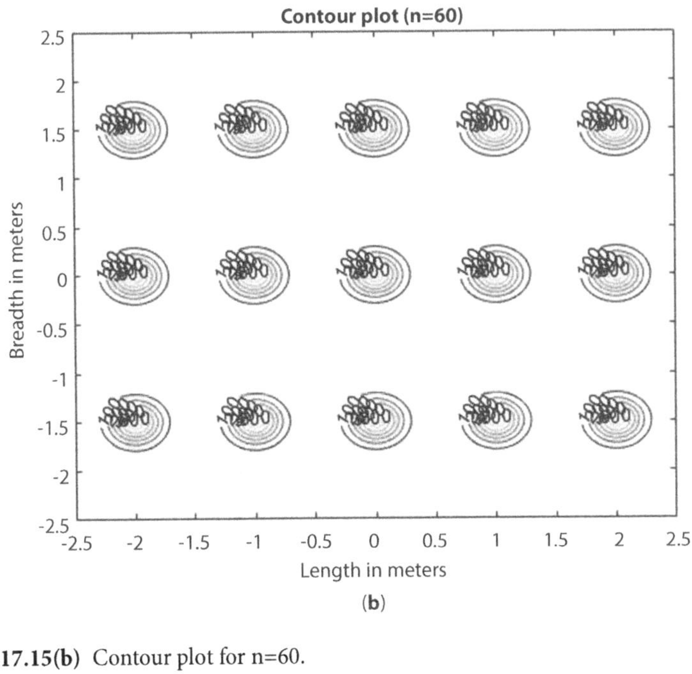

Figure 17.15(b) Contour plot for n=60.

Conclusions

To enhance illuminance, it is important to work with more LEDs that have a high luminous intensity value. Figure 17.15(a) demonstrates the illuminance spread with n = 60, each having a luminous intensity of 11,200 mcd.

Code 2: Evaluation of received power for the LED layout, as shown in Figure 17.13, for LOS configuration

```
% LED Part No.:                 VLHW5100
% Manufacturer:                 Vishay Semiconductors
% Description Standard          5mm
LEDs:
% Luminous Intensity:           11200 mcd=12.2cd
% Viewing angle:                10
% Forward current:              20 mA
% Forward voltage:              2.7 V

%Transmitted optical power
p_total=100e-3;                 %Power for simulation=20
                                dBm
g_fil=1;                        %The gain of optical fil-
                                ter
rho=0.8;                        %The reflection coeffi-
                                cient of wall
R=0.55;                         %Responsivity of photode-
                                tector A/W
Adet=7.5e-6;                    %The detector physical
                                area of a PD in meters
index=1.5;                      %Refractive index of lens
fov=60;                         %FOV of the receiver
g_con=(index^2)/(sind           %Gain of concentrator
(FOV).^2);

% Listing of LED physical parameters from the data-
sheet
hpa=10;                         %Semi-angle at half power
LI=11.2;                        %Center luminous intensi-
                                ty in candela of a single
                                LED
n=8;                            %Number of LEDs
LI_tot=n*LI;                    %Total center illuminance
```

```
m=-log(2)/log(cosd(h-     %Mode number
pa));

%Define room dimensions in meters
lx=5; ly=5; lz=3;
Nx=lx*50; Ny=ly*50;         %Number of subpoints
x=-lx/2:lx/Nx:lx/2;         %Define x-axis
y=-ly/2:ly/Ny:ly/2;         %Define y-axis
[XR,YR]=meshgrid(x,y);      %Receiver plane grid

%Define distance between transmitter and receiver
dtr_1=1;

%Define the positions of the LEDs
XTrans1=-2;    YTrans1=1.5;    %LED-1
XTrans2=-1;    YTrans2=1.5;    %LED-2
XTrans3=0;     YTrans3=1.5;    %LED-3
XTrans4=1;     YTrans4=1.5;    %LED-4
XTrans5=2;     YTrans5=1.5;    %LED-5

XTrans6=-2;    YTrans6=0;      %LED-6
XTrans7=-1;    YTrans7=0;      %LED-7
XTrans8=0;     YTrans8=0;      %LED-8
XTrans9=1;     YTrans9=0;      %LED-9
XTrans10=2;    YTrans10=0;     %LED-10

XTrans11=-2;   YTrans11=-1.5;  %LED11
XTrans12=-1;   YTrans12=-1.5;  %LED12
XTrans13=0;    YTrans13=-1.5;  %LED13
XTrans14=1;    YTrans14=-1.5;  %LED14
XTrans15=2;    YTrans15=-1.5;  %LED15

%Evaluate the distance vector
D1=sqrt((XR-XTrans1(1,1)).^2+(YR-YTrans1(1,1)).^2+
dtr_1^2);
D2=sqrt((XR-XTrans2(1,1)).^2+(YR-YTrans2(1,1)).^2+
dtr_1^2);
D3=sqrt((XR-XTrans3(1,1)).^2+(YR-YTrans3(1,1)).^2+
dtr_1^2);
D4=sqrt((XR-XTrans4(1,1)).^2+(YR-YTrans4(1,1)).^2+
dtr_1^2);
D5=sqrt((XR-XTrans5(1,1)).^2+(YR-YTrans5(1,1)).^2+
```

```
dtr_1^2);
D6=sqrt((XR-XTrans6(1,1)).^2+(YR-YTrans6(1,1)).^2+
dtr_1^2);
D7=sqrt((XR-XTrans7(1,1)).^2+(YR-YTrans7(1,1)).^2+
dtr_1^2);
D8=sqrt((XR-XTrans8(1,1)).^2+(YR-YTrans8(1,1)).^2+
dtr_1^2);
D9=sqrt((XR-XTrans9(1,1)).^2+(YR-YTrans9(1,1)).^2+
dtr_1^2);
D10=sqrt((XR-XTrans10(1,1)).^2+(YR-YTrans10(1,1)).^2+
dtr_1^2);
D11=sqrt((XR-XTrans11(1,1)).^2+(YR-YTrans11(1,1)).^2+
dtr_1^2);
D12=sqrt((XR-XTrans12(1,1)).^2+(YR-YTrans12(1,1)).^2+
dtr_1^2);
D13=sqrt((XR-XTrans13(1,1)).^2+(YR-YTrans13(1,1)).^2+
dtr_1^2);
D14=sqrt((XR-XTrans14(1,1)).^2+(YR-YTrans14(1,1)).^2+
dtr_1^2);
D15=sqrt((XR-XTrans15(1,1)).^2+(YR-YTrans15(1,1)).^2+
dtr_1^2);

%Evaluate the irrandiance angle
coseno_phi1=dtr_1./D1;
coseno_phi2=dtr_1./D2;
coseno_phi3=dtr_1./D3;
coseno_phi4=dtr_1./D4;
coseno_phi5=dtr_1./D5;
coseno_phi6=dtr_1./D6;
coseno_phi7=dtr_1./D7;
coseno_phi8=dtr_1./D8;
coseno_phi9=dtr_1./D9;
coseno_phi10=dtr_1./D10;
coseno_phi11=dtr_1./D11;
coseno_phi12=dtr_1./D12;
coseno_phi13=dtr_1./D13;
coseno_phi14=dtr_1./D14;
coseno_phi15=dtr_1./D15;
```

```
%Defining the DC channel gain
H_A1=((m+1)*Adet.*coseno_phi1.^(m+1))./(2*pi.*D1.^2);
H_A2=((m+1)*Adet.*coseno_phi2.^(m+1))./(2*pi.*D2.^2);
H_A3=((m+1)*Adet.*coseno_phi3.^(m+1))./(2*pi.*D3.^2);
H_A4=((m+1)*Adet.*coseno_phi4.^(m+1))./(2*pi.*D4.^2);
H_A5=((m+1)*Adet.*coseno_phi5.^(m+1))./(2*pi.*D5.^2);
H_A6=((m+1)*Adet.*coseno_phi6.^(m+1))./(2*pi.*D6.^2);
H_A7=((m+1)*Adet.*coseno_phi7.^(m+1))./(2*pi.*D7.^2);
H_A8=((m+1)*Adet.*coseno_phi8.^(m+1))./(2*pi.*D8.^2);
H_A9=((m+1)*Adet.*coseno_phi9.^(m+1))./(2*pi.*D9.^2);
H_A10=((m+1)*Adet.*coseno_phi10.^(m+1))./
(2*pi.*D10.^2);
H_A11=((m+1)*Adet.*coseno_phi11.^(m+1))./
(2*pi.*D11.^2);
H_A12=((m+1)*Adet.*coseno_phi12.^(m+1))./
(2*pi.*D12.^2);
H_A13=((m+1)*Adet.*coseno_phi13.^(m+1))./
(2*pi.*D13.^2);
H_A14=((m+1)*Adet.*coseno_phi14.^(m+1))./
(2*pi.*D14.^2);
H_A15=((m+1)*Adet.*coseno_phi15.^(m+1))./
(2*pi.*D15.^2);

%Evaluate received power
P_rec_A1=p_total.*H_A1.*Ts.*G_Con;
P_rec_A2=p_total.*H_A2.*Ts.*G_Con;
P_rec_A3=p_total.*H_A3.*Ts.*G_Con;
P_rec_A4=p_total.*H_A4.*Ts.*G_Con;
P_rec_A5=p_total.*H_A5.*Ts.*G_Con;
P_rec_A6=p_total.*H_A6.*Ts.*G_Con;
P_rec_A7=p_total.*H_A7.*Ts.*G_Con;
P_rec_A8=p_total.*H_A8.*Ts.*G_Con;
P_rec_A9=p_total.*H_A9.*Ts.*G_Con;
P_rec_A10=p_total.*H_A10.*Ts.*G_Con;
P_rec_A11=p_total.*H_A11.*Ts.*G_Con;
P_rec_A12=p_total.*H_A12.*Ts.*G_Con;
P_rec_A13=p_total.*H_A13.*Ts.*G_Con;
P_rec_A14=p_total.*H_A14.*Ts.*G_Con;
P_rec_A15=p_total.*H_A15.*Ts.*G_Con;
```

```
%Apply the receiver FOV condition
P_rec_A1(find(abs(recevier_angle1)>FOV))=0;
P_rec_A2(find(abs(recevier_angle2)>FOV))=0;
P_rec_A3(find(abs(recevier_angle3)>FOV))=0;
P_rec_A4(find(abs(recevier_angle4)>FOV))=0;
P_rec_A5(find(abs(recevier_angle5)>FOV))=0;
P_rec_A6(find(abs(recevier_angle6)>FOV))=0;
P_rec_A7(find(abs(recevier_angle7)>FOV))=0;
P_rec_A8(find(abs(recevier_angle8)>FOV))=0;
P_rec_A9(find(abs(recevier_angle9)>FOV))=0;
P_rec_A10(find(abs(recevier_angle10)>FOV))=0;
P_rec_A11(find(abs(recevier_angle11)>FOV))=0;
P_rec_A12(find(abs(recevier_angle12)>FOV))=0;
P_rec_A13(find(abs(recevier_angle13)>FOV))=0;
P_rec_A14(find(abs(recevier_angle14)>FOV))=0;
P_rec_A15(find(abs(recevier_angle15)>FOV))=0;

%Evaluate the received power
P_rec_total=P_rec_A1+P_rec_A2+P_rec_A3+P_rec_A4+P_
rec_A5+P_rec_A6+P_rec_A7+P_rec_A8+P_rec_A9+P_rec_
A10+P_rec_A11+P_rec_A12+P_rec_A13+P_rec_A14+P_rec_
A15;
P_rec_total1os=P_rec_total.*1;
P_rec_dBm=10*log10(P_rec_total1os);

figure(1)
meshc(x,y,P_rec_dBm);
colorbar;
xlabel('Length in meters');
ylabel('Breadth in meters');
zlabel('Total power in dBm');
title('Power distribution in dBm for LOS');

figure(2)
contour(x,y,P_rec_dBm,'ShowText','on');
xlabel('Length in meters');
ylabel('Breadth in meters');
title('Contour plot (n=5)');
```

Figure 17.16(a) depicts the received power distribution plot using 60 LEDs in a grid. Figure 17.16(b) shows the contour plot of the distribution.

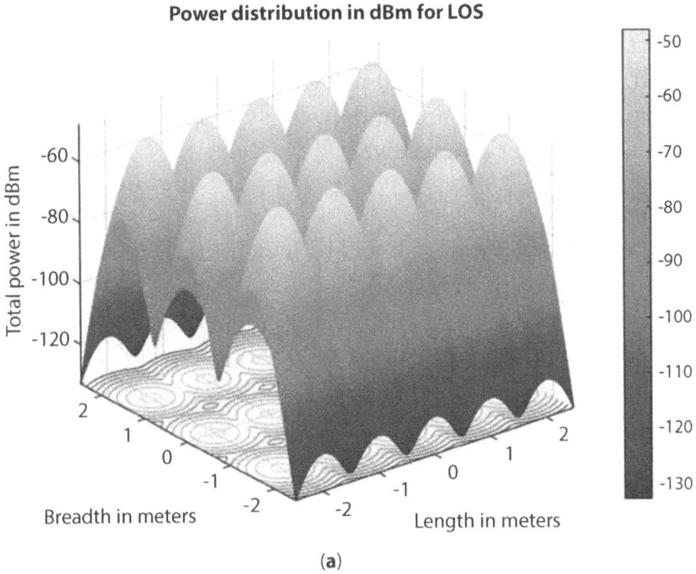

Figure 17.16(a) Received power plot for n=60.

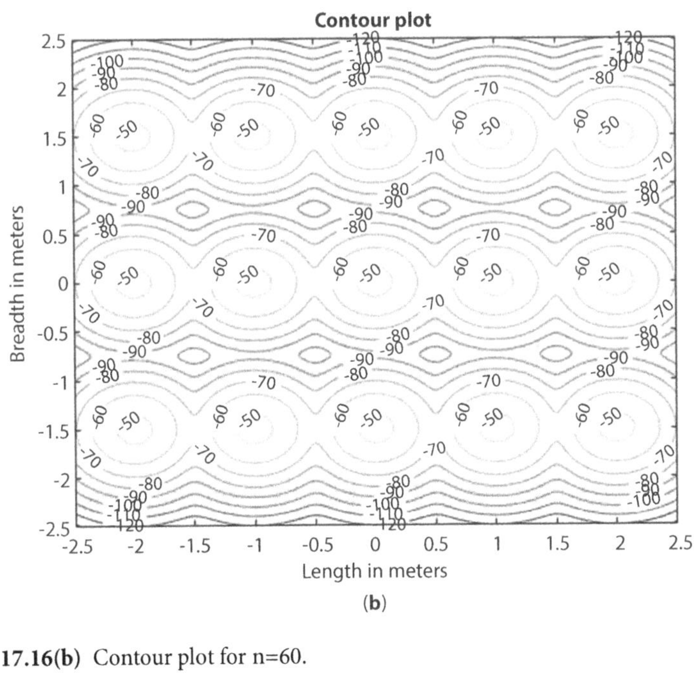

Figure 17.16(b) Contour plot for n=60.

Observations

As per equations (17.6) and (17.8), the received power depends on the DC channel gain and total transmitted power. The DC channel gain is directly proportional to the detector area and inversely proportional to the distance between the transmitter and receiver.

Conclusions

To enhance the received power, it will be beneficial to work with photodetectors in a larger sensitive area.

Code 3: Evaluation of signal-to-noise ratio (SNR) for LOS configuration

```
% LED Part No.:                VLHW5100
% Manufacturer:                Vishay Semiconductors
% Description Standard         5mm
LEDs:
% Luminous Intensity:          11200 mcd=12.2cd
% Viewing angle:               10
% Forward current:             20 mA
% Forward voltage:             2.7 V

%Transmitted optical power
p_total=100e-3;                %Power for simulation=20
                               dBm
g_fil=1;                       %The gain of optical filter
rho=0.8;                       %The reflection coefficient
                               of wall
R=0.55;                        %Responsivity of photode-
                               tector A/W
Adet=7.5e-6;                   %The detector physical
                               area of a PD in meters
index=1.5;                     %Refractive index of lens
fov=60;                        %FOV of the receiver
g_con=(index^2)/(sind(-        %Gain of concentrator
FOV).^2);

%Listing of LED physical parameters from the data-
sheet
hpa=10;                        %Semi-angle at half power
LI=11.2;                       %Center luminous intensity
                               in candela of a single LED
n=8;                           %Number of LEDs
```

```
LI_tot=n*LI;                 %Total center illuminance
m=-log(2)/log(cosd(hpa));  %Mode number

%Define room dimensions in meters
lx=5; ly=5; lz=3;
Nx=lx*50; Ny=ly*50;          %Number of subpoints
x=-lx/2:lx/Nx:lx/2;          %Define x-axis
y=-ly/2:ly/Ny:ly/2;          %Define y-axis
[XR,YR]=meshgrid(x,y);       %Receiver plane grid

%Define distance between transmitter and receiver
dtr_1=1;

%Define the positions of the LEDs
XTrans1=-2;    YTrans1=1.5;    %LED-1
XTrans2=-1;    YTrans2=1.5;    %LED-2
XTrans3=0;     YTrans3=1.5;    %LED-3
XTrans4=1;     YTrans4=1.5;    %LED-4
XTrans5=2;     YTrans5=1.5;    %LED-5

XTrans6=-2;    YTrans6=0;      %LED-6
XTrans7=-1;    YTrans7=0;      %LED-7
XTrans8=0;     YTrans8=0;      %LED-8
XTrans9=1;     YTrans9=0;      %LED-9
XTrans10=2;    YTrans10=0;     %LED-10

XTrans11=-2;  YTrans11=-1.5;  %LED11
XTrans12=-1;  YTrans12=-1.5;  %LED12
XTrans13=0;   YTrans13=-1.5;  %LED13
XTrans14=1;   YTrans14=-1.5;  %LED14
XTrans15=2;   YTrans15=-1.5;  %LED15

%Evaluate the distance vector
D1=sqrt((XR-XTrans1(1,1)).^2+(YR-YTrans1(1,1)).^2+
dtr_1^2);
D2=sqrt((XR-XTrans2(1,1)).^2+(YR-YTrans2(1,1)).^2+
dtr_1^2);
D3=sqrt((XR-XTrans3(1,1)).^2+(YR-YTrans3(1,1)).^2+
dtr_1^2);
D4=sqrt((XR-XTrans4(1,1)).^2+(YR-YTrans4(1,1)).^2+
dtr_1^2);
```

```
D5=sqrt((XR-XTrans5(1,1)).^2+(YR-YTrans5(1,1)).^2+
dtr_1^2);
D6=sqrt((XR-XTrans6(1,1)).^2+(YR-YTrans6(1,1)).^2+
dtr_1^2);
D7=sqrt((XR-XTrans7(1,1)).^2+(YR-YTrans7(1,1)).^2+
dtr_1^2);
D8=sqrt((XR-XTrans8(1,1)).^2+(YR-YTrans8(1,1)).^2+
dtr_1^2);
D9=sqrt((XR-XTrans9(1,1)).^2+(YR-YTrans9(1,1)).^2+
dtr_1^2);
D10=sqrt((XR-XTrans10(1,1)).^2+(YR-YTrans10(1,1)).^2+
dtr_1^2);
D11=sqrt((XR-XTrans11(1,1)).^2+(YR-YTrans11(1,1)).^2+
dtr_1^2);
D12=sqrt((XR-XTrans12(1,1)).^2+(YR-YTrans12(1,1)).^2+
dtr_1^2);
D13=sqrt((XR-XTrans13(1,1)).^2+(YR-YTrans13(1,1)).^2+
dtr_1^2);
D14=sqrt((XR-XTrans14(1,1)).^2+(YR-YTrans14(1,1)).^2+
dtr_1^2);
D15=sqrt((XR-XTrans15(1,1)).^2+(YR-YTrans15(1,1)).^2+
dtr_1^2);

%Evaluate the irrandiance angle
coseno_phi1=dtr_1./D1;
coseno_phi2=dtr_1./D2;
coseno_phi3=dtr_1./D3;
coseno_phi4=dtr_1./D4;
coseno_phi5=dtr_1./D5;
coseno_phi6=dtr_1./D6;
coseno_phi7=dtr_1./D7;
coseno_phi8=dtr_1./D8;
coseno_phi9=dtr_1./D9;
coseno_phi10=dtr_1./D10;
coseno_phi11=dtr_1./D11;
coseno_phi12=dtr_1./D12;
coseno_phi13=dtr_1./D13;
coseno_phi14=dtr_1./D14;
coseno_phi15=dtr_1./D15;
```

```
%Defining the DC channel gain
H_A1=((m+1)*Adet.*coseno_phi1.^(m+1))./(2*pi.*D1.^2);
H_A2=((m+1)*Adet.*coseno_phi2.^(m+1))./(2*pi.*D2.^2);
H_A3=((m+1)*Adet.*coseno_phi3.^(m+1))./(2*pi.*D3.^2);
H_A4=((m+1)*Adet.*coseno_phi4.^(m+1))./(2*pi.*D4.^2);
H_A5=((m+1)*Adet.*coseno_phi5.^(m+1))./(2*pi.*D5.^2);
H_A6=((m+1)*Adet.*coseno_phi6.^(m+1))./(2*pi.*D6.^2);
H_A7=((m+1)*Adet.*coseno_phi7.^(m+1))./(2*pi.*D7.^2);
H_A8=((m+1)*Adet.*coseno_phi8.^(m+1))./(2*pi.*D8.^2);
H_A9=((m+1)*Adet.*coseno_phi9.^(m+1))./(2*pi.*D9.^2);
H_A10=((m+1)*Adet.*coseno_phi10.^(m+1))./
(2*pi.*D10.^2);
H_A11=((m+1)*Adet.*coseno_phi11.^(m+1))./(2*pi.*D11.
^2);
H_A12=((m+1)*Adet.*coseno_phi12.^(m+1))./(2*pi.*D12.
^2);
H_A13=((m+1)*Adet.*coseno_phi13.^(m+1))./(2*pi.*D13.
^2);
H_A14=((m+1)*Adet.*coseno_phi14.^(m+1))./(2*pi.*D14.
^2);
H_A15=((m+1)*Adet.*coseno_phi15.^(m+1))./(2*pi.*D15.
^2);

%Evaluate received power
P_rec_A1=p_total.*H_A1.*Ts.*G_Con;
P_rec_A2=p_total.*H_A2.*Ts.*G_Con;
P_rec_A3=p_total.*H_A3.*Ts.*G_Con;
P_rec_A4=p_total.*H_A4.*Ts.*G_Con;
P_rec_A5=p_total.*H_A5.*Ts.*G_Con;
P_rec_A6=p_total.*H_A6.*Ts.*G_Con;
P_rec_A7=p_total.*H_A7.*Ts.*G_Con;
P_rec_A8=p_total.*H_A8.*Ts.*G_Con;
P_rec_A9=p_total.*H_A9.*Ts.*G_Con;
P_rec_A10=p_total.*H_A10.*Ts.*G_Con;
P_rec_A11=p_total.*H_A11.*Ts.*G_Con;
P_rec_A12=p_total.*H_A12.*Ts.*G_Con;
P_rec_A13=p_total.*H_A13.*Ts.*G_Con;
P_rec_A14=p_total.*H_A14.*Ts.*G_Con;
P_rec_A15=p_total.*H_A15.*Ts.*G_Con;
```

```
%Apply the receiver FOV condition
P_rec_A1(find(abs(recevier_angle1)>FOV))=0;
P_rec_A2(find(abs(recevier_angle2)>FOV))=0;
P_rec_A3(find(abs(recevier_angle3)>FOV))=0;
P_rec_A4(find(abs(recevier_angle4)>FOV))=0;
P_rec_A5(find(abs(recevier_angle5)>FOV))=0;
P_rec_A6(find(abs(recevier_angle6)>FOV))=0;
P_rec_A7(find(abs(recevier_angle7)>FOV))=0;
P_rec_A8(find(abs(recevier_angle8)>FOV))=0;
P_rec_A9(find(abs(recevier_angle9)>FOV))=0;
P_rec_A10(find(abs(recevier_angle10)>FOV))=0;
P_rec_A11(find(abs(recevier_angle11)>FOV))=0;
P_rec_A12(find(abs(recevier_angle12)>FOV))=0;
P_rec_A13(find(abs(recevier_angle13)>FOV))=0;
P_rec_A14(find(abs(recevier_angle14)>FOV))=0;
P_rec_A15(find(abs(recevier_angle15)>FOV))=0;

%Evaluate the received power
P_rec_total=P_rec_A1+P_rec_A2+P_rec_A3+P_rec_A4+P_
rec_A5+P_rec_A6+P_rec_A7+P_rec_A8+P_rec_A9+P_rec_
A10+P_rec_A11+P_rec_A12+P_rec_A13+P_rec_A14+P_rec_
A15;

%SNR Parameters
noisebandwidth=0.562;   % Define noise bandwidth
datarate=51200;         %Define data rate in bps
bn=noisebandwidth*datarate;
q=1.6*10-19;            %Electronic charge
sigma_shot=2*q*R*(P_rec_total)*bn;
                        %Evaluating the shot noise
ba=4.5e6;               %Amplifier bandwidth
amp_curr=0.01;          %Amplifier current
sigma_amp=amp_curr^2*ba;
sigma_tot=sigma_shot+sigma_amp;
snr=(R*P_rec_total)^2./sigma_tot;
snrdb=10*log10(snr);
figure(1)
meshc(x,y,snrdb);
colorbar;
xlabel('Length in meters');
```

```
ylabel('Breadth in meters');
zlabel('SNR in dBm');
title('SNR distribution in dBm for LOS');
```

Code 4: Evaluating channel impulse response for NLOS configuration

```
close all;
p_total=100e-3;              %Transmitted optical power
                             for simulation=20dBm
C=3e8*1e-9;                  %Distance traveled by
                             light in 1 ns=0.3
hpa=30;                      %Semi angle at half power
m=-log(2)/log(cosd(hpa));    %mode no, cosd is used to
                             get the angle in degree
%---------------------------------------------------
%Defining time and receiver dimensions
%FOV of receiver is larger than hpa of LED
delta_t=0.5;                 %Delay parameter
Adet=7.5e-6;                 %The detector physical
                             area of a PD in meters
rho=0.8;                     %The reflection coefficient
                             of wall
FOV=85;                      %FOV of the receiver
%---------------------------------------------------
%Defining room dimensions
lx=5; ly=5;lz=3;
Nx=lx*15;
Ny=ly*15;Nz=round(lz*15);
dA=lz*ly/(Ny*Nz);            %Will be used for diffuse
                             channel
x=linspace(-lx/2,lx/2,Nx);   %75 points on x-axis from
                             -2.5 to +2.5
y=linspace(-ly/2,ly/2,Ny);   %75 points on y-axis from
                             -2.5 to +2.5
z=linspace(-lz/2,lz/2,Nz);   %45 points on z-axis from
                             -1.5 to +1.5
[XR,YR,ZR] = meshgrid(x-     %Receiver mesh grid. The
,y,-lz/2);                   receiver is placed at the
                             bottom
```

```
dtr_1=1;                    %Distance between trans-
                            mitter and receiver
%----------------------------------------------------

%Define the positions of the transmitters LEDs
%TP1=[0 0 lz/2];
TP1=[-lx/2.5 ly/3.333 lz/2];  % LED 1 Transmitter po-
                              sition
for ii=1:Nx
    for jj=1:Ny
        RP1=[x(ii) y(jj) -lz/2]; %We are considering
        all receiver positions
        t_vector=0:25/0.3333; % time vector in ns (75
        points)
        h_vector1=zeros(1,length(t_vector)); %Create
        a row to store h vector
        D1(ii,jj)=sqrt(dot(TP1-RP1,TP1-RP1));
        cosphi(ii,jj)= dtr_1/D1(ii,jj);
        tau0(ii,jj)=D1(ii,jj)/C; %tau0 is measured in
        ns
        index1(ii,jj)=find(round(tau0(ii,jj)/0.5)==t_
        vector);
        if abs(acosd(cosphi(ii,jj)))<=FOV
h_vector1(index1(ii,jj))=h_vector1(index1(ii,jj))+
((m+1)*Adet.*cosphi(ii,jj).^(m+1))./(2*pi.*D1(ii,jj).
^2);
        end
%---------------------------------------------------
        %The NLOS part is starting from this point
        count1=1;
        for kk=1:Ny           %Y direction is variable
            for ll=1:Nz       %Z direction is variable
            WP1=[-lx/2 y(kk) z(ll)]; %This is the
            position of left wall
            Dnlos1=sqrt(dot(TP1-WP1,TP1-WP1));
            cos_phi1= abs(WP1(3)-TP1(3))/Dnlos1;
            cos_alpha1 = abs(TP1(1)-WP1(1))/Dnlos1;
```

```
                %Since these are absolute values,
                the position of TP1,WP1
                %or RP does not matter
                Dnlos2=sqrt(dot(WP1-RP1,WP1-RP1));
                cos_beta1=abs(WP1(1)-RP1(1))/Dnlos2;
                cos_psi1=abs(WP1(3)-RP1(3))/Dnlos2;
                tau1=(Dnlos1+Dnlos2)/C;
                index1=find(round(tau1/0.5)==t_vec-
                tor);
                if abs(acosd(cos_psi1))<=FOV
h_vector1(index1)=h_vector1(index1)+(m+1)*Ade-
t*rho*dA*cos_phi1^m*cos_alpha1*cos_beta1*cos_psi1/
(2*pi^2*Dnlos1^2*Dnlos2^2);
                end
                count1=count1+1;
            end
        end

        %Reflection from 2nd wall WP2
        count2=1;
        for mm=1:Ny
            for nn=1:Nz
                WP2=[lx/2 y(mm) z(nn)]; %This is the
                position of right wall
                Dnlos3=sqrt(dot(TP1-WP2,TP1-WP2));
                cos_phi12=abs(WP2(3)-TP1(3))/Dnlos3;
                cos_alpha2=abs(TP1(1)-WP2(1))/Dn-
                los3;
                Dnlos4=sqrt(dot(WP2-RP1,WP2-RP1));
                cos_beta3=abs(WP2(1)-RP1(1))/Dnlos4;
                cos_psi3=abs(WP2(3)-RP1(3))/Dnlos4;
                tau2=(Dnlos3+Dnlos4)/C;
                index1=find(round(tau2/delta_t)==t_
                vector);
                if abs(acosd(cos_psi3))<=FOV
h_vector1(index1)=h_vector1(index1)+(m+1)*Ade-
t*rho*dA*cos_phi12^m*cos_alpha2*cos_beta3*cos_psi3/
(2*pi^2*Dnlos3^2*Dnlos4^2);
```

```
                end
                count2=count2+1;
            end
        end

        %Reflection from 3rd wall WP3
        count3=1;
        for oo=1:Nx
            for pp=1:Nz
                WP3=[x(oo) -ly/2 z(pp)]; %This is
                the position of behind wall
                Dnlos5=sqrt(dot(TP1-WP3,TP1-WP3));
                cos_phi13=abs(WP3(3)-TP1(3))/Dnlos5;
                cos_alpha3=abs(TP1(2)-WP3(2))/Dn-
                los5;
                Dnlos6=sqrt(dot(WP3-RP1,WP3-RP1));
                cos_beta4=abs(WP3(2)-RP1(2))/Dnlos6;
                cos_psi4=abs(WP3(3)-RP1(3))/Dnlos6;
                tau3=(Dnlos5+Dnlos6)/C;
                index1=find(round(tau3/delta_t)==t_
                vector);
                if abs(acosd(cos_psi4))<=FOV
h_vector1(index1)=h_vector1(index1)+(m+1)*Ade-
t*rho*dA*cos_phi13^m*cos_alpha3*cos_beta4*cos_psi4/
(2*pi^2*Dnlos5^2*Dnlos6^2);
                end
                count3=count3+1;
            end
        end

        %Reflection from 4th wall WP4
        count4=1;
        for qq=1:Nx
            for rr=1:Nz
                WP4=[x(qq) ly/2 z(rr)]; %This is the
                position of front wall
                Dnlos7=sqrt(dot(TP1-WP4,TP1-WP4));
                cos_phi14=abs(WP4(3)-TP1(3))/Dnlos7;
                cos_alpha4=abs(TP1(2)-WP4(2))/Dn-
                los7;
```

```
                Dnlos8=sqrt(dot(WP4-RP1,WP4-RP1));
                cos_beta5=abs(WP4(2)-RP1(2))/Dnlos8;
                cos_psi5=abs(WP4(3)-RP1(3))/Dnlos8;
                tau4=(Dnlos7+Dnlos8)/C;
                index1=find(round(tau4/delta_t)==t_
                vector);
                if abs(acosd(cos_psi5))<=FOV
%
h_vector5(index5)=h_vector5(index5)+(m+1)*Ade-
t*rho*dA*cos_phi14^m*cos_alpha4*cos_beta5*cos_psi5/
(2*pi^2*Dnlos7^2*Dnlos8^2);

h_vector1(index1)=h_vector1(index1)+(m+1)*Ade-
t*rho*dA*cos_phi14^m*cos_alpha4*cos_beta5*cos_psi5/
(2*pi^2*Dnlos7^2*Dnlos8^2);
                end
                count4=count4+1;
            end
        end
        t_vector=t_vector*delta_t;
        mean_delay1(ii,jj)=sum((h_vector1).^2.*t_vec-
        tor)/sum(h_vector1.^2);
        Drms1(ii,jj)= sqrt(sum((t_vector-mean_de-
        lay1(ii,jj)).^2.*h_vector1.^2)/sum(h_vec-
        tor1.^2));
    end
end
figure (1)
plot(t_vector*delta_t, h_vector1)
figure (2)
meshc(x,y, Drms1); %This will give rms delay wrt to
only one transmitter
TP1;
    axis([-lx/2 lx/2 -ly/2 ly/2 min(min(Drms1)) max(max
    (Drms1))]);
```

Figure 17.17 shows the channel impulse response for first order refelection coefficient.

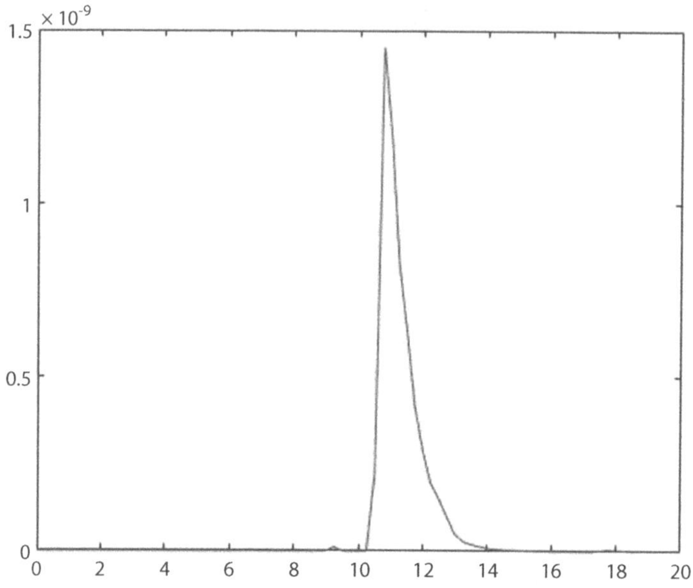

Figure 17.17 Channel impulse response.

References

1. Matheus, L.E.M., Vieira, A.B., Vieira, L.F.M., Vieira, M.A.M., Gnawali, O., Visible Light Communication: Concepts, Applications and Challenges. *IEEE Commun. Surv. Tutor.*, 21, 4, 3204–3237, 2019.
2. Pathak, P.H., Feng, X., Hu, P., Mohapatra, P., Visible Light Communication, Networking, and Sensing: A Survey, Potential and Challenges. *IEEE Commun. Surv. Tutor.*, 17, 4, 2047–2077, 2015.
3. Karunatilaka, D., Zafar, F., Kalavally, V., and XXXR. Parthiban, LED Based Indoor Visible Light Communications: State of the Art. *IEEE Commun. Surv. Tutor.*, 17, 3, 1649–1678, 2015.
4. Khan, L.U., Visible Light Communications: Applications, architecture, standardization and research challenges. *Sci. Direct Digital Commun. Netw.*, 3, 2, 2018.
5. Burchardt, H., Serafimovski, N., Tsonev, D., Videv, S., Haas, H., VLC: Beyond point-to-point communication. *IEEE Commun. Mag.*, 52, 7, 98–105, 2014.
6. Ji, R., Wang, S., Liu, Q., Lu, W., High-speed visible communications: Enabling technologies and state of the art. *Appl. Sci.*, 8, 4, 589, 2018.

7. Vappangi, S. and Mani, V.V., Concurrent illumination and communication: A survey on Visible Light Communication. *Phys. Commun.*, 33, 90–114, 2019.
8. Rehman, S.U., Ullah, S., Chong, P.H.J., Yongchareon, S., Komosny, D., Visible light communication: a system perspective—overview and challenges. *Sensors*, 19, 1153, 2019.
9. Lian, J., Vatansever, Z., Noshad, M., Brandt-Pearce, M., Indoor visible light communications, networking, and applications. *J. Phys.: Photonics*, 1, 1, 2019.
10. Mapunda, G.A., Ramogomana, R., Marata, L., Basutli, B., Khan, A.S., Chuma, J.M., Indoor Visible Light Communication: A Tutorial and Survey. *Wireless Commun. Mobile Comput.*, 101, 2020.
11. Ibhaze, A.E., Orukpe, P.E., Edeko, F.O., High capacity data rate system: Review of visible light communications technology. *J. Electron. Sci. Technol.*, 18, 100055, 2020.
12. Rahman, M.T., Bakibillah, A.S.M., Parthiban, R., Bakaul, M., Review of advanced techniques for multi-gigabit visible light communication. *IET Optoelectron.*, 14, 359–373, 2020.
13. Yu, T.C., Huang, W.T., Lee, W.B., Chow, C.W., Chang, S.W., Kuo, H.C., Visible light communication system technology review: Devices, architectures, and applications. *Crystals*, 11, 1098, 2021.
14. Merdan, F.A.B., Thiagarajah, S.P., Dambul, K., Non-line of sight visible light communications: A technical and application-based survey. *Optik*, 259, 168982, 2022.
15. Vappangi, S. and Mani, V.V., A survey on the integration of visible light communication with power line communication: Conception, applications and research challenges. *Optik*, 266, 169582, 2022.
16. Sejan, M.A.S., Rahman, M.H., Aziz, M.A., Kim, D.-S., You, Y.-H., Song, H.-K., A Comprehensive Survey on MIMO Visible Light Communication: Current Research, Machine Learning and Future Trends. *Sensors, 23*, 739, 2023.
17. Zakavi, M.J., Alireza Nezamalhosseini, S., Lawrence, R., Chen., Multiuser Massive MIMO-OFDM for Visible Light Communication Systems. *IEEE Access*, 11, 2259–2273, 2023.
18. Almadani, Y., Plets, D., Bastiaens, S., Joseph, W., Ijaz, M., Ghassemlooy, Z., Rajbhandari, S., Visible light communications for industrial applications—Challenges and potentials. *Electronics*, 9, 2157, 2020.
19. Reguera, V.A., Teixeira, L., Barriquello, C.H., Thomas, D.H., Costa, M.A.D., Efficient and Low Complexity Rate and Dimming Control of VLC for Industrial IoT Applications. *IEEE J. Emerging Sel. Top. Ind. Electron.*, 3, 1087 – 1095, 2022.
20. Costa, W., Camporez, H., Segatto, M., Rocha, H., Silva, J., Towards AI-enhanced VLC Systems. Optical Fiber Communication Conference. *Optica Publ. Group*, W3I–7, 2022.

21. BA.Vijayalakshmi, B., Arunsundar, B., Gopalan, A., An exploration on VLC channel model and characteristics using LEDs in underground mining. *J. Opt.*, 52, 1399–1404, 2023.
22. Li, X., Ghassemlooy, Z., Zvanovec, S., Haigh, P.A., Experimental Demonstration of a 40 Mb/s VLC System Using a Large Off-the-Shelf LED Panel. *IEEE 12th Int. Symp. on Commun. Systems Netw. Digit. Signal Process. (CSNDSP)*, pp. 1–5, 2020.
23. Xicong, L., Ghassemlooy, Z., Zvánovec, S., Haigh, P.A., A 40 Mb/s VLC system reusing an existing large LED panel in an indoor office environment. *Sensors*, 21, 1697, 2021.
24. Muñoz, S., Iglesias, C.A., Scheianu, A., Suciu, G., Semantic Modeling of a VLC-Enabled Task Automation Platform for Smart Offices. *Electronics*, 11, 326, 2022.
25. Vijayalakshmi, A.B. and Nesasudha, M., Data transmission and inoffensive communication by dimmed LEDs using visible light communication technology. *J. Opt.*, 52, 1, 154–161, 2023.
26. Idris, S., Mohammed, U., Sanusi, J., Thomas, S., Visible light communication: A potential 5G and beyond communication technology. *IEEE 15th International Conference on Electronics, Computer and Computation (ICECCO)*, pp. 1–6, 2019.
27. Yang, H., Zhong, W., Chen, C., Alphones, A., Integration of visible light communication and positioning within 5G networks for internet of things. *IEEE Netw.*, 34, 134–140, 2020.
28. Ariyanti, S. and Suryanegara, M., Visible light communication (VLC) for 6G technology: The potency and research challenges. *Fourth World Conference on Smart Trends in Systems, Security and Sustainability (WorldS4)*, pp. 490–493, 2020.
29. Katz, M. and Ahmed, I., Opportunities and challenges for visible light communications in 6G. 2nd 6G wireless summit (6G SUMMIT), pp. 1–5, 2020.
30. Menaka, D., Sabitha Gauni, C.T., Megalai, M., Kalimuthu, K., Vision of IoUT: Advances and future trends in optical wireless communication. *J. Opt.*, 50, 3, 439–452, 2021.
31. Gupta, A. and Fernando, X., Exploring secure visible light communication in next-generation (6G) internet-of-things. *International Wireless Communications and Mobile Computing (IWCMC)*, pp. 2090–2097, 2021.
32. Georlette, V., Moeyaert, V., S.Bette, N., Point, Visible light communication challenges in the frame of smart cities. *IEEE 22nd International Conference on Transparent Optical Networks (ICTON)*, pp. 1–4, 2020.
33. Georlette, V., Véronique, M., Bette, S., Point, N., Outdoor Optical Wireless Communication: Potentials, standardization and challenges for Smart Cities. *IEEE 29th Wireless Opt. Commun. Conf. (WOCC)*, pp. 1–6, 2020.
34. Sarkar, A., Chakraborty, R., Dutta, H., LiFi-Based Energy-Efficient Traffic Sensing and Controlling System Management for Smart City Application, in:

Environmental Informatics: Challenges and Solutions, pp. 213–226, Springer Nature Singapore, Singapore, 2022.
35. Mishra, P. and Singh, G., 6G-IoT Framework for Sustainable Smart City: Vision and Challenges, in: *Sustainable Smart Cities: Enabling Technologies, Energy Trends and Potential Applications*, pp. 97–117, Springer International Publishing, Cham, 2023.
36. Dahri, F.A., Mangrio, H.B., Baqai, A., Umrani, F.A., Experimental evaluation of intelligent transport system with VLC vehicle-to-vehicle communication. *Wireless Pers Commun.*, 106, 1885–1896, 2019.
37. Ardi, A.P., Aulia, I.S., Priramadhi, R.A., Darlis, D., VLC-based car-to-car communication. *Jurnal Elektronika dan Telekomunikasi*, 20, 1, 16–22, 2020.
38. Meucci, M., Seminara, M., Nawaz, T., Caputo, S., Mucchi, L., Catani, J., Bidirectional Vehicle-to-Vehicle Communication System Based on VLC: Outdoor Tests and Performance Analysis. *IEEE Trans. Intell. Transp. Syst.*, 23, 11465–11475, 2021.
39. Sharda, P., Reddy, G.S., Bhatnagar, M.R., Ghassemlooy, Z., A Comprehensive Modeling of Vehicle-To-Vehicle Based VLC System under Practical Considerations, an Investigation of Performance, and Diversity Property. *IEEE Trans. Commun.*, 70, 3320–3332, 2022.
40. Refas, S., Acheli, D., Yahia, S., Meraihi, Y., Ramdane-Cherif, A., N.V.V., T.D.H., Performance Analysis of Bidirectional Multi-Hop Vehicle-to-Vehicle Visible Light Communication. *IEEE Access*, 11, 129436–129448, 2023.
41. El-Garhy, S.M., Khalaf, A.A.M., Abaza, M., *et al.*, Intelligent transportation system using wireless optical communication: a comparative study. *Opt. Quant. Electron*, 56, 247, 2024.
42. Datasheet of VLHW5100, https://www.farnell.com/datasheets/2245864.pdf.
43. Komine, T. and Nakagawa, M., Fundamental analysis for visible-light communication system using LED lights. *IEEE Trans. Consum. Electron.*, 50, 1, 100–107, 2004.
44. Lu, H., Su, Z., Yuan, B., SNR and optical power distribution in an indoor visible light communication system. *7th International Congress on Image and Signal Processing*, pp. 1063–1067, 2014.
45. Nguyen, H.Q., *et al.*, MATLAB-based simulation program for indoor visible light communication system, A., *7th International Symposium on Communication Systems, Networks & Digital Signal Processing (CSNDSP 2010)*, pp. 537–541, 2010.
46. BPW34 datasheet, https://www.vishay.com/docs/81521/bpw34.pdf.
47. Keiser, G., *Optical Fiber Communications*, fifth edition, Mc Graw Hill Education, Newton Center, MA, USA, 2021.
48. SN74LS194A datasheet, https://www.ti.com/product/SN74LS194A.
49. SN74LS86N datasheet, https://www.ti.com/lit/ds/symlink/sn54s86.pdf.
50. SN7400 datasheet, https://www.ti.com/product/SN7400/.
51. TLO81datasheet, https://www.ti.com/lit/ds/symlink/tl082.pdf?ts=1646200024816&ref_url=https%253A%252F%252Fwww.google.com%252F.

52. VLHW5100 data sheet, https://www.vishay.com/docs/81159/vlhw5100.pdf.
53. 7410 Datasheet, https://www.futurlec.com/74/IC7410.shtml.
54. Wan, R., Wang, L., Huang, J., Yi, X., Kuo, H.C., Li, J., Improving the modulation bandwidth of GaN-Based Light Emitting Diodes for High speed Visible Light Communication: countermeasures and challenges, in: *Advanced Photonics Research*, vol. 2, p. 12, 2021.
55. Mukherjee, M. and Noronha, K., Experimental analysis of received power for OOK-NRZ visible light communication system using off-the-shelf components. *Int. J. Inf. Tecnol.*, 14, 2839–2853, 2022.
56. Mukherjee, M. and Noronha, K., Experimental estimation of quality of service parameters at divergent wavelengths and luminous intensities for indoor visible light communication using OOK-NRZ modulation. *J. Opt.*, 53, 3617–3636, 2023.

Index

1G, 3, 8, 15
2G, 3, 9, 15
3D antennas, 219
3G, 3, 10, 16
4G, 3, 11, 16
5G, 3, 12, 267, 352, 357, 358
5G network in agriculture, 357, 358
6G, 3, 14, 22, 311–313, 317–320
6G network, 327–329
6G technology, 89, 98, 106
6G wireless networks, 161–162, 164–167, 171

Ad hoc networks, 265
Adaptive beamforming, 254
Aforementioned, 36, 43
Agnostic, 35, 43
Agriculture, 352
AI-driven autonomous networks, 208
Alani, 37
Alfadhl, 52
Algorithm, 191
Alice and Bob, 90, 92, 96
Amplifying 6G, 272
Amplitude modulation, 17
Android application, 359, 360
ANN, 230
Applications, 75, 85
Arduino, 359, 362
Artificial intelligence, 75, 143, 144, 167, 289
Artificial neural network, 295
Augmented reality (AR), 170, 279, 289
Automated machine learning (AutoML), 150
Automation, 354, 360
Autonomous vehicles, 278

Battery life, 277
BB84 protocol, 96, 100
Beamforming, 168
Beamforming training (BT), 248, 252
Bell state, 91
Bellavista, 52
Bias and fairness, 204
Bioinformatics, 151
Bipartite system, 92
Bloch sphere, 128
Bluetooth, 7

Case studies, 277
Categorization, 48
Cellular networks, 266
Challenges, 199, 320
Challenges and solutions, 275
Characterization, 39
CIP, 131
Climate control systems, 358
Clustering, 46
Cognitive radio networks, 129
Compatibility, 202
Cryptographic algorithms, 305
Cryptographic attacks, 95, 105
Cryptography, 78
Current research trends, 209
Cybersecurity, 78, 157

Data augmentation, 257
Data availability, 200
Data preprocessing techniques, 195
Data privacy, 301
Data quality, 199
Data sources, 194
DC channel gain, 380
Deep learning (DL), 150, 151, 152
Deep neural network (DNN), 254
Depicts, 31, 32, 39
Deployed, 34
Deploying, 48, 50
Deployment, 30, 48, 196
Depth, 47
Derivation, 50
Derive, 50
Described, 34, 40
Desired, 37
Device identifiers, 98
Device-to-device, 263
Discrete logarithm problem, 95, 106

Eavesdropping, 94, 96, 100
ECIES, 106
Edge computing, 167, 169
Edge Intelligence, 172
Elliptic Curve Diffie-Hellman (ECDH), 95, 106
Emerged, 29
Emergence, 30
Emerging technologies, 208
Emissions, 49
Emphasis, 47
Emphasize, 41
Emphasizing, 47
Employ, 44
Encrypt and decrypt, 119–120
Energy efficiency, 258, 275, 354
Entanglement, 90–92, 291
Error correction, 79
Ethical considerations, 203
Ethical implications, 206
European broadcast communications guidelines organization (ETSI), 121

Fault detection, 192
Feasible, 31, 41
Feature selection and engineering, 195
Features, 31
Federated learning, 129
FeMBMS, 50
FFL, 132
Field condition management, 158
Fifth generation, 218
Flexible antenna, 219
Fourth Industry Revolution (4IR), 143, 157
Fraud detection, 157
Frequency modulation, 17
Fully autonomous networks, 208

Gathering, 33
Gaussian, 39
Gaussian mixture model (GMM), 253
Gener, 52
GPS, 7
Grover's algorithm, 95, 105

Half beam angle, 376
Hall effect, 131
Hall voltage, 131
HBF (hybrid beamformer), 247, 248
Healthcare, 278
Heuristic, 49
Hexagonal, 34
Higher, 34, 41, 49
Human-machine collaboration, 208

Identifier flaws in 5G, 98
Illuminance, 377
Immersive media, 279
In-band, 264
Indicates, 34
Industry collaborations, 210
Interference management, 273
Interference mitigation, 175–176
Internet of Things (IoT), 288, 293
Interoperability, 201
Intrusion detection system, 293

IoT (Internet of Things), 352, 354
Irrigation, 352

Keep, 31
Keeping, 31
Key encapsulation mechanism (KEM), 107
Key generation rate, 103
K-nearest neighbor (KNN), 252
Kyber algorithm, 110, 111, 112

Latency, 276
Light emitting diode (LED), 367, 369, 373–376, 382, 384
LightSaber protocol, 110, 111, 112
Link, 41
Linkages, 37
Load balancing, 193
LTE, 11
Luminous flux, 376
Luminous intensity, 376, 389

Machine learning, 76, 162, 164–178, 221, 225, 227–232, 268, 285, 289, 291, 305
Machine learning fundamentals, 190
Machine learning program, 145
Measurement-device-independent QKD (MDI), 101, 102
Membership, 50
Methods to achieve, 317
  6G URLLC, 317
  hardware development, 317
MIMO, 168, 224, 230, 289
Mobility management, 275
Model training, 196
Monte Carlo simulations, 77
Moore's law, 118
MRAM, 131
Multi-modal learning (MML), 150
Multiple input multiple output, 17

Need for standardization, 202
Network automation, 189
Network intelligence, 124, 311– 323
Network management, 166–167
Network security in vehicular communication, 327, 336–338
Network slicing, 167
Neural Information Processing Systems or NIPS, 149
No-cloning theorem, 93, 94
Non-orthogonal multiple access (NOMA), 244

OOK-NRZ, 374, 382
Open-source projects, 211
Orthogonal frequency division multiplexing, 17
Out-band, 265

Peer-to-peer, 265
Phase shift keying, 17
Photodetector, 389–390
Photonic QC, 132
Photons, 120
Post-quantum cryptography, 89, 99, 105
PRBS, 383
Predictive maintenance, 192
Preprocessing, 194
Privacy, 275
Pseudo-random number seed key construction (PRNSKC), 104

QEC, 320–321
QKD, 315, 318, 322
QKD/quantum key distribution, 117, 121
Q-learning, 155
QML (quantum machine learning), 311, 313, 319, 323
QoS prediction, 159
Quadrature amplitude modulation, 17
Quality of service (QoS), 129, 254, 327, 343
Quality of service (QoS) optimization, 193

Quantum algorithms, 64, 67–69, 71, 77, 85
Quantum attacks, 301, 302
Quantum bits, 133
Quantum computer, 59–60, 70, 77
Quantum computing, 57–62, 69–71, 76–79, 85, 89, 90, 94, 95, 127
Quantum computing (QC), 285, 287, 288, 298, 293, 294, 305
Quantum cryptography, 117, 119, 121, 285, 287, 301
Quantum decoherence, 78
Quantum error correction, 129
Quantum Fourier transform, 65–66
Quantum gates, 62–63
Quantum hardware, 72–74, 79, 85
Quantum identifiers, 100, 104
Quantum key distribution (QKD), 96, 100
Quantum machine learning (QML), 285, 287, 293, 294, 305, 327, 328, 329
Quantum mechanical properties, 90
Quantum mechanics, 123
Quantum registers, 61, 66
Quantum security, 99, 105, 106
Quantum software, 74, 80–81, 85
Quantum states, 76
Quantum supremacy, 130
Quantum-assisted wireless artificial intelligence (QAWAI), 319
Qubit, 60, 62, 66, 73
Qubit space, 316
Quantum information technology (QIT), 287
Quantum key distribution (QKD), 120, 287, 288

Radiant sensitive area, 379
Random polarization, 120
Raspberry Pi, 353
Real-time handling, 276
Recurrent neural network (RNN), 254
Regulatory compliance, 205
Regulatory considerations, 203
Reinforcement learning (RL), 154, 190, 270, 253
Resource allocation, 175–176, 258, 273, 314, 321
Resource allocation in 6G, 300
Resource constraints, 201
Resource management, 327, 340
Responsivity, 378
Rise time, 378
RSA algorithm, 118

Scalability, 79, 200
Security, 275
Security flaws in classical algorithms, 99
Semi-supervised learning, 154
Sensors, 355, 358, 363
SHSTNO, 130
Signal denoising, 175–176
Sixth generation, 218
Sixth generation (6G) network, 285, 289, 293, 300, 301, 305
Smart cities, 277
Smart farming, 358, 359
Smart irrigation, 352, 362
Software-defined network (SDN), 293
Soil moisture, 355, 356
Spectrum management, 273
Speech recognition, 153
Spin transfer torque, 131
Spin-orbit coupling, 128
Spin-orbit torque, 131
Spintronic QC, 127
Sprinkler, 352
SQLite, 359
Standards, 201
Subscriber Concealed Identifier (SUCI), 105, 106

Supervised, 190
Supervised learning, 153, 252, 268
Support vector machine (SVM), 149, 155

Tensiometer, 356
Terahertz communication, 26
Traffic engineering, 193
Traffic prediction, 327, 332
Traffic prediction in 6G networks, 332–336
Trans impedance amplifier (TIA), 375, 382, 390
Turing test, 148

Unsupervised, 190
Unsupervised learning, 153, 252, 269
Urban IoT networks, 277
Use case, 191

Vehicle-to-everything (V2X), 255
Vehicular communication, 278
Vendor-specific challenges, 203
Virtual reality (VR), 170, 289, 316
Visible light communication (VLC), 368–383, 392

Water conservation, 354, 363
Water holding capacity, 356
Wearable devices, 278
WiFi, 7
Wireless communication, 3–8

Also of Interest

Check out these published and forthcoming titles in the "Industry 5.0 Transformation Applications" series from Scrivener Publishing

Cyber-Physical Systems for Innovating and Transforming Society 5.0
Edited by Tanupriya Choudhury, Abhijit Kumar, Ravi Tomar, S. Balamurugan and Ankit Vishnoi
Published 2025. ISBN 978-1-394-19771-2

Distributed Time-Sensitive Systems
Edited by Tanupriya Choudhury, Rahul Kumar Singh, Ravi Tomar, S. Balamurugan, J. C. Patni
Published 2025. ISBN 978-1-394-19772-9

Generative Artificial Intelligence
Concepts and Applications
Edited by R. Nidhya, D. Pavithra, Manish Kumar, A. Dinesh Kumar, and S. Balamurugan
Published 2025. ISBN 978-1-394-20922-4

Intelligent Robots and Cobots
Concepts and Applications for Industry 5.0 Transformation
Edited by Ramasamy V., S. Balamurugan, and Sheng-Lung Peng
Published 2025. ISBN 978-1-394-19817-7

Smart Factories for Industry 5.0 Transformation
Edited by R. Nidhya, Manish Kumar, S. Karthik, Rishabh Anand and S. Balamurugan
Published 2025. ISBN 978-1-394-19995-2

Optimized Computational Intelligence Driven Decision-Making Theory, Application and Challenges
Edited by Hrudaya Kumar Tripathy, Sushruta Mishra, Minakhi Rout, S. Balamurugan and Samaresh Mishra
Published 2024. ISBN 978-1-394-24253-5

Welding Practices for Industry 5.0
Edited by Syed Quadir Moinuddin, Shaik Himam Saheb, Ashok Kumar Dewangan, Muralimohan Cheepu and S. Balamurugan
Published 2024. ISBN 978-1-394-17241-2

Metaverse and Immersive Technologies
An Introduction to Industrial, Business and Social Applications
Edited by Chandrashekhar A., Shaik Himam Saheb, Sandeep Kumar Panda, S. Balamurugan and Sheng-Lung Peng
Published 2023. ISBN 978-1-394-17454-6

www.scrivenerpublishing.com

Printed in the USA/Agawam, MA
September 16, 2026

910661.145